DOCTORAL DISSERTATIONS ON CHINA, 1971-1975

A Bibliography of Studies
in Western Languages

Compiled and edited by
FRANK JOSEPH SHULMAN

UNIVERSITY OF WASHINGTON PRESS
SEATTLE AND LONDON

This work has been published as a supplement to *Doctoral Dissertations on China: A Bibliography of Studies in Western Languages, 1945-1970*, compiled and edited by Leonard H. D. Gordon and Frank J. Shulman (Seattle and London: published for the Association for Asian Studies by the University of Washington Press, 1972).

Library of Congress Cataloging in Publication Data

Shulman, Frank Joseph, 1943-
   Doctoral dissertations on China, 1971-1975.

   Supplement to Doctoral dissertations on China ;
a bibliography of studies in Western languages,
1945-1970, by L. H. D. Gordon and F. J. Shulman.
   Includes index.
   1. China--Bibliography. 2. Dissertations,
Academic--Bibliography. I. Gordon, Leonard H. D.,
1928 -   Doctoral dissertations on China.
II. Title.
Z3106.G65 Suppl.   [DS706]   016.951   77-15188
ISBN 0-295-95592-9
ISBN 0-295-95593-7 pbk.

Is the scholar human?

        -- Vitali Rubin *

DEDICATED TO

Lucien Bianco

Wm. Theodore de Bary

Irene Eber

David N. Keightley

Steven I Levine

Rhoads Murphey

Harold Z. Schiffrin

and all others who
responded to an
appeal that could
not go ignored.

* "An Open Letter to American Sinologists."
New York Review of Books.
October 5, 1972.   p.36.

Contents

CONTENTS

CONTENTS

CONTENTS

CONTENTS

CONTENTS

Introduction

The vast expansion of Chinese Studies in the West since World War II has been accompanied by a rapid increase in the number of doctoral degrees awarded for work relating to China. Between 1945 and 1970, approximately 2200 dissertations dealing in some way with Chinese affairs were completed in Australia, central and western Europe, and North America. For the most part, they have been recorded in *Doctoral Dissertations on China: A Bibliography of Studies in Western Languages, 1945-1970*, by Leonard H.D. Gordon and Frank J. Shulman (University of Washington Press, 1972). Nearly as many dissertations have been accepted by institutions of higher learning since then. This phenomenal development underscores the necessity for the type of bibliographical control which the present volume--and future five-year supplements to *Doctoral Dissertations on China*--is designed to provide.

Like its parent volume, this bibliography is a comprehensive, interdisciplinary, classified listing of doctoral research dealing in whole or in part with China before and after 1949 as well as with Hong Kong, Mongolia, Tibet, and the overseas Chinese communities. With the exception of Soviet theses, for which adequate up-to-date information has been unavailable, all dissertations that are known to deal in any way with Chinese affairs (including work about the impact of Chinese culture upon the West, about Western academic programs concerned with the study of China, and about China within a broad, global context) have been included. As an underlying principle, the selection of all bibliographical items has been based strictly on the relevance of their contents, not on their intrinsic value or merit. No attempt has been made to assess the quality of the research listed.

The main body of this volume (pp.3-221) contains 1573 entries. These have been arranged along subject lines primarily on the basis of their content and only secondarily in accordance with the academic discipline in which their authors have specialized. As a result, most dissertations in the social sciences pertaining to China before 1949 are to be found under "History", and all theses concerning Chinese communities outside of East Asia are entered solely under "Overseas Chinese Communities." Throughout the volume, cross-references leading the reader from one section to related entries elsewhere are provided. Within each section and subsection, the dissertations are arranged strictly in chronological order according to the calendar year of their completion or formal acceptance. This approach will help the interested reader discern long-term trends in many areas of doctoral research, especially when he also has *Doctoral Dissertations on China...1945-1970* on hand. An extensive appendix (pp.223-57) lists 228 theses completed before 1971 which were unknown to the authors at the time the parent volume was compiled. This is followed by two tables which (1) summarize the distribution of dissertations on China throughout the entire postwar period by the country in which they were written and by their calendar year of completion, and (2) indicate the distribution of American dissertations by degree-awarding institution during the years 1971-1975. Details on the availability of the doctoral dissertation typescripts are provided on pages 261-76. Three indexes --(a) an alphabetical listing by author; (b) an index by degree-awarding institution (arranged alphabetically on a country-by-country basis); and (c) a modified subject index limited primarily to geographical, literary and personal names--should also be useful for many readers.

The information furnished for each dissertation entry within both the main body and the appendix appears in the following order:

(1) the consecutive entry number

(2) the author's name in full

(3) the complete title and subtitle of the dissertation, together with a translation of foreign-language titles

(4) the name of the degree-awarding university or institution in abbreviated form (the full name of each university may be found within the institutional index)

(5) the calendar year in which the author received his degree or, when unknown, the year in which his dissertation was completed and defended

(6) the type of degree awarded and the name either of the academic department/school for which the thesis was written or the author's field of specialization (this usually is expressed as "Ph.D. in X," "Ed.D. in Y," "Doctorat de 3^e cycle en X," "Dr., Y Fakultät," etc.)

(7) the number of pages in the microfilm copy of the dissertation as noted in *Dissertation Abstracts International* or the pagination of the actual dissertation typescript (whichever is most readily at hand)

(8) the *Dissertation Abstracts International* (DAI) volume, issue and page numbers citing the location of a readily available six hundred word summary whenever this is applicable

(9) the University Microfilms International order number (UM) where appropriate, or a statement explaining how to obtain a copy of the dissertation from some other source

(10) details about the publication of a book-length manuscript by the author that is either based on the dissertation or is closely related to his doctoral research (to the extent that this information has been readily available prior to the completion of this bibliography)

(11) a brief annotation where the title of a dissertation has failed to specify its relevance for this bibliography, where it has been necessary to indicate the appropriateness for entering a particular dissertation under one section rather than under another, or where other special circumstances have dictated the inclusion of information describing a dissertation's contents and scope

Regretfully, in a few cases (especially where French dissertations are concerned), certain basic bibliographical information has not become available in time for inclusion within this volume.

In compiling any bibliography of this nature, the author must impose continually upon the cooperation, goodwill and patience of his colleagues and associates. Many individuals--among them university reference librarians and faculty members--have contributed to this book. Especially noteworthy assistance has been received from: The Association for Asian Studies, Inc. (Ann Arbor, Michigan), which permitted the publication of bibliographical information that first appeared in the author's ongoing column of doctoral research within various AAS publications; Enid Bishop (Australian National University Library) and Barry C. Bloomfield (SOAS Library, University of London), who supplied important details about theses at their respective institutions; Harley Holden (Harvard University Archives), who enabled the author to work within the Archives and answered numerous inquiries by mail over the years;

INTRODUCTION

Eva Kraft (Ostasienabteilung, Staatsbibliothek Preussischer Kulturbesitz), Gert Naundorf (Institut für Sinologie der Julius-Maximilians-Universität Würzburg), and Wolfgang Seuberlich (Marburg/Lahn), who frequently alerted the author to pertinent German doctoral research; Michel Popoff (Bibliothèque de la Sorbonne, Paris) and Mlle. E. Dartiguenave (Centre de Documentation Sciences Humaines, C.N.R.S., Paris), who greatly facilitated the author's efforts in June 1974 to cover French doctoral theses; the Scientific Information Service, Institute for World Economics of the Hungarian Academy of Sciences (Budapest), which provided the author with a listing of dissertations from which all of the Hungarian entries within the present volume have been drawn; the staff of The University of Michigan's Harlan Hatcher Library, who helped in many ways before the author moved to College Park from Ann Arbor; Carl Jacobson and Margaret Yamashita, who contributed their time when the initial compilation was underway; Hans Wellisch (University of Maryland, College Park), Irene Eber (Hebrew University of Jerusalem) and Robert Ruhlmann (Université de Paris), who assisted the author in translating the titles of selected German, Polish, and French-language dissertations; Kuang-yao Fan, Connie Tomita Galmeijer and Ellen A. Nollman (East Asia Collection, University of Maryland Libraries), who prepared the Chinese-language introduction to this volume and helped out in many other ways as the bibliography was being completed for publication; Beverly L. Hughes (Greenbelt, Maryland), who patiently and carefully typed portions of the camera-ready copy; and the Center for Japanese Studies at The University of Michigan and the administration of the University of Maryland Libraries, which provided essential office space and typing facilities. To all of these individuals and institutions, the author expresses his most sincere appreciation. This bibliography could not have been prepared in its present form without their help.

Corrections and additions to this volume as well as contributions to forthcoming five-year supplements will always be very welcome. The author hopes that readers will take the initiative to alert him to pertinent research by writing him at the East Asia Collection, McKeldin Library, University of Maryland, College Park, Maryland 20742 (USA).

Frank Joseph Shulman

College Park, Maryland

December 1977

前 言

　　自從二次世界大戰以來西方國家對中國研究學習之擴展導致了對這方面的博士學位之授予迅速增加, 從1945到1970年之間, 在澳洲, 中歐與西歐以及北美大約有2200有關中國之博士論文完成. 按這些論文大部份已收入 Leonard H.D. Gordon 與 Frank J. Shulman 合著之 *Doctoral Dissertations on China: A Bibliography of Studies in Western Languages, 1945-1970* (見 1972年華盛頓大學版本) 自該書出版後, 又有幾乎等量的論文提出並已被各院校接受. 這種發展情形促進了編輯本目錄之需要.

　　一如其母書 1972版, 本目錄係一有關中國之綜合性及多學科的分類博士研究目錄. 這些論文有的全部或局部討論1949以前或以後之中國, 並包括香港, 蒙古, 西藏以及華僑社會.

　　除了有關蘇俄之論文 因資料不全之故　所有已知有關中國之論文均已收入. 本目錄編輯之標準以內容是否與中國有關為主. 致於論文之評鑑將超出本目錄之範圍.

　　本目錄主要部分 (pp.3-221) 收有1573項, 各項之主題排列以內容為主, 作者之專門學科為副. 由是之故 1949年前之社會科學論文被列入 "歷史" 項下. 其他有關東亞以外之中國社會之論文均收在 "華僑社會" 項下. 為便於讀者參閱起見, 本目錄自始至終大量使用 "交互參考" 方法. 各部之論文均按該論文之提出或正式

被接受之年代的先後排列. 如果參照 Doctoral Dissertations on China...1945 這個方法兼可有助於研判對這方
面博士研究之臺期趨向. 本目錄附有一詳盡之附錄. 這
個附錄 (pp.223-57) 列有228項於1971年前所完成之博士
論文 按這些論文因故未被收入1972母書. 附錄後又
附加兩個圖表. 一個是各國於戰後所提出有關中國之
博士論文 以年代先後排列 之分佈情形, 一個是1971-
1975期間美國各博士學位授予院校之分佈情形. 讀
者可在 (pp.261-76) 頁內找到有關如何購得或借閱各論文打
字稿之詳細說明. 本目錄並提供三種索引, 它們將有
助於讀者使用本目錄

按字母先後排列之作者索引
學位授予院校之索引 按字母先後之國家排列
簡易地名, 文學與人名索引
本目錄所收之博士論文(主要部份及附錄)以下
列次序排列之
連續性之論文編号
作者之全名
論文之名稱及副題 如非用英文撰寫者, 並附
有英文繙譯.
各學位授予之院校簡稱.
論文作者獲得博士學位之年代, 或論文完成
與辯護之年代
學位之種類及接受論文之學系, 或院校之名
稱, 或作者之專門學科. (此以 "Ph.D. in X,"
"Ed.D. in Y," "Doctorat de 3e cycle en X," "Dr.,
Y Fakultät" 示之)
在 Dissertation Abstracts International (DAI) 內所
記載之論文頁數或打字稿的實際頁數
說明何處可借閱或購得 DAI 卷期, 頁數之記載
UM (University Microfilms International) 訂購号碼
或其他可獲得某論文之方法.

以博士論文為主或相似所出版之書的有關資料
如有下列需要，將加以註釋
　論文名稱無法說明是否與本目錄有關者
　如將某論文列入甲部較佳於乙部者
　論文之內容與範圍有說明之必要者
令人遺憾者，因若干基本目錄資料不全，故某些論
文無法列入．尤以法文論文為最
　　從事此類目錄編纂工作，作者盡其所能以求正
確完整，然而，遺漏與錯誤在所難免．如讀者
諸君有所指正無任歡迎，並請直接函示

Frank Joseph Shulman
East Asia Collection, McKeldin Library
University of Maryland
College Park, Maryland 20742 (USA)

Abbreviations

DAI; DA *Dissertation Abstracts International* (before July 1969, *Dissertation Abstracts*) with volume, issue and page numbers of the published abstract.

Example: DAI 36, no.2 (Aug. 1975): 960-61-A

(A 600 word summary of the thesis will be found on pages 960-A and 961-A of the August 1975--volume 36, no.2--issue of *Dissertation Abstracts International*)

UM University Microfilms International order number for use when purchasing microfilm and xerographic copies of dissertation typescripts that are available from University Microfilms International.

Example: UM 75-12,310.

... Indicates that the title of the book is identical with the title of the dissertation, which is provided in full within the same entry.

Example: Published as Tseng...Bureaucracy.

(The title of the book is the same as that of the dissertation: *Tseng Kuo-fan's Private Bureaucracy*.)

A.D. Doctor of Arts

Akad.avh. Akademisk avhandling (Swedish: Academic Thesis)

D.B.A. Doctor of Business Administration

D.Crim. Doctor of Criminology

D.Eng. Doctor of Engineering

D.L.S. Doctor of Library Science

D.Min. Doctor of Ministry

ABBREVIATIONS

D.Miss.   Doctor of Missiology

D.N.S.   Doctor of Nursing Science

D.Phil.   Doctor of Philosophy   (used in Great Britain)

D.Sc.   Doctor of Science

D.S.S.   Doctor of Social Science

D.S.W.   Doctor of Social Welfare

Dr.P.H.   Doctor of Public Health

Dr.U.   Doctor of the University   (used in Hungary)

Ed.D.   Doctor of Education

J.S.D.   Doctor of Juridical/Judicial Sciences

kand.   Kandidat   (Candidate's degree)

LL.D.   Legum Doctor   (Doctor of Laws)

M.D.   Doctor of Medicine)

Ph.D.   Doctor of Philosophy

S.J.D.   Scientiae Juridicae Doctor   (Doctor of Juridical
                      Sciences)

Th.D.   Doctor of Theology

The Wade-Giles transcription system has been used for Chinese
names and terms within the translations of European-language
dissertation titles, the annotations, and the modified subject
index.

Doctoral Dissertations
on China, 1971-1975

ANTHROPOLOGY

General and Miscellaneous Studies

See also entry 1409 and the section "Overseas Chinese Communities" (pp.161-81).

1 NETTLESHIP, Martin Anderson. *Background to an Experiment in Applied Anthropology among the Atayal of Taiwan*. London, 1971 (Ph.D. in Anthropology, London School of Economics). 427p.

2 FRIEDMAN, Jonathan Ames. *System, Structure and Contradiction in the Evolution of "Asiatic" Social Formations*. Columbia, 1972 (Ph.D. in Anthropology). 405p. DAI 36, no. 2 (Aug. 1975): 960-61-A; UM 75-12,310. Deals in part with ancient Chinese states in present-day Yünnan.

3 PILLSBURY, Barbara Linné Kroll. *Cohesion and Cleavage in a Chinese Muslim Minority*. Columbia, 1973 (Ph.D. in Anthropology). 316p. DAI 35, no.7 (Jan. 1975): 3962-A; UM 74-29,644. Studies the community in Taipei during the 1950s and 1960s.

4 ROHSENOW, Hill Gates. *Prosperity Settlement: The Politics of Paipai in Taipei, Taiwan*. Michigan, 1973 (Ph.D. in Anthropology). 211p. DAI 35, no.1 (July 1974): 16-17-A; UM 75-15,837. Paipai are cyclical religious festivals of rural and urban communities in Taipei.

5 JEN, Shien-min. *Cybernetic Analysis of Chinese Cultural Evolution*. Wisconsin, 1974 (Ph.D. in Behavioral Cybernetics). 191p. DAI 35, no.5 (Nov. 1974): 2405-06-B; UM 74-19,336. Focuses on cultural adaption and control in ancient China.

6 KENNY, James Andrew. *A Numerical Taxonomy of Ethnic Units*

3

Using Murdock's 1967 World Sample.   Indiana, 1974 (Ph.D.
in Anthropology).   309p.   DAI 35, no.4 (Oct. 1974):
1789-A; UM 74-22,737.   Includes consideration of the Manchu, Min Chinese, and Tibetans.

7   NAMMOUR, Valerie Wheeler.   *Drums and Guns: A Cross-Cultural Study of the Nature of War*.   Oregon, 1974 (Ph.D. in
Anthropology).   559p.   DAI 35, no.12 (June 1975): 7460-A;
UM 75-12,554.   Nammour studied sociocultural and warfare
variables in 186 societies throughout the world including
the Chinese, Manchu and Khalka Mongol societies.

8   RAUBER, Hanna.   *Der Schmied und sein Handwerk im traditionellen Tibet*.   [German: The Blacksmith and His Craft in
Traditional Tibet.]   Zürich, 1975 (D.Phil., Ethnologisches
Seminar).   233p.   A copy is available at the Zentralbib-
liothek Zürich.

9   SCHENK-SANDBERGEN, Louise Charlotte.   *Vuil werk, schone
toekomst? Het leven van straatvegers en vuilruimers.
Een onderzoek in Bulsar, India, en verkenningen in Peking,
Shanghai, Tientsin en Tangshan, China*.   [Dutch, with a
summary in English: Dirty Work, Fine Future? The Life of
Road-Sweepers and Refuse-Collectors. An Investigation
Conducted in Bulsar, India; together with Observations
Made in Peking, Shanghai, Tientsin and Tangshan in China.]
Amsterdam Gemeentelijke, 1975 (Dr.).

10 YIN, Chien-chung.   *Migration and Voluntary Associations
in Rural and Urban Taiwan: A Study of Group Adaptative
Strategies in Social Change*.   Hawaii, 1975 (Ph.D. in Anthropology).   295p.   DAI 36, no.9 (Mar. 1976): 6180-A;
UM 76-6563.

Community and Regional Studies

See also entries 1422, 1425, 1427, 1554, and 1564.

11 YOUNG, John Aubrey.   *Interpersonal Networks and Economic
Behavior in a Chinese Market Town*.   Stanford, 1971 (Ph.D.
in Anthropology).   272p.   DAI 32, no.3 (Sept. 1971):
1336-B; UM 71-23,574.   Deals with the market town of Yuen
Long in the New Territories of Hong Kong.

12 WALKER, Anthony Rupert.   *The Lahu of the Yunnan-Indochina
Borderlands: Ethnic Group and Village Community*.   Oxford,
1972 (D.Phil. in Anthropology and Geography).   xx, 448p.

13 CRISSMAN, Lawrence William.   *Town and Country: Central-
Place Theory and Chinese Marketing Systems, with Particular*

Reference to Southwestern Changhua Hsien, Taiwan. Cornell, 1973 (Ph.D. in Anthropology). 472p. DAI 34, no.10 (Apr. 1974): 4796-B; UM 74-6296.

14 DeGLOPPER, Donald Robert. *City on the Sands: Social Structure in a Nineteenth-Century Chinese City.* Cornell, 1973 (Ph.D. in Anthropology). 282p. DAI 34, no.10 (Apr. 1974): 4796-97-B; UM 74-6297. About the social and political structure of Lukang when it was the main seaport of central Taiwan.

15 AZIZ, Barbara Norma. *The People of Dingri: A Socio-Historical Portrait of a Community in Southwestern Tibet.* London, 1974 (Ph.D. in Arts, School of Oriental and African Studies). 422p. + appendixes.

16 BEATTIE, Hilary Jane. *Land and Lineage in China: A Study of T'ung-ch'eng County, Anhwei, in the Ming and Ch'ing Dynasties.* Cambridge, 1974 (Ph.D. in Oriental Studies). iii, 391p.

17 BLAKE, Charles Fredric. *Negotiating Ethnolinguistic Symbols in a Chinese Market Town.* Illinois, 1975 (Ph.D. in Anthropology). 464p. DAI 36, no.5 (Nov. 1975): 2937-A; UM 75-24,263. On the political economy of Sai Kung market in rural Hong Kong.

18 CHEN, Chung-min. *Ying-ting: A Cultural-Ecological Study of a Chinese Mixed Cropping Village in Taiwan.* Michigan State, 1975 (Ph.D. in Anthropology). 262p. DAI 36, no. 12 (June 1976): 8146-A; UM 76-12,415.

19 FEUCHTWANG, Stephan David Raphael. *The Social Bases of Religion and Religious Change in a Market Town on the Mountainous Rim of the Taipei Basin, Northern Taiwan.* London, 1975 (Ph.D. in Anthropology; External). 562p. Order copies from the British Library Lending Division, Boston Spa, Yorkshire, order no.D13320/75.

Family and Kinship Studies

See also entry 1556.

20 MOODY, Edward Jones. *Chinese Family Structure and Personality: The Relation of Authority to the Development of Achievement Motivation.* California (Berkeley), 1971 (Ph.D. in Anthropology). v, 531p. Order copies from the Library Photographic Service, General Library, University of California at Berkeley.

21 MARK, Lindy Li. *Taiwanese Lineage Enterprises: A Study
    of Familial Entrepreneurship.* California (Berkeley),
    1972 (Ph.D. in Anthropology). xvii, 153p. Order copies
    from the Library Photographic Service, General Library,
    University of California at Berkeley.

22 CHIU, Chi-chien. *Kinship Structure of the Bunun.* Geor-
    gia, 1973 (Ph.D. in Anthropology). 280p. DAI 34, no.7
    (Jan. 1974): 3056-57-B; UM 73-31,869. On sedentary culti-
    vators living in the mountains of Formosa.

23 TANG, Mei-chun. *Life and Family Structure in a Chinese
    City: Taipei, Taiwan.* Columbia, 1973 (Ph.D. in Anthro-
    pology). 405p. DAI 35, no.2 (Aug. 1974): 641-A; UM
    74-17,908.

24 SUNG, Lung-sheng. *Inheritance and Kinship in North Tai-
    wan.* Stanford, 1975 (Ph.D. in Anthropology). 257p. DAI
    35, no.12 (June 1975): 7464-A; UM 75-13,608. Examines
    the social structure of landowning kinship groups since
    the 1800s.

Physical Anthropology

25 SCHANFIELD, Melvin Samuel. *Population Studies on the Gm
    and Inv Antigens in Asia and Oceania.* Michigan, 1971
    (Ph.D. in Human Genetics). 147p. DAI 32, no.7 (Jan.
    1972): 3797-98-B; UM 72-4971. Includes the Chinese and
    the aborigines of Taiwan.

26 SO, Joseph Kwok-fai. *Genetic, Acclimatizational and An-
    thropometric Factors in Cold-Induced Temperature Responses
    among Asian and European Populations: A Study in Adaptive
    Human Biology.* State University of New York at Buffalo,
    1974 (Ph.D. in Anthropology). 98p. DAI 35, no.10 (Apr.
    1975): 6293-A; UM 75-7800. Focuses on people of northern
    and southern Chinese ancestry.

Values and Attitudes

See also entries 20, 145, 151, and 280.

27 ALEXANDER, James McKenzie (III). *Tibetan National Char-
    acter.* Washington (Seattle), 1971 (Ph.D. in Anthropolo-
    gy). 214p. DAI 32, no.3 (Sept. 1971): 1329-B; UM
    71-24,017. Based on data from the period 1912-1951.

28 NUTTING, Margaret Wickes Gibbons. *The Fate of the*

Confucian Ideal in "Reading" Textbooks of Taiwan and the China Mainland: A Study of Continuity and Change. Syracuse, 1973 (Ph.D. in Anthropology). 506p. DAI 35, no.2 (Aug. 1974): 640-A; UM 74-17,605. Measures modern textbook definitions of the culturally competent citizen against the traditional values represented by the Confucian chun tzu ideal.

29 PAN, Margaret Tai-li. *The Attitudes of Taiwan Businessmen toward the Entertaining Girls of the City of Taipei.* New York, 1973 (Ph.D., School of Education). 208p. DAI 34, no.6 (Dec. 1973): 2432-33-B; UM 73-30,107.

30 SCHAK, David Carl. *From Mang-hun ya-chia to Tsu-yu lien-ai: The Evolution of Dating and Free Courtship in Modern China as Manifested in Taipei, Taiwan.* California (Berkeley), 1973 (Ph.D. in Anthropology). 263p. DAI 34, no.7 (Jan. 1974): 3065-B; UM 73-25,387. Published as Dating and Mate-Selection in Modern Taiwan (Taipei: Chinese Association for Folklore, 1975. iii, x, 253p. [Asian folklore and social life monographs]).

ARCHAEOLOGY

See also entries 37, 42, 44, 53, 63, 397, 949, and 1574.

31 MARSZEWSKI, Tomasz. *Problem czasu i miejsca wprowadzenia uprawy kukurydzy do Azji oraz jego znaczenie dla badań nad przedkolumbijskimi kontaktami między ludami Starego i Norwego Świata.* [Polish: The Problem of Determining the Time and Place of the Introduction of Corn Products into Asia and Implications for Research on Pre-Columbian Contacts between Peoples of the Old and New Worlds.] Uniwersytet Jagielloński w Krakowie, 1972 (Doktor habilitowany, Wydz. Biologii i Nauk o Ziemi).

32 WONG, Yin-wai. *Yin-chou ch'ing-t'ung-ch'i shang-tz'u ming-wen yen-shiu.* [Chinese, with a summary in English: Inscribed Bronze Vessels of Yin and Chou Recording the Granting of Benefices.] Australian National, 1972 (Ph.D. in Chinese). 221p. + 20p. English-language summary.

33 CHOI, Mou-chang. *Le paléolithique de la Chine.* [French: The Paleolithic Age of China.] Paris I (Panthéon-Sorbonne), 1973 (Doctorat de 3e cycle en préhistoire). 280p. A copy is available at the Bibliothèque de la Sorbonne, library catalogue no. I 2320-4°.

34 HSÜ, Chin-hsiung. *Scapulimantic Techniques and Periodic Classification.* Toronto, 1974 (Ph.D. in East Asian Studies). iii, 529p. DAI 37, no.12 (June 1977): 7826-A; Order copies directly from the Canadian Theses Division, National Library of Canada at Ottawa; available only in microfiche format. Focuses on oracle bone inscriptions.

35 HUDSON, Dee Travis. *The Holocene Prehistory of Old World Arid Lands: A Research Appraisal.* Arizona State, 1974 (Ph.D. in Anthropology). 444p. DAI 35, no.11 (May 1975): 6864-A; UM 75-10,043. Includes coverage of the Turkestan, Takla-Makan, and Gobi regions of central Asia.

36 LUCHTERHAND, Kubet Emil. *Mid-Pleistocene Hominid Distribution and Adaptation in Eastern Asia.* Chicago, 1974 (Ph.D. in Anthropology). vi, 315p. Order copies from the Photoduplication Department, Joseph Regenstein Library, University of Chicago. Covers sites in China, mainland Southeast Asia, and Java.

ART AND ARCHITECTURE

General and Miscellaneous Studies

See also entry 786 and the sections "Chinese Influence on Foreign Art, Music, and Ideology" (pp.20-21), "Urban and Regional Planning" (p.221) and--within the Appendix-- "Art and Architecture" (pp.223-25).

37 BLECKMAN, Walter Ralph. *Some Dongson Motifs: Their Iconographical Analysis and Identification in Related Cultures.* Pittsburgh, 1972 (Ph.D. in Fine Arts). 414p. DAI 33, no. 8 (Feb. 1973): 4274-75-A; UM 73-5004. This is a study of the art of the first bronze using culture of Southeast Asia (ca.800 B.C.-220 A.D.). It includes information about ancient Chinese culture.

38 ECKE, Betty Tseng Yu-ho. *Emperor Hui Tsung, the Artist: 1082-1136.* New York, 1972 (Ph.D. in Fine Arts). 412p. DAI 34, no.1 (July 1973): 221-A; UM 73-16,562. On Hui Tsung's role as artist, collector, and imperial sponsor of the arts.

39 GOEPPER, Roger. *Shu-p'u. Der Traktat zur Schriftkunst des Sun Kuo-ting.* [German: Shu-p'u: The Treatise on Calligraphy by Sun Kuo-t'ing.] Köln, 1972 (Habilitationsschrift). Published as Shu-p'u...Sun Kuo-t'ing (Wiesbaden: Steiner, 1974. 512p. [Studien zur ostasiatischen schriftkunst, 2]).

40 JOHNSTON, Robert Stewart. *Planning and Architectural Design in China*. Nottingham, 1972 (Ph.D. in Architecture). 330p.

41 KAO, Mayching Margaret. *China's Response to the West in Art: 1898-1937*. Stanford, 1972 (Ph.D. in Art). 390p. DAI 33, no.8 (Feb. 1973): 4276-77-A; UM 73-4529.

42 LINDUFF, Katheryn McAllister. *Tradition, Phase, and Style of Shang and Chou Bronze Vessels*. Pittsburgh, 1972 (Ph.D. in Fine Arts). 258p. DAI 33, no.8 (Feb. 1973): 4277-78-A; UM 73-4154.

43 DOHRENWEND, Doris Joan. *The Human Image in Chinese Art before Buddhism: The Mask*. Harvard, 1973 (Ph.D. in Fine Arts). 446 + 243p. (2 vols.). Available at the Harvard University Archives, Pusey Library, call no.HU 90.10337.20.

44 JULIANO, Annette L. *Teng-hsien: An Important Six Dynasties Tomb*. New York, 1974 (Ph.D. in Fine Arts). 217p. DAI 37, no.3 (Sept. 1976): 1734-35-A; UM 76-21,339. Focuses on the tomb's importance for understanding the period's non-Buddhist pictorial and landscape art.

45 SUN, Shirley Hsiao-ling. *Lu Hsün and the Chinese Woodcut Movement: 1929-1936*. Stanford, 1974 (Ph.D. in Art). 270p. DAI 35, no.10 (Apr. 1975): 6603-04-A; UM 74-27,123. On Lu Hsün's revival of woodblock printing and his efforts to promote an appealing popular art form.

46 BHATTACHARYA, Chhaya. *Studies in the Wooden Objects of the Berlin Central Asian Art Collection*. Freie Universität Berlin, 1975 (Dr., Fachbereich Kunstwissenschaft). 420p.

47 SASAGUCHI, Rei. *The Image of the Contemplating Bodhisattva in Chinese Buddhist Sculpture of the Sixth Century*. Harvard, 1975 (Ph.D. in Fine Arts). 270p. Available at the Harvard University Archives, Pusey Library, call no. HU 90.10847.

48 WONNE, Mirang. *Couleurs et société Han*. [French: Colors and Han Society.] Paris I (Panthéon-Sorbonne), 1975 (Doctorat de 3e cycle en esthétique). 382p. A copy is available at the Bibliothèque de la Sorbonne, library catalogue no.I 3415-4°.

Painting

See also the section within the Appendix entitled "Art and
Architecture" (pp.223-25).

49   CHANG, Cornelius Patrick. *A Study of the Paintings of
      the Water-Moon Kuan-yin*. Columbia, 1971 (Ph.D. in Art
      History and Archaeology). 185p. DAI 32, no.6 (Dec.
      1971): 3178-79-A; UM 72-1286. Focuses on paintings from
      the Sung through Ming periods.

50   CHIN, Ming-ming. *Li Tch'eng, 918-967, peintre chinois du
      Xème siècle, sa vie, son oeuvre et son influence sur le
      développement de l'art du paysage en Chine*. [French: Li
      Ch'êng, 918-967, a Tenth Century Chinese Painter: His
      Life, His Work, and His Influence on the Development of
      Landscape Painting in China.] Paris I (Panthéon-Sor-
      bonne), 1971 (Doctorat de 3ᵉ cycle ès lettres). v, 244p.
      A copy is available at the Bibliothèque de la Sorbonne,
      library catalogue no. I 1559-4°.

51   CLAPP, Anne de Coursey. *Wen Cheng-ming: The Ming Artist
      and Antiquity*. Harvard, 1971 (Ph.D. in Fine Arts). i,
      249 + ii, 170p. + v p., 58 plates (3 vols.). Available
      at the Harvard University Archives, Pusey Library, call
      no.HU 90.9926. Published as Wen Cheng-ming...Antiquity
      (Ascona: Artibus Asiae Publishers, 1975. xii, 102p.
      [Artibus Asiae: Supplementum, 34]).

52   COLEMAN, Earle Jerome. *Philosophy of Painting by Shih-
      T'ao: A Translation and Exposition of His Hua-p'u (Trea-
      tise on the Philosophy of Painting)*. Hawaii, 1971 (Ph.D.
      in Philosophy). 268p. DAI 32, no.9 (Mar. 1972): 5281-A;
      UM 72-10,163. On this contribution to the theory of art
      by Tao-chi (Shih-t'ao), 1641-1717(?).

53   FONG, Mary Helena. *Secular Figure Painting of the T'ang
      Dynasty, A.D. 618-906: Based on Archaeological Finds and
      Sources of Unquestioned Authenticity (The Tun-huang Cave
      Shrines and the Shōsō-in Treasury)*. New York, 1972 (Ph.D.
      in Fine Arts). 519p. DAI 33, no.11 (May 1973): 6254-A;
      UM 73-11,695.

54   RICKERT, Richard Frederick. *Aesthetic Interpreting and
      Describing: Their Functions in Regard to the "Transinter-
      pretive" Art of Kafka and Zen*. North Carolina, 1972
      (Ph.D. in Philosophy). 258p. DAI 33, no.8 (Feb. 1973):
      4480-A; UM 73-4869. Includes a study of "Persimmons," a
      Zen painting of the Sung artist Mu Ch'i.

55   WEINSTEIN, Vicki Frances. *Painting in Yang-chou, 1710-*

1765: Eccentricity or the Literati Tradition? Cornell,
1972 (Ph.D. in History of Art and Archaeology). 448p.
DAI 33, no.3 (Sept. 1972): 1092-93-A; UM 72-23,889.

56 ROSENZWEIG, Daphne Lange. *Court Painters of the K'ang-
hsi Period.* Columbia, 1973 (Ph.D. in Art History and Archaeology). 455p. DAI 37, no.6 (Dec. 1976): 3241-A; UM
76-29,304.

57 SILBERGELD, Jerome Leslie. *Political Symbolism in the
Landscape Painting and Poetry of Kung Hsien (c.1620-1689).*
Stanford, 1974 (Ph.D. in Art). 322p. DAI 35, no.6 (Dec.
1974): 3598-A; UM 74-27,114.

58 WEY, Nancy. *Mu-ch'i and Zen Painting.* Chicago, 1974
(Ph.D. in Art). vii, 235p. Order copies from the Photoduplication Department, Joseph Regenstein Library, University of Chicago. On Mu-ch'i (1177-1239), the leader and
greatest master of the Southern Sung Ch'an movement.

59 LINN, John William. *The Phenomenological Analysis of
Sung Painting.* Georgia, 1975 (Ph.D. in Art). 263p. DAI
36, no.9 (Mar. 1976): 5608-A; UM 76-6419.

60 ROREX, Robert Albright. *Eighteen Songs of a Nomad Flute:
The Story of Ts'ai Wen-chi.* Princeton, 1975 (Ph.D. in
Art and Archaeology). 699p. DAI 36, no.7 (Jan. 1976):
4086-A; UM 76-266. Published as Eighteen Songs of a Nomad Flute: The Story of Lady Wen-chi; A Fourteenth-Century
Handscroll in the Metropolitan Museum of Art. Coauthored
with Wen Fong (New York: Metropolitan Museum of Art, 1974.
1 vol. [unpaged]). Studies important Southern Sung narrative paintings.

61 WILKINSON, Stephen Adams. *Depictions of Su Shih's Prose
Poems on the Red Cliff and the Development of Scholar-Art-
ist Theory and Practice in Sung Times.* Harvard, 1975
(Ph.D. in Fine Arts). ix, 195p. + 96 figures. Available
at the Harvard University Archives, Pusey Library, call
no.HU 90.11088.10.

Pottery and Porcelain

See also entry 1577.

62 PARK, Sook-Hi. *Chinesisches Auftragsporzellan der Osta-
siatischen Handelskompanie in Emden.* [German: The China
Trade Porcelain of the Ostasiatische Handelskompanie in
Emden.] Münster, 1971 (Dr., Fachbereich Philosophie).
Published as Chinesisches...Emden (Aurich: Verlag

Ostfriesische Landschaft, 1973. 55 + 98p. [Abhandlungen und Vorträge zur Geschichte Ostfrieslands, 55]). On the Asiatische Compagnie in Emden nach Canton und China.

63   HUBER, Louisa Galt Fitzgerald. *The Traditions of Chinese Neolithic Pottery.* Harvard, 1974 (Ph.D. in Fine Arts). xvi, 311p. + 106p. of photographic plates. Available at the Harvard University Archives, Pusey Library, call no. HU 90.10565.20.

CHINA AND CHINESE CIVILIZATION ABROAD

China as a Subject of Academic Study
among Foreigners

In the United States

--On the Secondary School Level--

See also entry 1590.

64   DENNIS, Donald Allen. *A Creative Approach to Involvement in Non-Western Culture by Secondary School Students.* Michigan State, 1971 (Ph.D. in Education). 165p. DAI 32, no.6 (Dec. 1971): 3002-A; UM 71-31,187. Does not deal with any specific culture but may be of particular interest to teachers of East Asian Studies.

65   WONG, Sheh. *China in High School Social Studies Textbooks.* Northwestern, 1971 (Ph.D. in Social Studies Education). 131p. DAI 32, no.6 (Dec. 1971): 2930-A; UM 71-30,989. Examines the quantitative and qualitative treatment of China in American textbooks.

66   DAVIS, Daniel Frederick. *The Role of East Asian Studies in American Secondary Education: An Evaluative and Comparative Conceptual Approach.* Ohio State, 1972 (Ph.D. in Education). 236p. DAI 33, no.4 (Oct. 1972): 1412-A; UM 72-26,995.

67   BARLOW, Janelle Mary Schlimgen. *The Images of the Chinese, Japanese and Koreans in American Secondary School World History Textbooks, 1900-1970.* California (Berkeley), 1973 (Ph.D. in Education). ii, 246p. Order copies from the Library Photographic Service, General Library, University of California at Berkeley.

68   FRANK, Dwayne Irving. *The Attitudes of High School United States History Teachers toward the Treatment of Oriental-*

Americans and the Far East in United States History Textbooks. Idaho, 1973 (Ed.D. in Secondary Education). 163p. DAI 34, no.11 (May 1974): 7071-72-A; UM 74-11,771.

69 WILK, Robert M. *Teaching Non-Western Studies in Secondary School: An In-Service Strategy.* Massachusetts, 1973 (Ed.D. in Education). 186p. DAI 34, no.10 (Apr. 1974): 6280-A; UM 74-8650. Includes non-Western area studies in Massachusetts high schools.

70 ABRAHAM, Timothy Joseph. *Curricular Change: A Study of the Relationship between a University and Three Selected Secondary Schools Teaching East Asian Studies.* Columbia (Teachers College), 1974 (Ed.D. in Curriculum and Teaching). 584p. DAI 35, no.2 (Aug. 1974): 792-A; UM 74-18,709. Deals with Seton Hall University and with high schools in New Jersey, New York and Ohio.

71 KAMBAYASHI, Kikuko. *The Expansion of Treatments of Japan in High School Textbooks in American History, 1951-1972.* Michigan, 1974 (Ph.D. in Education). 276p. DAI 36, no.3 (Sept. 1975): 1344-A; UM 75-20,378. Includes textbook treatment of the Manchurian Incident and Japanese expansion into China as an issue in U.S.-Japanese relations.

72 SCHMIDT, Kenneth Charles. *The Treatment of East Asia in World History Textbooks.* Syracuse, 1974 (Ph.D. in Cultural Foundations of Education). 164p. DAI 36, no.10 (Apr. 1976): 6519-A; UM 76-7937.

73 YUN, Sei Chul. *An Analysis of Modernization in China (1842-1949) for Teaching Secondary Social Studies.* Northwestern, 1974 (Ph.D. in Social Science Education). 304p. DAI 35, no.6 (Dec. 1974): 3547-A; UM 74-28,786. Yun sought to interpret the problems of China's modernization and to determine how to present this in a document that high school teachers could use when assessing the adequacy of textbook chapters on China.

74 SCHNIEDEWIND, Nancy. *A Model Integrating Personal and Social Change in Teacher Education: Its Implementation in a Racism and Sexism Training Program.* Massachusetts, 1975 (Ed.D. in Teacher Education). 354p. DAI 36, no.9 (Mar. 1976): 6025-26-A; UM 76-5395. An examination of educational programs arising out of the Cultural Revolution in China was included within this model which Schniedewind designed for classroom use in the United States.

--On the University and Community College Level--

See also entries 70, 1009, and 1591.

75 BATNAG, Beatrice DeKang. *The Teaching of Introductory Asian Civilization/History Courses in the Undergraduate Schools of American Colleges and Universities, 1969-1970.* Columbia (Teachers College), 1971 (Ed.D.). 350p. DAI 32, no.10 (Apr. 1972): 5560-A; UM 72-12,798.

76 DE ROCHER, James Edward, Jr. *An Analysis of Certain Factors of Divergent and Convergent Production as Related to Achievement in Military Intensive Language Courses.* American, 1972 (Ph.D. in Education). 162p. DAI 33, no.8 (Feb. 1973): 4171-A; UM 73-4658.

77 HOOPER, Paul Franklin. *A History of Internationalism in Hawaii between 1900 and 1940.* Hawaii, 1972 (Ph.D. in American Studies). 298p. DAI 33, no.9 (Mar. 1973): 5091-A; UM 73-5273. Focuses in part on the Institute of Pacific Relations and on American academic interest in China.

78 DRYSDALE, Thomas Townsend. *A Status Study of Non-Western Curricular Offerings at the Undergraduate Level within the Consortium of Universities of the Washington Metropolitan Area in 1973.* George Washington, 1973 (Ed.D.). 230p. DAI 35, no.5 (Nov. 1974): 2643-A; UM 74-16,739. Includes East Asian Studies.

79 KUKLIS, Robert Darryle. *General Education and the Social Science at Amherst College: A Study of Inquiry and Learning.* Columbia (Teachers College), 1973 (Ed.D.). 445p. DAI 34, no.2 (Aug. 1973): 593-A; UM 73-19,349. Includes a case study of a course on modernization in China.

80 BIGGERS, Earl Robert Francis. *A Study of Ethnocentrism among Community College Transfer Students Enrolled in Asian Studies and Non-Asian Studies Courses at Five Illinois Public Community Colleges.* Northern Illinois, 1974 (Ed.D.). 94p. DAI 35, no.12 (June 1975): 7604-A; UM 75-13,154.

81 COTTLE, Ronald Eastwood. *Religious Studies in California Public Higher Education with Special Reference to Community Colleges.* Southern California, 1974 (Ed.D.). 319p. DAI 34, no.10 (Apr. 1974): 6407-08-A; UM 74-9063. Includes the study of Chinese religion in Californian schools.

82 HOLMES, David Robert. *A Comparative Study of Student Learning Style in Non-Traditional and Traditional*

Education. Denver, 1974 (Ph.D. in Education). 296p.
DAI 35, no.7 (Jan. 1975): 4190-A; UM 75-1871. Includes a
study of the Sung China component of the University of
Denver's Humanities Program.

83 ARUM, Stephen Marshall. *Early Stages of Foreign Language
and Area Studies in the U.S.: 1915-1941.* Columbia (Teachers College), 1975 (Ed.D. in Higher and Adult Education).
678p. DAI 37, no.3 (Sept. 1976): 1421-A; UM 76-20,864.
Includes American studies of China.

84 WOOD, Diana Marston. *Alienated Intellectuals in China:
1500-1968. A College Curriculum.* Carnegie-Mellon, 1975
(D.A. in History). 340p. DAI 36, no.9 (Mar. 1976):
6235-A; UM 76-638. An experimental, introductory course
prepared for American college students.

In Other Countries

See also entry 1589.

85 O'COLLINS, Ellen Maev. *Policy Formulation in Australian
Education: The Establishment of the Advisory Committee on
the Teaching of Asian Languages and Cultures.* Columbia,
1972 (D.S.W.). 268p. DAI 33, no.1 (July 1972): 405-06-A;
UM 72-20,058. Includes the teaching of Chinese in Australia.

86 GATES, Robert Michael. *Soviet Sinology: An Untapped
Source for Kremlin Views and Disputes Relating to Contemporary Events in China.* Georgetown, 1974 (Ph.D. in History). 306p. DAI 35, no.4 (Oct. 1974): 2171-A; UM
74-21,652.

87 TAM, Yue-him. *In Search of the Oriental Past: The Life
and Thought of Naitō Konan (1866-1934).* Princeton, 1975
(Ph.D. in East Asian Studies). 361p. DAI 37, no.2 (Aug.
1976): 1151-52-A; UM 76-18,488. Naitō was an influential
Sinologist in Japan who founded the Kyoto School of Sinology.

China in Foreign Literary Works

American and British

See also entries 1013 and 1076.

88 LEVITIN, Alexis Anthony. *A Study in Revision: W. H. Auden's "A Voyage" and "Sonnets from China".* Columbia, 1971

15

(Ph.D. in English and Comparative Literature).   269p.
DAI 35, no.7 (Jan. 1975): 4532-33-A; UM 74-29,617.   Auden's
two groups of poems deal with his trip to war-torn China
of the late 1930's.

89   MOTSCH, Monika. *Ezra Pound und China.* [German: Ezra
Pound and China.] Heidelberg, 1971 (Dr., Neuphilologische
Fakultät). Published as Ezra...China (Heidelberg: Winter,
1976. 180p. [Heidelberger Forschungen; H.17]).

90   COHEN, Derek Michael. *Nicholas Rowe's The Biter: A Literary and Historical Study with an Edition.* New York, 1972
(Ph.D. in English). 192p. DAI 33, no.11 (May 1973):
6347-A; UM 73-11,681. Includes Rowe's interest in and use
of Chinese customs and references in this comic drama (produced in 1705).

91   WAND, David Happell Hsin-fu. *Cathay Revisited: The Chinese
Tradition in the Poetry of Ezra Pound and Gary Snyder.*
Southern California, 1972 (Ph.D. in Comparative Literature). 212p. DAI 33, no.9 (Mar. 1973): 5205-06-A; UM
73-787.

92   JUSTIN, Jeffrey Arthur. *Unknown Land Poetry: Walt Whit-
man, Robert Bly, and Gary Snyder.* Michigan, 1973 (Ph.D.
in English Language and Literature). 189p. DAI 35, no.1
(July 1974): 457-58-A; UM 74-15,770. Includes a discussion of their respective links with Taoism.

93   SAKURAI, Emiko. *The Oriental Tradition in the Poetry of
Kenneth Rexroth.* Alabama, 1973 (Ph.D. in English). 229p.
DAI 34, no.5 (Nov. 1973): 2577-78-A; UM 73-27,319. Includes the influence of Chinese history, art, philosophy,
literature, mythology and drama upon the poetry of this
20th century American poet.

94   CLARKSON, William Ellis. *A Rage for Order: The Development
of Ezra Pound's Poetics and Politics, 1910-1945.* Virginia,
1974 (Ph.D. in English). 184p. DAI 35, no.8 (Feb. 1975):
5391-A; UM 75-2062. Deals extensively with the Chinese influence upon his writing.

95   KNIPPS, Charles Christopher. *Types of Orientalism in
Eighteenth-Century England.* California (Berkeley), 1974
(Ph.D. in Comparative Literature). 346p. DAI 35, no.5
(Nov. 1974): 2944-45-A; UM 74-24,674. Includes a study of
Oliver Goldsmith's book The Citizen of the World, or,
Letters from a Chinese Philosopher, Residing in London, to
His Friends in the East (published in London).

97 OLSSON, Theodore Charles Alexander. *Usura: Economics and Ethics in the Cantos of Ezra Pound*. California (Santa Barbara), 1974 (Ph.D. in English). 376p. DAI 35, no.6 (Dec. 1974): 3758-59-A; UM 74-27,707. Includes Pound's literary use of Confucian themes.

97 CARMICHAEL, Frank Charles, Jr. *Ezra Pound, Romanticism, and Explanation*. South Carolina, 1975 (Ph.D. in English). 264p. DAI 36, no.11 (May 1976): 7418-19-A; UM 76-10,446. One section examines the influence of Chinese thought and literature upon Ezra Pound.

98 YU, Yuh-chao. *Pearl S. Buck's Fiction: A Cross-Cultural Interpretation*. Hawaii, 1975 (Ph.D. in American Studies). xxv, 293p. Order copies from the Interlibrary Loan Department, University of Hawaii Library. Largely on China.

French

See also entry 1592.

99 GELBER, Lynne Levick. *The Art Criticism of Paul Claudel*. Colorado, 1971 (Ph.D. in French). 193p. DAI 32, no.4 (Oct. 1971): 2088-89-A; UM 71-25,823. Includes this French writer's interests in China and Japan.

100 PARK, Young-hai. *L'Orphelin de la Chine de Voltaire: étude d'ensemble*. [French: Voltaire's Orphelin de la Chine: A Comprehensive Study.] Paris IV (Paris-Sorbonne), 1971 (Doctorat de 3e cycle ès lettres). 381p. A copy is available at the Bibliothèque de la Sorbonne, library catalogue no. I 1667-4°. On a 3-act play by Voltaire (1694-1778) set in China and involving Genghis Khan.

101 BIEN, Gloria. *Victor Segalen's Knowledge of Chinese Culture*. [Portions of the text in French] Washington (Seattle), 1973 (Ph.D. in Comparative Literature). 162p. DAI 34, no.8 (Feb. 1974): 5091-A; UM 74-2242. Studies the Chinese sources which inspired and influenced the literary work of Victor Segalen (1878-1919), a poet, Sinologist, archaeologist, and physician.

102 HUE, Bernard. *Littératures et arts de l'Orient dans l'oeuvre de Claudel*. [French: Eastern literature and Art in the Work of Claudel.] Haute Bretagne, 1973. 595p. DAI 37, no.1 (Autumn 1976): Vol.C--entry no.1/115c. Includes the interest of Paul Claudel (1868-1955), a French poet and dramatist, in Chinese literature and religion. (See entry 1592 for a related thesis by Bernard Hue.)

103   LEKI, Ilona Nina. *The Travel Literature of Henri Michaux.*
       Illinois, 1974 (Ph.D. in French). 238p. DAI 35, no.11
       (May 1975): 7312-13-A; UM 75-11,724. Includes the prose
       works of this French intellectual (1899-1971) based on
       his 1930 trip to China, Southeast Asia and India.

104   SISHUPAL, Karthy. *L'Asie dans l'oeuvre d'André Malraux.*
       [French: Asia in the Writings of André Malraux.] Paris
       III (Sorbonne Nouvelle), 1974 (Doctorat de 3e cycle en
       littérature française). 317p. A copy is available at
       the Bibliothèque de la Sorbonne. Includes this author
       and politician's literary works about China and Hong Kong
       during the 1920s.

105   STEINSIECK, Wolf. *Die Funktion der Reise- und Brieflitera-*
       tur in der Aufklärung untersucht am Beispiel der "Lettres
       Chinoises" des Marquis d'Argens. [German: The Function
       of Travel Books and Letters during the Age of Enlighten-
       ment Exemplified by the Case of the Lettres chinoises of
       the Marquis d'Argens (1704-1771).] Technische Hochschule
       Aachen, 1974 (Dr., Philosophische Fakultät). Published
       as Die Funktion...d'Argens (Aachen: I.A. Mayer, 1975.
       216p.). On the Lettres chinoises, ou Correspondance phi-
       losophique, historique et critique, entre un chinois
       voyageur à Paris et ses correspondans à la Chine...(La
       Haye, 1739-40).

                         German and Austrian

106   BERG-PAN, Renata. *The Chinese Influence on the Drama-*
       turgy of Bertolt Brecht. Harvard, 1971 (Ph.D. in Ger-
       manic Languages and Literatures). iv, 218p. Available
       at the Harvard University Archives, Pusey Library, call
       no.HU 90.9910.10. On Bertolt Brecht (1898-1956), German
       playwright and poet.

107   MISTRY, Freny. *Hugo von Hofmannsthal: A Study of His*
       Relation to East Asia and Its Significance for His De-
       velopment. Toronto, 1971 (Ph.D. in German). viii, 428p.
       DAI 34, no.8 (Feb. 1974): 5194-A; Order copies directly
       from the Canadian Theses Division, National Library of
       Canada at Ottawa; available only in microfiche format.
       On this Austrian poet and playwright's interest in China
       and Japan, especially during the early 1900s.

108   GRIMES, James Milton. *The Nature of Hesse's Glass Bead*
       Game and Its Function in the Novel Das Glasperlenspiel.
       [Portions of text in German.] Vanderbilt, 1972 (Ph.D.

in German). 204p. DAI 33, no.8 (Feb. 1973): 4413-A; UM
73-1619. Chapter 3 explores the analogy between the Bead
Game and I Ching.

109 GUIRGUIS, Fawzy D. *Bild und Funktion des Orients in
Werken der deutschen Literatur des 17. und 18. Jahrhun-
derts*. [German: Image and Function of the Orient in Ger-
man Literary Works of the 17th and 18th Centuries.] Freie
Universität Berlin, 1972 (Dr., Fachbereich Germanistik).
Published as Bild...Jahrhunderts (Berlin, 1972. 358p.).
Focuses on the Middle East but also includes coverage of
China.

110 LEE, Inn-Ung. *Ostasiatische Anschauungen im Werk Hermann
Hesses*. [German: East Asian Concepts in the Writings of
Hermann Hesse.] Würzburg, 1972 (Dr., Philosophische
Fakultät). Published as Ostasiatische...Hesses (Würzburg,
1972. iv, 269p.). Hermann Hesse (1877-1962), German nov-
elist and Nobel laureate who was interested in China.

111 FUSSY, Herbert. *Die neuere deutsche Lyrik und Ostasien*.
[German: Modern German Lyric Poetry and East Asia.] Graz,
1974 (Dr., Philosophische Fakultät). 364p.

112 CHI, Ursula K. *Die chinesischen Einflüsse in Hermann
Hesse's Glasperlenspiel*. [German: The Chinese Influences
in Hermann Hesse's Glassbead Game.] Washington (Seattle),
1975 (Ph.D. in Germanics). 271p. DAI 37, no.2 (Aug.
1976): 997-A; UM 76-17,429. Published as Die Weisheit
Chinas und Das Glasperlenspiel (Frankfurt a.M.: Suhrkamp,
1976. 235p.).

113 LAZDA, Irene Galins. *Brecht's Concept of Wisdom and Its
Related Attitude with Special Reference to Mo-tzu and
Lao-tzu*. Pittsburgh, 1975 (Ph.D. in Germanic Languages
and Literature). 172p. DAI 36, no.10 (Apr. 1976):
6722-A; UM 76-8807. Analyzes the influence of Chinese
philosophy on the literary works of Bertolt Brecht (1898-
1956).

Other European

See also entry 1584.

114 MAGGS, Barbara Widenor. *China in the Literature of
Eighteenth-Century Russia*. Illinois, 1973 (Ph.D. in
Comparative Literature). 380p. DAI 34, no.9 (Mar. 1974):
5919-20-A; UM 74-5629. Compares and contrasts the images
that Russian diplomats, missionaries and intellectuals
had of China.

115   TOM, Henry Yuk Kong. *The Wonderful Voyage: Chivalric and Moral Asia in the Imagination of Sixteenth-Century Italy, Spain, and Portugal*. Chicago, 1975 (Ph.D. in History). v, 276p. DAI 36, no.7 (Jan. 1976): 4700-01-A; Order copies from the Photoduplication Department, Joseph Regenstein Library, University of Chicago. Includes literary accounts and views of China.

Japanese

116   CHENG, Ching-mao. *Nagai Kafū and Chinese Tradition*. Princeton, 1971 (Ph.D. in East Asian Studies). 262p. DAI 32, no.4 (Oct. 1971): 2076-A; UM 71-23,350. Investigates the relationship of this major Japanese author (1879-1959) with Chinese tradition (especially Confucian concepts and Chinese literature).

117   SESAR, Carl Gordon. *Nō Drama and Chinese Literature*. Columbia, 1971 (Ph.D. in East Asian Languages and Cultures). 233p. DAI 35, no.2 (Aug. 1974): 1060-61-A; UM 74-17,905. Examines the use of Chinese materials in the writing and performance of Japanese Noh plays.

Chinese Influence on Foreign Art, Music, and Ideology

See also entries 377, 429, 1139, 1141, 1545, 1586, and 1593.

118   KANG, Thomas Hosuck. *The Making of Confucian Societies in Tokugawa Japan and Yi Korea: A Comparative Analysis of the Behavior Patterns in Accepting the Foreign Ideology, Neo-Confucianism*. American, 1971 (Ph.D. in International Studies). 346p. DAI 32, no.4 (Oct. 1971): 2155-56-A; UM 71-25,284.

119   REAVES, R. B., Jr. *Sir William Chambers: A Study of Georgian Taste*. Wisconsin, 1971 (Ph.D. in English). 321p. DAI 32, no.8 (Feb. 1972): 4576-A; UM 72-437. Includes the interest that this 18th century English architectural scholar had in Chinese gardening and architecture.

120   SCHLOTTERBACK, Thomas. *The Basis for Chinese Influence in American Art, 1784-1850*. Iowa, 1972 (Ph.D. in Art History). 502p. DAI 33, no.4 (Oct. 1972): 1617-A; UM 72-26,733.

121   REICHEL, Friedrich. *Die Chinoiserie in Sachsen*. [German:

Chinoiserie in Saxony.] Halle-Wittenberg, 1973 (Dr.,
Philosophische Fakultät). 255p.

122 al-GAILANI, 'Abd Al-Raḥmān Maḥmūd. *The Origins of Islamic Art and the Role of China.* Edinburgh, 1974 (Ph.D. in
Arts). xix, 422p. On the existence of motifs and arti-
facts of Chinese origin in Islamic paintings, 'Abbasid
pottery and minarets, and Kufic inscriptions.

123 CHI, Chul Young. *The Influence of Chinese Music on Korean
Music.* Northern Colorado, 1975 (Ed.D. in Curriculum and
Instruction). 171p. DAI 36, no.2 (Aug. 1975): 589-90-A;
UM 75-16,833.

Foreign Accounts, Knowledge, and Views of China

See also entries 366, 368, 438, 656, 678, 1328, 1416, 1477,
1585, and 1587. For academic studies of China, *see* the section "China as a Subject of Academic Study among Foreigners"
(pp.12-15).

124 VAN HUNG MAI [MAI, Van-hung]. *Malebranche à la recherche
de l'absolu chez les philosophes chinois.* [French: Nicolas
de Malebranche (1638-1715) in Search of the Absolute among
the Chinese Philosophers.] Lyon II, 1971 (Doctorat de 3e
cycle ès lettres). 242p.

125 NINOMIYA, Kazuo Z. *A View of the Outside World during
Tokugawa Japan: An Analysis of Reports of Travel by Cast-
aways, 1636 to 1856.* Washington (Seattle), 1972 (Ph.D. in
Geography). 262p. DAI 33, no.8 (Feb. 1973): 3708-09-B;
UM 73-3764. Includes the reports of Japanese who visited
the Chinese mainland and Taiwan.

126 NITTI, John Joseph. *An Edition, Study and Vocabulary of
the Unique Aragonese Book of Marco Polo, Translated by
Juan Fernández de Heredia.* Wisconsin, 1972 (Ph.D. in
Spanish and Portugese). 1945p. DAI 33, no.8 (Feb. 1973):
4357-A; UM 72-31,550.

127 SHBOUL, Ahmad Mohamad Hadi. *Al-Mas'ūdī, with Special Reference to His Treatment of Non-Muslim History and Religion.*
London, 1972 (Ph.D. in Arts, Royal Holloway College).
419p. Includes a discussion of this Moslem traveller's
writings about China during the 10th century.

128 SONG, Du-Yul. *Die Bedeutung der asiatischen Welt bei
Hegel, Marx und Max Weber.* [German: The Importance of the
Asiatic World in the Works of Hegel, Marx and Max Weber.]
Frankfurt, 1972 (Dr., Fachbereich Philosophie). Published

as Die Bedeutung...Weber (Frankfurt, 1972. 196p.).
Focuses entirely on their views of and knowledge about
China and India.

129 WALRAVENS, Hartmut. *Die Deutschland-Kenntnisse der
     Chinesen (bis 1870). Nebst einem Exkurs über die Dar-
     stellung fremder Tiere im K'un-yü t'u-shuo des P. Verbiest.*
     [German: What the Chinese Knew about Germany (until 1870),
     together with an Excursus on the Representation of Out-
     landish Animals in the K'un-yü t'u-shuo of Ferdinand
     Verbiest (1623-1688).] Köln, 1972 (Dr., Philosophische
     Fakultät). Published as Die Deutschland...Verbiest (Köln,
     1972. iii, 277p.).

130 TU, Henry Yuanli. *A Study of American Press Coverage on
     the Rural People's Communes in Communist China.* Fordham,
     1973 (Ph.D. in Political Science). 301p. DAI 34, no.8
     (Feb. 1974): 5277-78-A; UM 74-2767. On press coverage
     for the period August 1958-April 1971.

131 ZIMMERMANN, Fritz. *John Clarks Werk über die Schiffs-
     medizin "Observations on the Diseases in Long Voyages to
     Hot Countries and Particularly on Those Which Prevail in
     the East Indies" 1773.* [German: John Clark's Work on
     Naval Medicine Entitled Observations on the Diseases in
     Long Voyages to Hot Countries and Particularly on Those
     Which Prevail in the East Indies, 1773.] Düsseldorf,
     1973 (Dr., Medizinische Fakultät). 133p. Includes
     Clark's account of his visits to Macao and southern China.

132 LA HAYE, Yves de. *La pharmacie chinoise: "information"
     et langage dans la presse quotidienne française.* [French:
     Chinese Pharmacy: "Information" and Language in the French
     Daily Press.] Paris V (René Descartes), 1974 (Doctorat
     de 3ᵉ cycle ès Lettres). A copy is available at the
     Bibliothèque de la Sorbonne.

133 NGUYEN THANH HUNG. *Zur Theorie der vorkapitalistischen
     Produktionsweisen bei K. Marx und F. Engels. Dargestellt
     anhand der Probleme der "asiatischen Produktionsweise".*
     [German: Towards the Theory of the Pre-Capitalist Means
     of Production in the Writings of Karl Marx and Friedrich
     Engels: Shown in Their Treatment of the Problems of the
     "Asiatic Means of Production".] Frankfurt, 1974 (Dr.,
     Fachbereich Gesellschaftswissenschaft). Published as Zur
     Theorie...Produktionsweise (Gaiganz: Politladen-Verlags-
     GmbH, 1975. 119p.). Deals in part with ancient China.

134 MENDE, Gunter S. *The Image of China in Germany, 1919-
     1939.* California (Irvine), 1975 (Ph.D. in History).
     310p. DAI 36, no.10 (Apr. 1976): 6866-A; UM 76-7242.

Based on a study of German middle-class newspapers.

135 TOBEL, Urs van. *China im Spiegel der britischen Presse 1896-1900.* [German: China Reflected in the British Press, 1896-1900.] Zürich, 1975 (Dr., Philosophische Fakultät I). vi, 243p.

DEMOGRAPHY, POPULATION, AND FAMILY PLANNING

See also entries 209, 1569, 1594, and 1595.

136 CHANG, Kung-kong. *A Decision Making System for a Family Planning Program: A Case Study of Taiwan.* North Carolina, 1971 (Dr.P.H.). 281p. DAI 32, no.6 (Dec. 1971): 3465-66-B; UM 71-30,620.

137 PIOTROW, Phyllis Tilson. *Population, Politics and Policy: A Study of the Development of United States Government Policy toward the Population Problem with Special Reference to the Developing Countries, 1959-1969.* Johns Hopkins, 1971 (Ph.D. in Political Science). 647p. DAI 34, no.8 (Feb. 1974): 5273-A; UM 73-31,232. Published as World Population Crisis: The United States Response (New York: Praeger, 1973. xxiii, 276p. [Law and population book series, 4] [Praeger special studies in international economics and development]). Deals in part with the People's Republic of China and the Republic of China.

138 RAO, Sethuramaiah Lakshminarayana N. *Age Distribution and Life Table Development: A Case Study of Selected Asian Countries.* Pennsylvania, 1971 (Ph.D. in Demography). 234p. DAI 32, no.12 (June 1972): 7105-A; UM 72-17,413. Includes Hong Kong, the Republic of China, and the largely Chinese-inhabited Republic of Singapore.

139 RUTSTEIN, Shea Oscar. *The Influence of Child Mortality on Fertility in Taiwan: A Study Based on Sample Surveys Conducted in 1967 and 1969.* Michigan, 1971 (Ph.D. in Economics). 238p. DAI 33, no.5 (Nov. 1972): 1931-A; UM 72-29,186.

140 WANG, I-shou. *Chinese Migration and Population Change in Manchuria, 1900-1940.* Minnesota, 1971 (Ph.D. in Geography). 243p. DAI 32, no.11 (May 1972): 6468-69-B; UM 72-14,394.

141 ARNOLD, Fred Sidney. *A Model Relating Education to*

Fertility in Taiwan. Michigan, 1972 (Ph.D. in Economics). 369p. DAI 33, no.9 (Mar. 1973): 4618-A; UM 73-6776.

142 BHATTACHARYYA, Amit Kumar. *Inequality as a Factor in the Theory of Demographic Transition*. Brown, 1972 (Ph.D. in Sociology). 178p. DAI 33, no.12 (June 1973): 7031-A; UM 73-14,547. Includes survey data from Taiwan.

143 HIDAY, Virginia Marie Aldigé. *Land Tenure and Population: A Study of the Effects of Land Tenure Structure on Population Growth and Distribution*. North Carolina, 1973 (Ph.D. in Sociology). 229p. DAI 35, no.1 (July 1974): 582-A; UM 74-15,346. Covers 24 countries including the Republic of China.

144 KOO, Helen Ping-ching [Mrs. Richard Billsborrow]. *Use of Induced Abortion and Contraception in Taiwan: A Multivariate Analysis*. Michigan, 1973 (Dr. P.H.). 301p. DAI 34, no.11 (May 1974): 7358-A; UM 74-11,216.

145 WILLIAMSON, Nancy Elizabeth. *Preference for Sons around the World*. Harvard, 1973 (Ph.D. in Sociology). 363p. DAI 34, no.2 (Aug. 1973): 880-81-A; UM 73-18,223. Published as Sons or Daughters: A Cross-Cultural Survey of Parental Preferences (Beverly Hills, Calif.: Sage Publications, 1976. 207p. [Sage library of social research, 31]). Includes a case study of Taiwanese families in Kungliao and Hsinchuang.

146 ANDERSON, John Ellis. *Areal Variation in Fertility Trends in Taiwan, 1952-1970: Diffusion or Development Process*. Michigan, 1974 (Ph.D. in Sociology). 218p. DAI 35, no.5 (Nov. 1974): 3137-38-A; UM 74-25,136.

147 AVERY, Roger Christopher. *The Age Pattern of Fertility and the Demographic Transition*. California (Berkeley), 1974 (Ph.D. in Demography). xv, 595p. Order copies from the Library Photographic Service, General Library, University of California at Berkeley. Focuses on the Republic of China.

148 BEDWANY, Therese Labib. *The Status of Women and Population Control: The Relationship of Gross Reproduction Rate and Selected Indicators of the Status of Women in Developed and Developing Countries*. Michigan State, 1974 (Ph.D. in Family and Child Sciences). 190p. DAI 35, no.11 (May 1975): 7417-A; UM 75-7113. Includes women in the Republic of China.

149 CHEN, Hsiao-chang. *An Analysis of the Field Workers' Performance in Recruiting IUD Acceptors in Taiwan*. Michigan, 1974 (Ph.D. in Sociology). 218p. DAI 35, no.11 (May 1975): 7418-A; UM 75-10,146.

150 KULKARNI, Purushottam Madhav. *On Populations with Chang-
     ing Fertility and Mortality.* Colorado State, 1974 (Ph.D.
     in Statistics). 112p. DAI 36, no.1 (July 1975): 316-B;
     UM 75-14,663. Studies the Republic of China and 3 other
     countries.

151 CERNADA, George Peter. *Basic Beliefs about Human Life
     Relating to Ethical Judgments Family Planning Field
     Workers Make about Induced Abortion: Taiwan, 1973.* Cali-
     fornia (Berkeley), 1975 (Dr.P.H.). 132p. DAI 37, no.1
     (July 1976): 140-41-A; UM 76-15,076.

ECONOMY (since 1949)

People's Republic of China

General and Miscellaneous Studies

See also entries 1314 and 1610.

152 CHOW, Chuen-tyi. *China's Internal Transport Problem:
     The Case of the Railways' First Century, 1866-1966.*
     Michigan State, 1972 (Ph.D. in Geography). 340p. DAI 33,
     no.9 (Mar. 1973): 4331-32-B; UM 73-5345.

153 SNEAD, William George. *An Economic Policy Model for the
     Urban People's Commune Movement in the People's Republic
     of China, 1958-1961.* California (Berkeley), 1972 (Ph.D.
     in Economics). x, 491p. Order copies from the Library
     Photograph Service, General Library, University of Cali-
     fornia at Berkeley.

154 UH, Zu-schon. *Die wirtschaftlichen Verflechtungen Ostas-
     iens in der jüngeren Vergangenheit und Gegenwart.* [German:
     The Economic Relationships of East Asia in the Recent Past
     and at the Present Time.] Technische Universität Braun-
     schweig, 1972 (Dr., Philosophische und Sozialwissenschaft-
     liche Fakultät). iii, 141p.

155 STOLZ, Günter. *Sozialistisch orientierte Planwirtschaft,
     dargestellt am Beispiel Chinas.* [German: Socialist Ori-
     ented Planned Economy Shown through the Example of China.]
     Hochschule für Welthandel (Wien), 1973 (Dr.).

156 ROLL, Charles Robert, Jr. *The Distribution of Rural In-
     comes in China: A Comparison of the 1930s and the 1950s.*
     Harvard, 1975 (Ph.D. in Economics). vii, 223p. Available
     at the Harvard University Archives, Pusey Library, call
     no.HU 90.10840.20.

157   ZEYLSTRA, Willem Gustaaf. *Aid or Development: The Rele-
      vance of Development Aid to Problems of Developing Coun-
      tries.* Amsterdam, 1975 (Dr.). Published as Aid...Coun-
      tries (Leiden: A.W. Sijthoff, 1975. xviii, 268p.). In-
      cludes some information on pre-1949 China and on the Peo-
      ple's Republic of China.

                              Agriculture

See also entries 130, 360, 1349, 1363, and--within the Appen-
dix--the section entitled "Economy (since 1949)" (pp.227-29).

158   LIPPIT, Victor David. *Land Reform in China: The Contri-
      bution of Institutional Change to Financing Economic De-
      velopment.* Yale, 1971 (Ph.D. in Economics). 186p.
      DAI 32, no.12 (June 1972): 6627-28-A; UM 72-16,672. Pub-
      lished as Land Reform and Economic Development in China:
      A Study of Institutional Change and Development Finance
      (White Plains, N.Y.: International Arts and Sciences
      Press, 1974. xi, 183p.). On land reform in the People's
      Republic of China during the 1950s.

159   WANG, Wen-tien. *Die Transformation der Produktions-
      verhältnisse in der chinesischen Landwirtschaft und die
      Diskussion innerhalb der KPCh 1921-1957.* [German: The
      Transformation of the Conditions of Chinese Agricultural
      Production and Its Discussion within the Chinese Commu-
      nist Party, 1921-1957.] Marburg, 1971 (Dr., Philosophi-
      sche Fakultät). viii, 271p.

160   DENNY, David Ladd. *Rural Policies and the Distribution
      of Agricultural Products in China: 1950-1959.* Michigan,
      1972 (Ph.D. in Economics). 422p. DAI 33, no.5 (Nov.
      1972): 1923-A; UM 72-29,029.

161   SCHWEIZER, Heinrich. *Sozialistische Agrartheorie und
      -praxis (Sowjetunion und China) und ihre Relevanz für
      Entwicklungsländer.* [German: Socialist Agrarian Theory
      and Practice (U.S.S.R. and China) and Its Relevance for
      Developing Nations.] Basel, 1972 (Dr. der Staatswissen-
      schaften). Published as Sozialistische Agrartheorie und
      Landwirtschaftspolitik in China und der Sowjetunion. Ein
      Modell für Entwicklungsländer? (Bern & Frankfurt a.M.:
      Lang, 1972. 266p.).

162   ABDULLATIF, Tarik. *Ziele, Prozesse und Auswirkungen der
      Ägrarreformen in Kuba, der Volksrepublik China und Ägypten;
      eine Untersuchung auf der Basis des Tuma'schen Ansatzes
      zu einer Agrarreformtheorie.* [German: Objectives, Pro-
      cedures and Consequences of Agrarian Reform in Cuba, the

People's Republic of China and Egypt: An Investigation on the Basis of Elias H. Tuma's Attempts at a Theory of Agrarian Reform.] Göttingen, 1973 (Dr., Landwirtschaftliche Fakultät). Published as Ziele...Agrarreformtheorie (Göttingen, 1973. vii, 371p.).

163   BROWN, Shannon Rafter. *A Comparative Study of Collective Farming in Russia and China.* California (Berkeley), 1974 (Ph.D. in Economics). vii, 245p. Order copies from the Library Photographic Service, General Library, University of California at Berkeley.

164   NICKUM, James Edward. *A Collective Approach to Water Resources Development: The Chinese Commune System, 1962-1972.* California (Berkeley), 1974 (Ph.D. in Economics). i, 344 + 154p. Order copies from the Library Photographic Service, General Library, University of California at Berkeley. Related publication by the author: Hydraulic Engineering and Water Resources in the People's Republic of China (Stanford: U.S.-China Relations Program, Stanford University, 1974. 122p.).

165   SANDERATNE, Nimal Ebenezer Herat. *The Political Economy of Asian Agrarian Reform: A Comparative Analysis with Case Studies of the Philippines and Sri Lanka (Ceylon).* Wisconsin, 1974 (Ph.D. in Development Studies). 546p. DAI 35, no.3 (Sept. 1974): 1338-A; UM 74-16,223. Part 3 includes a survey of agrarian reform in the People's Republic of China and the Republic of China.

166   TISSIER, Patrick. *Les communes populaires et la voie chinoise vers le socialisme.* [French: The People's Communes and the Chinese Path towards Socialism.] Paris I (Panthéon-Sorbonne), 1974 (Doctorat d'Etat ès sciences économiques).

167   ASH, Robert Fairbanks. *Development and Institutional Change in Chinese Agriculture: A Case Study of Kiangsu Province, 1946-1959.* London, 1975 (Ph.D. in Economics, School of Oriental and African Studies). 592p. Order copies from the British Library Lending Division, Boston Spa, Yorkshire, order no. D13309/75.

168   STEIDLMAYER, Paul Kelly. *The Da Zhai Model in Chinese Agriculture, 1964-1974.* Stanford, 1975 (Ph.D., Food Research Institute). 594p. DAI 36, no.4 (Oct. 1975): 2330-A; UM 75-21,901. On the Tachai brigade model in the People's Republic of China.

169   VOLTI, Rudolph, Robert. *Agricultural Development and Organizational Change: Agrotechnical Extension Services*

in the People's Republic of China. Rice, 1975 (Ph.D. in Sociology). 227p. DAI 36, no.4 (Oct. 1975): 2445-A; UM 75-22,074.

Business, Commerce, Finance, and Industry

See also entries 179, 180, 1361, 1369, 1599, and 1628.

170 BRUGGER, William Christian. *"Democratisation" and "Enterprise" in the Chinese Industrial Enterprise: A Socio-Political Perspective.* London, 1972 (Ph.D. in Economics, School of Oriental and African Studies). 440p. Published as Democracy and Organisation in the Chinese Industrial Enterprise (1948-1953) (Cambridge, Eng. & New York: Cambridge University Press, 1972. 374p. [Contemporary China Institute publications]).

171 CHEN, Chien-jen. *Die Lohnstruktur der Volksrepublik China.* [German: The Wage Structure in the People's Republic of China.] Freiburg, 1972 (Dr. der Wirtschafts- und Sozialwissenschaften). Published as Die Lohnstruktur ...China (Bern: Schweizerisches Ost-Institut, 1972. viii, 198p.).

172 RAWSKI, Thomas George. *The Economics of Chinese Machine-Building, 1931-1967.* Harvard, 1972 (Ph.D. in Economics). xiii, 521p. Available at the Harvard University Archives, Pusey Library, call no.HU 90.10244.20.

173 VEILLEUX, Louis. *The Paper Industry in China from 1891 to the Cultural Revolution.* Hong Kong, 1972 (Ph.D. in Geography). 320p. Available from the Library, University of Hong Kong.

174 BUCKNALL, Kevin Barry. *The Cotton Textile Industry as a Case Study of the Planning of Economic Development in China, 1949-1961.* Australian National, 1973 (Ph.D. in Economics). xiv, 232, x p.

175 DAVIES, Ian Graham. *The Chinese Iron and Steel Industry: An Economic and Regional Analysis.* Sydney, 1974 (Ph.D. in Geography). 1377p. For copies contact the Fisher Library, University of Sydney, Sydney, Australia.

176 LARDY, Nicholas Richard. *Central Control and Redistribution in China: Central-Provincial Fiscal Relations since 1949.* Michigan, 1975 (Ph.D. in Economics). 290p. DAI 36, no.6 (Dec. 1975): 3872-73-A; UM 75-29,274. On the central control of resource allocation and its impact on economic growth and the distribution of social services.

28

Labor

See also entries 262, 1355, and 1366.

177 AWANOHARA, Susumu. *Economics of Labor Mobilization: A Tentative Model of Chinese Economic Development.* Yale, 1973 (Ph.D. in Economics). 167p. DAI 34, no.11 (May 1974): 6848-A; UM 74-10,331. Deals with the People's Republic of China.

178 SEZGIN, Oya. *Le système syndical en Chine populaire.* [French: The Trade-Union System in the People's Republic of China.] Paris I (Panthéon-Sorbonne), 1974 (Doctorat d'Etat ès sciences politiques).

Management

See also entries 170 and 1357.

179 ANDORS, Stephen P. *Factory Management in China: The Politics of Modernization in a Revolutionary Society, 1958-1969.* Columbia, 1974 (Ph.D. in Political Science). iv, 567p. Will eventually be available from University Microfilms International. Related publication by the author: China's Industrial Revolution: Politics, Planning, and Management, 1949 to the Present (New York: Pantheon Books, 1977. xviii, 344p. [The Pantheon Asia library]).

180 CHUNG, Chongwook. *Ideology and the Politics of Industrial Management in the People's Republic of China: 1949-1965.* Yale, 1975 (Ph.D. in Political Science). 372p. DAI 36, no.12 (June 1976): 8267-68-A; UM 76-13,700.

Republic of China and Hong Kong

General and Miscellaneous Studies

See also entries 358, 1388, and 1606.

181 CHANG, Se-Moon. *Transformation of Dual Economies with Special Reference to Internal Migration and Marginal Product of Farm Labor.* Florida State, 1971 (Ph.D. in Economics). 204p. DAI 32, no.10 (Apr. 1972): 5424-A; UM 72-10,018. Focuses on postwar Japan, Taiwan, and Korea.

182 SEAKS, Terry Gilpin. *An Econometric Model of Taiwan, 1952 to 1970.* Duke, 1972 (Ph.D. in Economics). 168p.

DAI 33, no.9 (Mar. 1973): 4629-A; UM 73-6595.

183 LU, Chung-chi. *The Role of Food Aid, Agricultural De-*
     velopment, and Capital Formation in Economic Development:
     A Case Study of Taiwan. Iowa State, 1973 (Ph.D. in Eco-
     nomics). 317p. DAI 34, no.1 (July 1973): 41-A; UM
     73-16,964.

184 HUANG, Kuo-shing. *An Econometric Analysis of the Taiwan*
     Economy. California (Berkeley), 1975 (Ph.D. in Agricul-
     tural Economics). 173p. DAI 37, no.1 (July 1976):
     463-64-A; UM 76-15,229.

                          Agriculture

See also entries 18, 165, 181, 183, 242, 356, 1530, 1602, and
1608 as well as the section "Export Economy" (pp.34-36).

185 TSENG, Chieh-hsin. *The Consumption and Demand for Soy-*
     beans in Taiwan, China. Ohio State, 1971 (Ph.D. in Agri-
     cultural Economics and Rural Sociology). 173p. DAI 32,
     no.11 (May 1972): 5975-76-A; UM 72-15,313.

186 WONG, Chen-ta. *Vegetable Farming in Hong Kong: A Study*
     in Agricultural Geography. Hong Kong, 1971 (Ph.D. in
     Geography and Geology). 524p.

187 WU, Craig Chi-yen. *The Contribution of Education to*
     Farm Production in a Transitional Farm Economy. Vander-
     bilt, 1971 (Ph.D. in Economics). 163p. DAI 32, no.5
     (Nov. 1971): 2267-68-A; UM 71-29,338. Empirically fo-
     cuses on the Republic of China during the mid-1960s.

188 ONG, Marcia Min-ron Lee. *Changes in Farm Level Savings*
     and Consumption in Taiwan, 1960-1970. Ohio State, 1972
     (Ph.D. in Agricultural Economics and Rural Sociology).
     167p. DAI 33, no.11 (May 1973): 5934-A; UM 73-11,551.

189 LEE, Paul Shen-tung. *An Econometric Analysis of the*
     Wheat Markets of Taiwan and Japan. Washington State,
     1973 (Ph.D. in Agricultural Economics). 202p. DAI 33,
     no.12 (June 1973): 6552-53-A; UM 73-14,764.

190 LIN, Wuu-long. *Economic Interactions in Taiwan: A Study*
     of Sectoral Flows and Linkages. Stanford, 1973 (Ph.D.,
     Food Research Institute). 192p. DAI 34, no.3 (Sept.
     1973): 969-70-A; UM 73-20,493. Examines sectoral inter-
     action between agriculture and industry, 1952-1970.

191 OLSON, Gary Lee. *Land Reform as a Political Instrument*

of American Foreign Policy: Consequences for Third World Development. Colorado, 1973 (Ph.D. in Political Science). 302p. DAI 34, no.7 (Jan. 1974): 4353-A; UM 73-32,575. Published as U.S. Foreign Policy and the Third World Peasant: Land Reform in Asia and Latin America (New York: Praeger, 1974. x, 153p. [Praeger special studies in international politics and government]). Includes American agrarian policies in Taiwan during the late 1940s.

192 WILLIAMS, Jack Francis. *The Conflict between Peasant and Public Interest in a Developing Country: A Case Study of the Taiwan Sugar Company, 1950-1970.* Hawaii, 1973 (Ph.D. in Geography). xii, 248p. Order copies from the Interlibrary Loan Department, University of Hawaii Library.

193 HUANG, Chin-Rong. *Analyse des Schweinemarktes in Taiwan.* [German: An Analysis of the Market for Hogs in Taiwan.] Göttingen, 1974 (Dr., Landwirtschaftliche Fakultät). 81p.

194 TRUONG QUANG CANH [CANH, Truong Quang]. *Income Instability and Consumption Behavior: A Study of Taiwanese Farm Households, 1964-1970.* Ohio State, 1974 (Ph.D. in Agricultural Economics). 140p. DAI 35, no.8 (Feb. 1975): 4823-A; UM 74-24,303.

195 COLLADO, Geronimo Miranda. *Financing Dimensions of Philippine Agriculture: The Management of Institutional Credit Delivery Programs for Rice and Sugar Farmers.* Harvard, 1975 (D.B.A.). 330p. DAI 36, no.10 (Apr. 1976): 6788-89-A; UM 76-7415. Includes an overview of farm credit programs in the Republic of China.

196 SHEN, Raphael. *Narrowing Taiwan's Per Capita Farm/Nonfarm Income Gap Via Increased Agricultural Production and Guaranteed Prices: Projections and Analysis, 1973-1984.* Michigan State, 1975 (Ph.D. in Agricultural Economics). 240p. DAI 36, no.9 (Mar. 1976): 6221-A; UM 76-5639.

197 SHIH, Jhi Tzeng. *Specification and Estimation of Farm Level Production Function from Combined Cross-Section Time Series Data in Taiwan.* Ohio State, 1975 (Ph.D. in Agricultural Economics and Rural Sociology). 158p. DAI 36, no.8 (Feb. 1976): 5432-33-A; UM 76-3553. This study utilized data from a record-keeping project for 53 Taiwanese farms covering the period 1964 through 1970.

Business, Industry, and Domestic Commerce

See also entries 11, 13, 17, 21, 190, 213, 228, 231, 351, 1002, and 1605 as well as the section "Export Economy" (pp.34-36).

198 LIN, Ching-yuan. *The Orientation of Policy Incentives, Trade, and Industrial Development: A Case Study on Taiwan, 1946-1970.* George Washington, 1971 (Ph.D. in Economics). 288p. DAI 32, no.9 (Mar. 1972): 4820-A; UM 72-9003. Published as Industrialization in Taiwan, 1946-1972: Trade and Import-Substitution Policies for Developing Countries (New York: Praeger, 1973. xix, 244p. [Praeger special studies in international economics and development]).

199 RIEDEL, James Charles. *The Industrialization of Hong Kong.* California (Davis), 1972 (Ph.D. in Economics). 233p. DAI 34, no.2 (Aug. 1973): 481-A; UM 73-19,105. Related publication by the author: The Hong Kong Model of Industrialization (Kiel: Kiel Institute of World Economy, 1973. 18p. [Kiel discussion paper, 29]).

200 MOXON, Richard Williams. *Offshore Production in the Less-Developed Countries by American Electronics Companies.* Harvard, 1973 (D.B.A.). 186p. DAI 34, no.5 (Nov. 1973): 2100-A; UM 73-27,541. Includes brief information on Hong Kong and the Republic of China.

201 CHEN, Robert Che-tong. *The Electronics Industry in Taiwan: A History and Analysis.* Santa Clara, 1974 (Ph.D. in Business). 205p. DAI 36, no.1 (July 1975): 389-A; UM 75-13,930.

202 MIRCHANDANI, Lal Naraindas. *A Comparison of Employment Performance in the Manufacturing Sector of Less Developed Countries: Empirical Tests of Alternative Hypotheses.* Southern California, 1974 (Ph.D. in Economics). 169p. DAI 35, no.5 (Nov. 1974): 2520-A; UM 74-23,604. Covers 20 countries for the 1960-69 period including the Republic of China.

203 TSE, Fu-yuen. *Street Trading in Modern Hong Kong.* London, 1974 (Ph.D. in Economics, London School of Economics and Political Science). xi, 376p.

204 WANG, George Shen-yuan. *An Empirical Study of the Marketing System of the Canning Industry in Taiwan.* Saint Louis, 1975 (Ph.D. in Business). 205p. DAI 36, no.6 (Dec. 1975): 3861-A; UM 75-26,337. Covers the period 1952 to 1972.

Economic Growth and Development
(General Studies)

See also entries 233, 301, and 1601.

205   HERRMANN, Michael. *Hong Kong versus Singapore. Ein Erklärungsversuch divergierender Entwicklungsverläufe.* [German, with a summary in English: Hong Kong versus Singapore: An Attempt at Explaining Diverging Trends in Development.] Hamburg, 1971 (Dr., Fachbereich Wirtschaftswissenschaft). Published as Hong Kong...Entwicklungsverläufe (Stuttgart: Gustav Fischer, 1970. viii, 134p. [Ökonomische Studien, Bd. 18]).

206   WU, Rong-i. *The Strategy of Economic Development: A Case Study of Taiwan.* Louvain, 1971 (Doctorat en science politique). Published as The Strategy...Taiwan (Louvain: Vander, 1971. vii, 217p. [Université catholique de Louvain. Faculté des sciences économiques, sociales et politiques, Nouv.ser., 90]).

207   ANG, Edwin Kian-An. *The Use of a Social Accounting Framework of Economic Growth for Long-Run Projections of the Taiwan Economy 1970-1979.* California (Berkeley), 1972 (Ph.D. in Economics). ix, 194p. Order copies from the Library Photographic Service, General Library, University of California at Berkeley.

208   GRAVEREAU, Jacques. *Hong-Kong: analyse d'un boom.* [French: Hong Kong: Analysis of a Boom.] Paris I (Panthéon-Sorbonne), 1973 (Doctorat de 3e cycle en économie). x, 503, xvi p. A copy is available at the Bibliothèque de la Sorbonne. Published as Hong-Kong...boom (Paris: Centre d'Etudes des Techniques Economiques Modernes: Editions Cujas, 1974. 446p. [TEM analyse; 1974, no.1]).

209   LIU, Paul Ke-chih. *Interactions between Population Growth and Economic Development in Taiwan.* Michigan State, 1973 (Ph.D. in Economics). 221p. DAI 34, no.6 (Dec. 1973): 2858-A; UM 73-29,739.

210   LIU, Tai-ying. *A Dynamic National Economic Planning Model: A Case Study of the Republic of China.* Cornell, 1974 (Ph.D. in Economics). 190p. DAI 35, no.9 (Mar. 1975): 5637-A; UM 75-1438.

211   VAN EATON, Charles David. *Adaptation of a Land-Scarce Economy: The Economic Growth and Trade of Hong Kong, 1950-1966.* Tulane, 1974 (Ph.D. in Economics). 343p. DAI 35, no.8 (Feb. 1975): 4820-A; UM 75-2952.

212   DE GUZMAN, Dante Q. *An Analysis of Some Factors Affecting Economic Growth.* Rensselaer Polytechnic Institute,

1975 (Ph.D. in Management). 154p. DAI 36, no.1 (July
1975): 391-A; UM 75-14,942. Provides extensive coverage
of Asian countries including the Republic of China.

Export Economy

See also entries 204, 1598, 1609, and 1611.

213 TSENG, Kuo-cheng. *An Analysis of the Growth of Selected
     Export Industries in Taiwan, 1952-1969.* Pennsylvania
     State, 1971 (Ph.D. in Economics). 383p. DAI 33, no.1
     (July 1972): 39-A; UM 72-19,394.

214 KERSHNER, Thomas Richard. *Commodity Demand, Market
     Shares, and Competition: The Foreign Trade of Japan and
     Pacific Asia, 1958-1970.* Harvard, 1972 (Ph.D. in Eco-
     nomics). vii, 404p. Available at the Harvard University
     Archives, Pusey Library, call no.HU 90.10169.15. Pub-
     lished as Japanese Foreign Trade (Lexington, Mass.:
     Lexington Books, 1975. xvi, 204p.). Includes Japanese
     trade with Hong Kong and the Republic of China.

215 LIU, Ching-chuang. *Strukturwandlungen im Agrarexports
     Taiwans; Arbeit aus dem Institut für Ausländische Land-
     wirtschaft an der Georg-August-Universität Göttingen.*
     [German: Structural Changes in the Agricultural Exports
     of Taiwan: A Study Undertaken at the Institute for For-
     eign Agriculture at the University of Göttingen.] Göt-
     tingen, 1972 (Dr., Landwirtschaftliche Fakultät). Pub-
     lished as Strukturwandlungen...Göttingen (Frankfurt:
     DLG-Verlag, 1972, vii, 215p.).

216 SANCHEZ, Nicolas. *The Economics of Sugar Quotas.*
     Southern California, 1972 (Ph.D. in Economics). 276p.
     DAI 33, no.7 (Jan. 1973): 3140-A; UM 73-769. Measures
     the effect of American sugar import quotas upon the rev-
     enues of such sugar exporting countries as the Republic
     of China.

217 GOH, Keng Leng. *Factors Influencing U.S. International
     Firms in Locationg Export-Oriented Manufacturing Facili-
     ties in Singapore, Taiwan and Hong Kong.* Indiana, 1973
     (D.B.A.). 194p. DAI 35, no.5 (Nov. 1974): 2465-A; UM
     74-20,681.

218 LEE, Gin-fu Larry. *The Structure of the Hardwood Ply-
     wood Industry in the Far East Exporting Countries: Japan,
     Republic of China, Republic of Korea, and the Philippines.*
     Oregon State, 1973 (Ph.D. in Forest Management). 214p.

DAI 34, no.5 (Nov. 1973): 2131-32-A; UM 73-25,356.

219   STOLLAR, Andrew John Thomas. *Cotton Textiles: An Empirical Evaluation of Voluntary Export Restraints.* Boston College, 1973 (Ph.D. in Economics). 315p. DAI 34, no.3 (Sept. 1973): 965-966-A; UM 73-19,853. Includes coverage of the Republic of China.

220   WEI, Wou. *The Effects of Price and Income Changes on Taiwan's Trade in Rice and Wheat.* Saint Louis, 1973 (Ph.D. in Economics). 92p. DAI 34, no.9 (Mar. 1974): 5428-29-A; UM 74-4590.

221   HSU, Paul Shih-chun. *The Adoption of New Export Marketing Techniques by Exporters in Taiwan: A Causal Model.* Michigan, 1974 (Ph.D. in Business Administration). 359p. DAI 35, no.5 (Nov. 1974): 2469-A; UM 74-25,223. Concerned with the use of training devices to introduce new techniques to a group of business firms currently engaged in exporting.

222   JEE, Hen-Jan. *Die Produktionsbedingungen taiwanesischer Gemusekonservenindustrie und ihre Absatzverhältnisse mit besonderer Berücksichtigung der Exportaussichten ausgewählter Produke auf dem westdeutschen Markt.* [German: The Production Conditions of the Taiwanese Canned Vegetables Industry and Its Market Conditions, with Particular Regard to the Export Prospects of Selected Products in the West German Market.] Bonn, 1974 (Dr., Landwirtschaftliche Fakultät). 218p.

223   KRISHNAKUMAR, Parameswar. *An Exploratory Study on the Influence of Country of Origin on the Product Images of Persons from Selected Countries.* Florida, 1974 (Ph.D. in Marketing). 231p. DAI 36, no.2 (Aug. 1975): 973-74-A; UM 75-16,403. The subjects included citizens of the Republic of China.

224   MALANGA, Vincent Joseph. *An Empirical Study of Fluctuations in the Export Proceeds of Underdeveloped Countries and Their Effect on Economic Development.* Fordham, 1974 (Ph.D. in Economics). 302p. DAI 35, no.6 (Dec. 1974): 3281-82-A; UM 74-25,119. Includes China.

225   SOUTAR, Geoffrey Norman. *Export Instability and Concentration in the Less Developed Countries: A Cross Sectional Analysis.* Cornell, 1974 (Ph.D. in Business and Public Administration). 185p. DAI 35, no.2 (Aug. 1974): 677-78-A; UM 74-17,129. Based on a sample of 48 countries including the Republic of China.

226   HEMPHILL, William Loehr. *The Effect of Foreign Exchange*

Receipts on Imports of Less Developed Countries. Princeton, 1975 (Ph.D. in Economics). 189p. DAI 36, no.7 (Jan. 1976): 4655-A; UM 76-251. Includes the Republic of China.

227 WAT, Sui-ying. *An Econometric Study of the U.S. Demand for Exports of Cotton Manufacturers of Developing Countries*. Stanford, 1975 (Ph.D. in Engineering in Economics). 95p. DAI 35, no.12 (June 1975): 7496-A; UM 75-13,614. Includes coverage of Hong Kong and the Republic of China, 1967-1972.

Management and Accounting

228 SILIN, Robert Henry. *Management in Large-Scale Taiwanese Industrial Enterprises*. Harvard, 1971 (Ph.D. in Anthropology). viii, 206p. Available at the Harvard University Archives, Pusey Library, call no.HU 90.10064.5. Published as Leadership and Values: The Organization of Large-Scale Taiwanese Enterprises (Cambridge, Mass.: East Asian Research Center, Harvard University, 1976. 226p. [Harvard East Asian monographs, 62]).

229 CHEN, Raymond Swei-cheng. *An Evaluation of Some Aspects of the Public Accounting Profession in Taiwan*. Missouri, 1973 (Ph.D. in Accounting). 225p. DAI 34, no.11 (May 1974): 6793-94-A; UM 74-9916.

230 CHEN, Ting-ko. *Management Transfer, Management Practice, and Management Performance: An Empirical Quantitative Study in Taiwan*. Michigan, 1973 (Ph.D. in Business Administration). 227p. DAI 34, no.4 (Oct. 1973): 1415-A; UM 73-24,540.

231 CHIU, James Sheng-hsiung. *An Empirical Investigation of Management Accounting Techniques in the Manufacturing Companies of Taiwan*. Missouri, 1973 (Ph.D. in Accountancy). 196p. DAI 35, no.2 (Aug. 1974): 625-26-A; UM 74-18,499.

Money, Banking, Investment, and Public Finance
See also entries 903 and 1607

232 JAO, Yu-ching. *Commercial Banking in Hong Kong: An Analysis of Its Growth, Structure, and Strains, 1954-1968*. Hong Kong, 1971 (Ph.D. in Economics). 500p.

233 LO, Mei-sho. *Les investissements et le développement
économique de Taiwan de 1965 à 1968 et le quatrième
plan quadriennal.* [French: Investments and Economic
Development in Taiwan, 1965-1968, and the Fourth Four-
Year Plan.] Paris I (Panthéon-Sorbonne), 1971 (Doctorat
d'Université ès sciences économiques). 264p.

234 PANDIT, Vishwanath. *Sources of Inflation in Developing
Economies: Case Studies of Colombia, India, Korea, and
Taiwan.* Pennsylvania, 1971 (Ph.D. in Economics). 361p.
DAI 32, no.8 (Feb. 1972): 4199-A; UM 72-6213.

235 ASSAD, Mohammed Naim. *Das zentralbankpolitische Instru-
mentarium in ausgewählten ostasiatischen Ländern. Indo-
nesien, Süd-Korea, Philippinen und Taiwan.* [German: The
Instruments of Central Banking Policy in Selected East
Asian Nations: Indonesia, South Korea, Philippines and
Taiwan.] Erlangen-Nürnberg, 1972 (Dr., Wirtschafts-
und Sozialwissenschaftliche Fakultät). xxvi, 255p.

236 KANE, Joseph Aloysius. *The Economic Significance of Industrial Development Banking in the Developing Countries.*
Temple, 1972 (Ph.D. in Economics). 529p. DAI 33, no.11
(May 1973): 5943-44-A; UM 73-8867. Published as Development Banking: An Economic Appraisal (Lexington, Mass.:
Lexington Books, 1975. xvi, 217p.). Deals in part with
the Republic of China.

237 KOO, Bon Ho. *The Role of Effective Exchange Rates in
Small, Overpopulated, and Semi-Industrialized Economies.*
Minnesota, 1972 (Ph.D. in Economics). 183p. DAI 33,
no.4 (Oct. 1972): 1278-A; UM 72-20,172. Focuses on the
experience of South Korea and the Republic of China.

238 LEE, Po-chih. *Foreign Assistance and Economic Development: The Case of Taiwan.* State University of New York
at Binghamton, 1972 (Ph.D. in Economics). 156p. DAI 33,
no.3 (Sept. 1972): 867-A; UM 72-23,266.

239 MYO MYINT [MYINT, Myo]. *Studium nad problemem tworzenia
kapitału i jego wpływ na wzrost gospodarczy w wybranych
krajach południowo-wschodniej Azji: Birmie, Taiwanie i
Syjamie.* [Polish: A Study of the Problem of Capital
Formation and Its Influence on Economic Growth in Selec-
ted Southeast Asian Countries: Burma, Taiwan, Thailand.]
Szkoła Główna Planowania i Statystyki w Warszawie, 1973
(Rozprawa doktorska, Wydz. Finansów i Statystyki).

240 SALEHIZADEH, Ali. *International Reserves and Balance of
Payments Adjustment Policies of Less Developed Countries.*
Pittsburgh, 1973 (Ph.D. in Economics). 163p. DAI 34,

no.10 (Apr. 1974): 6214-15-A; UM 74-6795.   Covers 10
countries including the Republic of China.

241   TINNIN, James Bernard.   *The Use of Local Taxation for
Urban Development in Developing Countries.*   Syracuse,
1973 (Ph.D. in Social Sciences).   143p.   DAI 35, no.2
(Aug. 1974): 705-A; UM 74-17,634.   Tinnin examined urban
land problems in Taipei, Hong Kong, and 3 other Asian
cities.

242   TUAN, Chyau.   *Determinants of Financial Savings in Taiwanese Farmers' Associations 1960-1970.*   Ohio State, 1973
(Ph.D. in Agricultural Economics and Rural Sociology).
142p.   DAI 34, no.11 (May 1974): 6837-38-A; UM 74-11,063.
Published as Determinants...1970 (Nankang, Taipei: Institute of Three Principles of the People, Academia
Sinica, 1976.   x, 132p.   [Monograph series, 1]).

243   CHINN, Dennis Leslie.   *Potential Effects of Income Redistribution on Economic Growth Constraints: Evidence
from Taiwan and South Korea.*   California (Berkeley), 1974
(Ph.D. in Economics).   146p.   DAI 34, no.11 (May 1974):
6822-A; UM 74-11,887.

244   IYENGAR, Ranganath Kadaba Ramanuja.   *Towards a Complete
Savings Expenditure System with an Application to Taiwan
Data.*   Wisconsin, 1974 (Ph.D. in Economics).   128p.   DAI
35, no.11 (May 1975): 6897-98-A; UM 75-7586.

245   MacDONALD, Maurice Marcus.   *Income Distribution and Economic Mobility in Taiwan.*   Michigan, 1974 (Ph.D. in Economics).   396p.   DAI 35, no.5 (Nov. 1974): 2493-A; UM
74-25,258.

246   YUNG, Tien-man.   *The Determinants of the Money Stock in
Taiwan: 1949-1969.*   Massachusetts, 1974 (Ph.D. in Economics).   175p.   DAI 35, no.9 (Mar. 1975): 5658-A; UM
75-6113.

247   CHOW, Frederick Chung-hsi.   *The Role of Taxation in Eco-
nomic Development: A Case Study of Taiwan, 1957-1970.*
Pennsylvania State, 1975 (Ph.D. in Economics).   196p.
DAI 37, no.2 (Aug. 1976): 1093-94-A; UM 76-17,156.

248   CHUNG, Yu-to.   *A Model of Government Budgeting in a Developing Country, Hong Kong.*   Indiana, 1975 (D.B.A.).
232p.   DAI 36, no.11 (May 1976): 7492-93-A; UM 76-10,378.

249   HO, Henry Chun Yuen.   *Developmental and Redistributive
Aspects of the Fiscal System of Hong Kong since 1945.*
London, 1975 (Ph.D. in Economics; External).   402p.

Transportation

250 BUTLER, Richard. *Bus Operation in Hong Kong: A Study of
Public and Private Enterprise*. London, 1971 (Ph.D. in
Economics; External). 291p.

251 LEE, David Tong Yong. *Development of a Mathematic Model
and Information System for Forecasting Intercity Trip
Demands for the Taipei, Taiwan Metropolitan Area*. Michigan State, 1972 (Ph.D. in Social Science). 138p. DAI
34, no.1 (July 1973): 450-A; UM 73-12,760.

252 PAN, William Shang-yi. *Transport Development and Economic Growth in Taiwan: 1953-1972*. Columbia, 1974 (Ph.D.
in Business). 188p. DAI 35, no.10 (Apr. 1975): 6338-A;
UM 75-9305.

EDUCATION (since 1949)

People's Republic of China

General and Miscellaneous Studies

See also entries 28 and 1623.

253 SWETZ, Frank Joseph. *A Survey of the Evolution of Mathematics Education in the People's Republic of China: Its
Content and Pedagogy as Dictated by National Goals*.
Columbia (Teachers College), 1972 (Ed.D.). 369p. DAI 35,
no.4 (Oct. 1974): 2127-28-A; UM 74-23,533. Published as
Mathematics Education in China: Its Growth and Development (Cambridge, Mass.: MIT Press, 1974. 364p.).

254 HAWKINS, John Noel. *The Educational Thought of Mao Tse-
tung*. George Peabody College for Teachers, 1973 (Ph.D.
in Education). 283p. DAI 34, no.10 (Apr. 1974):
6425-A; UM 73-32,631.

255 SINAGA, Hulman. *A Comparative Analysis of Aims of Educa-
tion in the United States, People's Republic of China and
Malaysia*. Wayne State, 1973 (Ph.D. in Education). 242p.
DAI 34, no.8 (Feb. 1974): 4718-A; UM 73-31,783.

256 GLASSMAN, Joel Norman. *The Implementation of Education
Policy in Communist China*. Michigan, 1974 (Ph.D. in
Political Science). 355p. DAI 35, no.7 (Jan. 1975):
4636-A; UM 75-699.

257 HATCH, John Davis (III). *Societal Relevance: An Issue
in Rural Primary Education*. Massachusetts, 1974. (Ed.D.).

207p.   DAI 35, no.1 (July 1974): 232-33-A; UM 74-15,019.
Includes a brief study of Chinese educational programs.

258   LANG, Ting-chih. *School Systems in Communist China
(1949-1963)*. Utah State, 1974 (Ed.D. in Educational
Administration). 182p. DAI 34, no.12 (June 1974):
7468-69-A; UM 74-13,235.

259   SHIRK, Susan Lee. *The Middle School Experience in China*.
Massachusetts Institute of Technology, 1974 (Ph.D. in
Political Science). 323p. Order copies from the Microreproduction Laboratory, Massachusetts Institute of Technology).

260   BURGESS, Clara Skipwith. *Decision-Making in the Education System in Selected Cities of the People's Republic
of China*. Fordham, 1975 (Ph.D. in Education). 162p.
DAI 36, no.8 (Feb. 1976): 4890-A; UM 76-4148.

261   TUQAN, Mustafa Izzat. *Education, Society and Development in Underdeveloped Countries*. Utrecht, 1975 (Dr. in
de Sociale Wetenschappen). DAI 37, no.1 (Autumn 1976):
Vol.C--entry no.1/325c. Published as Education...Coun-
tries (The Hague: Centre for the Study of Education in
Changing Societies, 1975. v, 278p.). Includes a case
study of the People's Republic of China.

Higher, Adult, and Teacher Education

262   WU, Chien-Sung. *Ideology, Higher Education, and Pro-
fessional Manpower in Communist China, 1949-1969*. New
Mexico, 1971 (Ph.D. in Education). 403p. DAI 32, no.2
(Aug. 1971): 763-64-A; UM 71-19,325.

263   HU, Shiao-chung. *Education in the People's Republic of
China, 1949-1971: Focus on the Teaching Profession*.
George Peabody College for Teachers, 1972 (Ed.D.). 749p.
DAI 33, no.7 (Jan. 1973): 3460-A; UM 72-34,195.

264   SHERMAN, James Charles. *Mao Tse-tung's Concept of Higher
Education*. Denver, 1972 (Ph.D. in Education). 187p.
DAI 33, no.6 (Dec. 1972): 2740-A; UM 72-31,657.

265   YAO, Katherine York-bing. *The Development of Science
and Technical Education in China: The Soviet Phase,
1949-1957*. Columbia (Teachers College), 1972 (Ph.D. in
Education). 228p. DAI 34, no.2 (Aug. 1973): 522-23-A;
UM 73-9057.

266   DORN, Jared Hugh. *The Principle of Combining Productive
Labor with Higher Education in China: A Historical*

Analysis. Southern Illinois, 1973 (Ph.D. in Education). 219p. DAI 34, no.9 (Mar. 1974): 5658-A; UM 74-6192. Covers the Communist Chinese implementation of this principle between 1921 and 1973.

267 YIN, Chih-peng. *The Cultural Revolution in Chinese Higher Education: The Mass Line*. Columbia (Teachers College), 1973 (Ed.D.). 139p. DAI 34, no.1 (July 1973): 152-A; UM 73-15,032.

268 TAYLOR, Robert Irvine Davison. *Policies Governing University Enrolment in the People's Republic of China since 1949*. London, 1974 (Ph.D. in Economics; External). 361p. Published in part as Education and University Enrolment Policies in China, 1949-1971 (Canberra: Australian National University Press, 1973. 56p. [Contemporary China papers, 6]).

269 WU, Hei-Tak. *The Institutionalization of Participation in Communist China: The Case of Two Universities in Peking*. Stanford, 1975 (Ph.D. in Education). 312p. DAI 36, no.5 (Nov. 1975): 3104-05-A; UM 75-25,631.

Politics and Education

See also the section on the Cultural Revolution (pp.186-88).

270 BIETZ, Gary Roy. *The Politics of Educational Reform in the People's Republic of China: Revolutionary Destruction, 1966-1968*. New York, 1972 (Ph.D. in History). 340p. DAI 33, no.11 (May 1973): 6264-65-A; UM 73-11,672.

271 HSU, Kuang-liang. *Chinese Communist Education: The Cultural Revolution and Aftermath*. George Peabody College for Teachers, 1972 (Ph.D. in Education). 547p. DAI 33, no.4 (Oct. 1972): 1472-73-A; UM 72-25,389. Related publication by the author: Chinese Education and Society, a Bibliographic Guide: The Cultural Revolution and Its Aftermath. Coauthored with Steward E. Fraser (White Plains, N.Y.: International Arts and Sciences Press, 1972. 204p.).

272 CHEN, Lin. *Politics of Education in Communist China, 1958-1968*. Chicago, 1973 (Ph.D. in Political Science). 284p. Order copies from the Photoduplication Department, Joseph Regenstein Library, University of Chicago.

273 EISEMAN, James Stephen. *Formal Education and the Education of the Masses: Politics and Education in the Peoples' Republic of China*. Boston University, 1975 (Ph.D. in

Political Science). 150p. DAI 35, no.6 (Dec. 1974):
3825-26-A; UM 74-26,455.

274   KIEFFER, William Joseph. *Educational Development and National Policy in the People's Republic of China: The Role of the School in Building a New State.* Michigan State, 1975 (Ph.D. in Educational Administration). 368p. DAI 36, no.3 (Sept. 1975): 1179-A; UM 75-20,851.

Republic of China and Hong Kong

General and Miscellaneous Studies

See also entries 28, 141, 187, 1395, 1480, 1616 and 1623.

275   CHOI, Jae Won. *A Comparative Analysis of National Income Elasticities of Educational and Non-Educational Government Expenditures among Selected Nations.* Illinois, 1971 (Ph.D. in Education). 179p. DAI 32, no.8 (Feb. 1972): 4272-A; UM 72-6891. Includes the Republic of China.

276   DASTUR, Dinoo Nari. *Development and Evaluation of a Televised Series "Nutrition and Man" for Use in Developing Countries.* Ohio State, 1971 (Ph.D. in Home Economics). 236p. DAI 32, no.3 (Sept. 1971): 1687-B; UM 71-22,462. The series was tested by women from various countries including the Republic of China.

277   HUANG, Kun-huei. *Historical Development of the Educational Administration System in the Republic of China, 1905-1970.* Northern Colorado, 1971 (Ed.D. in Educational Administration). 304p. DAI 32, no.7 (Jan. 1972): 3612-A; UM 72-3271.

278   LEE, Hong-Woo. *A Multivariate Analysis of Education and Unemployment: Toward a Strategy of Planning Education and Training in Developing Countries.* Columbia (Teachers College), 1971 (Ed.D. in International Educational Development). 210p. DAI 32, no.3 (Sept. 1971): 1191-A; UM 71-24,155. Covers many countries including the Republic of China.

279   BETTELHEIM, Ruth Colette. *Futures of the Unborn: Political, Economic and Educational Socialization in Asian Preschools.* California (Los Angeles), 1972 (Ph.D. in Education). 318p. DAI 33, no.8 (Feb. 1973): 4235-A; UM 73-1684. Related publication by the author: <u>Early Schooling in Asia</u>. Coauthored with Ruby Takanishi (New

York: McGraw-Hill, 1976.   xviii, 202p.   [I/D/E/A reports
on schooling]).   Includes children in Hong Kong and the
Republic of China.

280   CHU, Nai-suon. *The Social Context of the Elementary
Classroom and the Socialization of National Sentiments
in Taiwan.* Cornell, 1973 (Ph.D. in Education).   224p.
DAI 34, no.5 (Nov. 1973): 2155-56-A; UM 73-28,284.

281   PEREZ DE TAGLE, Oscar G. *The Stage Theory of Balanced
Educational-Economic Development and Its Application to
Developing Countries with Educated Unemployment.* Wis-
consin, 1973 (Ph.D. in Educational Administration).
284p.   DAI 34, no.10 (Apr. 1974): 6322-A; UM 73-30,340.
Includes the Republic of China.

282   SHEU, Tian-way. *Survey of Teacher Competencies Needed
and Teaching Problems Encountered by Teachers of the
Physically Handicapped in Taiwan, The Republic of China.*
Northern Colorado, 1974 (Ed.D. in Special Education and
Rehabilitation).   195p.   DAI 35, no.2 (Aug. 1974): 914-A;
UM 74-16,896.

283   HADLEY, Lawrence Hamilton. *An International Comparative
Analysis of Educational Strategies in Underdeveloped
Countries Incorporating Rates of Return to Education.*
Connecticut, 1975 (Ph.D. in Education).   233p.   DAI 36,
no.7 (Jan. 1976): 4624-A; UM 76-1676.   Covers 51 coun-
tries including the Republic of China.

284   LANGAN, Martin Joseph. *Educational Developments in the
Republic of China, 1960-1970: Their Impact on Nation-
Building Efforts.* St. John's, 1975 (Ph.D. in Asian
History).   206p.   DAI 36, no.8 (Feb. 1976): 4872-73-A;
UM 76-2994.

285   NUCKOLS, Margaret Lynn. *A Comparative Analysis of Selected United Nations Documents Related to Educational
Opportunities for Women during the First Development
Decade (1960-1970).* Florida State, 1975 (Ph.D. in Educational Management Systems).   135p.   DAI 36, no.6 (Dec.
1975): 3454-A; UM 75-26,802.   Provides worldwide coverage
including China.

286   ROGERS, Charles. *Status, Ability, Encouragement, Sex
Roles, and Educational Aspirations of Adolescents in
Taiwan: A Replicative Study of the Sewell Model.* Illi-
nois, 1975 (Ph.D. in Education).   124p.   DAI 36, no.9
(Mar. 1976): 5955-56-A; UM 76-6932.

287   WU, Wu-tien. *Classroom Climates in Chinese and American
Elementary Schools: A Cross-Cultural Study.* Kentucky,

1975 (Ph.D. in Education).   204p.   DAI 36, no.10 (Apr. 1976): 6575-A; UM 76-7741.   Compares schools in Taiwan and Indiana.

High School Level Education

288 CHIANG, George Chi-yung. *An Evaluation of Seventh and Eighth Grade Mathematics Curriculum in Taiwan, Republic of China.* Pittsburgh, 1971 (Ph.D. in Curriculum and Supervision). 96p. DAI 32, no.8 (Feb. 1972): 4322-23-A; UM 72-7883.

289 YAO, Esther Shu-shin Lee. *The Efficacy of Child Development and Family Life Courses for Chinese Students in Different Types of High Schools in the Republic of China.* Purdue, 1971 (Ph.D. in Education). 146p. DAI 32, no.6 (Dec. 1971): 3013-14-A; UM 72-1981.

290 YIEH, Molly Cheng-li. *Relationships between Locus of Control and Some Familial and Demographic Variables in Educable Mental Retardates.* Ohio State, 1971 (Ph.D. in Education). 127p. DAI 32, no.4 (Oct. 1971): 1951-A; UM 71-27,586. The subjects were junior high school students in Taipei.

291 YU, Bosco Shu-mou. *The Notion of Leader of High School Students in Taiwan.* Louvain, 1971 (Doctorat de 3e cycle ès sciences de l'éducation). 106p.

292 CHAO, Chung-ho. *A Comparative Study of Education in the Junior High Schools in the State of Utah and the Province of Taiwan.* Brigham Young, 1972 (Ed.D. in Educational Administration). 76p. DAI 33, no.3 (Sept. 1972): 914-A; UM 72-23,381.

293 JUANG, Hwai-I. *Rates of Return to Investment in Education in Taiwan and Their Policy Implications: A Cost-Benefit Analysis of the Academic High School and the Vocational High School.* Columbia (Teachers College), 1972 (Ed.D.). 214p. DAI 33, no.1 (July 1972): 108-A; UM 72-19,517.

294 LANTRY, Jay Harold. *A Study of Faculty-Principal Participation in Decision-Making in the Seventh-Day Adventist Secondary Schools of the Far East.* Colorado, 1972 (Ph.D. in Education). 738p. DAI 34, no.3 (Sept. 1973): 1032-33-A; UM 73-18,578. Lantry's research--in Hong Kong, the Republic of China, and elsewhere--examined different perceptions of decision-making participation patterns.

295   CHEN, Jeching. *A Comparison of Junior High School Princi-palships in Missouri and Taiwan.* Missouri, 1973 (Ed.D.). 191p.   DAI 35, no.2 (Aug. 1974): 741-A; UM 74-18,496.

296   GRIMLEY, Liam K. *A Cross-Cultural Study of Moral Devel-opment.* Kent State, 1973 (Ph.D. in Education). 209p. DAI 34, no.7 (Jan. 1974): 3990-A; UM 73-32,344. The subjects included secondary school and college students from Hong Kong.

297   CHAO, Chin-chi. *A Study of Conceptual Elements Involved in Two Physics Terms for Students of Different Cultural Backgrounds.* Ohio State, 1974 (Ph.D. in Education). 246p.   DAI 35, no.8 (Feb. 1975): 5146-47-A; UM 75-3024. Compares American and Taiwanese students.

Higher, Adult, and Teacher Education

See also entries 311, 323, 1398, and 1406.

298   CHEN, John Allen. *Higher Education in the Republic of China (Taiwan).* Southern California, 1971 (Ed.D.). 167p.   DAI 32, no.7 (Jan. 1972): 3714-A; UM 72-3764.

299   JACKSON, Malan Robert. *The Role of Higher Education in the Realization of the National Goals of the Republic of China.* Arizona State, 1971 (Ph.D. in Educational Administration and Supervision). 383p.   DAI 32, no.2 (Aug. 1971): 753-A; UM 71-14,431.

300   ROSS, Helen Stapley. *Changes Effected in Cross-Cultural T-Groups.* California (Berkeley), 1971 (Ed.D. in Adult Education). vii, 166p.   Order copies from the Library Photographic Service, General Library, University of California at Berkeley. Studied individuals from 10 countries including the Republic of China.

301   YANG, Edward Chung-chong. *High-Level Manpower Policy and Process in Economic Development: The Case of Nation-alist China, 1949-1965.* New York, 1971 (Ph.D. in Higher Education). 447p.   DAI 32, no.11 (May 1972): 5986-87-A; UM 72-11,487. On changes in the Republic of China's institutions of higher learning and the impact of these changes upon high-level manpower and economic development.

302   HASTINGS, Greg A. *A Study to Assess the Relevance of the Activities and Programs of the Asian Institute for Teacher Educators to the Development of Teacher Education in Asia.* Michigan State, 1972 (Ph.D. in Social and Phil-osophical Foundations). 159p.   DAI 33, no.5 (Nov. 1972):

1977-78-A; UM 72-29,987. Includes the Republic of China.

303 KU, Peter Chia-shan. *Master Plan for Community Colleges in the Republic of China.* Duke, 1972 (Ph.D. in English). 271p. DAI 33, no.6 (Dec. 1972): 2736-A; UM 72-31,577.

304 TSENG, Shihchang. *The Demand for Higher Education: A Case Study of Taiwan, 1950-1969.* Oklahoma, 1972 (Ph.D. in Economics). 121p. DAI 33, no.3 (Sept. 1972): 871-A; UM 72-23,120.

305 FRANCUS, Stanley Edward. *The Community College Concept and the Developing World: A Planning Strategy with a Focus on Asia.* Southern California, 1973 (Ph.D. in Education). 212p. DAI 34, no.7 (Jan. 1974): 3906-A; UM 73-31,343. The Republic of China is one of thirteen countries covered.

306 LU, Ching-ming. *Personality Characteristics of Prospective Teachers in China.* Northern Colorado, 1973 (Ph.D. in Education). 173p. DAI 34, no.8 (Feb. 1974): 4878-79-A; UM 74-1628. The subjects were students at the Hsinchu Teachers College in Taiwan.

307 CHEN, Mason Mei-sheng. *An Analysis of Performance-Based Teacher Education for Developing a Model for Elementary Teacher Education for the Republic of China.* Tennesee, 1974 (Ed.D. in Curriculum and Instruction). 224p. DAI 35, no.8 (Feb. 1975): 5183-A; UM 75-3579.

308 SUZUKI, Michael Glenn. *Cross-National Comparison of Educational Programming Preferences, Ratings of Severity, and Classification of Learning or Behavioral Problems.* Kentucky, 1975 (Ed.D. in Special Education). 173p. DAI 36, no.10 (Apr. 1976): 6606-07-A; UM 76-7738. Compares normal school, college and university students from 4 countries including the Republic of China.

Vocational and Religious Education

See also entries 293, 294, and 1620.

309 NEE, Nelson Ven-chung. *A Proposal for an Advanced Program in Industrial Education for Taiwan, Republic of China.* Tennessee, 1971 (Ed.D. in Educational Administration and Supervision). 176p. DAI 32, no.5 (Nov. 1971): 2457-A; UM 71-29,482.

310 CHEN, Kuan-yu. *A Century of Chinese Christian Education: An Analysis of the True Light Seminary and Its Successors in Canton and Hong Kong.* Connecticut, 1972 (Ph.D. in

Education).   313p.   DAI 33, no.6 (Dec. 1972): 2609-A; UM
72-32,209 .

311   CHANG, Tien-jin Frank. *Industrial Technical Education
Teacher Preparation and Economic Growth in Taiwan: A
Case Study*. Pennsylvania State, 1974 (Ph.D. in Industrial Arts Education). 146p.   DAI 35, no.11 (May 1975):
7187-A; UM 75-9765.

312   HO, Kam-Fai. *Factors Predictive of Successful Performance in Social Work Education*. Columbia, 1974 (D.S.W.).
195p.   DAI 35, no.9 (Mar. 1975): 6237-A; UM 75-5223.
The author's sample consisted of applicants to the Chinese University of Hong Kong.

313   SAAH, Maurice Kwamina. *Review and Synthesis of Research
on Agricultural Education in Developing Countries*. Ohio
State, 1974 (Ph.D. in Agricultural Education). 234p.
DAI 35, no.5 (Nov. 1974): 1996-B; UM 74-24,396. Includes
research about the Republic of China

314   CHU, Mark Ping-hsin. *Cross-Cultural Study of Vocational
Interests Measured by the SCII*. Wisconsin, 1975 (Ph.D.
in Counseling and Guidance). 262p.   DAI 36, no.7 (Jan.
1976): 4438-A; UM 75-19,060. Compares Chinese and American college students in connection with the Strong-Camp-
bell Interest Inventory.

American Schools in Hong Kong and Taipei

315   ULMER, Francis Charles. *An Investigation of Physics Instruction through Overhead Projection of Experiments
and Demonstrations*. Arizona State, 1972 (Ed.D. in
Secondary Education). 133p.   DAI 32, no.12 (June 1972):
6826-A; UM 72-15,618. The study was conducted at the
Taipei American School (Taipei, Taiwan) in 1969/70.

316   RUSSELL, Juanita G. *A Descriptive Study of the Elementary English Language Arts Program of American-Sponsored
International Schools*. State University of New York at
Buffalo, 1973 (Ed.D. in Elementary and Remedial Education). 410p.   DAI 34, no.1 (July 1973): 72-A; UM
73-15,471. Includes schools in Hong Kong and the Republic of China.

317   WIRE, Howard Russell. *A Study of Personality Factors
Affecting Cultural Adjustment of American Teachers Overseas*. Southern California, 1973 (Ph.D. in Education).
95p.   DAI 34, no.7 (Jan. 1974): 4014-A; UM 74-950. The

subjects were the American teachers of the Taipei American School.

Chinese Students at Foreign Universities

See also entry 1403 and--within the Appendix--the section entitled "Education (since 1949)" (pp.229-31).

318   CHANG, Shu-yuan Hsieh. *The Views and Contributions of Chinese Students and Intellectuals in the United States.* Utah, 1971 (Ph.D. in Political Science). 135p. DAI 32, no.6 (Dec. 1971): 3399-400-A; UM 71-31,125. Focuses on students who came from the Republic of China during the 1960s.

319   DIAS, Milagres Constancio Nepomoceno. *The Effect of Counseling on Adjustment of Foreign Students.* California (Los Angeles), 1971 (Ed.D. in Counseling). 223p. DAI 32, no.11 (May 1972): 6123-A; UM 72-13,602. This study of Asian and European students includes a number of Chinese students.

320   JONES, Theodore Alan. *The Value to Foreign Student Alumni of Their Education in the United States of America.* Northern Colorado, 1971 (Ph.D. in Education). 210p. DAI 32, no.7 (Jan. 1972): 3721-22-A; UM 72-3274. Includes Chinese alumni of the Universities of Denver and Northern Colorado.

321   TJIOE, Loan Eng. *Asiaten über Deutsche: Kulturkonflikte ostasiatischer Studentinnen in der Bundesrepublik.* [German: Asians on Germans: The Cultural Conflict of East Asian Female Students in West Germany.] Bonn, 1971 (Dr., Philosophische Fakultät). Published as Asiaten... Bundesrepublik (Frankfurt: Thesen-Verlag, 1972. 252p. [Sozialpsychologie, no.2]). Discusses what Asians think about Germans.

322   CHANG, Hwa-bao. *A Study of Some Attributes of Chinese Students in the United States.* Texas, 1972 (Ph.D. in Sociology). 182p. DAI 33, no.7 (Jan. 1973): 3787-A; UM 73-416.

323   HWANG, Philip Ong. *Cross-Cultural Orientation and Adaptation: A Four-Summer Program and Research.* Marquette, 1972 (Ph.D. in Education). 122p. DAI 33, no.9 (Mar. 1973): 5492-93-A; UM 73-8279. Studies a program conducted at Fu Jen University (Taipei) on behalf of Chinese students planning to come to the U.S. for higher education.

324   KHALIDI, Ata Fuad. *Foreign Students in the United States:*
      The Effects of Some Cultural and Situational Variables
      on the Adaptation of Far Eastern and North European
      Students. Wayne State, 1972 (Ph.D. in Education). 168p.
      DAI 33, no.11 (May 1973): 6091-92-A; UM 73-12,550. In-
      cludes students from the Republic of China.

325   KIYUNA, Kenneth Mitsugi. *The Effect of Two Group Treat-*
      ments on the Relationship between Asian and American Uni-
      versity Students. Pennsylvania State, 1972 (Ph.D. in
      Counselor Education). 133p. DAI 33, no.12 (June 1973):
      6593-A; UM 73-14,003. Includes students from Hong Kong
      and the Republic of China as well as students of Chinese
      ancestry from Singapore.

326   THARPE, Gertrude Addis. *The Identification of the Es-*
      sential Elements of a Predeparture Orientation Program
      for Hong Kong College Students. George Peabody College
      for Teachers, 1972 (Ed.D.). 177p. DAI 33, no.4 (Oct.
      1972): 1468-A; UM 72-25,367. About students who planned
      to study in American institutions of higher education.

327   COONEY, David Thomas. *The Foreign Student Program in*
      Florida Public Community Junior Colleges: Present Status
      and Future Development. Florida State, 1973 (Ph.D. in
      Education). 167p. DAI 35, no.2 (Aug. 1974): 741-42-A;
      UM 74-17,988. Includes unspecified groups of Asian stu-
      dents; Chinese students are presumably among them.

328   HAMANN, James Robert. *A Study of the Relationship be-*
      tween Value Differences and Learning Satisfaction in a
      Cross-Cultural Adult Education Setting. Wisconsin, 1973
      (Ph.D. in Cooperative Extension Education). 135p. DAI
      35, no.1 (July 1974): 155-56-A; UM 74-9184. Hamann's
      subjects were graduate students from the Republic of
      China and four other countries.

329   el SENOUSSI, Veronica. *The UCLA Foreign Alumni Study,*
      1945-70. California (Los Angeles), 1973 (Ed.D. in Coun-
      seling and Guidance). 298p. DAI 34, no.6 (Dec. 1973):
      3085-A; UM 73-28,691. Includes alumni from Hong Kong
      and the Republic of China.

330   CULHA, Meral Ulker. *Needs and Satisfactions of Foreign*
      Students at the University of Minnesota. Minnesota,
      1974 (Ph.D. in Psychology). 176p. DAI 35, no.8 (Feb.
      1975): 4141-B; UM 75-2095. Includes students from Hong
      Kong and the Republic of China.

331   WILCOX, Lee Owen. *The Prediction of Academic Success of*
      Undergraduate Foreign Students. Minnesota, 1974 (Ph.D.

in Psychology). 127p. DAI 35, no.12 (June 1975): 6084-B; UM 73-12,178. Includes a study of 99 freshmen attending American schools from Hong Kong.

332 ABADZI, Helen. *Evaluation of Foreign Students Admission Procedures Used at the University of Alabama.* Alabama, 1975 (Ph.D. in Administration and Higher Education). 143p. DAI 36, no.12 (June 1976): 7754-A; UM 76-13,884. Covers 71 students including 8 from Hong Kong and 9 from the Republic of China.

333 BARNES, Carol Ruth. *A Study of the Processes of Attitude Formation and Change as Applied to Foreign Students.* Texas, 1975 (Ph.D. in Sociology). 339p. DAI 37, no.1 (July 1976): 612-A; UM 76-14,413. Includes students from Hong Kong and the Republic of China.

334 HAN, Pyung Eui. *A Study of Goals and Problems of Foreign Graduate Students from the Far East at the University of Southern California.* Southern California, 1975 (Ed.D.). 199p. DAI 36, no.1 (July 1975): 68-A; UM 75-15,536. Includes students from Hong Kong and the Republic of China.

335 KEMPF, Margaret Kohler (Jang). *A Study of English Proficiency Level and the Composition Errors of Incoming Foreign Students at the University of Cincinnati during 1969-1974.* Ohio State, 1975 (Ph.D. in Humanities Education). 235p. DAI 36, no.6 (Dec. 1975): 3636-A; UM 75-26,605. Includes speakers of Chinese.

336 QUINN, Walter Albert (II). *A Study of Selected Preferences and Priorities of Stanford University Foreign Students.* Stanford, 1975 (Ph.D. in Education). 506p. DAI 35, no.12 (June 1975): 7576-A; UM 75-13,580. This study includes students from Hong Kong and the Republic of China at Stanford during the 1971/72 academic year.

337 RAZAVI, Masoumeh Zinat. *Personality Correlates Relating to the Brain Drain among Foreign Students from Far Eastern and South American Countries.* Southern California, 1975 (Ph.D. in Education). 135p. DAI 36, no.1 (July 1975): 136-37-A; UM 75-15,569.

338 RODRIGUEZ, Orlando. *Social Determinants of Non-Return: A Study of Foreign Students from Developing Countries in the United States.* Columbia, 1975 (Ph.D. in Sociology). 237p. DAI 36, no.6 (Dec. 1975): 4059-A; UM 75-27,458. Some students were from Hong Kong and the Republic of China.

339 WILSON, W. Douglas. *Social Relationships of International Students Attending Oklahoma State University.*

Oklahoma State, 1975 (Ed.D.). 94p. DAI 36, no.11 (May
1976): 7223-A; UM 76-9800. Includes students from the
Republic of China.

Language Study (Teaching and Learning)

See also entries 76, 85, and 1282.

340 LUM, John Bernard. *An Effectiveness Study of English
     as a Second Language (ESL) and Chinese Bilingual Methods.*
     California (Berkeley), 1971 (Ph.D. in Education). viii,
     116p. Order copies from the Library Photographic Ser-
     vice, General Library, University of California at Berke-
     ley.

341 VOCI, Frank. *An Analysis of Linguistic Problems of
     Cantonese Students of English as a Second Language.*
     California (Berkeley), 1971 (Ph.D. in Education). vi,
     134p. Order copies from the Library Photographic Ser-
     vice, General Library, University of California at Berke-
     ley.

342 CHEN, Shang-chun. *Computer-Aided Learning of the Writing
     of Chinese Characters.* Washington (St. Louis), 1973
     (D.Sc. in Electrical Engineering). 121p. DAI 34, no.12
     (June 1974): 5994-B; UM 74-13,802.

343 HUANG, Pi-chun Liu. *A Study of the Relationships between
     the Native Chinese Speaker's Spoken English Proficiency
     and His Attitudes, Motivation, and Backgrounds in Learn-
     ing English.* Southern Illinois, 1973 (Ph.D. in Educa-
     tion). 117p. DAI 34, no.9 (Mar. 1974): 5481-82-A; UM
     74-6212.

344 BENNION, Roy Billings. *Response Mode and Memory Coding
     Strategies: A Study in Learning of Chinese-English Pairs.*
     Brigham Young, 1974 (Ph.D. in Educational Psychology).
     71p. DAI 35, no.6 (Dec. 1974): 3505-A; UM 74-28,388.

345 CHIANG, Alice. *Instructional Algorithms Derived from
     Mathematical Learning Models: An Application in Computer
     Assisted Instruction of Paired-Association Items.* City
     University of New York, 1974 (Ph.D. in Education). 160p.
     DAI 35, no.3 (Sept. 1974): 1492-A; UM 74-20,351. Chiang's
     experiments involved learning Chinese vocabulary using
     a computer controlled system.

346 HUANG, Tsan-sui. *A Contrastive Analysis of the Syntactic
     Errors in English Made by Chinese Students and Its Impli-
     cations for the Teaching of English Syntax to Chinese.*

Southern Illinois, 1974 (Ph.D. in Education). 166p.
DAI 34, no.9 (Mar. 1974): 5482-A; UM 74-6213.

347 FU, Gail Bertha Schaefer. *A Hong Kong Perspective:*
English Language Learning and the Chinese Student. Mich-
igan, 1975 (Ph.D. in English and Education). 254p.
DAI 36, no.10 (Apr. 1976): 6526-A; UM 76-9399.

GEOGRAPHY

See also entries 140, 186, 410, 1570, 1627, and 1628.

348 HUDSON, Brian James. *Land Reclamation in Hong Kong*.
Hong Kong, 1971 (Ph.D. in Architecture). 315p.

349 KOCH, Wilfried. *Funktionale Strukturwandlungen in Tai-*
wan. Das Beispiel Luchou im Umland der Millionenstadt
Taipei. [German: Functional Structural Changes within
Taiwan: The Case of Luchou Near the Metropolis of Taipei.]
Köln, 1971 (Dr., Math.-Naturwissenschaftliche Fakultät).
Published as Funktionale...Taipei (Wiesbaden: F. Stein-
er, 1971. viii, 261, 40p. [Kölner geographische Ar-
beiten, H.26]).

350 PANNELL, Clifton W. *T'ai-chung, T'ai-wan: Structure and*
Function. Chicago, 1971 (Ph.D. in Geography). xii,
200p. Order copies from the Photoduplication Department,
Joseph Regenstein Library, University of Chicago. Published as T'ai-chung...Function (Chicago: Dept. of Geography, University of Chicago, 1973. xii, 200p. [Re-
search paper, 144]).

351 SELYA, Roger Mark. *The Industrialization of T'aiwan: A*
Geographic Analysis. Minnesota, 1971 (Ph.D. in Geography). 332p. DAI 32, no.5 (Nov. 1971): 2788-B; UM
71-28,284. Published as The Industrialization of Taiwan:
Some Geographic Considerations (Jerusalem: Jerusalem Academic Press, 1974. 117p. [Jerusalem studies on Asia]).

352 CHUNG, Yuet-ping. *Residential Changes of Households in*
Kowloon, Hong Kong. Minnesota, 1972 (Ph.D. in Geography).
180p. DAI 33, no.10 (Apr. 1973): 4855-B; UM 73-10,665.

353 LIANG, Chi-sen. *Kowloon: A Factorial Study of Urban*
Land Use and Retail Structure. London, 1972 (Ph.D. in
Geography, University College). xv, 331p. Related
publication by the author: Urban Land Use in Hong Kong
and Kowloon (Hong Kong: Research Institute of Far Eastern Studies, Chinese University of Hong Kong, 1966.
[Geography research paper, 1]).

354 NETOLITZKY, Almut. *Ling-wai tai-ta von Chou Chü-fei,
     eine Landeskunde Südchinas aus dem 12. Jahrhundert.*
     [German: The Ling-wai tai-ta of Chou Chü-fei: Geography
     of South China in the 12th Century.] München, 1972/73
     (Dr.).

355 BLADEN, Wilford Allen. *Levels of Viability of Sovereign
     States.* Kentucky, 1973 (Ph.D. in Geography). 139p.
     DAI 34, no.3 (Sept. 1973): 1145-46-B; UM 73-20,574.
     Measures the geographical variations of viability among
     66 nations including the Republic of China.

356 VANDER MEER, Paul. *Farm Plot Dispersal: Luliao Village,
     Taiwan, 1967.* Michigan, 1973 (Ph.D. in Geography).
     471p. DAI 34, no.8 (Feb. 1974): 3852-53-B; UM 74-3740.

357 LIN, Gong-Yuh. *Surface Synoptic Flow Types and Their
     Relation to Rainfall over the Island of Taiwan.* Hawaii,
     1974 (Ph.D. in Geography). xv, 353p. Order copies from
     the Interlibrary Loan Dept., University of Hawaii Library.

358 CHAO, Thomas Kang. *The Spatial Distribution of Urban
     Land Values in the City of Taipei, Taiwan, China, 1964-
     1972.* Kentucky, 1975 (Ph.D. in Geography). 126p. DAI
     36, no.6 (Dec. 1975): 2687-B; UM 75-26,442.

359 CHIANG, Tao-chang. *The Salt Industry of China, 1644-
     1911: A Study in Historical Geography.* Hawaii, 1975
     (Ph.D. in Geography). 349p. DAI 36, no.9 (Mar. 1976):
     6304-05-A; UM 76-6554.

360 GREER, Charles Edwin. *Chinese Water Management Strate-
     gies in the Yellow River Basin.* Washington (Seattle),
     1975 (Ph.D. in Geography). 249p. DAI 37, no.2 (Aug.
     1976): 672-B; UM 76-17,478.

        HEALTH, MEDICINE, AND SOCIAL WELFARE

See also entries 132, 276, 312, 1150, 1225, 1129, 1241, and
1253, as well as the sections entitled "Demography, Population, and Family Planning" (pp.23-25) and--within the Ap-
pendix--"Health, Medicine and Social Welfare" (p.232).

361 RALL, Jutta Maria. *Die vier grossen Medizinschulen der
     Mongolenzeit. Stand und Entwicklung der chinesischen
     Medizin in der Chin- und Yüan-Zeit.* [German: The Four
     Great Medical Schools of the Mongol Period: The Position
     and Development of Chinese Medicine during the Chin
     and Yüan Periods.] Hamburg, 1971 (Habilitationsschrift,
     Seminar für Sprache und Kultur Chinas). Published as

Die vier...Yüan-Zeit (Wiesbaden: Steiner, 1970. viii,
114p. [Münchener ostasiatische Studien; Bd.7]).

362 UNSCHULD, Paul Ulrich. *Die Praxis des traditionellen
chinesischen Heilsystems unter Einschluss der Pharmazie
dargestellt an der heutigen Situation auf Taiwan.* [Ger-
man: The Practice of the Traditional Chinese Healing
System: A Description of Its Current Situation in Taiwan,
Including Pharmacy.] München, 1971 (Dr., Philosophische
Fakultät). Published as Die Praxis...Taiwan (Wiesbaden:
Steiner, 1973. viii, 182p. + 36 illustrations [Münchener
ostasiatische Studien, 8]).

363 LIU, I-jung. *An Investigation of the Motivations in the
Assistance Programs for Retired Servicemen in the Republic of China.* Oklahoma, 1972 (D.B.A.). 233p. DAI
33, no.5 (Nov. 1972): 1908-A; UM 72-29,898.

364 POUTCHKOVSKY, Michel. *Bases de la médecine chinoise.*
[French: Bases of Chinese Medicine.] Aix-Marseille II,
1972 (Doctorat d'Etat en médecine). 93p.

365 UNSCHULD, Ulrike. *Das T'ang-yeh pen-ts'ao und die Über-
tragung der klassischen chinesischen Medizintheorie auf
die Praxis der Drogenanwendung.* [German: The T'ang-yeh
pen-ts'ao and the Application of the Classical Chinese
Medical Theories to Drug Use.] München, 1972 (Dr.,
Philosophische Fakultät). 227p. An abbreviated version
has been published under the title "Traditional Chinese
Pharmacology: An Analysis of its Development in the
Thirteenth Century".

366 GRÜNBECK, Wolfgang. *Akupunktur in Deutschland; umfassen-
der Entwicklungsbericht und derzeitiger Standpunkt.*
[German: Acupuncture in Germany: Comprehensive Report on
Its Development and Present Position.] Erlangen-Nürnberg,
1973 (Dr., Medizinische Fakultät). Published as Akupunktur...Standpunkt (Erlangen: Verlag für Lehrmittel, Wissenschaft und Forschung, 1975. 115p.).

367 PORKERT, Manfred. *Die theoretischen Grundlagen der
chinesischen Medizin: Das Entsprechungssystem.* [German:
The Theoretical Foundations of Chinese Medicine: The
System of Analogies.] München, 1973 (Habilitationsschrift, Philosophische Fakultät). Published as Die
theoretischen...Entsprechnungssystem (Wiesbaden: Steiner,
1973. 300, xx p. [Münchener ostasiatische Studien,
5]).

368 ARNOLD, Hans-Jürgen. *Die Geschichte der Akupunktur in
Deutschland.* [German: The History of Acupuncture in

Germany.] Köln, 1974 (Dr., Medizinische Fakultät).
150p. Published as Die Geschichte...Deutschland (Heidelberg: Haug, 1976. 128p.).

369 BULLOCK, Mary Hopper Brown. *The Rockefeller Foundation in China: Philanthropy, Peking Union Medical College, and Public Health.* Stanford, 1974 (Ph.D. in History). 494p. DAI 34, no.9 (Mar. 1974): 5854-A; UM 74-6454.

370 ISMADI, Mieke. *Untersuchungen über das Vorhandensein des Matratzenphänomens bei Chinesen im Bereich der Oberschenkelhaut.* [German: Investigations on the Existence of the Mattress Syndrome in the Skin Area of the Thigh of Chinese.] Mainz, 1974 (Dr., Fachbereich Medizin).

371 LAMPTON, David Michael. *The Politics of Public Health in China: 1949-1969.* Stanford, 1974 (Ph.D. in Political Science). 495p. DAI 34, no.12 (June 1974): 7866-A; UM 74-13,653. Published as Health, Conflict, and the Chinese Political System (Ann Arbor: Center for Chinese Studies, University of Michigan, 1974. xii, 149p. [Michigan papers in Chinese Studies, 18]), and as The Politics of Medicine in China: The Political Process, 1949-1977 (Boulder, Colo.: Westview Press, 1977 [Westview special studies on China and East Asia]).

372 RENARD, Paul. *Pathologie, psychologie et acupuncture.* [French: Pathology, Psychology and Acupuncture.] Paris V (René Déscartes), 1974 (Doctorat de 3ᵉ cycle en psychologie). 272p. A copy is available at the Bibliothèque de la Sorbonne, library catalogue no. I 2609-4°. On the use and effectiveness of acupuncture and on its relations to other psychotherapeutic techniques.

373 TAM, Maisie. *Medical Personnel and Health Care in the People's Republic of China.* Yale Medical School, 1974 (M.D.). 55p. Order copies directly from the Medical School.

HISTORY

General and Miscellaneous Studies

See also entry 1673.

374 ALLEN, Terence Michael. *Crossroads of Destiny: A History of Marine Corps Base Camp Pendelton through the Ages.* New Mexico, 1971 (Ph.D. in History). 357p. DAI 32, no.9 (Mar. 1972): 5130-A; UM 72-8349. From his study of a California site, Allen concludes that "Asians and Chinese are definitely connected to the exploration of

North America prior to Columbus."

375 COHEN, Alvin Philip. *The Avenging Ghost: Moral Judge-
ment in Chinese Historical Texts*. California (Berkeley),
1971 (Ph.D. in Oriental Languages). 481p. Order
copies from the Library Photographic Service, General
Library, University of California at Berkeley.

376 SUEBSAENG PROMBOON [PROMBOON, Suebsaeng]. *Sino-Siamese
Tributary Relations, 1282-1853*. Wisconsin, 1971 (Ph.D.
in History). 377p. DAI 32, no.1 (July 1971): 343-A;
UM 71-14,163.

377 WADA, Hiroshi. *Prokops Rätselwort Serinda und die
Verpflanzung des Seidenbaus von China nach dem oströmi-
schen Reich*. [German: Prokop's Use of the Riddle Word
"Serinda" and the Transplantation of Sericulture from
China to the Byzantine Empire.] Köln, 1971 (Dr.,
Philosophische Fakultät). Published as Prokops...Reich
(Köln, 1970? v, 101p.).

378 MARSCHALL, Wolfgang. *Transpazifische Kulturbeziehungen.
Studien zu ihrer Geschichte*. [German: Transpacific Cultural Relationships: Studies towards Their History.]
Tübingen, 1972 (Habilitationsschrift, Fachbereich Alter-
tums- und Kulturwissenschaft). Published as Transpazifische...Geschichte (München: Renner, 1972. 292, viiip.).
Deals extensively with China, India and Southeast Asia.

379 VATANKHAH, Mostafa. *Historischer Materialismus und
Revolution in nichtindustrialisierten Ländern: am Beispiel Russlands und Chinas*. [German: Historical Material-
ism and Revolution in Nonindustrialized Countries: The
Examples of Russia and China.] Freie Universität Berlin, 1973 (Dr., Fachbereich Politische Wissenschaft).
Published as Historischer...Chinas (Berlin: Merve-Verlag,
1973. 383p.).

380 KANG, Soon Heung. *The Problems of Autonomy for Korea
amid Rivalries of Great Powers: The Search for a New
Order*. Iowa, 1974 (Ph.D. in History). 473p. DAI 35,
no.12 (June 1975): 7838-39-A; UM 75-13,771. Includes
Chinese involvement in Korean affairs from earliest times
through the 1960s.

381 WANG, Ming-yu. *The Involvement in Recurrent Power Struggles of the Han, T'ang, and Ming Eunuchs*. St. John's,
1974 (Ph.D. in History). 205p. DAI 35, no.8 (Feb. 1975):
5272-73-A; UM 75-3281.

382 EBREY, Patricia Buckley. *Prestige and Power in Early
Imperial China: A Case Study of the Po-ling Ts'ui Family.*

Columbia, 1975 (Ph.D. in East Asian Languages and Cultures). 355p. DAI 36, no.6 (Dec. 1975): 3951-52-A; UM 75-27,401. Published as The Aristocratic Families of Early Imperial China: A Case Study of the Po-ling Ts'ui Family (Cambridge, Eng. and New York: Cambridge University Press, 1977 [Cambridge studies in Chinese history, literature and institutions]). Coverage extends from the family's first recorded appearance in the Former Han period until the Five Dynasties period (907-960).

383   HSU, Wen-hsiung. *Chinese Colonization of Taiwan.* Chicago, 1975 (Ph.D. in Far Eastern Languages and Civilizations). xiii, 756p. DAI 36, no.7 (Jan. 1976): 4690-A; Order copies from the Photoduplication Department, Joseph Regenstein Library, University of Chicago. Covers the 12th century to 1895.

From Earliest Times through the Ch'in (206 B.C.)

See also entries 2, 37, 1431, 1636, 1643, 1647, and 1655, as well as the section on Archaeology (pp.7-8).

384   CHAO, Lin. *Shang Government.* Chicago, 1972 (Ph.D. in Far Eastern Languages and Civilizations). 184p. Order copies from the Photoduplication Department, Joseph Regenstein Library, University of Chicago.

385   LANDERS, James Russel. *The Political Thought of Han Fei.* Indiana, 1972 (Ph.D. in East Asian Languages and Literatures). 192p. DAI 33, no.2 (Aug. 1972): 788-A; UM 72-21,394.

386   MATHIEU, Rémi. *Le Mu Tianzi Zhuan.* [French: The Mu T'ien-tzu chuan.] Paris VII, 1973 (Doctorat de 3e cycle). A copy is available at the Bibliothèque de la Sorbonne. On the Biography of the Son of Heaven, Mu, an ancient work about the purported travels of King Mu (fl.900 B.C.) to regions outside of China.

387   PAIRAULT, Thierry Claude. *La dynastie Zhou: éléments d'histoire économique et sociale.* [French: The Chou Dynasty: Elements of Economic and Social History.] Paris II, 1973 (Doctorat d'Etat ès sciences économiques). 442p. A copy is available at the Bibliothèque Cujas de Droit et des Sciences Economiques de Paris, library catalogue no. DZ 1973/168.

388   ROSEN, Sydney. *In Search of the Historical Kuan Chung.* Chicago, 1973 (Ph.D. in Far Eastern Languages and Civilizations). 254p. Order copies from the Photoduplication

Department, Joseph Regenstein Library, University of
Chicago. Kuan Chung (Kuan-tzu) served as an advisor to
Duke Huan of Ch'i in ancient times.

389 ALLAN, Sarah Meyers. *The Heir and the Sage: A Struc-*
tural Analysis of Ancient Chinese Dynastic Legends.
California (Berkeley), 1974 (Ph.D. in Oriental Languages).
vi, 214p. Order copies from the Library Photographic
Service, General Library, University of California at
Berkeley.

390 BYRNE, Rebecca Zerby. *Harmony and Violence in Classical*
China: A Study of the Battles in the Tso-chuan. Chicago,
1974 (Ph.D. in Political Science). ix, 267p. Order
copies from the Photoduplication Department, Joseph Regenstein Library, University of Chicago.

391 PILLAI, Padmanabh Vijai. *The King in Two Lands: An Anal-*
ysis of Attitudes toward Political Power in India and
China between c. Seventh to Second Centuries B.C. Michigan, 1974 (Ph.D. in History). 329p. DAI 35, no.11
(May 1975): 7210-A; UM 75-10,258. Pillai's sources included the Confucian Analects, Mencius, Hsün-tzu, Tao
te ching, Chuang-tzu, Mo-tzu, and Han Fei tzu.

392 LAGERWEY, John. *A Translation of The Annals of Wu and*
Yüeh, Part I, with a Study of Its Sources. Harvard, 1975
(Ph.D. in East Asian Languages and Civilizations). 380p.
Available at the Harvard University Archives, Pusey Library, call no.HU 90.10791. Wu and Yüeh were important
political states in the Yangtze valley area and Chekiang
during the Eastern Chou period.

393 SARGENT, Howard Wayne. *A Preliminary Study of the Kuo-*
yü. Chicago, 1975 (Ph.D. in Far Eastern Languages and
Civilizations). iv, 161p. DAI 37, no.2 (Aug. 1976):
1151-A; Order copies from the Photoduplication Department, Joseph Regenstein Library, University of Chicago.
Argues that this ancient book was written as political
propaganda.

394 SMITH, Cortlandt Bross. *The Bureaucratic Vision of Han*
Fei Tzu. California (Berkeley), 1975 (Ph.D. in Political Science). 223p. Order copies from the Library Photographic Service, General Library, University of California at Berkeley.

395 VANDERMEERSCH, Leon. *Wangdao ou la voie royale. Rech-*
erche sur l'esprit des institutions de la Chine archaïque.
[French: Wang tao or the Royal Way: Research into the
Spirit of the Institutions of Ancient China.] Paris VII,

1975 (Doctorat d'Etat ès lettres). 958, xiii, 245p. A
copy is available at the Bibliothèque de la Sorbonne,
library catalogue no.W 1975 (37)-4 .

The Two Han Dynasties (206 B.C. - 220 A.D.)

See also entries 405 and 1634.

396 LEBAN, Carl. *Ts'ao Ts'ao and the Rise of Wei: The Early
Years*. Columbia, 1971 (Ph.D. in East Asian Languages
and Cultures). 504p. DAI 35, no.2 (Aug. 1974): 990-A;
UM 74-17,880. Focuses on Ts'ao Ts'ao's military career,
ca.180-200 A.D.

397 PIRAZZOLI, Michèle. *La civilisation du royaume de Dian*.
[French: The Civilization of the Kingdom of Tien.]
Paris VII, 1971 (Doctorat d'Etat). A copy is available
at the Bibliothèque de la Sorbonne. Published as La
civilisation du royaume de Dian à l'époque Han: d'après
le matériel exhumé à Shizhai shan, Yunnan. By Michèle
Pirazzoli-t'Serstevens. Paris: Ecole française d'Extrême-
Orient, 1974. 339p. [Publications de l'Ecole française
d'Extrême-Orient, 94]).

398 STREFFER, Johann Michael. *Das Kapitel 86 (76) des Hou
Han shu*. [German: Chapter 86 (76) of the Hou Han shu.]
Tübingen, 1971 (Dr., Fachbereich Altertums- und Kultur-
wissenschaft). Published as Das Kapitel...shu (Göppingen:
Kümmerle, 1971. 163p.). On the History of the Later
Han Dynasty.

399 TAO, Tien-yi. *The Recruitment of Officials on Grounds
Other Than Ability during the Former Han Dynasty (206
B.C. - 8 A.D.)*. Chicago, 1972 (Ph.D. in Far Eastern
Languages and Civilizations). 150p. Order copies from
the Photoduplication Department, Joseph Regenstein Li-
brary, University of Chicago.

400 CHA, Joseph Hyosup. *The Historical Significance of the
Reigns of Emperors Wen and Ching of the Former Han Dynasty, 180-141 B.C.* Chicago, 1973 (Ph.D. in History).
236p. Order copies from the Photoduplication Department,
Joseph Regenstein Library, University of Chicago.

401 LIN, Ruey-lin. *An Inquiry into the Directionality of
Change: A Case Study of Chinese Society*. California
(Los Angeles), 1974 (Ph.D. in Sociology). 200p. DAI 35,
no.10 (Apr. 1975): 6821-22-A; UM 75-9414. Focuses on the
cultural perspective and structural characteristics of

society in the Han dynasty.

402   BERNHARD, Elmar Maria. *Die Yüan-hou und die gesell-*
      schaftliche und politische Stellung der Kaiserinnen
      gegen Ende der Ch'ien-Han Periode. [German: The Yüan-
      hou and the Social and Political Position of Empresses
      towards the End of the Former Han Dynasty.] Göttingen,
      1975 (Dr., Philosophische Fakultät). iv, 222p. DAI 37,
      no.3 (Spring 1977): Vol.C--entry no.1/3524c.

403   JUGEL, Ulrike. *Politische Funktion und soziale Stellung*
      der Eunuchen zur späten Hanzeit (25-220 n.Chr.). [Ger-
      man: The Political Function and Social Position of the
      Eunuchs during the Later Han Period (25-220 A.D.).]
      München, 1975 (Dr., Philosophischer Fachbereich Alter-
      tumskunde und Kulturwissenschaft). Published as Po-
      litische...220 n.Chr. (Wiesbaden: Steiner, 1976. xvi,
      451 + 16p. [Münchener ostasiatische Studien; Bd.15]).

                    Six Dynasties and Sui Periods
                          (220-618 A.D.)

See also entry 1038.

404   MEYER, Hektor. *Wang Tao--Gründungsminister der Ost-Chin;*
      eine kritische Darstellung nach dem Shih-shuo-hsin-yü
      und seinem Kommentar. [German: Wang Tao, Founding Minis-
      ter of the Eastern Chin: A Critical Presentation Accord-
      ing to the Shih shuo hsin yü and Its Commentary.] Freie
      Universität Berlin, 1972 (Dr., Fachbereich Philosophie
      und Sozialwissenschaft). Published as Wang...Kommentar
      (Berlin, 1973. 206p.).

405   NIENHAUSER, William H., Jr. *An Interpretation of the*
      Literary and Historical Aspects of the Hsi-ching tsa-chi
      (Miscellanies of the Western Capital). Indiana, 1972
      (Ph.D. in East Asian Languages and Literatures). 234p.
      DAI 33, no.9 (Mar. 1973): 5134-A; UM 73-6505. On a work
      probably compiled by Hsiao Pen (ca. A.D. 495-552) that
      was designed as a handbook for scholars interested in
      the Former Han Dynasty.

T'ang Period and the Five Dynasties Era
(618-960 A.D.)

See also entries 127, 786, and 1055.

406 CARLSON, Marianne Louise. *The Rationale of Eunuch Power in the Government of T'ang China, 618-805.* Chicago, 1971 (Ph.D. in Far Eastern Languages and Civilizations). 476p. Order copies from the Photoduplication Department, Joseph Regenstein Library, University of Chicago.

407 KROMPART, Robert James. *The Southern Restoration of T'ang: Counsel, Policy, and Parahistory in the Stabilization of the Chiang-Huai Region, 887-943.* California (Berkeley), 1973 (Ph.D. in History). iii, 423p. Order copies from the Library Photographic Service, General Library, University of California at Berkeley.

408 KWAN, Lai-hung. *The Factional Struggle of China, 820-850 A.D.* London, 1973 (Ph.D. in Arts). xi, 659p.

409 DALBY, Michael Thomas. *Court Politics in Late T'ang Times, 750-860 A.D.* Harvard, 1974 (Ph.D. in History and East Asian Languages). 295p. Available at the Harvard University Archives, Pusey Library, call no. HU 90.10528.20.

410 LAM, Chi-hung. *Political Activities of the Christian Missionaries in the T'ang Dynasty.* Denver, 1975 (Ph.D. in History). 261p. DAI 36, no.11 (May 1976): 7564-A; UM 76-10,289.

411 SOMERS, Robert Milton. *The Collapse of the T'ang Order.* Yale, 1975 (Ph.D. in History). 390p. DAI 37, no.1 (July 1976): 510-A; UM 76-14,561. Focuses on political developments during the years 860-907.

Sung, Liao, and Chin Periods (960-1279)

See also entries 354, 786, 999, 1531, 1639, 1645, 1654, and 1664.

412 MA, Laurence Jun-chao. *Commercial Development and Urban Change in Sung China.* Michigan, 1971 (Ph.D. in Geography). 202p. DAI 32, no.7 (Jan. 1972): 4004-B; UM 72-4927. Published as Commercial...China (Ann Arbor: Department of Geography, University of Michigan, 1971. xv, 196p. [Michigan geographical publications, 6]).

413 TCHANG, Fou-jouei. *La vie et l'oeuvre de Hong Mai*

(1123-1202). [French: The Life and Works of Hung Mai (1123-1202).] Paris VII, 1971 (Doctorat de 3e cycle). A copy is available at the Bibliothèque de la Sorbonne. Hung was the author of <u>Jung chai sui pi</u> (Jottings from the Leisure Studio), a contribution to our knowledge of social and political history.

414   GOLAS, Peter John. *The Sung Wine Monopoly*. Harvard, 1972 (Ph.D. in History and Far Eastern Languages). iii, 173p. Available at the Harvard University Archives, Pusey Library, call no.HU 90.10149.5.

415   HATCH, George Cecil, Jr. *The Thought of Su Hsun (1009-1066): An Essay in the Social Meaning of Intellectual Pluralism in Northern Sung*. Washington (Seattle), 1972 (Ph.D. in History). 499p. DAI 33, no.12 (June 1973): 6825-A; UM 73-13,831.

416   IZGI, Özkan. *The Itinerary of Wang Yen-te to Kao-ch'ang (981-984)*. Harvard, 1972 (Ph.D. in Far Eastern Languages). xxxi, 127p. Available at the Harvard University Archives, Pusey Library, call no.HU 90.10162.10. On the <u>Hsi chou ch'eng chi</u>, a Sung government official's account of his trip to a small country outside of central China.

417   KUNG, Tsung-tsai. *Tchao Ming-Tch'eng (1081-1129): sa vie et son oeuvre*. [French: Chao Ming-ch'êng (1081-1129): His Life and His Work.] Paris VII, 1972 (Doctorat de 3e cycle ès études extrême-orientales). 190p. A copy is available at the Bibliothèque de la Sorbonne. On a scholar and antiquarian, author of a treatise on ancient stone inscriptions entitled <u>Chin shih lu</u>.

418   PHAIRE, Barbara Rose. *Papal Motivations for an Asian Apostolate (1245-1254): An Analysis*. New York, 1972 (Ph.D. in History). 107p. DAI 33, no.11 (May 1973): 6262-A; UM 73-11,752. Includes Papal contacts with the Tartars.

419   DARS, Jacques. *La marine chinoise du Xème au XIVème siècle*. [French: The Chinese Navy and Seamanship between the 10th and 14th Centuries.] Paris VII, 1973 (Doctorat d'Etat). A copy is available at the Bibliothèque de la Sorbonne.

420   FRANTZELL, Lennart. *Dr. Her's Comprehensive Essays on the Art of War: The <u>Her Bor-shyh Bey Luenn</u>, Translation with Prolegomena*. Stockholm, 1973 (Akad. avh.). Published as <u>Dr. Her's...Prolegomena</u> (Stockholm: Stockholms Universitet, Institutionen für orientaliska sprak, 1973.

173p.). On <u>Ho po shih pei lun</u>, a work by a little known Sung scholar named Ho Ch'ü-fei.

421 FREEMAN, Michael Dennis. *Lo-yang and the Opposition to Wang An-shih: The Rise of Confucian Conservatism, 1068-1086.* Yale, 1973 (Ph.D. in History). 282p. DAI 34, no.11 (May 1974): 7140-A; UM 74-11,474.

422 MORPER, Cornelia. *Ch'ien Wei-yen (977-1034) und Feng Ching (1021-1094) als Prototypen eines ehrgeizigen, korrupten und eines bescheidenen, korrekten Ministers der Nördlichen Sung-Dynastie.* [German: Ch'ien Wei-yen (977-1034) and Feng Ching (1021-1094) as Prototypes of an Ambitious and Corrupt Minister and of a Modest and Proper Minister of the Northern Sung Dynasty.] Würzburg, 1973 (Dr., Philosophische Fakultät). Published as <u>Ch'ien...Sung-Dynastie</u> (Bern & Frankfurt a.M.: Lang, 1975. iii, 154p. [Würzburger Sino-Japonica, 4]).

423 VITTINGHOFF, Helmolt. *Proskription und Intrige gegen Yüan-yu-Parteigänger. Ein Beitrag zu den Kontroversen nach den Reformen des Wang an-Shih, dargestellt an den Biographien des Lu Tien (1042-1102) und des Ch'en Kuan (1057-1124).* [German: Proscription and Intrigue against Members of Yüan-yu. A Contribution to the Quarrels Following the Reforms of Wang an-shih, Shown in the Biographies of Lu Tien (1042-1102) and Ch'en Kuan (1057-1124).] Würzburg, 1973 (Dr., Seminar für Sinologie). Published as <u>Proskription...1124</u> (Bern & Frankfurt a.M.: Lang, 1975. 206p. [Würzburger Sino-Japonica, 5]).

424 LEE, Thomas Hong-chi. *Education in Northern Sung China.* Yale, 1974 (Ph.D. in History). DAI 36, no.1 (July 1975): 459-A; UM 75-15,340.

425 OLSSON, Karl Frederick. *The Structure of Power under the Third Emperor of Sung China: The Shifting Balance after the Peace of Shan-yuan.* Chicago, 1974 (Ph.D. in Far Eastern Languages and Civilizations). 264p. Order copies from the Photoduplication Department, Joseph Regenstein Library, University of Chicago.

426 WONG, Hon-chiu. *Government Expenditures in Northern Sung China (960-1127).* Pennsylvania, 1975 (Ph.D. in History). 293p. DAI 36, no.8 (Feb. 1976): 5462-A; UM 76-3232.

Yüan Dynasty (1279-1368)

See also entries 126, 361, 419, 1000, and 1633.

427   DREYER, Edward Leslie. *The Emergence of Chu Yüan-chang,*
      1360-1365. Harvard, 1971 (Ph.D. in History and Far
      Eastern Languages). iv, 573p. Available at the Harvard
      University Archives, Pusey Library, call no.HU 90.9940.10.
      On the activities of the founder of the Ming Dynasty
      during the years immediately preceding the fall of the
      Yüan Dynasty.

428   MANGOLD, Gunther. *Das Militärwesen in China unter der*
      Mongolen-Herrschaft. [German: The Military Establish-
      ment in China under Mongol Rule.] München, 1971 (Dr.,
      Philosophische Fakultät). Published as Das Militär-
      wesen...Mongolen-Herrschaft (Bamberg: Aku Fotodruck, 1971.
      252p.).

429   SEIDEN, Jacob. *The Mongol Impact on Russia from the*
      Thirteenth Century to the Present: Mongol Contributions
      to the Political Institutions of Muscovy, Imperial Rus-
      sia, and the Soviet State. Georgetown, 1971 (Ph.D. in
      Russian Area Studies). 1101p. DAI 32, no.7 (Jan. 1972):
      3934-A; UM 72-4219.

430   HEYDE, Doris. *Der Kampf um die Wiedereinführung des*
      staatlichen Prüfungssystems unter der Yuan-Dynastie.
      [German: The Struggle for the Reestablishment of the
      State Examination System under the Yüan Dynasty.] Hum-
      boldt-Universität Berlin, 1972 (Dr., Gesellschafts-
      wissenschaftliche Fakultät). xii, 145p.

431   KWANTEN, Luc Herman M. *Tibetan-Mongol Relations during*
      the Yuan Dynasty, 1207-1368. South Carolina, 1972
      (Ph.D. in History). 238p. DAI 34, no.1 (July 1973):
      225-A; UM 73-16,308.

432   LANGER, Lawrence N. *The Russian Medieval Town: From the*
      Mongol Invasions to the End of the Fifteenth Century.
      Chicago, 1972 (Ph.D. in History). 630p. Order copies
      from the Photoduplication Department, Joseph Regenstein
      Library, University of Chicago.

433   LANGLOIS, John Dexter, Jr. *Chin-hua Confucianism under*
      the Mongols (1279-1368). Princeton, 1973 (Ph.D. in His-
      tory). 447p. DAI 35, no.2 (Aug. 1974): 994-A; UM
      74-17,469. Examines a movement of cultural preserva-
      tionism in Chin-hua, central Chekiang, in order to under-
      stand the Confucian response to Mongol domination.

434   TOGAN, Isenbike. *The Chapter on Annual Grants in the*

Yüan shih. Harvard, 1973 (Ph.D. in East Asian Languages
and Civilizations). cxxx, 559p. Available at the Harvard University Archives, Pusey Library, call no.HU
90.10670.

435 WU, Pai-nan Rashid. *The Fall of Baghdad and the Mongol
Rule in al-^CIrāq, 1258-1335*. Utah, 1974 (Ph.D. in History). 356p. DAI 35, no.10 (Apr. 1975): 6621-A; UM
75-9617.

436 CLARK, Larry Vernon. *Introduction to the Uyghur Civil
Documents of East Turkestan (13th-14th Centuries)*. Indiana, 1975 (Ph.D. in Uralic and Altaic Studies). 503p.
DAI 36, no.8 (Feb. 1976): 5461-62-A; UM 76-2795. On
documents from Turfan and Kucha dealing with social and
economic life under Mongol rule.

437 MARTINEZ, Arsenio Peter. *Interregional Trade Cycles,
Bullion Transfers and Economic Policy in Mongol Western
Asia*. Columbia, 1975 (Ph.D. in Middle East Languages
and Cultures). 705p. DAI 36, no.3 (Sept. 1975):
1698-99-A; UM 75-18,417. Focuses on Mongol rule in
Persia under the Ilkhans (1256-1349).

Ming Dynasty (1368-1644)

See also entries 427, 462, 1479, 1648, 1656, 1661, and 1669.

438 CHEN, Min-sun. *Three Contemporary Western Sources on
the History of Late Ming and the Manchu Conquest of
China*. Chicago, 1971 (Ph.D. in History). 254p. Order
copies from the Photoduplication Department, Joseph Regenstein Library, University of Chicago.

439 KELLY, Edward Thomas. *The Anti-Christian Persecution of
1616-1617 in Nanking*. Columbia, 1971 (Ph.D. in East
Asian Languages and Cultures). 389p. DAI 32, no.3
(Sept. 1971): 1427-28-A; UM 71-23,601.

440 KU, Helen Pui-king. *Chu Chun-shui: His Life and Influence*. St. John's, 1971 (Ph.D. in History). 187p. DAI
32, no.5 (Nov. 1971): 2586-A; UM 71-30,228. On a Chinese philosopher (lived 1600-1682) who fled from the
Manchus to Japan.

441 WALKER, Hugh Dyson. *The Yi-Ming Rapprochement: Sino-
Korean Foreign Relations, 1392-1592*. California (Los
Angeles), 1971 (Ph.D. in History). 355p. DAI 32, no.6
(Dec. 1971): 3189-90-A; UM 72-1511.

442   HSI, Angela Ning-jy Sun. *Social and Economic Status of
      the Merchant Class of the Ming Dynasty, 1368-1644*. Il-
      linois, 1972 (Ph.D. in History). 239p. DAI 33, no.6
      (Dec. 1972): 2845-A; UM 72-19,851.

443   CHEANG, Eng-chew. *Li Chih as a Critic: A Chapter of the
      Ming Intellectual History*. Washington (Seattle), 1973
      (Ph.D. in Asian Languages and Literature). 384p. DAI
      34, no.8 (Feb. 1974): 5095-A; UM 74-2246. On Li's social,
      philosophical and literary criticism.

444   EBERSTEIN, Bernd. *Bergbau und Bergarbeiter zur Ming-
      Zeit (1368-1644)*. [German: Mining and Miners during the
      Ming Period (1368-1644).] Hamburg, 1973 (Dr.phil., Sem-
      inar für Sprache und Kultur Chinas). Published as Berg-
      bau...1644 (Hamburg: Gesellschaft für Natur- und Völker-
      kunde Ostasiens, 1974. 243p. [Its Mitteilungen, Bd.57]).

445   KU, Joseph King-hap. *Hsu Kuang-chi: Chinese Scientist
      and Christian (1562-1633)*. St. John's, 1973 (Ph.D. in
      History). 175p. DAI 34, no.7 (Jan. 1974): 4124-25-A;
      UM 73-29,965.

446   WIENS, Mi Chu. *Socioeconomic Change during the Ming
      Dynasty in the Kiangnan Area*. Harvard, 1973 (Ph.D. in
      History and East Asian Languages). vi, 433p. Available
      at the Harvard University Archives, Pusey Library, call
      no.HU 90.10491.

447   RYAN, Michael Timothy. *New Worlds of Pagan Religion in
      the Seventeenth Century*. New York, 1974 (Ph.D. in His-
      tory). 530p. DAI 35, no.11 (May 1975): 7233-34-A; UM
      75-9695. Deals in part with European activities in
      China, focusing on Matteo Ricci (1552-1610) and the Je-
      suits.

448   ATWELL, William Stewart. *Ch'en Tsu-lung (1608-1647): A
      Scholar-Official of the Late Ming Dynasty*. Princeton,
      1975 (Ph.D. in East Asian Studies). 218p. DAI 36, no.4
      (Oct. 1975): 2390-A; UM 75-23,179.

449   HANDLIN, Joanna Flug. *Lü K'un (1536-1618): The Reorien-
      tation of a Scholar-Official*. California (Berkeley),
      1975 (Ph.D. in History). v, 215p. Order copies from
      the Library Photographic Service, General Library, Uni-
      versity of California at Berkeley.

450   LEE, Lawrence Yu-kam. *A Systems Analysis of the Ming
      Censorial System in China (1368-1644)*. Pittsburgh, 1975
      (Ph.D. in History). 550p. DAI 36, no.4 (Oct. 1975):
      2438-A; UM 75-22,418.

451 LI, Gertrude Roth. *The Rise of the Early Manchu State: A Portrait Drawn from Manchu Sources to 1636.* Harvard, 1975 (Ph.D. in History and East Asian Languages). 235p. Available at the Harvard University Archives, Pusey Library, call no.HU 90.10796.20.

452 MEI, June Yuet. *Kaifeng, a Chinese City in the Ming Dynasty.* Harvard, 1975 (Ph.D. in History and East Asian Languages). 370p. Available at the Harvard University Archives, Pusey Library, call no.HU 90.10992.10.

Early Ch'ing Period (1644-1800)

Internal Affairs

See also entries 359, 451, 498, 1651, 1659, and 1667.

453 JONES, Susan Louise Mann. *Hung Liang-chi (1746-1809): The Perception and Articulation of Political Problems in Late Eighteenth Century China.* Stanford, 1972 (Ph.D. in Asian Languages). 234p. DAI 32, no.12 (June 1972): 6867-A; UM 72-16,731. Focuses on this scholar-official's extensive critique of government policy and bureaucratic practices.

454 DENNERLINE, Jerry Paul. *The Mandarins and the Massacre of Chia-ting: An Analysis of the Local Heritage and the Resistance to the Manchu Invasion of 1645.* Yale, 1973 (Ph.D. in History). 474p. DAI 34, no.11 (May 1974): 7132-A; UM 74-10,665.

455 RIDLEY, Charles Price. *Educational Theory and Practice in Late Imperial China: The Teaching of Writing as a Specific Case.* Stanford, 1973 (Ph.D. in Asian Languages). 555p. DAI 34, no.3 (Sept. 1973): 1110-A; UM 73-20,512. Based on a study of works by Lu Shih-i (1611-1672), Wang Yün (1784-1854), and Chang Hsüeh-ch'eng (1738-1801).

456 TORBERT, Preston McCullough. *The Ch'ing Imperial Household Department: A Study of Its Organization and Principal Functions, 1662-1796.* Chicago, 1973 (Ph.D. in History). 295p. Order copies from the Photoduplication Department, Joseph Regenstein Library, University of Chicago.

457 FISHER, Thomas Stephen. *Lü Liu-liang (1629-83) and the Tseng Ching Case (1728-33).* Princeton, 1974 (Ph.D. in History). 502p. DAI 36, no.4 (Oct. 1975): 2361-A; UM 75-23,198. On a major literary case of the Yung-chen Period.

458 KÄMPFE, Hans-Rainer. *Die soziale Rolle des 2. pekinger
     Lcan skya-qutuqtu rol pa'i rdo rje (1717-1786); Beiträge
     zu einer Analyse anhand tibetischer und mongolischer
     Biographien.* [German: The Social Role of the Second
     Peking Lcan skya-qutuqtu rol pa'i rdo rje (1717-1786):
     Contributions to an Analysis on the Basis of Tibetan
     and Mongolian Biographies.] Bonn, 1974 (Dr., Philoso-
     phische Fakultät). Published as Die soziale...Biographien
     (Bonn: Rheinische Friedrich-Wilhelms-Universität, 1974.
     394p.).

459 LEGRAND, Jacques. *L'administration dans la domination
     sino-mandchoue en Mongolie Qalq-a (fin du XVIIIe-début
     du XIXe siècle). La version mongole du Lifan yuan zeli.*
     [French: Administration in Khalka Mongolia during the
     Period of the Sino-Manchu Domination (Late 18th-Early
     19th Centuries): The Mongol Version of the Li-fan Yuan
     tse-li.] Paris VII, 1974 (Doctorat de 3e cycle ès études
     extrême-orientales). iv, 391p. A copy is available at
     the Bibliothèque de la Sorbonne, library catalogue no.
     I 2698-4°.

460 MILLER, Harold Lyman. *Factional Conflict and the Inte-
     gration of Ch'ing Politics, 1661-1690.* George Washing-
     ton, 1974 (Ph.D. in History). 213p. DAI 35, no.4 (Oct.
     1974): 2157-A; UM 74-22,260.

461 ROPP, Paul Stanley. *Early Ch'ing Society and Its Critics:
     The Life and Times of Wu Ch'ing-tzu (1701-1754).* Michi-
     gan, 1974 (Ph.D. in History). 353p. DAI 35, no.11 (May
     1975): 7233-A; UM 75-10,275.

462 STRUVE, Lynn Ann. *Uses of History in Traditional Chinese
     Society: The Southern Ming in Ch'ing Historiography.*
     Michigan, 1974 (Ph.D. in History). 323p. DAI 35, no.7
     (Jan. 1975): 4407-08-A; UM 75-828.

463 COLE, James Hillard. *Shaohsing: Studies in Ch'ing Social
     History.* Stanford, 1975 (Ph.D. in History). 280p. DAI
     36, no.4 (Oct. 1975): 2357-A; UM 75-21,858. On Shaohsing
     prefecture, Chekiang province.

464 SYMONS, Van Jay. *The Ch'ing Ginseng Monopoly.* Brown,
     1975 (Ph.D. in Asian History). 226p. DAI 37, no.1
     (July 1976): 529-A; UM 76-15,725.

465 WILL, Pierre-Etienne. *Bureaucratie et famine dans la
     Chine du XVIIIème siecle.* [French: Bureaucracy and
     Famine Relief in Eighteenth China.] Paris V (René Des-
     cartes), 1975 (Doctorat de 3e cycle). vi, 302p. Fo-
     cuses on the 1743-44 drought in Chihli.

Foreign Relations and Foreign Trade

See also entries 62, 125, 129, 528, and 1657.

466 ABEL, Anne-Marie J. *La pauvreté dans la pensée et
     l'oeuvre de Jean-Martin Moye.* [French: Poverty in the
     Thought and Works of Jean-Martin Moye.] Paris IV (Paris-
     Sorbonne), 1972 (Doctorat de 3e cycle en histoire).
     432p. A copy is available at the Bibliothèque de la
     Sorbonne. Moye (1730-1793) was a priest from Lorraine
     who spent part of his life in China.

467 FIELD, Alvin Robert. *Himalayan Diplomacy (1767-1793).*
     American, 1972 (Ph.D. in International Relations and
     Organization). 321p. DAI 33, no.7 (Jan. 1973): 3739-A;
     UM 73-1348. On early Sino-Indian relations.

468 SCOTT, Gordon Alistair Keith. *The Formation of the
     Turkestan Frontier between Russia and China in the Eigh-
     teenth Century.* Oxford, 1972 (D.Phil. in Modern History).
     iii, 273p.

469 GOLDSTEIN, Jonathan. *The China Trade from Philadelphia,
     1682-1846: A Study of Interregional Commerce and Cul-
     tural Interaction.* Pennsylvania, 1973 (Ph.D. in History).
     239p. DAI 34, no.12 (June 1974): 7675-76-A; UM 74-14,066.
     Published as Philadelphia and the China Trade, 1682-1846:
     Commercial, Cultural, and Attitudinal Effects (University
     Park: Pennsylvania State University Press, 1977).

470 WITEK, John Wayne, S.J. *An Eighteenth-Century Frenchman
     at the Court of the K'ang-hsi Emperor: A Study of the
     Early Life of Jean Francois Foucquet.* Georgetown, 1973
     (Ph.D. in History). 767p. DAI 35, no.1 (July 1974):
     388-89-A; UM 74-14,928.

471 INOGUCHI, Takashi. *Wars as International Learning: Chi-
     nese, British and Japanese in East Asia.* Massachusetts
     Institute of Technology, 1974 (Ph.D. in Political Sci-
     ence). 628p. Order copies from the Microreproduction
     Laboratory, Massachusetts Institute of Technology. In-
     cludes 22 case studies of international conflict between
     the early 1600s and 1945, among them Ch'ing period con-
     flicts with Burma, Great Britain, Korea and Vietnam, and
     various Sino-Japanese wars.

472 SARASIN VIRAPHOL [VIRAPHOL, Sarasin]. *Sino-Siamese
     Trade, 1652-1853.* Harvard, 1974 (Ph.D. in History and
     East Asian Languages). viii, 651p. Available at the
     Harvard University Archives, Pusey Library, call no.
     HU 90.10674. Published as Tribute and Profit: Sino-
     Siamese Trade, 1652-1853 (Cambridge, Mass.: Council

on East Asian Studies, Harvard University, 1977 [Harvard East Asian Monographs, 76]).

Late Ch'ing Period (1800-1911)
Biographical Studies

This section is limited to biographical studies of Chinese. Studies of Westerners in China may be found in sections on foreign relations and on missions and missionaries (pp.76-86).

473 BAYS, Daniel Henry. *Chang Chih-tung and the Politics of Reform in China, 1895-1905.* Michigan, 1971 (Ph.D. in History). 281p. DAI 33, no.5 (Nov. 1972): 2275-A; UM 72-28,997.

474 CHUANG, Chen-kuan. *Liang Ch'i-Ch'ao (1873-1929): A Political Study.* Alberta, 1971 (Ph.D. in History). vii, 220p. Order copies directly from the Canadian Theses Division, National Library of Canada at Ottawa; available only in microfilm format, film no.8067, @ $2.50.

475 DES FORGES, Roger Van Vranken. *Hsi-liang: a Portrait of a Late Ch'ing Patriot.* Yale, 1971 (Ph.D. in History). 522p. DAI 32, no.5 (Nov. 1971): 2596-A; UM 71-28,158. Published as Hsi-liang and the Chinese National Revolution (New Haven: Yale University Press, 1973. xviii, 274p. [Yale historical publications. Miscellany, 99]).

476 DRAKE, Fred William. *Hsü Chi-yü and His Ying-huan chih-lüeh (1848): An Early Modern View of the Non-Chinese World.* Harvard, 1971 (Ph.D. in History and Far Eastern Languages). iv, 410p. Available at the Harvard University Archives, Pusey Library, call no.HU 90.9940. Published as China Charts the World: Hsü Chi-yü and His Geography of 1848 (Cambridge, Mass.: East Asian Research Center, Harvard University, 1975. ix, 272p. [Harvard East Asian monographs, 64]).

477 KEHNEN, Johannes. *Cheng Kuan-ying, Unternehmer und Reformer der späten Ch'ing-Zeit.* [German: Cheng Kuan-ying, Entrepreneur and Reformer of the Late Ch'ing Period.] Bochum, 1971 (Dr., Abteilung für Geschichtswissenschaft). Published as Cheng...Ch'ing-Zeit (Wiesbaden: Harrassowitz, 1975. viii, 179p. [Veröffentlichungen des Ostasien-Instituts der Ruhr-Universität Bochum; Bd. 14]).

478 LEONARD, Jane Kate. *Wei Yüan and the Hai-kuo t'u-chih: A Geographical Analysis of Western Expansion in Maritime*

Asia. Cornell, 1971 (Ph.D. in History). 223p. DAI 32, no.4 (Oct. 1971): 2013-A; UM 71-24,517. On the "Illustrated Treatise on the Maritime Kingdoms" by the prominent scholar Wei Yüan (1794-1856).

479 MACHETZKI, Rüdiger. *Liang Ch'i-ch'ao und die Einflüsse deutscher Staatslehren auf den monarchischen Reformnationalismus in China nach 1900.* [German: Liang Ch'i-ch'ao and the Influence of German Political Theory on the Monarchical Reform Nationalism in China after 1900.] Hamburg, 1971 (Dr., Philosophische Fakultät). Published as Liang...1900 (Hamburg, 1973. x, 169, xxiv p.).

480 MacKINNON, Stephen Robert. *Yüan Shih-k'ai in Tientsin and Peking: The Sources and Structure of His Power, 1901-1908.* California (Davis), 1971 (Ph.D. in History). 275p. DAI 32, no.10 (Apr. 1972): 5716-A; UM 72-9902.

481 PORTER, Jonathan. *Tseng Kuo-fan's Private Bureaucracy.* California (Berkeley), 1971 (Ph.D. in History). iii, 306p. Published as Tseng...Bureaucracy (Berkeley: Center for Chinese Studies, University of California, 1972. 151p. [China research monographs, no.9]).

482 FIELDS, Lanny Bruce. *Tso Tsung-T'ang (1812-1885) and His Campaigns in Northwestern China, 1868-1880.* Indiana, 1972 (Ph.D. in History). 175p. DAI 33, no.10 (Apr. 1973): 5653-A; UM 73-9759. On the Moslem uprisings.

483 HOWARD, Richard Campbell. *The Early Life and Thought of K'ang Yu-wei, 1858-1895.* Columbia, 1972 (Ph.D. in East Asian Languages and Cultures). 672p. DAI 33, no.1 (July 1972): 253-A; UM 72-20,045.

484 LAI, Jin-nan. *Hong Rengan (1822-1864).* [French: Hung Jen-kan (1822-1864).] Paris VII, 1972 (Doctorat de 3e cycle en histoire). vii, 268p. A copy is available at the Bibliothèque de la Sorbonne, library catalogue no. I 2205-4°. Hung served as prime minister and regent of the Taiping Kingdom.

485 ROBEL, Ronald Ray. *The Life and Thought of T'an Ssu-t'ung.* Michigan, 1972 (Ph.D. in History). 469p. DAI 33, no.5 (Nov. 1972): 2306-A; UM 72-29,181. On an outspoken advocate of reform during the late Ch'ing period.

486 TENG, Tony Yung-yuan. *Prince Kung and the Survival of Ch'ing Rule, 1858-1898.* Wisconsin, 1972 (Ph.D. in History). 274p. DAI 33, no.12 (June 1973): 6821-22-A; UM 73-9227.

487 WONG, John Yue-wo. *The Political Career of Yeh Ming-ch'en, 1807-1859.* Oxford, 1972 (D.Phil. in Modern

History). xxvii, 480p.

488 WORDEN, Robert Leo. *A Chinese Reformer in Exile: The North American Phase of the Travels of K'ang Yu-wei, 1899-1909*. Georgetown, 1972 (Ph.D. in History). 380p. DAI 33, no.7 (Jan. 1973): 3567-68-A; UM 72-34,191.

489 KAMACHI, Noriko. *Huang Tsun-hsien (1848-1905): His Response to Meiji Japan and the West*. Harvard, 1973 (Ph.D. in History and East Asian Languages). 410p. Available at the Harvard University Archives, Pusey Library, call no.HU 90.10376.10.

490 LEE, Chi-fang. *Wang T'ao (1828-1897): His Life, Thought, Scholarship, and Literary Achievement*. Wisconsin, 1973 (Ph.D. in Chinese). 344p. DAI 35, no.1 (July 1974): 461-A; UM 74-10,251.

491 VEIT, Veronika. *Arad-un Qatan Bayatur Maysurǰab (1878-1927). Eine Untersuchung über das Leben und die Bedeutung eines mongolischen Generals*. [German: Arad-un Qatan Bayatur Maysurǰab (1878-1927): An Investigation of the Life and Importance of a Mongolian General.] Bonn, 1973 (Dr., Philosophische Fakultät). Published as <u>Arad-un Qatan Bayatur Maysurǰab... Generals</u> (Bonn: Rheinische Friedrich-Wilhelms-Universität, 1974. 170p.).

492 WU, Chang-chuan. *Cheng Kuan-ying: A Case Study of Merchant Participation in the Chinese Self-Strengthening Movement (1878-1884)*. Columbia, 1974 (Ph.D. in History). 382p. DAI 35, no.10 (Apr. 1975): 6649-A; UM 75-7548.

493 CHUNG, Sue Fawn. *The Much Maligned Empress Dowager: A Revisionist Study of the Empress Dowager Tz'u-hsi in the Period 1898 to 1900*. California (Berkeley), 1975 (Ph.D. in History). 304p. DAI 37, no.2 (Aug. 1976): 1150-A; UM 76-15,140.

494 HSIEH, Andrew Cheng-kuang. *Tseng Kuo-fan, a Nineteenth-Century Confucian General*. Yale, 1975 (Ph.D. in History). 245p. DAI 36, no.12 (June 1976): 8234-A; UM 76-14,045.

495 OCKO, Jonathan Kevin. *Ting Jih-ch'ang and Restoration Kiangsu, 1864-1870: Rhetoric and Reality*. Yale, 1975 (Ph.D. in History). 401p. DAI 37, no.1 (July 1976): 521-A; UM 76-14,583. On Ting's tenure as Kiangsu financial commissioner and governor.

496 TSAI, Jung-fang. *Comprador Ideologists in Modern China: Ho Kai (Ho Ch'i, 1859-1914) and Hu Li-yüan (1847-1916)*. California (Los Angeles), 1975 (Ph.D. in History). 379p. DAI 36, no.6 (Dec. 1975): 3953-A; UM 75-26,999.

Internal Affairs

--General and Miscellaneous Studies--

See also entries 463, 464, 600, 621, and 623.

497 FUNG, Edmund Shiu Kay. *The Hupeh Revolutionary Move-
     ment 1900-1912: A Study of the Role of the New-Style
     Army*. Australian National, 1971 (Ph.D. in Far Eastern
     History). 376p.

498 ROZMAN, Gilbert Friedell. *Urban Networks in Ch'ing China
     and Tokugawa Japan*. Princeton, 1971 (Ph.D. in Sociology).
     454p. DAI 32, no.7 (Jan. 1972): 4131-A; UM 72-2743.
     Published as Urban...Japan (Princeton: Princeton Univer-
     sity Press, 1974. xiv, 355p.). Includes studies of
     Peking and Chihli Province.

499 WONG, Young-tsu. *Remolders of Tradition: Reformist
     Thought in Nineteenth Century China*. Washington (Se-
     attle), 1971 (Ph.D. in History). 370p. DAI 32, no.5
     (Nov. 1971): 2581-A; UM 71-28,496. Focuses on the prob-
     lems encountered by 14 reformist thinkers and on their
     solutions.

500 ROSENBAUM, Arthur Lewis. *China's First Railway: The
     Imperial Railways of North China, 1880-1911*. Yale, 1972
     (Ph.D. in History). 592p. DAI 32, no.12 (June 1972):
     6903-04-A; UM 72-17,164.

501 LIN, Tsung-kuang. *The Compradore in Modern Chinese
     Politics, 1840-1911*. Fletcher School of Law and Diplo-
     macy, 1974 (Ph.D.). iv, 530p. Order copies from the
     Edwin Ginn Library, Fletcher School of Law and Diplomacy,
     Tufts University.

502 NAQUIN, Susan. *Millenarian Rebellion in China: The
     Eight Trigrams Uprising of 1813*. Yale, 1974 (Ph.D. in
     History). 535p. DAI 36, no.1 (July 1975): 488-A; UM
     75-15,347. Published as Millenarian...1813 (New Haven:
     Yale University Press, 1976. xii, 384p. [Yale his-
     torical publications: miscellany, 108]).

503 HAYES, James William. *South East China in the Late
     Ch'ing: Some Rural Settlements in the Hong Kong Region of
     Kwangtung, with Special Reference to the Period 1850-1899*.
     London, 1975 (Ph.D. in History). vii, 350p. Order copies
     from the British Library Lending Division, no.D15658/76.

504 LAU, Siu Kai. *The Confucian Elite, Power and Social
     Stability in Traditional China: Toward a Theory of Seg-
     mental Cooperation*. Minnesota, 1975 (Ph.D. in Sociology).
     444p. DAI 36, no.4 (Oct. 1975): 2437-A; UM 75-21,063.

Lau's hypotheses are tested with historical data from 19th century China.

505   SKOCPOL, Theda R. *Social Revolutions in France, Russia, and China: A Comparative-Historical and Structural Analysis*. Harvard, 1975 (Ph.D. in Sociology). iv, 556p. Available at the Harvard University Archives, Pusey Library, call no.HU 90.11053.10. Focuses on the late Ch'ing period and the 20th century.

--The Economy--

See also entries 152, 173, 359, 360, 477, 492, 495, and 632.

506   CHAN, Wellington Kam-kong. *Merchants, Mandarins and Modern Enterprise in Late Ch'ing China (1872-1911)*. Harvard, 1972 (Ph.D. in History). vi, 378p. Available at the Harvard University Archives, Pusey Library, call no. HU 90.10119.15. Published as Merchants...China (Cambridge, Mass.: East Asian Research Center, Harvard University, 1977. xiv, 323p. [Harvard East Asian monographs, 79]).

507   LOJEWSKI, Frank Arno. *Confucian Reformers and Local Vested Interests: The Su-Sung-T'ai Tax Reduction of 1863 and Its Aftermath*. California (Davis), 1973 (Ph.D. in History). 453p. DAI 34, no.10 (Apr. 1974): 6569-A; UM 74-8522. Explores problems in the grain tribute administration of an area within southern Kiangsu.

508   LIU, Ts'ui-jung. *Trade on the Han River and Its Impact on Economic Development, c. 1800-1911*. Harvard, 1974 (Ph.D. in History and East Asian Languages). vi, 289p. Available at the Harvard University Archives, Pusey Library, call no.HU 90.10585.

509   HAMILTON, Gary Glen. *Cathay and the Way Beyond: Modernization, Regionalism and Commerce in Imperial China*. Washington (Seattle), 1975 (Ph.D. in Sociology). 311p. DAI 37, no.2 (Aug. 1976): 1236-37-A; UM 76-17,488. Focuses on 19th century China.

510   McELDERRY, Andrea Lee. *Shanghai Old-Style Banks (Ch'ien-chuang), 1800-1935: A Traditional Institution in a Changing Society*. Michigan, 1975 (Ph.D. in History). 285p. DAI 36, no.3 (Sept. 1975): 1727-28-A; UM 75-20,404. Published as Shanghai...Society (Ann Arbor: Center for Chinese Studies, University of Michigan, 1976. viii, 230p. [Michigan papers in Chinese studies, 25]).

--Taiping Movement and the Moslem Rebellions--

See also entries 482 and 484.

511 WU, Thomas Dong. *A Model for Revolutions That Failed:
     A Case Study of the Taiping Mass Movement in China,
     1850-1864.* Southern Illinois, 1971 (Ph.D. in Government).
     177p. DAI 32, no.9 (Mar. 1972): 5318-A; UM 72-10,313

512 SMITH, Richard Joseph. *Barbarian Officers of Imperial
     China: Ward, Gordon and the Taiping Rebellion.* Cali-
     fornia (Davis), 1972 (Ph.D. in History). v, 471p. Con-
     tact the University of California library for copies.
     On the American military adventurer Frederick Townsend
     Ward and the British captain Charles George Gordon.

513 HUANG, Wen-chih. *Das Taiping-Christentum. Eine Analyse
     seiner Entstehung, Entwicklung sowie seiner Lehre mit
     besonderer Berücksichtigung seiner Einflüsse auf die
     Revolutionsbewegung der Taipings.* [German: Taiping
     Christianity: An Analysis of Its Origin, Development and
     Doctrines with Particular Regard to Its Influence upon
     the Taiping Revolutionary Movement.] Erlangen-Nürnberg,
     1973 (Dr., Philosophische Fakultat). DAI 37, no.3 (Spring
     1977): Vol.C--entry no.1/3317c. Published as Das
     Taiping-Christentum...Taipings (Erlangen: Hogl, 1973.
     147p.).

514 LIANG, Kenneth Chok-king. *Mass Action Disturbances in
     China, 1796-1911: Their Nature and Social Sources.*
     Pittsburgh, 1973 (Ph.D. in Sociology). 224p. DAI 34,
     no.5 (Nov. 1973): 2781-82-A; UM 73-27,178.

515 CHANG, Chung-yun. *The Organization, Training, and Leader-
     ship of a Victorious Army: The Hsiang-chun, 1853-1865.*
     St. John's, 1974 (Ph.D. in Asian History). 364p. DAI
     35, no.8 (Feb. 1975): 5290-A; UM 75-3238.

516 CHOW, Hun Lin. *The Taiping Rebellion and Its Foreign
     Relations.* Santo Tomas [Manila], 1974 (Ph.D. in His-
     tory). ix, 502p.

517 ISRAELI, Raphael. *Chinese versus Muslims: A Study of
     Cultural Confrontation.* California (Berkeley), 1974
     (Ph.D. in History). 417p. DAI 35, no.6 (Dec. 1974):
     3192-A; UM 74-27,175. Focuses on the Muslim community
     and the Muslim rebellions during the 19th century.

518 WEI, Alice Bihyün Gan. *The Moslem Rebellion in Yunnan,
     1855-1873.* Chicago, 1974 (Ph.D. in History). xi, 335p.
     Order copies from the Photoduplication Department,
     Joseph Regenstein Library, University of Chicago.

Foreign Relations, Trade, and Investment

--General and Miscellaneous Studies--

See also entries 472, 516, 786, 856, 994, 1640, 1641, 1652, and 1657, as well as the many subsections under "Overseas Chinese Communities" (pp.161-81).

519   IRICK, Robert Lee. *Ch'ing Policy toward the Coolie Trade, 1847-1878.* Harvard, 1971 (Ph.D. in History and Far Eastern Languages). 608p. Available at the Harvard University Archives, Pusey Library, call no.HU 90.9977.10.

520   LEE (LI), En-han. *China's Quest for Recovery of Railway Rights, 1904-1911: Economic Nationalism in Action.* California (Santa Barbara), 1971 (Ph.D. in History). xiii, 378p. Order copies directly from the Department of Special Collections, University of California at Santa Barbara Library.

521   HANSON, John Robert (II). *The 19th Century Exports of the Less Developed Countries.* Pennsylvania, 1972 (Ph.D. in Economics). 383p. DAI 33, no.4 (Oct. 1972): 1300-A; UM 72-25,581. Includes China.

522   WAUNG, William Šui Kǐng. *The Opium Question in China, 1860-1887.* London, 1972 (Ph.D. in History, School of Oriental and African Studies). 450p.

523   CARRINGTON, George Williams. *Foreigners in Formosa, 1841-1874.* Oxford, 1973 (D. Phil. in Modern History). 352p. DAI 34, no.7 (Jan. 1974): 4142-A; UM 73-31,197. On Americans, Europeans and Japanese.

524   GODLEY, Michael Richard. *The Mandarin-Capitalists from Nanyang: Overseas Chinese Enterprise and the Modernization of China, 1893-1911.* Brown, 1973 (Ph.D. in Asian History). 373p. DAI 34, no.9 (Mar. 1974): 5865-A; UM 74-3017.

525   MOULDER, Frances Valentine. *Development and Underdevelopment in Japan and China: The International Context.* Columbia, 1973 (Ph.D. in Sociology). 310p. DAI 37, no.7 (Jan. 1977): 4634-35-A; UM 76-29,381. Published as Japan, China and the Modern World Economy: Towards a Reinterpretation of East Asian Development ca.1600-ca. 1918 (Cambridge, Eng. & New York: Cambridge University Press, 1977. x, 255p.). Focuses on the impact of the relationships of China and Japan to the 19th century world political-economy.

526 WU, Juin-yih. *Les concessions de Shanghai: étude sociale.*
     [French: The Foreign Concessions at Shanghai: A Social
     Study.]   Paris VII, 1974 (Doctorat d'Université ès études
     extrême-orientales).   246p.   A copy is available at the
     Bibliothèque de la Sorbonne, library catalogue no. W
     Univ. 1975 (8)-4°.   Focuses on the period 1895-1910.

527 BASU, Dilip Kumar. *Asian Merchants and Western Trade:
     A Comparative Study of Calcutta and Canton 1800-1840.*
     California (Berkeley), 1975 (Ph.D. in History).   xi,
     441p.   Order copies from the Library Photographic Ser-
     vice, General Library, University of California at
     Berkeley.

528 CUSHMAN, Jennifer Wayne. *Fields from the Sea: Chinese
     Junk Trade with Siam during the Late Eighteenth and Early
     Nineteenth Centuries.*   Cornell, 1975 (Ph.D. in History).
     267p.   DAI 36, no.4 (Oct. 1975): 2358-A; UM 75-22,982.

529 LI, Lillian Ming-tse. *Kiangnan and the Silk Export
     Trade, 1842-1937.*   Harvard, 1975 (Ph.D. in History and
     East Asian Languages).   465p.   Available at the Harvard
     University Archives, Pusey Library, call no.HU
     90.10796.20.   Focuses on the trade's impact upon the
     traditional system of silk manufacture and commerce.

530 REYNOLDS, Bruce Lloyd. *The Impact of Trade and Foreign
     Investment on Industrialization: Chinese Textiles, 1875-
     1931.*   Michigan, 1975 (Ph.D. in Economics).   349p.   DAI
     36, no.6 (Dec. 1975): 3876-A; UM 75-29,310.

--With Continental European Countries--

See also entries 545, 547, 1637, 1642, 1658, and 1663.

531 LAFFEY, Ella Sapira. *Relations between Chinese Pro-
     vincial Officials and the Black Flag Army, 1883-1885.*
     Cornell, 1971 (Ph.D. in History).   318p.   DAI 32, no.4
     (Oct. 1971): 2034-A; UM 71-25,165.   Focuses on a band of
     former Chinese rebels active in Tonkin (northern Vietnam)
     during the Sino-French War.

532 LEE, Kya Ha. *China und Österreich-Ungarn. Die politi-
     schen, diplomatischen, militärischen, wirtschaftlichen
     und kulturellen Beziehungen von ihrer Aufnahme (1869) bis
     zum Ausbruch des Ersten Weltkrieges.*   [German: China
     and Austria-Hungary: Political, Diplomatic, Military,
     Economic and Cultural Relations from Their Inception
     (1869) until the Outbreak of the First World War.]   Wien,
     1971 (Dr., Philosophische Fakultät).   iv, 335p.

533   MENDE, Erling von. *Die wirtschaftlichen und konsulären Beziehungen Norwegens zu China von der Mitte des 19. Jahrhunderts bis zum 1. Weltkrieg.* [German: Norwegian Economic and Consular Relations with China from the Middle of the 19th Century until World War I.] Köln, 1971 (Dr., Philosophische Fakultät). Published as Die wirtschaftlichen...Weltkrieg (Köln, 1971. viii, 238p.).

534   ENGLISH, Christopher John Basil. *Napolean III's Intervention in China, 1856-1861: A Study of Policy, Press and Public Opinion.* Toronto, 1972 (Ph.D. in History). vi, 395p. DAI 34, no.8 (Feb. 1974): 5055-56-A; Order copies directly from the Canadian Theses Division, National Library of Canada at Ottawa; available only in microfiche format. Centers on French military expeditions to China in 1857-58 and 1860.

535   GANZ, Albert Harding. *The Role of the Imperial German Navy in Colonial Affairs.* Ohio State, 1972 (Ph.D. in History). 305p. DAI 33, no.4 (Oct. 1972): 1639-A; UM 72-27,006. Focuses in part on the Navy's acquisition and administration of Kiaochow (Shantung Province).

536   SMITH, Woodruff D. *The Ideology of German Colonialism, 1840-1918.* Chicago, 1972 (Ph.D. in History). 568p. Order copies from the Photoduplication Department, Joseph Regenstein Library, University of Chicago. Part of chapter 4, "Colonial Ideology and Colonial Policy 1885-1905," deals with Kiaochow (Shantung Province).

537   METZGAR, Harold Dart, Jr. *Foreign Penetration and the Rise of Nationalism in Yünnan, 1895-1903.* Harvard, 1973 (Ph.D. in History). 282p. Available at the Harvard University Archives, Pusey Library, call no.HU 90.10596.20.

538   SINCLAIR, Michael Loy. *The French Settlement of Shanghai on the Eve of the Revolution of 1911.* Stanford, 1973 (Ph.D. in History). 423p. DAI 34, no.9 (Mar. 1974): 5886-A; UM 74-6552.

539   BILOF, Edwin George. *The Imperial Russian General Staff and China in the Far East 1880-1888: A Study of the Operations of the General Staff.* Syracuse, 1974 (Ph.D. in History). 245p. DAI 35, no.11 (May 1975): 7218-A; UM 75-10,525.

540   GLATFELTER, Ralph Edward. *Russia in China: The Russian Reaction to the Boxer Rebellion.* Indiana, 1975 (Ph.D. in History). 272p. DAI 36, no.8 (Feb. 1976): 5468-A; UM 76-2818. Focuses on the Russian diplomatic response in Chihli and Manchuria during the years 1900-1902.

541 JUDGE, Edward Henry. *The Russia of Plehve: Programs and Policies of the Ministry of Internal Affairs, 1902-1904.* Michigan, 1975 (Ph.D. in History). 650p. DAI 36, no.10 (Apr. 1976): 6880-A; UM 76-9433. Includes a chapter on the Far Eastern Question and Russia's policy towards China.

542 LIMA, Jude M. de. *La question d'Extrême-Orient vue par la diplomatie française (1894-1904).* [French: The Far Eastern Question as Seen by the French Foreign Office, 1894-1904.] Paris IV (Paris-Sorbonne), 1975 (Doctorat d'Université ès lettres). iii, 236p. A copy is available at the Bibliothèque de la Sorbonne library, catalogue no. W 1975(4)-4°.

543 SCHMIDT, Vera. *Die deutsche Eisenbahnpolitik in Shantung, 1898-1914. Ein Beitrag zur Geschichte des deutschen Imperialismus in China.* [German: The German Railway Policy in Shantung, 1898-1914: A Contribution to the History of German Imperialism in China.] Bochum, 1975 (Dr., Abteilung für Geschichtswissenschaft). Published as Die deutsche...China (Wiesbaden: Harrassowitz, 1976. viii, 240p. [Veröffentlichungen des Ostasien-Instituts der Ruhr-Universität Bochum; Bd. 16]).

--With Great Britain--

See also entries 135, 471, and 512.

544 VINNAI, Volker. *Die Entstehung der Überseebanken und die Technik des Zahlungsverkehrs im Asienhandel von 1850 bis 1875.* [German: The Rise of Overseas Banks and the Technique of Financial Transactions in the Trade with Asia, 1850-1875.] Frankfurt, 1971 (Dr., Wirtschafts- und Sozialwissenschaftliche Fakultät). Published as Die Entstehung...1875 (Frankfurt a.M., 1971 (viii, 237p.). Deals extensively with Britain's trade with China.

545 BECKER, Robert Dean. *Anglo-Russian Relations, 1898-1910.* Colorado, 1972 (Ph.D. in History). 217p. DAI 34, no.2 (Aug. 1973): 684-85-A; UM 73-18,547. Includes policies involving Tibet.

546 GREENHUT, Frederic Adolph (II). *The Tibetan Frontier Dispute from Curzon to the Colombo Conference.* Syracuse, 1972 (Ph.D. in Social Science). 208p. DAI 32, no.10 (Apr. 1972): 5712-A; UM 72-12,939.

547 BOYD, Thomas Frank. *Anglo-Russian Colonial Relations 1907-1914.* Tennessee, 1973 (Ph.D. in History). 341p.

DAI 34, no.5 (Nov. 1973): 2505-A; UM 73-27,716.   Includes their differences over Tibet.

548   CHOY, Timothy Young Chu. *A Rhetorical Study of Parliament's Attempts to Inquire into British Foreign Policy during 1832-1865.* Pennsylvania State, 1973 (Ph.D. in Speech). 205p. DAI 35, no.1 (July 1974): 608-09-A; UM 74-16,002. The debate on Richard Cobden's motion of February 26, 1857 on the Arrow Affair in China was one of the author's four case studies.

549   McLEAN, David Alexander. *British Banking and Government in China: The Foreign Office and the Hongkong and Shanghai Bank, 1895-1914.* Cambridge, 1973 (Ph.D. in History). ix, 276, 7p.

550   MARSHALL, Martha Elizabeth Hulsey. *Britain in India and China during the Administration of Governor-General Auckland, 1836-1842.* Georgia, 1974 (Ph.D. in History). 308p. DAI 35, no.8 (Feb. 1975): 5309-A; UM 75-2618.

551   BUCKLEY, Edgar Vincent. *Colonial Office Policy to Constitutional Change in Cyprus, Hong Kong, Mauritius and Ceylon, 1878-1890.* London, 1975 (Ph.D. in Arts, Birkbeck College). 335p. Order copies from the British Library Lending Division, Boston Spa, Yorkshire, order no.D14018/75.

552   SIEGLER, Sylvia Hopkins. *Imperial Servant: The Life and Times of Sir Claude MacDonald.* Claremont, 1975 (Ph.D. in History). 470p. DAI 36, no.3 (Sept. 1975): 1733-A; UM 75-19,671. Includes MacDonald's activities in Peking as a British diplomat (1896-1900).

553   STURDEVANT, Saundra Pollock. *A Question of Sovereignty: Railways and Telegraphs in China, 1861-1878.* Chicago, 1975 (Ph.D. in History). ii, 242p. DAI 36, no.7 (Jan. 1976): 4692-A; Order copies from the Photoduplication Department, Joseph Regenstein Library, University of Chicago. On the attempts of British and American capitalists to construct a railway at Shanghai and telegraph lines at Foochow.

--With Japan and Korea--

See also entries 471, 575, 675, 1644, and 1646.

554   BIX, Herbert Philip. *Japanese Imperialism and Manchuria, 1890-1931.* Harvard, 1972 (Ph.D. in History and Far

Eastern Languages). iii, 325p. Available at the Harvard University Archives, Pusey Library, call no.HU 90.10111.

555 CHOW, Jen-hwa. *The History of Chinese Diplomatic Missions in Japan, 1877-1911.* Australian National, 1972 (Ph.D. in Far Eastern History). v, 456p. Published as China and Japan: The History of Chinese Diplomatic Missions in Japan, 1877-1911 (Singapore: Chopmen Enterprises, 1975. 318p.).

556 KIM, Dalchoong. *Korea's Quest for Reform and Diplomacy in the 1880's: With Special Reference to Chinese Intervention and Control.* Fletcher School of Law and Diplomacy, 1972 (Ph.D.). x, 589p. Order copies from the Edwin Ginn Library, Fletcher School of Law and Diplomacy, Tufts University.

557 BLAKER, Michael Kent. *Patterns in Japan's International Negotiating Behavior before World War II.* Columbia, 1973 (Ph.D. in Political Science). 424p. DAI 37, no.6 (Dec. 1976): 3885-86-A; UM 76-29,291. Published as Japanese International Negotiating Style (New York: Columbia University Press, 1977). Deals extensively with Sino-Japanese relations between 1895 and 1922.

558 McWILLIAMS, Wayne Cully. *Soejima Taneomi: Statesman of Early Meiji Japan, 1868-1874.* Kansas, 1973 (Ph.D. in History). 540p. DAI 34, no.6 (Dec. 1973): 3310-11-A; UM 73-30,843. Includes Soejima's expansionist foreign policy designed to extend Japanese sovereignty over Formosa and his diplomatic mission to Peking in 1873.

559 HAYASE, Yukiko. *The Career of Gotō Shinpei: Japan's Statesman of Research, 1857-1929.* Florida State, 1974 (Ph.D. in History). 283p. DAI 35, no.2 (Aug. 1974): 1008-A; UM 74-18,076. Includes Gotō's work as civil governor of Taiwan and as president of the South Manchurian Railway Company.

560 KWAN, Siu-hing. *Japanese and Chinese Attitudes towards the Idea of a Sino-Japanese Special Relationship, 1895-1911.* London, 1974 (Ph.D. in Arts, School of Oriental and African Studies). 298p.

561 OH, Bonnie Bongwan. *The Background of Chinese Policy Formation in the Sino-Japanese War of 1894-95.* Chicago, 1974 (Ph.D. in History). 515p. Order copies from the Photoduplication Department, Joseph Regenstein Library, University of Chicago.

562 HWANG, In Kwan. *The Korean Reform Movement of the 1880s and Fukuzawa Yukichi.* Washington (St. Louis), 1975

(Ph.D. in Chinese and Japanese). 276p. DAI 36, no.12
(June 1976): 8241-A; UM 76-14,062. The movement was
particularly concerned with the problem of Korea's ties
with China.

563 KIM, Key Hiuk. *The Last Phase of the East Asian World
Order: The Sino-Japanese Rivalry and the Opening of
Korea, 1870-1882.* California (Davis), 1975 (Ph.D. in
History). 398p. Order copies from the Interlibrary
Loan Service, Shields Library, University of California
at Davis.

--With the United States, 1800-1894--

See also entries 469, 512, 553, and 592, as well as the section "Overseas Chinese Communities" (pp.170-81).

564 HU, Hua-ling Wang. *American Diplomatic and Commercial
Relations with Taiwan up to 1872.* Colorado, 1971 (Ph.D.
in History). 267p. DAI 32, no.7 (Jan. 1972): 3894-A;
UM 72-3666.

565 PAOLINO, Ernest Nicholas. *William Henry Seward and the
Foundations of the American Empire.* Rutgers, 1972
(Ph.D. in History). 304p. DAI 32, no.12 (June 1972):
6902-A; UM 71-17,858. Published as The Foundations of
the American Empire: William Henry Seward and U.S. Foreign Policy (Ithaca, N.Y.: Cornell University Press,
1973. xii, 235p.). Deals in part with Seward's policies
vis-à-vis China.

566 PUDELKA, Leonard William. *American Whig Party's Far
Eastern Foreign Policy: A Prelude to Imperialism.* Syracuse, 1972 (Ph.D. in History). 270p. DAI 34, no.3
(Sept. 1973): 1196-97-A; UM 73-19,840. Focuses on the
first half of the nineteenth century.

567 RING, Martin Robert. *Anson Burlingame, S. Wells Williams
and China, 1861-1870: A Great Era in Chinese-American
Relations.* Tulane, 1972 (Ph.D. in History). 344p. DAI
33, no.8 (Feb. 1973): 4318-A; UM 73-2210.

568 ANDERSON, David Louis. *To the Open Door: America's
Search for a Policy in China, 1861-1900.* Virginia, 1974
(Ph.D. in History). 312p. DAI 35, no.8 (Feb. 1975):
5282-A; UM 75-2057.

569 KUEBEL, Mary Veronica. *Merchants and Mandarins: The
Genesis of American Relations with China.* Virginia,
1974 (Ph.D. in History). 489p. DAI 35, no.8 (Feb. 1975):

5306-07-A; UM 75-2017.   Examines the sixty years of Sino-
American contact that preceded the Treaty of Wanghsia
(1844).

570   MORKEN, William Hubert. *America Looks West: The Search
      for a China Policy, 1876-1885*. Claremont, 1974 (Ph.D.
      in History). 211p. DAI 35, no.8 (Feb. 1975): 5311-A;
      UM 75-2269.

571   WOODWARD, William H., Jr. *America Meets China, 1839-
      1846: Politics, Expansion, and the Formal Beginnings of
      Sino-American Relations*. Georgetown, 1974 (Ph.D. in
      History). 405p. DAI 36, no.5 (Nov. 1975): 3056-A; UM
      75-24,489.

572   BIGGS, Jeffrey Robert. *The Origins of American Diplo-
      macy with China: The Cushing Mission of 1844 and the
      Treaty of Wang-hsia*. George Washington, 1975 (Ph.D. in
      American Studies). 448p. DAI 37, no.1 (July 1976):
      512-A; UM 76-10,607.

573   COVELL, Ralph Ruluf. *The Life and Thought of W.A.P.
      Martin: Agent and Interpreter of Sino-American Contact
      in the Nineteenth and Early Twentieth Century*. Denver,
      1975 (Ph.D. in History). 615p. DAI 36, no.2 (Aug. 1975):
      1022-A; UM 75-14,487. On an American missionary-educa-
      tor who served in China between 1850 and 1916.

574   SIU, Sister Victoria M. Cha-tsu, R.S.C.J. *Sino-American
      Relations, 1882-1885: The Mission of John Russell Young*.
      Georgetown, 1975 (Ph.D. in History). 669p. DAI 37,
      no.2 (Aug. 1976): 1147-A; UM 76-18,316.

          --With the United States, 1894-1911--

See also entries 568, 573, 601, 681, and 687.

575   DORWART, Jeffrey Michael. *The Pigtail War: The American
      Response to the Sino-Japanese War of 1894-1895*. Massa-
      chusetts, 1971 (Ph.D. in History). 256p. DAI 32, no.3
      (Sept. 1971): 1434-35-A; UM 71-24,247. Published as The
      Pigtail War: American Involvement in the Sino-Japanese
      War of 1894-1895 (Amherst: University of Massachusetts
      Press, 1975. 168p.).

576   FORD, Andrew Thomas. *The Diplomacy of the Boxer Upris-
      ing, with Special Reference to American Foreign Policy*.
      Wisconsin, 1971 (Ph.D. in History). 310p. DAI 32, no.6
      (Dec. 1971): 3203-04-A; UM 71-25,720.

577 HUNT, Michael Houston. *Frontier Defense and the Open Door: Manchuria in Chinese-American Relations, 1895-1911.* Yale, 1971 (Ph.D. in History). 415p. DAI 32, no.5 (Nov. 1971): 2604-A; UM 71-28,182. Published as Frontier... 1911 (New Haven: Yale University Press, 1973. xiv, 281p. [Yale historical publications. Miscellany, 95]).

578 DARNELL, Michael Russell. *Henry P. Fletcher and American Diplomacy, 1902-1929.* Colorado, 1972 (Ph.D. in History). 527p. DAI 33, no.4 (Oct. 1972): 1633-34-A; UM 72-25,153. Includes Fletcher's economic diplomacy while serving as First Secretary of Legation and Chargé in China, 1907-1910.

579 WILSON, Donald Gordon. *Imperialist Thought in the United States as Expressed in General Periodicals, 1898-1913: The Impact of Expansion on the American Mind.* State University of New York at Albany, 1972 (Ph.D. in History). 531p. DAI 34, no.3 (Sept. 1973): 1229-30-A; UM 73-19,713. Includes American views of China.

580 CHANG, Chung-tung. *China's Response to the Open Door, 1898-1906.* Michigan State, 1973 (Ph.D. in History). 184p. DAI 34, no.3 (Sept. 1973): 1202-A; UM 73-20,322. Focuses on Sino-American relations.

581 PAPAGEORGE, Linda Madson. *The United States Diplomats' Response to Rising Chinese Nationalism, 1900-1912.* Michigan State, 1973 (Ph.D. in History). 277p. DAI 34, no.9 (Mar. 1974): 5881-A; UM 74-6102.

582 THOMAS, Gerald Eustis. *William D. Leahy and America's Imperial Years, 1893-1917.* Yale, 1973 (Ph.D. in History). 180p. DAI 34, no.11 (May 1974): 7172-73-A; UM 74-11,926. Leahy participated in the events of the Boxer Rebellion.

583 BICKERTON, Ian James. *Bankers, Businessmen, and the Open Door Policy, 1899-1911.* Claremont, 1974 (Ph.D. in History). 316p. DAI 35, no.11 (May 1975): 7217-A; UM 75-2245. Examines the relationship between American financial and business interests and the U.S. State Department.

584 GOLL, Eugene Wilhelm. *The Diplomacy of Walter Q. Gresham, Secretary of State, 1893-1895.* Pennsylvania State, 1974 (Ph.D. in History). 231p. DAI 35, no.6 (Dec. 1974): 3632-33-A; UM 74-28,958. Includes his policies vis-à-vis East Asia.

585 NUTTER, Thomas Edward. *American Telegraphy and the Open Door Policy in China, 1900-1930.* Missouri, 1974 (Ph.D.

in History). 243p. DAI 35, no.9 (Mar. 1975): 6070-71-A; UM 75-5779.

586 ROZANSKI, Mordechai. *The Role of American Journalists in Chinese-American Relations, 1900-1925.* Pennsylvania, 1974 (Ph.D. in History). 447p. DAI 36, no.1 (July 1975): 462-A; UM 75-14,618.

587 TALBERT, Betty Weaver. *The Evolution of John Hay's China Policy.* North Carolina, 1974 (Ph.D. in History). 501p. DAI 35, no.8 (Feb. 1975): 5323-A; UM 75-4874. Primarily on Hay's China-oriented activities while serving as U.S. Secretary of State, 1898-1905.

588 BUSSELLE, James Arthur. *The United States in the Far East, 1894-1905: The Years of Illusion.* Virginia, 1975 (Ph.D. in History). 389p. DAI 36, no.8 (Feb. 1976): 5464-A; UM 75-26,087.

589 CHAO, Lin. *John Hay and the Open Door: A Rhetorical Analysis.* Indiana, 1975 (Ph.D. in Speech). 265p. DAI 36, no.11 (May 1976): 7043-A; UM 76-11,455. On American and European policies vis-à-vis China.

590 COCHRAN, Sherman Gilbert. *Big Business in China: Sino-American Rivalry in the Tobacco Industry, 1890-1930.* Yale, 1975 (Ph.D. in History). 506p. DAI 36, no.5 (Nov. 1975): 3035-36-A; UM 75-24,511.

591 HAAS, Martin R. *Prophets and Observers: Two Statisticians of the New American Empire.* Rutgers, 1975 (Ph.D. in History). 223p. DAI 36, no.10 (Apr. 1976): 6863-64-A; UM 76-7294. Includes some information relating to American policy vis-à-vis China following the Spanish-American War.

Missions and Missionaries in China (1800-1911)

See also entries 573, 616, 658, and 1635.

592 COUGHLIN, Margaret Morgan. *Strangers in the House: J. Lewis Shuck and Issachar Roberts, First American Baptist Missionaries to China.* Virginia, 1972 (Ph.D. in History). 341p. DAI 33, no.2 (Aug. 1972): 691-92-A; UM 72-22,632. Covers primarily the 1840s and early 1850s.

593 BARNETT, Suzanne Wilson. *Practical Evangelism: Protestant Missions and the Introduction of Western Civilization into China, 1820-1850.* Harvard, 1973 (Ph.D. in History and East Asian Languages). iii, 444p. Available

at the Harvard University Archives, Pusey Library, call
no. HU 90.10308.10.

594 KUEPERS, Jacobus Joannes Antonius Mathias. *China und
die katholische Mission in Süd-Shantung, 1882-1900*.
Die Geschichte einer Konfrontation. [German, with a
summary in English: China and the Roman Catholic Mission
in South Shantung, 1882-1900: The History of a Confrontation.] Nijmegen Katholieke, 1974 (Dr.). Published as
China...Konfrontation (Steul: Missiehuis, 1974. 232p.).

595 SHAW, Yu-ming. *John Leighton Stuart: The Mind and Life
of an American Missionary in China, 1876-1941.* Chicago,
1975 (Ph.D. in History). vii, 374p. DAI 36, no.7 (Jan.
1976): 4684-A; Order copies from the Photoduplication
Department, Joseph Regenstein Library, University of
Chicago. Focuses on his missionary work and activities
as president of Yenching University.

The Republican Revolution of 1911

596 CHAN, Rose Pik-siu. *The Great Powers and the Chinese
Revolution, 1911-1913.* Fordham, 1971 (Ph.D. in History).
359p. DAI 32, no.2 (Aug. 1971): 873-A; UM 71-20,156.

597 ESHERICK, Joseph Wharton. *Reform, Revolution and Reaction: The Chinese Revolution of 1911 in Hunan and
Hupeh.* California (Berkeley), 1971 (Ph.D. in History).
iv, 642p. Order copies from the Library Photographic
Service, General Library, University of California at
Berkeley. Published as Reform and Revolution in China:
The 1911 Revolution in Hunan and Hubei (Berkeley: University of California Press, 1976. xi, 324p. [Michigan
studies on China]).

598 LEE, Thomas Ben-king. *The Canton Revolution of 1911.*
St. John's, 1972 (Ph.D. in History). 237p. DAI 33,
no.6 (Dec. 1972): 2861-62-A; UM 72-31,029.

599 BARLOW, Jeffrey Garrigus. *Vietnam and the Chinese Revolution of 1911.* California (Berkeley), 1973 (Ph.D. in
History). x, 592p. Order copies from the Library Photographic Service, General Library, University of California at Berkeley.

600 KUPPER, Samuel Yale. *Revolution in China: Kiangsi Province, 1905-1913.* Michigan, 1973 (Ph.D. in History).
436p. DAI 34, no.4 (Oct. 1973): 1829-A; UM 73-24,611.
Examines the relationship of social, economic and political factors to the revolutionary movement in China.

601   CRANE, Daniel Matthew. *The United States and the Chinese Republic: Profit, Power, and the Politics of Benevolence.* Virginia, 1974 (Ph.D. in History). 341p. DAI 35, no.8 (Feb. 1975): 5292-93-A; UM 75-4674. Focuses on American policy towards China during the 1911 Revolution.

Republican Period (1911-1949)

Biographical Studies

602   GEWURTZ, Margo Speisman. *Tsou T'ao-fen: The Sheng-huo Years, 1925-1933.* Cornell, 1972 (Ph.D. in History). 268p. DAI 33, no.7 (Jan. 1973): 3537-38-A; UM 73-345. Examines the Nationalist Government's alienation of intellectuals through a case study of the editor of the journal Sheng huo chou k'an.

603   WANG, Jan-chih. *General Chiang Pai-li and His Military Thought.* St. John's, 1972 (Ph.D. in History). 215p. DAI 33, no.2 (Aug. 1972): 713-A; UM 72-21,738.

604   HAYFORD, Charles Wishart. *Rural Reconstruction in China: Y.C. James Yen and the Mass Education Movement.* Harvard, 1973 (Ph.D. in History and East Asian Languages). iv, 333p. Available at the Harvard University Archives, Pusey Library, call no.HU 90.10361.

605   OLENIK, John Kenneth. *Left Wing Radicalism in the Kuomintang: Teng Yen-ta and the Genesis of the Third Party Movement in China, 1924-1931.* Cornell, 1973 (Ph.D. in History). 345p. DAI 34, no.11 (May 1974): 7163-64-A; UM 74-10,889.

606   SIGEL, Louis Tepperman. *T'ang Shao-yi (1860-1938): The Diplomacy of Chinese Nationalism.* Harvard, 1973 (Ph.D. in History). ii, 431p. Available at the Harvard University Archives, Pusey Library, call no.HU 90.10450.15.

607   SPELMAN, Douglas Gordon. *Ts'ai Yuan-p'ei, 1868-1923.* Harvard, 1973 (Ph.D. in History and East Asian Languages). 362p. Available at the Harvard University Archives, Pusey Library, call no.HU 90.10656.10. Focuses on Ts'ai's activities as a classical scholar, Tung meng hui member, education minister, and chancellor of Peking National University.

608   JEANS, Roger Bailey, Jr. *Syncretism in Defense of Confucianism: An Intellectual and Political Biography of the*

87

Early Years of Chang Chün-mai, 1887-1923. George Washington, 1974 (Ph.D. in History). 598p. DAI 35, no.9 (Mar. 1975): 6062-63-A; UM 75-5276.

609   SULESKI, Ronald Stanley. *Manchuria under Chang Tso-lin.* Michigan, 1974 (Ph.D. in History). 251p. DAI 35, no.5 (Nov. 1974): 2919-20-A; UM 74-25,338. On this warlord's rule between 1916 and 1918.

610   WANG, Jonathan Cheng-ming. *Sun Yat-sen's New Policy in 1924: The Role of Liao Chung-k'ai.* St. John's, 1974 (Ph.D. in Asian History). 306p. DAI 36, no.8 (Feb. 1976): 5477-A; UM 76-3021.

611   ALITTO, Guy Salvatore. *Chinese Cultural Conservatism and Rural Reconstruction: A Biography of Liang Shu-ming.* Harvard, 1975 (Ph.D. in History and East Asian Languages). 536p. Available at the Harvard University Archives, Pusey Library, call no.HU 90.10701. Liang attempted a new formulation of Confucianism and served as a leader in the rural reconstruction movement during the 1920s and 1930s.

612   CHAN, Fook-lam Gilbert. *A Chinese Revolutionary: The Career of Liao Chung-k'ai (1878-1925).* Columbia, 1975 (Ph.D. in East Asian Languages and Cultures). 507p. DAI 38, no.1 (July 1977): 421-22-A; UM 77-15,277.

613   ODANI, Akira. *Wang Ching-wei and the Fall of the Chinese Republic, 1905-1935.* Brown, 1975 (Ph.D. in Asian History). 256p. DAI 37, no.1 (July 1976): 522-A; UM 76-15,682.

Internal Affairs

--Throughout the Republican Period--

See also entries 173, 277, 510, 595, 1300, 1372, 1390, 1535, 1553, and 1649.

614   RAWLING, Karen Eide. *The Political Socialization of Inner Mongol Elites.* North Carolina, 1972 (Ph.D. in Political Science). 170p. DAI 33, no.8 (Feb. 1973): 4501-A; UM 73-4867. Covers the 1920s through the 1940s.

615   WIENS, Thomas Burnett. *The Microeconomics of Peasant Economy: China, 1920-1940.* Harvard, 1973 (Ph.D. in Economics). viii, 512p. Available at the Harvard University Archives, Pusey Library, call no.HU 90.10491.10.

616 CAMPFIELD, Mary Tarpley. *Oberlin-in-China, 1881-1951.* Virginia, 1974 (Ph.D. in History). 404p. DAI 36, no.8 (Feb. 1976): 5464-65-A; UM 75-22,168. On Oberlin College-sponsored educational activities in Shansi and elsewhere.

617 TSAI, Wen-hui. *Patterns of Political Elite Mobility in Modern China, 1912-1949.* California (Berkeley), 1974 (Ph.D. in Sociology). xiii, 362p. Order copies from the Library Photographic Service, General Library, University of California at Berkeley.

618 GROVE, Linda Ann. *Rural Society in Revolution: The Gaoyang District, 1910-1947.* California (Berkeley), 1975 (Ph.D. in History). 346p. DAI 37, no.1 (July 1976): 528-A; UM 76-15,201. On the Kaoyang district in Hopeh province.

--1911-1927--

See also entry 1675.

619 NATHAN, Andrew James. *Factionalism in Early Republican China: The Politics of the Peking Government, 1918-1920.* Harvard, 1971 (Ph.D. in Government). 564, vi p. Available at the Harvard University Archives, Pusey Library, call no.HU 90.10021. Published as Peking Politics, 1918-1923: Factionalism and the Failure of Constitutionalism (Berkeley: University of California Press, 1976. xix, 299p. [Michigan studies on China]).

620 SUTTON, Donald Sinclair. *The Rise and Decline of the Yunnan Army, 1909-1925.* Cambridge, 1971 (Ph.D. in Oriental Studies). 360p.

621 BUCK, David Douglas. *Tsinan, Shantung: Political and Social History of a Chinese City, 1900-1925.* Stanford, 1972 (Ph.D. in History). 498p. DAI 32, no.12 (June 1972): 6881-82-A; UM 72-16,699. Published as Urban Change in China: Politics and Development in Tsinan, Shantung, 1890-1949 (Madison: University of Wisconsin Press, 1977).

622 KU, Hung-ting. *Urban Mass Politics in Southern China, 1923-1927: Some Case Studies.* Ohio State, 1973 (Ph.D. in History). 283p. DAI 34, no.11 (May 1974): 7156-57-A; UM 74-10,994.

623 SAARI, Jon Leonard. *The Passage to Modernity: The Early Years of a Disinherited Generation of Chinese Intellectuals.* Harvard, 1973 (Ph.D. in History). 372p. Available at the Harvard University Archives, Pusey Library,

call no. HU 90.10438.15.   Focuses on the period 1890–1930.

624 BILLINGSLEY, Philip Richard. *Banditry in China, 1911 to 1928, with Particular Reference to Henan Province.* Leeds, 1974 (Ph.D. in Chinese Studies). vii, 585p. Focuses on Honan Province.

625 CHOU, Min-chih Maynard. *Science and Value in May Fourth China: The Case of Hu Shih.* Michigan, 1974 (Ph.D. in History). 214p. DAI 35, no.5 (Nov. 1974): 2891–A; UM 74-25,174.

626 JOHNSON, Carl Edward. *A Twentieth-Century Seeker: A Biography of James Vincent Sheean.* Wisconsin, 1974 (Ph.D. in Mass Communication). 785p. DAI 35, no.10 (Apr. 1975): 6654–A; UM 75-2460. Includes his journalistic work in China (1920s).

627 LEE, Peter King-hung. *Key Intellectual Issues Arising from the May Fourth Movement in China: With Particular Reference to Hu Shih, Li Ta-chao, and Liang Sou-ming.* Boston University, 1974 (Th.D.). 223p. DAI 35, no.4 (Oct. 1974): 2179–A; UM 74-23,168.

628 MA, King-cheuk. *A Study of the* Hsin ch'ing nien *(New Youth) Magazine, 1915-1926.* London, 1974 (Ph.D. in Arts, School of Oriental and African Studies). 363p. Studies the magazine as a reflection of changes in the intelligentsia's political attitudes.

629 SŁAWIŃSKI, Maria Roman. *La Société des Piques Rouges et le mouvement paysan en Chine en 1926-1927.* [French: The Society of Red Spears (Hung ch'iang hui) and the Peasant Movement in China, 1926-1927.] Uniwersytet Warszawski, 1974 (Doktor habilitowany, Wydz. Filologii Obcych). Published as La Société...1927. By Roman Sławiński (Warszawa: Wydaw, Uniwersytet Warszawski, 1975. 201p. [Rozprawy Uniwersytetu Warszawskiego, 82]).

630 BERGÈRE, Marie-Claude. *Les problèmes du développement et le rôle de la bourgeoisie chinoise: la crise économique de 1920-1923.* [French: The Problems of Development and the Role of the Chinese Bourgeoisie: The Economic Crisis of 1920-1923.] Paris VII, 1975 (Doctorat d'Etat ès lettres). iv, 808 + 766p. A copy is available at the Bibliothèque de la Sorbonne, library catalogue no. W 1975 (35)-4°.

631 BULLERT, Gary Byron. *John Dewey in Politics.* Claremont, 1975 (Ph.D. in Government). 581p. DAI 36, no.5 (Nov. 1975): 3106–A; UM 75-25,80. Includes John Dewey's

two-year stay in China, 1919-1921.

632 CHAN, Ming-Kou. *Labor and Empire: The Chinese Labor Movement in the Canton Delta, 1895-1927*. Stanford, 1975 (Ph.D. in History). 516p. DAI 36, no.5 (Nov. 1975): 3059-A; UM 75-25,504.

633 McDONALD, Angus William, Jr. *The Urban Origins of Rural Revolution: Elites and the Masses in Hunan Province, 1911-1927*. California (Berkeley), 1975 (Ph.D. in History). xlix, 593p. Order copies from the Library Photographic Service, General Library, University of California at Berkeley.

634 SCHOPPA, Robert Keith. *Politics and Society in Chekiang, 1907-1927: Elite Power, Social Control, and the Making of a Province*. Michigan, 1975 (Ph.D. in History). 474p. DAI 36, no.3 (Sept. 1975): 1732-33-A; UM 75-20,441.

635 WILLIAMSEN, Thomas Marvin. *Political Training and Work at the Whampoa Military Academy prior to the Northern Expedition*. Duke, 1975 (Ph.D. in History). 279p. DAI 36, no.7 (Jan. 1976): 4686-87-A; UM 75-29,554.

--1927-1945--

See also entries 156, 172, and 1670.

636 GILLESPIE, Richard Eugene. *Whampoa and the Nanking Decade (1924-1936)*. American, 1971 (Ph.D. in International Studies). 565p. DAI 32, no.6 (Dec. 1971): 3204-A; UM 72-1718. On the contributions of the faculty and graduates of the Whampoa Military Academy to Chinese Nationalist and Chinese Communist causes.

637 NEUGEBAUER, Ernst. *Anfänge pädagogischer Entwicklungshilfe unter dem Völkerbund in China: 1931-1935*. [German: The Beginnings of Educational Development Aid under the auspices of the League of Nations in China, 1931-1935.] Hamburg, 1971 (Dr., Fachbereich Erziehungswissenschaft). Published as Anfänge...1931-1935 (Hamburg: Institut für Asienkunde, 1971. 422p. [Mitteilungen des Instituts für Asienkunde Hamburg, Nr.39]).

638 HALL, John Christopher Stephen. *The Provincial Warlord Faction in Yünnan, 1927-1937*. Leeds, 1972 (Ph.D. in Chinese Studies). v, 461p.

639 HSIAO, Hsin-i. *Economie et société rurale du Sichuan de 1927 à 1945*. [French: The (Agricultural) Economy and

Rural Society of Szechwan Province from 1927 to 1945.]
Paris VII, 1972 (Doctorat de 3e cycle ès études êxtreme-orientales). 309p. A copy is available at the Biblio-thèque de la Sorbonne, library catalogue no. I 2240-4°.

640 SEPS, Jerry Bernard. *German Military Advisers and Chiang Kai-shek, 1927-1938*. California (Berkeley), 1972 (Ph.D. in History). vii, 678p. Order copies from the Library Photographic Service, General Library, University of California at Berkeley.

641 SHYU, Lawrence Nae-lih. *The People's Political Council and China's Wartime Problems, 1937-1945*. Columbia, 1972 (Ph.D. in History). 254p. DAI 33, no.5 (Nov. 1972): 2309-A; UM 72-28,100.

642 UPSHUR, Jiu-hwa Lo. *China under the Kuomintang: The Problem of Unification, 1928-1937*. Michigan, 1972 (Ph.D. in History). 316p. DAI 33, no.11 (May 1973): 6292-A; UM 73-11,282.

643 DIRLIK, Arif. *Revolution and History: Debates on Chinese Social History, 1928-1933*. Rochester, 1973 (Ph.D. in History). 329p. DAI 34, no.5 (Nov. 1973): 2509-10-A; UM 73-25,802.

644 MINER, Noel Ray. *Chekiang: The Nationalist's Effort in Agrarian Reform and Construction, 1927-1937*. Stanford, 1973 (Ph.D. in History). 305p. DAI 34, no.6 (Dec. 1973): 3313-14-A; UM 73-30,446.

645 WANG, Chih-yen. *A Study of the Social Studies Program in Chinese Secondary Schools 1929-1949*. Temple, 1973 (Ed.D. in Secondary Education). 234p. DAI 34, no.4 (Oct. 1973): 1600-01-A; UM 73-23,369.

646 CHAN, Kei-on. *The Kwangtung Military Establishment, 1927-1936*. Chicago, 1974 (Ph.D. in History). 377p. Order copies from the Photoduplication Department, Joseph Regenstein Library, University of Chicago.

647 DAVIN, Delia. *Women in China: Policy Developments from the 1930's to the 1950's*. Leeds, 1974 (Ph.D. in Chinese Studies). vii, 238, xxxv p. Published as Woman-Work: Women and the Party in Revolutionary China (Oxford: Clarendon Press, 1976. 244p.).

648 COBLE, Parks McLendon, Jr. *The Shanghai Capitalist Class and the Nationalist Government, 1927-1937*. Illinois, 1975 (Ph.D. in History). 379p. DAI 36, no.9 (Mar. 1976): 6252-A; UM 76-6727.

649 REYNOLDS, Douglas Robertson. *The Chinese Industrial*

Cooperative Movement and the Political Polarization of Wartime China, 1938-1945. Columbia, 1975 (Ph.D. in History). 505p. DAI 36, no.12 (June 1976): 8241-42-A; UM 76-13,192.

Missions and Missionaries in China
(1911-1949)

See also entries 595 and 1473.

650 SUELFLOW, Roy Arthur. *The Mission Enterprise of the Lutheran Church-Missouri Synod in Mainland China, 1913-1952.* Wisconsin, 1971 (Ph.D. in History). 405p. DAI 32, no.4 (Oct. 1971): 2044-45-A; UM 71-20,694.

651 BRESLIN, Thomas Aloysius. *American Catholic China Missionaries, 1918-1941.* Virginia, 1972 (Ph.D. in History). 310p. DAI 33, no.7 (Jan. 1973): 3524-A; UM 72-33,351.

652 JONSON, Jonas. *Lutheran Missions in a Time of Revolution: The China Experience 1944-1951.* Uppsala, 1972 (Akad.avh.). Published as <u>Lutheran...1944-1951</u> (Uppsala: Svenska institutut för missionsforskning, Tvåväga, 1972. 230p. [Studia missionalia Upsaliensia, 18]). On the Lutheran church missions in China.

653 LINDBERG, David Lloyd. *The Oriental Education Commission's Recommendation for Mission Strategy in Higher Education.* Chicago, 1972 (Ph.D., Divinity School). 218p. Order copies from the Photoduplication Department, Joseph Regenstein Library, University of Chicago. Deals with the work of Dr. Ernest DeWitt Burton (American theologian and educator, 1856-1925) on the OEC and focuses on China and Japan in particular.

654 ADCOCK, Cynthia Letts. *Revolutionary Faithfulness: The Quaker Search for a Peaceable Kingdom in China, 1939-1951.* Bryn Mawr, 1974 (Ph.D. in History). 335p. DAI 36, no.1 (July 1975): 468-A; UM 75-13,939.

655 EILERT, Håkan. *Boundlessness: Studies in Karl Ludvig Reichelt's Missionary Thinking with Special Regard to the Bouddhist-Christian Encounter.* Uppsala, 1974 (Th.D.). Published as <u>Boundlessness:...Encounter</u> (Århus: Forlaget Aros, 1974. 253p. [Studia missionalia upsaliensia, 24]). Studies Reichelt's (1877-1952) life as a missionary in China and his views of Buddhism.

656 GREENAWALT, Bruce Stephan. *Missionary Intelligence from*

China: American Protestant Reports, 1930-1950. North
Carolina, 1974 (Ph.D. in History). 385p. DAI 35, no.8
(Feb. 1975): 5300-01-A; UM 75-4823.

657   THORNBERRY, Milo Lancaster, Jr. *American Missionaries
and the Chinese Communists: A Study of Views Expressed
by Methodist Episcopal Church Missionaries, 1921-1941.*
Boston University, 1974 (Th.D. in Missions, Ecumenics
and World Religions). 437p. DAI 35, no.4 (Oct. 1974):
2391-A; UM 74-22,701.

658   WONG, Paul Yat-keung. *The History of Baptist Missions
in Hong Kong.* Southern Baptist Theological Seminary,
1974 (Ph.D. in Missions). 368p. DAI 36, no.1 (July
1975): 364-65-A; UM 75-14,960. Coverage is from the
late Ch'ing period to the 1970s.

659   VONINSKI, Paul. *Reciprocal Change: The Case of American Protestant Missionaries to China.* Syracuse, 1975
(Ph.D. in Anthropology). 203p. DAI 37, no.4 (Oct.
1976): 2281-A; UM 76-18,571.

Origins and Activities of the
Chinese Communist Movement
(1921-1949)

See also entries 159, 266, 618, 636, 657, 1020, 1320, 1321,
1322, and 1666.

660   GRIFFIN, Patricia E. Peck. *The Chinese Communist Treat-
ment of Counter-revolutionaries: 1924-1949.* Pennsyl-
vania, 1971 (Ph.D. in International Relations). 380p.
DAI 32, no.12 (June 1972): 7066-77-A; UM 72-17,363.
Published as The Chinese...1949 (Princeton: Princeton
University Press, 1976. xi, 257p.).

661   HSÜ, King-yi. *Agrarian Policies of the Chinese Soviet
Republic, 1931-1934.* Indiana, 1971 (Ph.D. in Political
Science). 544p. DAI 32, no.10 (Apr. 1972): 5854-A; UM
72-9980.

662   DORRILL, William Franklin. *Mao and the Returned Students: Issues of Policy and Power in the Chinese Communist Movement, 1930-1932.* Harvard, 1972 (Ph.D. in
Government). iii, 332p. Available at the Harvard University Archives, Pusey Library, call no.HU 90.10133.

663   GOLDSTEIN, Steven Martin. *Chinese Communist Perspectives on International Affairs, 1937-1941.* Columbia,

1972 (Ph.D. in Political Science). 561p. DAI 36, no.5 (Nov. 1975): 3106-A; UM 75-25,685.

664 RUSSELL, Charles Alvin. *Cuban Theories of Revolutionary War Examined in a Comparative Context*. American, 1972 (Ph.D. in International Studies). 283p. DAI 33, no.5 (Nov. 1972): 2535-A; UM 72-30,111. Includes a comparison with Chinese Communist guerrilla doctrines.

665 ANDERSON, Dennis Joseph. *K'ang Sheng: A Political Biography, 1924-1970*. St. John's, 1973 (Ph.D. in History). 216p. DAI 34, no.6 (Dec. 1973): 2816-A; UM 73-29,935. On a major, long-standing Chinese Communist Party member.

666 CHAN, Sucheng. *The Long March: Its Historiography and Political Context*. California (Berkeley), 1973 (Ph.D. in Political Science). viii, 814p. Order copies from the Library Photographic Service, General Library, University of California at Berkeley.

667 HO, Kuo-cheng. *The Status and Role of Women in the Chinese Communist Movement, 1946-1949*. Indiana, 1973 (Ph.D. in Political Science). 288p. DAI 33, no.11 (May 1973): 6481-A; UM 73-12,331.

668 CHAN, Adrian Man-cheong. *The Development and Nature of Chinese Communism: The Early Years to 1925*. Australian National, 1974 (Ph.D. in Far Eastern History). vii, 412p.

669 DONOVAN, Peter Williams. *The Chinese Red Army in the Kiangsi Soviet, 1931-1934*. Cornell, 1974 (Ph.D. in History). 225p. DAI 35, no.5 (Nov. 1974): 2896-A; UM 74-24,281. Published as The Red Army in Kiangsi, 1931-1934 (Ithaca, N.Y.: China-Japan Program, Cornell University, 1976. 209p. [Cornell University East Asia papers, 10]).

670 PRICE, Jane Lois. *The Training of Revolutionary Leadership in the Chinese Communist Party, 1920-1945*. Columbia, 1974 (Ph.D. in History). 510p. DAI 35, no.9 (Mar. 1975): 6072-A; UM 75-5240. Published as Cadres, Commanders and Commissars: The Training of the Chinese Communist Leadership, 1920-1945 (Boulder, Colo.: Westview Press, 1976. viii, 226p. [Westview special studies in China and East Asia]).

671 SHAFFER, Lynda Norene (Womack). *Mao Tse-tung and the Hunan Labor Movement*. Columbia, 1974 (Ph.D. in History). 383p. DAI 35, no.9 (Mar. 1975): 6077-A; UM 75-5250.

Examines Mao's work in Hunan (1921-23) on behalf of the
Chinese Communist Party.

Foreign Relations and Trade

--Throughout the Republican Period--

See also entries 369, 529, 530, 585, 590, 856, 1637, 1638,
and 1660.

672 WEST, Philip. *Yenching University and American-Chinese
     Relations 1917-1937*. Harvard, 1971 (Ph.D. in History
     and Far Eastern Languages). xii, 607p. Available at
     the Harvard University Archives, Pusey Library, call
     no.HU 90.10088. Published as Yenching University and
     Sino-Western Relations, 1916-1952 (Cambridge, Mass.:
     Harvard University Press, 1976. x, 327p. [Harvard East
     Asian series, 85]).

673 DOWER, John William. *Yoshida Shigeru and the Great
     Empire of Japan 1878-1945*. Harvard, 1972 (Ph.D. in
     History and Far Eastern Languages). ii, 422p. Avail-
     able at the Harvard University Archives, Pusey Library,
     call no.HU 90.10133.15. Includes information about
     Sino-Japanese relations during the 1920s and 1930s.

674 CHEN, Chi. *Die Beziehungen zwischen Deutschland und
     China bis 1933*. [German: Relations between Germany and
     China until 1933.] München, 1973 (Dr., Philosophische
     Fakultät). Published as Die Beziehungen...1933 (Ham-
     burg: Institut für Asienkunde, 1973. 341p. [Mittei-
     lungen des Instituts für Asienkunde Hamburg, Nr. 56]).

675 CHEN, Shih-ta. *Enclave Growth in an Open Agrarian Econo-
     my: Manchuria under Japanese Colonialism*. Cornell, 1973
     (Ph.D. in Economics). 345p. DAI 34, no.10 (Apr. 1974):
     6198-99-A; UM 74-6374. Focuses on the years between
     ca.1906 and ca.1935.

676 MAY, Gary Arthur. *The China Service of John Carter Vin-
     cent, 1924-1953*. California (Los Angeles), 1974 (Ph.D.
     in History). 585p. DAI 35, no.7 (Jan. 1975): 4393-A;
     UM 74-29,268. Examines the activities of an American
     diplomat in China.

677 TRIPLETT, Lynn Gordon. *Mori Kaku, 1883-1932: A Political
     Biography*. Arizona, 1974 (Ph.D. in Oriental Studies).
     174p. DAI 35, no.8 (Feb. 1975): 5269-A; UM 75-4942.
     Includes Mori's activities as a businessman in China
     (1900-1919) and his subsequent advocacy of Japanese

expansion in China.

678 WILLIS, Sabine Hedwig. *The Formation of Australian At-
     titudes towards China: 1918-1941.* New South Wales, 1974
     (Ph.D. in History). xiii, 412p. DAI 36, no.2 (Aug.
     1975): 1023-24-A; For copies contact the Librarian, Uni-
     versity of New South Wales.

679 YANG, Yun Yuan. *Nehru and China, 1927-1949.* Virginia,
     1974 (Ph.D. in History). 284p. DAI 35, no.8 (Feb.
     1975): 5329-A; UM 75-2070. On Nehru's relationship with
     Nationalist and Communist leaders.

                        --1911-1922--

See also entries 554, 557, 586, 704, 1152, 1653, and 1674.

680 ENGLISH, Howard Lawrence, Jr. *Great Britain and the
     Problem of Imperial Defense: The Far East, 1919-1923.*
     Fordham, 1971 (Ph.D. in History). 357p. DAI 32, no.4
     (Oct. 1971): 2024-A; UM 71-26,966. Focuses on the Im-
     perial Conferences of 1921 and 1923 and on the Washing-
     ton Conference.

681 GANSCHOW, Thomas William. *A Study of Sun Yat-sen's
     Contacts with the United States prior to 1922.* Indiana,
     1971 (Ph.D. in History). 241p. DAI 32, no.5 (Nov.
     1971): 2600-A; UM 71-29,572.

682 YOUNG John William. *The Japanese Military and the China
     Policy of the Hara Cabinet, 1918-1921.* Washington
     (Seattle), 1971 (Ph.D. in History). 300p. DAI 32, no.11
     (May 1972): 6362-A; UM 72-15,165.

683 CHRISTIE, Clive John. *The Problem of China in British
     Foreign Policy, 1917-1921.* Cambridge, 1972 (Ph.D. in
     History). iv, 368p.

684 DAVIS, Clarence Baldwin. *The Defensive Diplomacy of
     British Imperialism in the Far East, 1915-1922: Japan
     and the United States as Partners and Rivals.* Wisconsin,
     1972 (Ph.D. in History). 726p. DAI 33, no.7 (Jan. 1973):
     3530-A; UM 72-23,309. Includes an examination of the 21
     Demands, Japanese investment in China during World War I,
     and China as an issue at the Washington Conference.

685 DAYER, Roberta Allbert. *Struggle for China: The Anglo-
     American Relationship, 1917-1925.* State University of
     New York at Buffalo, 1972 (Ph.D. in History). iv, 456p.
     DAI 35, no.3 (Sept. 1974): 1590-A; For copies, write

directly to the author at 143 Woodbridge Ave., Buffalo,
NY 14214.

686 GLADECK, Frederick Robert. *The Peking Government and
the Chinese Eastern Railway Question, 1917-1919*. Pennsylvania, 1972 (Ph.D. in International Relations). 545p.
DAI 33, no.7 (Jan. 1973): 3739-40-A; UM 73-1392.

687 MOORE, John Allphin, Jr. *The Chinese Consortiums and
American-China Policy: 1909-1917*. Claremont, 1972
(Ph.D. in History). 202p. DAI 33, no.5 (Nov. 1972):
2298-A; UM 72-30,562.

688 SMITH, Ephraim Koch, Jr. *Robert Lansing and the Paris
Peace Conference*. Johns Hopkins, 1972 (Ph.D. in History). 672p. DAI 36, no.10 (Apr. 1976): 6870-71-A: UM
76-8499. Includes the issue of Shantung.

689 GLAIM, Lorne Eugene. *Sino-German Relations, 1919-1925:
German Diplomatic, Economic, and Cultural Reentry into
China after World War I*. Washington State, 1973 (Ph.D.
in History). 188p. DAI 33, no.12 (June 1973): 6839-A;
UM 73-14,752.

690 SCANLAN, Patrick John. *No Longer a Treaty Port: Paul S.
Reinsch and China, 1913-1919*. Wisconsin, 1973 (Ph.D.
in History). 458p. DAI 34, no.5 (Nov. 1973): 2533-A;
UM 73-20,275.

691 DIGNAN, Donald Keith. *The Indian Seditionist Problem in
British Diplomacy during the First World War*. Queensland, 1974 (Ph.D. in History). xiv, 490p. Deals extensively with the way in which the defense of British
interests in China was related to the security of British India.

692 ELLISON, Duane Conan. *The United States and China,
1913-1921: A Study of the Strategy and Tactics of the
Open Door Policy*. George Washington, 1974 (Ph.D. in
History). 653p. DAI 35, no.3 (Sept. 1974): 1590-91-A;
UM 74-17,402.

693 HAN, Sang Il. *Uchida Ryōhei and Japanese Continental
Expansionism, 1874-1916*. Claremmont, 1974 (Ph.D. in
Asian Studies). 352p. DAI 35, no.12 (June 1975):
7837-A; UM 75-2255. Includes Uchida's involvement in
the Chinese revolution and the Manchuria-Mongolia independence movement between 1911 and 1916.

694 HARTIG, Thomas Henry. *Robert Lansing: An Interpretive
Biography*. Ohio State, 1974 (Ph.D. in History). 482p.
DAI 35, no.8 (Feb. 1975): 5301-02-A; UM 75-3086. In-
cludes his policies towards East Asia as U.S. Secretary

of State (1915-1920).

695 METALLO, Michael Vincent. *The United States and Sun Yat-sen, 1911-1925.* New York, 1974 (Ph.D. in History). 307p. DAI 35, no.7 (Jan. 1975): 4395-A; UM 74-30,018.

696 BENSIMON, Simon C. *Political and Economic Developments in Shantung Province, 1914-1919.* Chicago, 1975 (Ph.D. in History). iv, 169p. DAI 37, no.1 (July 1976): 511-12-A; Order copies from the Photoduplication Department, Joseph Regenstein Library, University of Chicago.

697 CANNING, Craig Noel. *The Japanese Occupation of Shantung during World War I.* Stanford, 1975 (Ph.D. in History). 303p. DAI 36, no.5 (Nov. 1975): 3034-35-A; UM 75-25,502.

698 McDONALD, James Kenneth. *British Naval Policy and the Pacific and Far East: From Paris to Washington 1919-1922.* Oxford, 1975 (D.Phil. in Modern History). xxi, 524p.

--1922-1931--

See also entries 554, 685, 689, 695, and 724.

699 HOYT, Frederick Bernard. *Americans in China and the Formation of American Policy, 1925-1937.* Wisconsin, 1971 (Ph.D. in History). 284p. DAI 32, no.6 (Dec. 1971): 3208-A; UM 71-25,191.

700 BURDEN, Gary Allen. *German Policy toward China and the Chinese Revolution, 1919-1931, with Special Reference to the Beginnings of Sino-German Military Cooperation.* Alberta, 1972 (Ph.D. in History). xi, 423p. Order copies directly from the Canadian Theses Division, National Library of Canada at Ottawa; available only in microfilm format, film no.13319, @ $3.50.

701 MOTZ, Earl John. *Great Britain, Hong Kong, and Canton: The Canton-Hong Kong Strike and Boycott of 1925-26.* Michigan State, 1972 (Ph.D. in History). 218p. DAI 33, no.5 (Nov. 1972): 2299-30-A; UM 72-30,014.

702 TOZER, Warren Wilson. *Response to Nationalism and Disunity: United States Relations with the Chinese Nationalists, 1925-1938.* Oregon, 1972 (Ph.D. in History). 383p. DAI 33, no.12 (June 1973): 6854-55-A; UM 73-13,776.

703 CLARK, Peter Gaffney. *Britain and the Chinese Revolution, 1925-1927.* California (Berkeley), 1973 (Ph.D. in

History). 706p. DAI 34, no.9 (Mar. 1974): 5856-57-A; UM 74-4639.

704 McQUILKIN, David Karl. *Soviet Attitudes towards China, 1919-1927.* Kent State, 1973 (Ph.D. in History). 206p. DAI 35, no.1 (July 1974): 375-A; UM 74-15,071.

705 MEGGINSON, William James (III). *Britain's Response to Chinese Nationalism, 1925-1927: The Foreign Office Search for a New Policy.* George Washington, 1973 (Ph.D. in History). 682p. DAI 34, no.5 (Nov. 1973): 2525-A; UM 73-25,091.

706 SINGER, David Glen. *The United States Confronts the Soviet Union, 1919-1933: The Rise and Fall of the Policy of Nonrecognition.* Loyola University of Chicago, 1973 (Ph.D. in History). 216p. DAI 34, no.1 (July 1973): 260-A; UM 73-16,834. Focuses in part on the role of the Far East in Soviet-American relations at that time.

707 WILSON, David Clive. *Britain and the Kuomintang, 1924-1928: A Study of the Interaction of Official Policies and Perceptions in Britain and China.* London, 1973 (Ph.D. in Arts, School of Oriental and African Studies). 734p.

708 DAVIES, Evan. *Britain in the Far East, 1922-1931: A Study in Foreign and Defence Policy.* Birmingham, 1974 (Ph.D. in History). 517p.

709 McCORMACK, Gavan Patrick. *Chang Tso-lin, the Mukden Military Clique and Japan, 1920-1928: The Development and Inter-relationships of Chinese Militarism and Japanese Imperialism in Northeast China.* London, 1974 (Ph.D. in Arts, School of Oriental and African Studies). 331p. Order copies from the British Library Lending Division, Boston Spa, Yorkshire, order no.D12061/75. Published as Chang Tso-lin in Northeast China, 1911-1928: China, Japan, and the Manchurian Idea (Stanford: Stanford University Press, 1977. 416p.).

710 WILSON, David Lee. *The Attitudes of American Consular and Foreign Service Officers toward Bolshevism in China, 1920-1927.* Tennessee, 1974 (Ph.D. in History). 304p. DAI 35, no.11 (May 1975): 7241-A; UM 75-11,208.

711 DAVIS, Kenneth Penn. *The Diplomatic Career of Jacob Gould Schurman.* Virginia, 1975 (Ph.D. in History). 337p. DAI 36, no.7 (Jan. 1976): 4708-A; UM 76-4. Includes Schurman's career as American minister to China during the early 1920s.

712 DeANGELIS, Richard Clarke. *Jacob Gould Schurman and American Policy toward China, 1921-1925.* St. John's, 1975

(Ph.D. in Asian History).   357p.   DAI 36, no.8 (Feb. 1976):
5466-A; UM 76-2977.

713   DUBOIS, Howard. *Britische Chinapolitik während der chine-*
sisch-nationalistischen Revolution 1925-1927. [German:
British Policy vis-à-vis China during the Chinese Nationalist Revolution, 1925-1927.] Zürich, 1975 (Dr., Philosophische Fakultät I). DAI 37, no.2 (Winter 1976/77):
Vol.C--entry no.1/1691c. Published as Britische...1927
(Zürich? 1975. 251p.).

714   KANE, Harold Edwin. *Sir Miles Lampson at the Peking Le-*
gation, 1926-1933. London, 1975 (Ph.D. in Economics, London School of Economics). v, 192p. Order copies from
the British Library Lending Division, Boston Spa, Yorkshire, order no. D15435/76.

715   NEWTON, Christina E. *Anglo-American Relations and Bureau-*
cratic Tensions, 1927-1930. Illinois, 1975 (Ph.D. in History). 263p. DAI 36, no.9 (Mar. 1976): 6245-A; UM
76-6888. Includes information on Anglo-American policies
vis-à-vis Kuomintang China in 1927.

716   RIGBY, Richard W. *The May 30 Movement: An Outline.* Australian National, 1975 (Ph.D. in Far Eastern History).
xii, 409p. On an anti-British demonstration in Shanghai
in the year 1925.

--1931-1937--

See also entries 699 and 702.

717   GRECO, John Frank. *A Foundation for Internationalism:*
The Carnegie Endowment for International Peace, 1931-1941.
Syracuse, 1971 (Ph.D. in History). 318p. DAI 32, no.3
(Sept. 1971): 1437-38-A; UM 71-23,444. Includes the Foun-
dation's response to the Manchurian crisis and the out-
break of the Sino-Japanese War.

718   HOLLINGSWORTH, James Lewis. *William R. Castle and Japa-*
nese-American Relations 1929-1933. Texas Christian, 1971
(Ph.D. in History). 261p. DAI 32, no.10 (Apr. 1972):
5713-A; UM 72-12,490. Deals extensively with American
reactions to the Japanese seizure of Manchuria in 1931.

719   PICKLER, Gordon Keith. *United States Aid to the Chinese*
Nationalist Air Force, 1931-1949. Florida State, 1971
(Ph.D. in History). 448p. DAI 35, no.2 (Aug. 1974):
1024-25-A; UM 74-18,019. On the role of the U.S. government and its nationals (e.g., Claire L. Chennault).

720   REID, Jack Justice. *The New York Times, 1931-1941: An
      Editorial Response to International Relations.* Kansas,
      1971 (Ph.D. in Political Science). 364p. DAI 32, no.10
      (Apr. 1972): 5860-61-A; UM 72-11,794. Includes this news-
      paper's response to Japanese expansion on the Chinese
      mainland.

721   BLICKENSTORFER, Christian. *Die Haltung der englischen
      Regierung während der Mandschurischen Krise (1931-1933).*
      [German: The Position of the English Government during
      the Manchurian Crisis (1931-1933).] Zürich, 1972 (Dr.,
      Philosophische Fakultät I). Published as Die Haltung...
      Krise (1931-1933) (Zürich: Juris-Verlag, 1972. xii,
      223p.).

722   FOX, John Patrick. *The Formulation of Germany's Far East-
      ern Policy, 1933-1936.* London, 1972 (Ph.D. in Economics,
      London School of Economics and Political Science). 351p.

723   MUGHAL, Nazir A. *The Manchurian Crisis, 1931-1933: The
      League of Nations, the World Powers, and the United
      States.* Southern Illinois, 1972 (Ph.D. in Government).
      484p. DAI 33, no.3 (Sept. 1972): 1211-A; UM 72-24,366.

724   PAYER, Cheryl Ann. *Western Economic Assistance to Nation-
      alist China, 1927-1937: A Comparison with Postwar Foreign
      Aid Programs.* Harvard, 1972 (Ph.D. in Government). iii,
      398p. Available at the Harvard University Archives, Pusey
      Library, call no.HU 90.10228.

725   PEATTIE, Mark Robert. *Ishiwara Kanji (1889-1949) and the
      Japanese Army.* Princeton, 1972 (Ph.D. in History). 494p.
      DAI 33, no.10 (Apr. 1973): 5659-60-A; UM 73-9636. Pub-
      lished as Ishiwara Kanji and Japan's Confrontation with
      the West (Princeton: Princeton University Press, 1975.
      xix, 430p.). Deals extensively with Ishiwara's role in
      the Manchurian incident, with his views on Manchuria's
      development as a multiracial state, and with his efforts
      to improve Sino-Japanese relations during the mid-1930s.

726   POWASKI, Ronald Edward. *Great Britain and the Manchurian
      Crisis, 1931-1933.* Case Western Reserve, 1972 (Ph.D. in
      History). 453p. DAI 33, no.5 (Nov. 1972): 2303-04-A;
      UM 72-26,196.

727   RUSSELL, Michael Blaine. *American Silver Policy and Chi-
      na, 1933-1936.* Illinois, 1972 (Ph.D. in History). 288p.
      DAI 33, no.10 (Apr. 1973): 5660-A; UM 73-10,039.

728   ANDERSON, Irvine Henry, Jr. *The Standard-Vacuum Oil Com-
      pany and United States Asian Policy, 1933-1941.* Cincinna-
      ti, 1973 (Ph.D. in History). 309p. DAI 34, no.8 (Feb.

1974): 5046-A; UM 74-1674. Published as The Standard-Vac-uum...1941 (Princeton: Princeton University Press, 1975. xii, 260p.). Includes this American company's business activities within China.

729 ENDICOTT, Stephen Lyon. *Diplomacy and Enterprise: British China Policy, 1933-1937*. Toronto, 1973 (Ph.D. in History). iii, 359p. DAI 35, no.9 (Mar. 1975): 6055-A; Order copies directly from the Canadian Theses Division, National Library of Canada at Ottawa; available only in microfiche format, fiche no.20559, @ $2.00. Published as Diplomacy ...1937 (Vancouver: University of British Columbia Press; Manchester: Manchester University Press, 1975. xv, 209p.).

730 HOLCOMB, Michael Howell. *Anglo-American Policy and the Manchurian Crisis: The Simon-Stimson Controversy*. Colorado, 1973 (Ph.D. in History). 350p. DAI 34, no.7 (Jan. 1974): 4157-A; UM 73-32,552.

731 LEE, Chung Sik. *Japan's Security Policy and the League of Nations*. Columbia, 1973 (Ph.D. in Political Science). 331p. DAI 37, no.6 (Dec. 1976): 3888-A; UM 76-28,322. Includes consideration of the Manchurian Incident.

732 TROTTER, Alison Ann. *British Policy in East Asia, 1933-1936*. London, 1973 (Ph.D. in Arts, London School of Economics and Political Science). iii, 311p. Published as Britain and East Asia, 1933-1937 (London & New York: Cambridge University Press, 1975. xi, 277p.).

733 BRADSHAW, Sister Susan Ann, O.S.F. *The United States and East Asia: Frank Ross McCoy and the Lytton Commission, 1931-1933*. Georgetown, 1974 (Ph.D. in History). 687p. DAI 35, no.6 (Dec. 1974): 3623-24-A; UM 74-26,429.

734 HAGGIE, Paul. *The Royal Navy and the Far Eastern Problem, 1931-1941*. Manchester, 1974 (Ph.D. in History). 452p.

735 KEENE, Thomas Harry. *The Foreign Office and the Making of British Foreign Policy, 1929-1935*. Emory, 1974 (Ph.D. in History). 436p. DAI 35, no.2 (Aug. 1974): 1014-15-A; UM 74-18,390. Among the five case studies analyzed is the British Foreign Office's performance during the Manchurian crisis.

736 MEYER, David Henry. *Collective Diplomacy in the Inter-War Era: A Re-examination of the Major Disputes Brought before the League of Nations*. Johns Hopkins, 1974 (Ph.D. in International Studies). 705p. DAI 35, no.9 (Mar. 1975): 6223-A; UM 74-27,920. Includes the Sino-Japanese conflict over Manchuria in this study of the evolution of the League of Nations and of the international system.

737   TUCK, Howard Kline. *Sir John Simon and British Government Policy, 1931-1940.* Delaware, 1974 (Ph.D. in History). 390p. DAI 35, no.5 (Nov. 1974): 2921-A; UM 74-26,148. Includes Simon's policies towards Japanese expansion in China (1931-1935) at the time he served as British Foreign Secretary.

738   ZUERCHER, Roger Lee. *Walter Lippmann and His Views of American Foreign Policy, 1914-1935.* Michigan State, 1974 (Ph.D. in History). 272p. DAI 35, no.6 (Dec. 1974): 3664-A; UM 74-27,509. Includes Lippmann's views of Japanese actions in Manchuria.

739   GER, Kai-hwa. *Unification versus Resistance: China's Reaction to Japanese Aggression, 1931-1937.* New Mexico, 1975 (Ph.D. in History). vii, 157p. For copies, contact Interlibrary Loan, Zimmerman Library, University of New Mexico, Albuquerque, New Mexico 87106.

740   GUBLER, Greg. *The Diplomatic Career of Satō Naotake (1882-1971): A Samurai in Western Clothing.* Florida State, 1975 (Ph.D. in History). 359p. DAI 36, no.4 (Oct. 1975): 2364-A; UM 75-21,419. Includes Satō's efforts to foster better relations between Japan and China while he served as foreign minister in the Hayashi Cabinet (1937).

741   VEATCH, Richard. *Canadian Foreign Policy and the League of Nations.* Genève, 1975 (Dr. ès sciences politiques). DAI 37, no.3 (Spring 1977): Vol.C--entry no.1/3526c. Published as Canadian...Nations (Toronto: University of Toronto Press, 1975. xii, 224p.). One chapter deals specifically with the Manchurian Crisis.

--1937-1945--

See also entries 663, 717, 719, 720, 893, 1650, 1665, and 1672.

742   BOYES, Jon Lippitt. *The Political Adviser (POLAD): The Role of the Diplomatic Adviser to Selected United States and North Atlantic Military Commanders.* Maryland, 1971 (Ph.D. in Government and Politics). 542p. DAI 32, no.6 (Dec. 1971): 3399-A; UM 72-608. Includes information about American advisers in China during World War II.

743   DURRENCE, James Larry. *Ambassador Clarence E. Gauss and United States Relations with China, 1941-1944.* Georgia, 1971 (Ph.D. in History). 260p. DAI 32, no.7 (Jan. 1972): 3915-A; UM 72-2475.

744   KRANZLER, David H. *The History of the Jewish Refugee*

Community of Shanghai, 1938-1945. Yeshiva, 1971 (Ph.D. in Modern History). 563p. DAI 32, no.10 (Apr. 1972): 5714-15-A; UM 72-11,159. Published as Japanese, Nazis and Jews: The Jewish Refugee Community of Shanghai, 1938-1945 (New York: Yeshiva University Press, 1976. 644p.).

745 LANGEN, Benita. *Die Gebietsverluste Japans nach dem Zweiten Weltkrieg. Eine völkerrechtliche Studie.* [German: Japan's Loss of Territory Following World War II: A Study in International Law.] Bonn, 1971 (Dr., Rechts- und Staatswissenschaftliche Fakultät). Published as Die Gebietsverluste...Studie (Berlin: Duncker und Humblot, 1971. 241p. [Schriften zum Völkerrecht, 19]). Includes the termination of Japanese occupation of Formosa and Manchuria.

746 LIBBY, Justin Harris. *The Irresolute Years: American Congressional Opinion towards Japan, 1937-1941.* Michigan State, 1971 (Ph.D. in History). 282p. DAI 32, no.6 (Dec. 1971): 3215-16-A; UM 71-31,253. Deals in part with the American reaction to Japanese expansion on the Chinese mainland.

747 TAO, Chia-lin Pao. *The Role of Wang Ching-wei during the Sino-Japanese War.* Indiana, 1971 (Ph.D. in History). 222p. DAI 32, no.11 (May 1972): 6356-A; UM 72-13,139.

748 WHYATT, Nelson Thomas. *Planning for the Postwar World: Liberal Journalism during World War II.* Minnesota, 1971 (Ph.D. in History). 429p. DAI 32, no.5 (Nov. 1971): 2628-A; UM 71-28,323. Includes American journalistic writing about East Asia and its future after the war.

749 HAUNER, Milan. *The Place of India in the Strategic and Political Considerations of the Axis Powers, 1939-1942.* Cambridge, 1972 (Ph.D. in History). Includes consideration of India's importance as a backdoor to China.

750 MULCH, Barbara E. Gooden. *A Chinese Puzzle: Patrick J. Hurley and the Foreign Service Officer Controversy.* Kansas, 1972 (Ph.D. in History). 670p. DAI 33, no.11 (May 1973): 6283-A; UM 73-11,930. On Hurley's controversy with the American Foreign Service Officers stationed in China, 1944-45.

751 SHAI, Aron. *British Policy towards China, 1937-1939: Sino-Japanese War.* Oxford, 1972 (D.Phil. in Social Studies). 314p. Published as Origins of the War in the East: Britain, China and Japan 1937-39 (London: Croom Helm, 1976. 267p.).

752 BAGLEY, John Francis. *The First Quebec Conference, August*

14-24, 1943: Decisions at the Crossroads. Georgetown, 1973 (Ph.D. in History). 329p. DAI 34, no.7 (Jan. 1974): 4134-A; UM 74-1428. Includes consideration of Allied wartime planning with regard to China.

753   BAUER, Boyd Heber. *General Claire Lee Chennault and China, 1937-1958: A Study of Chennault, His Relationship with China, and Selected Issues in Sino-American Relations.* American, 1973 (Ph.D. in International Studies). 202p. DAI 35, no.1 (July 1974): 550-A; UM 74-14,855.

754   ERRICO, Charles Joseph, Jr. *Foreign Affairs and the Presidential Election of 1940.* Maryland, 1973 (Ph.D. in History). 405p. DAI 35, no.2 (Aug. 1974): 1003-A; UM 74-17,961. Includes the growing American hostility towards Japan and support for war-embattled China.

755   LAUER, Thomas Leroy. *German Attempts at Mediation of the Sino-Japanese War, 1937-1938.* Stanford, 1973 (Ph.D. in History). 196p. DAI 34, no.3 (Sept. 1973): 1212-A; UM 73-20,490.

756   LAZALIER, James Herbert. *Surrogate Diplomacy: Franklin D. Roosevelt's Personal Envoys, 1941-1945.* Oklahoma, 1973 (Ph.D. in History). 269p. DAI 34, no.9 (Mar. 1974): 5875-76-A; UM 74-6966. Includes information about President Roosevelt's envoys to China.

757   PAWLAK, Stanisław Michał. *Polityka Stanów Zjednoczonych wobec Chin (1941-1955).* [Polish: American Policy towards China, 1941-1955.] Uniwersytet Warszawski, 1973 (Doktor habilitowany, Wydz. Nauk Społecznych).

758   PRINCE, Gregory Smith, Jr. *The American Foreign Service in China, 1935-1941: A Case Study of Political Reporting.* Yale, 1973 (Ph.D. in American Studies). 342p. DAI 34, no.11 (May 1974): 7165-A; UM 74-11,868.

759   DeGROOT, Peter Tanguy. *Myth and Reality in American Policy toward China: Patrick J. Hurley's Missions, 1944-1945.* Kent State, 1974 (Ph.D. in History). 220p. DAI 35, no.9 (Mar. 1975): 6051-52-A; UM 75-7085.

760   FRIEDRICH, K. Marlin. *In Search of a Far Eastern Policy: Joseph Grew, Stanley Hornbeck, and American-Japanese Relations, 1937-1941.* Washington State, 1974 (Ph.D. in History). 309p. DAI 35, no.10 (Apr. 1975): 6633-34-A; UM 75-7638. Includes information about American views of Japanese aggression in China.

761   GRACE, Richard John. *Anglo-American Relations Regarding the Far East, 1937-1941.* Fordham, 1974 (Ph.D. in History). 855p. DAI 35, no.3 (Sept. 1974): 1591-92-A; UM 74-19,661.

762   LEE, Bradford Adams. *Britain and the Sino-Japanese War, 1937-1939*. Cambridge, 1974 (Ph.D. in History). vi, 338p. Published as **Britain and the Sino-Japanese War, 1937-1939: A Study in the Dilemmas of British Decline** (Stanford: Stanford University Press, 1973. ix, 319p.).

763   SBREGA, John Joseph. *Anglo-American Relations and the Politics of Coalition Diplomacy in the Far East during the Second World War*. Georgetown, 1974 (Ph.D. in History). 1188p. DAI 36, no.6 (Dec. 1975): 3938-39-A; UM 75-29,096. Focuses on Anglo-American relations with China during the years 1943-1945.

764   SCHALLER, Michael Robert. *The United States and China, 1938-1945*. Michigan, 1974 (Ph.D. in History). 480p. DAI 35, no.7 (Jan. 1975): 4404-05-A; UM 75-797.

765   BROWN, Frances Cummings. *Anglo-American Co-operation in China, 1937-1941*. Cornell, 1975 (Ph.D. in History). 281p. DAI 36, no.4 (Oct. 1975): 2355-A; UM 75-22,973.

766   DORRIS, Carl Eugene. *People's War in North China: Resistance in the Shansi-Chahar-Hopeh Border Region, 1938-1945*. Kansas, 1975 (Ph.D. in History). 373p. DAI 36, no.7 (Jan. 1976): 4689-90-A; UM 75-30,023.

767   PHILLIPS, Richard Taverner. *Regions of China under Japanese Occupation, 1937-1945*. Cambridge, 1975 (Ph.D. in Oriental Studies). ii, 324p.

768   TOWELL, William Patrick. *Cognitive Complexity of a Foreign Policy Decision-Maker under Conditions of Rising Threat: Joseph Grew and U.S.-Japan Relations, 1938-1941*. Illinois, 1975 (Ph.D. in Political Science). 198p. DAI 36, no.9 (Mar. 1976): 6295-A; UM 76-6992. Deals in part with the Sino-Japanese War.

Japanese Colonial Rule in Taiwan (1895-1945)

See also entry 1474.

769   TSURUMI, Elisabeth Patricia. *Japanese Colonial Education in Taiwan, 1895-1945*. Harvard, 1971 (Ph.D. in History and Far Eastern Languages). v, 307p. Available at the Harvard University Archives, Pusey Library, call no. HU 90.10077.10. Published as **Japanese...1945** (Cambridge, Mass.: Harvard University Press, 1977. xiii, 334p. [Harvard East Asian series, 88]).

770   CH'EN, Ch'ing-ch'ih. *Japanese Socio-Political Control in*

Taiwan, 1895-1945. Harvard, 1973 (Ph.D. in History and East Asian Languages). vi, 596p. Available at the Harvard University Archives, Pusey Library, call no. HU 90.10325.10.

Chinese Civil War (1945-1949)

See also entry 1672.

771 FORMAN, Eric Michael. *Competitive Intervention in Civil War: Great Power Reaction to Civil Strife.* Johns Hopkins, 1971 (Ph.D. in International Studies). 391p. DAI 32, no.5 (Nov. 1971): 2771-A; UM 71-29,146. Includes a case study of the American and Soviet involvement in the Chinese civil war during the 1940s.

772 HOUCHINS, Lee Stretton. *American Naval Involvement in the Chinese Civil War, 1945-1949.* American, 1971 (Ph.D. in International Studies). 271p. DAI 32, no.4 (Oct. 1971): 2163-64-A; UM 71-25,286.

773 LEVINE, Steven I. *Political Integration in Manchuria, 1945-1949.* Harvard, 1972 (Ph.D. in Political Science). ii, 511p. Available at the Harvard University Archives, Pusey Library, call no. HU 90.10180.10.

774 PEPPER, Suzanne. *The Politics of Civil War: China, 1945-1949.* California (Berkeley), 1972 (Ph.D. in Political Science). 740p. Order copies from the Library Photographic Service, General Library, University of California at Berkeley.

775 WETZEL, Carroll Robbins, Jr. *From the Jaws of Defeat: Lin Piao and the 4th Field Army in Manchuria.* George Washington, 1972 (Ph.D. in Political Science). 283p. DAI 33, no.4 (Oct. 1972): 1667-68-A; UM 72-25,070. On Communist Chinese military activities, 1945-1948.

776 FENG, Chi-jen. *The Politics of Intervention: America's Role in the Chinese Civil War.* New York, 1973 (Ph.D. in Politics). 254p. DAI 34, no.7 (Jan. 1974): 4362-63-A; UM 74-1884.

777 URKEN, Arnold Bernard. *Coalitions in the Chinese Civil War.* New York, 1973 (Ph.D. in Politics). 249p. DAI 34, no.8 (Feb. 1974): 5285-86-A; UM 74-1978. A methodological study dealing with the 1945-49 civil war.

778 KUAN, John Chung. *The Kuomintang-Communist Party Negotiations, 1944-1946: The Failure of Efforts to Avoid Civil*

War. Fletcher School of Law and Diplomacy, 1974 (Ph.D.). viii, 686p. Order copies from the Edwin Ginn Library, Fletcher School of Law and Diplomacy, Tufts University.

779 THAXTON, Ralph A., Jr. *When Peasants Took Power: Toward a Theory of Peasant Revolution in China.* Wisconsin, 1975 (Ph.D. in Political Science). 772p. DAI 36, no.9 (Mar. 1976): 6288-89-A; UM 75-26,532. On the Communist Party's activities in the Yellow River region during the 1940s.

American Reaction to the Outcome of the Civil War

See also entry 676.

780 THOMAS, John Nichols. *Charge and Countercharge: The Institute of Pacific Relations.* Fletcher School of Law and Diplomacy, 1971 (Ph.D.). v, 211p. Order copies from the Edwin Ginn Library, Fletcher School of Law and Diplomacy, Tufts University. Published as The Institute of Pacific Relations: Asian Scholars and American Politics (Seattle: University of Washington Press, 1974. ix, 187p.). Deals exclusively with China, especially with the controversial American "loss" of China to the Communists and with the Institute's alleged responsibility for this development.

781 GRIMMETT, Richard Fieldon. *The Politics of Containment: The President, the Senate and American Foreign Policy, 1947-1956.* Kent State, 1973 (Ph.D. in History). 359p. DAI 34, no.7 (Jan. 1974): 4153-54-A; UM 73-32,345. Deals extensively with Sino-American relations and with American efforts to contain the Chinese Communists.

782 WHITED, Fred Elmer, Jr. *The Rhetoric of Senator Patrick Anthony McCarran.* Oregon, 1973 (Ph.D. in Speech). 315p. DAI 34, no.3 (Sept. 1973): 1401-A; UM 73-20,226. Includes McCarran's investigation of the Institute of Pacific Relations (1951-52) and his accusations regarding the Institute's responsibility for the American "loss" of China.

783 CHERN, Kenneth Stephen. *A Prelude to Cold War: The United States Senate and the Abortive China Debate, 1945.* Chicago, 1974 (Ph.D. in History). v, 338p. DAI 36, no.1 (July 1975): 473-74-A; Order copies from the Photoduplication Department, Joseph Regenstein Library, University of Chicago. Discusses the major trends of American thought about China (e.g., Chiang Kai-shek's weakness, the expanding Chinese Communist revolution, Russia's growing capability in East Asia) at the end of the Second World War.

784 HAWLEY, Sandra McNair. *The China Myth at Mid-Century: Case Study of an Illusion.* Case Western Reserve, 1974 (Ph.D. in History). 404p. DAI 35, no.1 (July 1974): 366-A; UM 74-16,490. On the American image of China and the "loss" of China to Communism in the late 1940s.

785 MARDEN, David Lane. *The Cold War and American Education.* Kansas, 1975 (Ph.D. in History). 489p. DAI 37, no.1 (July 1976): 548-A; UM 76-16,749. Includes coverage of the Chinese Communists between 1945 and 1953.

INTERNATIONAL ECONOMIC AND POLITICAL RELATIONS
(since 1949)

General and Miscellaneous Studies

See also entries 1686 and 1690.

786 SCHMOTZER, John Stephen, S.J. *The Graphic Portrayal of "All under Heaven" (T'ien-hsia): A Study of Chinese World Views through Pictorial Representations.* Georgetown, 1973 (Ph.D. in Government). 358p. DAI 35, no.10 (Apr. 1975): 6788-89-A; UM 75-7867. Centers upon the T'ang and Sung periods, the closing decades of the Ch'ing era, and the years 1949-1965.

Chinese Representation in the United Nations

See also entry 804.

787 WENG, (Byron) Song-jan. *Continuity and Change in Peking's UN Policy, 1949-1969.* Wisconsin, 1971 (Ph.D. in Political Science). 510p. DAI 32, no.2 (Aug. 1971): 1055-A; UM 71-16,107. Published as Peking's UN Policy: Continuity and Change (New York: Praeger Publishers, 1972. xviii, 337p. [Prager special studies in international politics and public affairs]).

788 DUNN, D. Elwood. *The Foreign Policy of the Republic of Liberia as Reflected in Selected Political Questions in the United Nations.* American, 1972 (Ph.D. in International Studies). 345p. DAI 33, no.5 (Nov. 1972): 2464-A; UM 72-30,089. Includes Liberia's stand on the China Representation Question.

789 TYLER, Gerry Ruth Sack. *A Contextual Analysis of Public*

Opinion Polls: The Question of the Admission of Communist China to the United Nations. Yale, 1972 (Ph.D. in International Relations). 317p. DAI 34, no.1 (July 1973): 383-A; UM 73-16,407. Analyzes changes in the polled opinion of Americans between 1949 and 1971.

790 BACHRACK, Stanley David. *"The Committee of One Million" and United States China Policy, 1953-1963: Access and Foreign Policy.* California (Los Angeles), 1973 (Ph.D. in Political Science). 426p. DAI 34, no.6 (Dec. 1973): 3480-A; UM 73-28,669. Published as The Committee of One Million: "China Lobby" Politics, 1953-1971 (New York: Columbia University Press, 1976. xi, 371p.). On the committee that was opposed to the admission of the People's Republic of China to the United Nations.

791 BRYNILDSEN, Richard John. *The World Outlook of India and Japan as Reflected in Their Participation in the United Nations, 1957-1966.* Southern California, 1973 (Ph.D. in Political Science). 439p. DAI 34, no.7 (Jan. 1974): 4361-A; UM 73-31,329. Includes the issues of (a) Tibet and (b) the representation of China within the United Nations.

792 CHOU, David Shieu. *China and UN Decolonization, 1946-1971.* Duke, 1973 (Ph.D. in Political Science). 345p. DAI 34, no.9 (Mar. 1974): 6080-A; UM 74-7526. About the Republic of China's position on controversial colonial issues debated at the United Nations.

The Two Chinas and Foreign Affairs

See also entries 836 and 1680.

793 KALICKI, Jan Henryk. *The Pattern of Sino-American Crises in the 1950's: Political-Military Interactions under Stress.* London, 1971 (Ph.D. in Economics, London School of Economics). 442p. Published as The Pattern of Sino-American Crises: Political-Military Interactions in the 1950s (London & New York: Cambridge University Press, 1975. xiv, 279p.).

794 KEMP, Geoffrey Thomas Howard. *A Mission-Specific Analysis of Military Force Structures in the Third World Strategic Environment and Some Alternative Arms Donor Policy Options.* Massachusetts Institute of Technology, 1971 (Ph.D. in Political Science). iii, 391p. Order copies from the Microreproduction Laboratory, Massachusetts Institute of Technology. Related publication by the author: Arms

<u>Traffic and Third World Conflicts</u> (New York: Carnegie Endowment for International Peace, 1970. 80p. [International conciliation, no.577]). Includes consideration of China.

795   LUI, T. J. *Diplomatic Relations between China and the U.S.A.* Santo Tomas [Manila], 1971 (Ph.D.). 648p.

796   WHITE, Nathan Newby. *An Analysis of Japan's China Policy under the Liberal Democratic Party, 1955-1970.* California (Berkeley), 1971 (Ph.D. in Political Science). 712p. DAI 32, no.5 (Nov. 1971): 2775-76-A; UM 71-27,861.

797   RINECKER, Helga. *Revision aus der Mitte; Änderungen in der Haltung der USA gegenüber China zwischen den MacArthur-Hearings 1951 und den China-Hearings 1966 im aussenpolitischen Ausschuss des Amerikanischen Senats.* [German: Revision from the Middle: Changes in the American Attitude towards China between the Time of the MacArthur Hearings in 1951 and the China Hearings of 1966 within the Committee on Foreign Relations of the United States Senate.] Freie Universität Berlin, 1972 (Dr., Fachbereich Philosophie und Sozialwissenschaft). Published as <u>Revision...Senats</u> (München: Verlag UNI-Druck, 1974. 331p.).

798   CHEN, Yuan-chyuan. *Die Fernost-Politik der Vereinigten Staaten im Spiegel der Kritik der nationalchinesischen Presse 1954-1972.* [German: The Far Eastern Policy of the United States as Reflected in the Criticism of the Nationalist Chinese Press, 1954-1972.] München, 1973 (Dr., Philosophische Fakultät I). Published as <u>Das Opfer: Nationalchina und die amerikanische Fernostpolitik</u> (München: Tuduv-Verlagsgesellschaft, 1975. 265p.).

799   DUNN, Lewis Austin. *Go Not Abroad in Search of Monsters to Destroy: An Analysis of the Non-Interventionist Critique of Postwar American Foreign Policy in the Third World.* Chicago, 1973 (Ph.D. in Political Science). v, 475p. Order copies from the Photoduplication Department, Joseph Regenstein Library, University of Chicago. Includes coverage of Sino-American relations.

800   HANDELMAN, James M. *The Secretary of State's Images of the World Arena: The Influence of Personality and Situational Factors.* Michigan, 1973 (Ph.D. in Political Science). 248p. DAI 34, no.4 (Oct. 1973): 1997-98-A; UM 73-24,582. Includes American images of the People's Republic of China and the Republic of China during the years 1946-1970.

801   MINTER, William Maynard. *The Council on Foreign Relations:*

*A Case Study in the Societal Bases of Foreign Policy For-
mation.* Wisconsin, 1973 (Ph.D. in Sociology). 384p.
DAI 34, no.12 (June 1974): 7892-A; UM 74-9012. Includes
a case study of U.S. foreign policy formation with regard
to China, 1969-1972.

802   HAGEN, Christopher George. *Responses in the United
States Senate to Issues of International Significance:
The Confluence of International and Domestic Considerations in Decision-Making.* Brown, 1974 (Ph.D. in Political Science). 253p. DAI 35, no.11 (May 1975): 7364-A;
UM 75-9166. Deals in part with China for the years 1965-
1968.

803   RAU, Robert Lincoln. *Singapore's Foreign Relations 1965-
1972 with Emphasis on the Five Power Commonwealth Group.*
Michigan, 1974 (Ph.D. in Political Science). 510p. DAI
35, no.6 (Dec. 1974): 3855-56-A; UM 74-25,303. Includes
Singapore's relations with the People's Republic of China,
Hong Kong, and the Republic of China.

Mongolian People's Republic

804   HENDERSON, Sister Mary Aline, O.S.F. *United Nations Admission of the Mongolian People's Republic.* Fordham, 1971
(Ph.D. in Political Science). 248p. DAI 32, no.4 (Oct.
1971): 2155-A; UM 71-26,976.

805   BARTOW, Barry George. *The Policy of the Mongolian People's Republic toward China, 1952-1973.* West Virginia,
1974 (Ph.D. in Political Science). 270p. DAI 35, no.4
(Oct. 1974): 2363-64-A; UM 74-21,839.

People's Republic of China

General and Miscellaneous Studies

See also entries 1155, 1693, and 1696.

806   DENNO, Bryce Frederic. *Communist China's Military Policy
and Foreign Relations.* American, 1971 (Ph.D. in International Relations). 407p. DAI 32, no.3 (Sept. 1971):
1595-A; UM 71-24,576.

807   KUO, Kwan-leung. *Les relations entre la Chine et les
pays de l'Europe de l'Est depuis 1956.* [French: Relations
between the People's Republic of China and the Countries

of Eastern Europe since 1956.] Strasbourg III, 1971 (Diplôme de l'Institut des hautes études européennes). 72p.

808 RHEE, Sang Woo. *Communist China's Foreign Behavior: An Application of Field Theory Model II*. Hawaii, 1971 (Ph.D. in Political Science). 273p. DAI 32, no.9 (Mar. 1972): 5323-A; UM 72-10,158. Published as Communist...Model II (Honolulu: Dept. of Political Science, University of Hawaii, 1971. xi, 262p. [Research report, 57]).

809 SMITH, Robert McKaine. *The Revolutionary Doctrine of Communist China*. American, 1971 (Ph.D. in International Studies). 430p. DAI 32, no.4 (Oct. 1971). 2166-A; UM 71-24,940. Analyzes the doctrine as a realistic model for revolutions and for "wars of liberation".

810 AMER, Omar Ali. *China and the Afro-Asian People's Solidarity Organization 1958-1967*. Genève, 1972 (Doctorat ès sciences politiques). Published as China...1967 (Genève: Université de Genève, Institut Universitaire de Hautes Etudes Internationales, 1972. viii, 258p.).

811 CAMILLERI, Joseph Anthony. *The French and Chinese Challenges to the Post-1945 Bipolar Equilibrium*. London, 1972 (Ph.D. in Economics, London School of Economics). 494p.

812 DIAL, Roger Lee. *Chinese Foreign Relations: Toward a Framework for Causal and Comparative Analysis*. California (Berkeley), 1972 (Ph.D. in Political Science). vi, 320p. Order copies from the Library Photographic Service, General Library, University of California at Berkeley.

813 FACKLER, Hartmut. *Aussen- und innenpolitische Aspekte der Strategiediskussion in der Volksrepublik China von 1949 bis 1969*. [German: Aspects of Strategy Discussions on Foreign and Domestic Policy in the People's Republic of China, 1949-1969.] Freie Universität Berlin, 1972 (Dr., Fachbereich Politische Wissenschaft). Published as Aussen- und...1969 (Berlin? 1972. 132, cxxx p.).

814 FATEMI, Khosrow. *Middle East Oil Producing Countries: A Systems View*. Southern California, 1972 (Ph.D. in International Relations). x, 147p. DAI 36, no.11 (May 1976): 7619-A; Order copies from the University of Southern California Library. Includes some information about the increasing influence of the Chinese within the region.

815 FEDLAM, Fruzsina Harsanyi. *Proletarian Internationalism: The Political Biography of an Idea*. American, 1972 (Ph.D. in Government). 390p. DAI 34, no.1 (July 1973): 375-A; UM 73-16,607. Includes a study of the Chinese Communist Party's interpretation of working-class or proletarian internationalism.

816 HOWARD, Robert Falconer. *United States Policy and Nuclear Proliferation in Asia*. Australian National, 1972 (Ph.D. in International Relations). ix, 454p. Includes consideration of the potential nuclear capabilities of the People's Republic of China.

817 OÑATE, Andres David. *Foreign and Domestic Conflict Behavior in Communist China, 1949-1970: A Quantitative Study*. Arizona, 1972 (Ph.D. in Government). 149p. DAI 33, no.3 (Sept. 1972): 1211-A; UM 72-23,355.

818 SCOTT, Gary Linn. *Chinese Treaties: The Post-Revolutionary Restoration of International Law and Order*. Washington (Seattle), 1973 (Ph.D. in Political Science). 206p. DAI 35, no.1 (July 1974): 557-A; UM 74-15,590. Published as <u>Chinese...Order</u> (Dobbs Ferry, N.Y.: Oceana Publications, 1975. xv, 312p.).

819 SICK, Gary Gordon. *The Politics of Exchange: Foreign Policy Behavior in the Indian Ocean Area, 1960-1970*. Columbia, 1973 (Ph.D. in Political Science). 427p. DAI 34, no.6 (Dec. 1973): 3510-A; UM 73-29,863. Deals in part with the interaction of the People's Republic of China with 28 nations around the rim of the Indian Ocean.

820 HERVOUET, Gérard. *Approches et concepts dans les études sur la politique étrangère chinoise*. [French: Approaches and Concepts in the Studies of Chinese Foreign Policy.] Paris I (Panthéon-Sorbonne), 1974 (Doctorat de 3e cycle ès sciences politiques).

821 KLEIN, Donald Walker. *The Chinese Foreign Ministry*. Columbia, 1974 (Ph.D. in Political Science). 344p. DAI 35, no.10 (Apr. 1975): 6774-A; UM 75-7512. Studies the structures and personnel involved in the foreign affairs of the People's Republic of China, 1949-1973.

822 LIN, Kuo-chung. *Classical Chinese Concepts of International Politics and Their Influence on Contemporary Chinese Foreign Policy*. Oklahoma, 1974 (Ph.D. in Political Science). 359p. DAI 35, no.2 (Aug. 1974): 1195-A; UM 74-17,207. Uses historical, theoretical and prescriptive analysis to explore conceptual linkages between ancient Chinese political concepts and Chinese Communist perceptions of world order.

823 RA, Pil-yull. *Ideological Foundations of Recent Chinese Foreign Policy as Reflected in English Language Publications*. Southern Illinois, 1974 (Ph.D. in Government). 159p. DAI 35, no.7 (Jan. 1975): 4658-A; UM 75-134. Analyzes the theoretical-ideological foundations of Chinese

Communist foreign policy.

824   COPPER, John Franklin. *China's Foreign Aid Program: An
       Analysis of an Instrument of Peking's Foreign Policy.*
       South Carolina, 1975 (Ph.D. in International Studies).
       319p. DAI 36, no.6 (Dec. 1975): 4002-A; UM 75-28,983.
       Discusses aid to the Communist Bloc, non-Communist Asia,
       the Middle East, and Africa.

825   OMEN, John E., Jr. *A Forecasting Model of International
       Conflict.* Hawaii, 1975 (Ph.D. in Political Science).
       viii, 215p. Order copies from the Interlibrary Loan De-
       partment, University of Hawaii Library. Deals in part
       with China.

826   SZYMANSKI, Christopher John. *Bureaucratic Development in
       the People's Republic of China: A Case Study of the For-
       eign Affairs System, 1949-1973.* Brown, 1975 (Ph.D. in Po-
       litical Science). 204p. DAI 37, no.1 (July 1976): 592-A;
       UM 76-15,726. Related publication by the author: The Chi-
       nese Foreign Ministry Elite and the Cultural Revolution.
       Coauthored with Ying-mao Kau (Edwardsville: Southern Il-
       linois University, 1973. 21p. [Asian studies: occasional
       paper series, 9]).

                        Relations with Africa

See also entry 810.

827   ALBRIGHT, David Edward. *The Soviet Union, Communist Chi-
       na, and Ghana, 1955-1966.* Columbia, 1971 (Ph.D. in Polit-
       ical Science). 667p. DAI 36, no.5 (Nov. 1975): 3105-A;
       UM 75-25,642. Focuses on Soviet and Chinese policies to-
       wards the Third World.

828   OGUNSANWO, Cornelius. *China's Policy in Africa, 1958-
       1968.* London, 1971 (Ph.D. in Economics, London School of
       Economics). 357p. Published as China's Policy in Africa,
       1958-1971 (London: Cambridge University Press, 1974.
       310p.).

829   BAILEY, Martin Dawson. *Tanzania's Relations with the
       Third World.* London, 1974 (Ph.D. in Economics, London
       School of Economics). 404p. Related publication by the
       author: Freedom Railway: China and the Tanzania-Zambia
       Link (London: Collings, 1976. xiii, 168p.). Includes in-
       formation about Tanzania's relations with the People's Re-
       public of China.

830   TING, David. *Les relations sino-africaines, 1960-1972.*

[French: Sino-African Relations, 1960-1972.] Paris I
(Panthéon-Sorbonne), 1974 (Doctorat d'Etat ès sciences
politiques).

831 GODONOU-APITHY, Félix Médard. *Les états socialistes dans
leurs relations avec l'Afrique Noire après la fin des an-
nées 50 (chapitres choisis traitant l'histoire des relations diplomatiques, économiques et autres des pays socialistes de l'Europe et de la Chine populaire avec le Dahomey, le Ghana, la Guinée et le Mali).* [French: The Socialist States and Their Relations with Black Africa after the End of the 1950s (Selected Chapters Treating the
History of Diplomatic, Economic and Other Relations of
the European Socialist Countries and the People's Republic
of China with Dahomey, Ghana, Guinea and Mali).] Paris I
(Panthéon-Sorbonne), 1975 (Doctorat de 3e cycle en histoire). 460p. A copy is available at the Bibliothèque
de la Sorbonne, library catalogue no. I 3417-4°.

832 MUNIU, George Njoroge. *The Chinese Model of Economic Aid
and Development: Its Relevance in Africa.* Oregon, 1975
(Ph.D. in Political Science). 171p. DAI 36, no.9 (Mar.
1976): 6292-A; UM 76-5195.

Relations within East Asia

See also entries 380, 791, 796, 805, 882, 1689, 1690, 1691,
and 1695.

833 CATRON, Gary Wayne. *China and Hong Kong, 1945-1967.* Harvard, 1971 (Ph.D. in Government). ii, 353p. Available
at the Harvard University Archives, Pusey Library, call
no. HU 90.9923.20.

834 RIGGS, James Richard. *Congress and the Conduct of the
Korean War.* Purdue, 1972 (Ph.D. in History). 455p. DAI
33, no.2 (Aug. 1972): 706-A; UM 72-21,259. Includes Congressional response to the Chinese Communist intervention
in the Korean War.

835 SIMMONS, Robert Richard. *The Strained Alliance: Peking,
P'yongyang, Moscow and the Politics of the Korean War.*
California (Los Angeles), 1972 (Ph.D. in Political Sci-
ence). 310p. DAI 33, no.8 (Feb. 1973): 4513-14-A; UM
73-1735. Published as The Strained...War (New York: Free
Press, 1975. xxiii, 287p.).

836 KUO, Shih-cheng. *Die Haltung der Volksrepublik China gegenüber dem Taiwanproblem.* [German: The Position of the

People's Republic of China towards the Problem of Taiwan.]
Köln, 1973 (Dr., Philosophische Fakultät). Published as
Die Haltung...Taiwanproblem (Witterschlick b. Bonn:
Schwarzbold, 1973. vii, 211, ix p.).

837 MAENO, John Rey. *Postwar Japanese Policy toward Communist
China, 1952-1972: Japan's Changing International Relations
and New Political Culture.* Washington (Seattle), 1973
(Ph.D. in Political Science). 250p. DAI 34, no.7 (Jan.
1974): 4367-A; UM 74-821.

838 LAI, Nathan Yu-jen. *United States Policy and the Diplomacy of Limited War in Korea: 1950-1951.* Massachusetts,
1974 (Ph.D. in Political Science). 345p. DAI 35, no.9
(Mar. 1975): 6221-A; UM 75-6046. Includes U.S. policy
towards Communist Chinese intervention in the Korean War
and U.S. responses to Chinese counteroffensives in Korea
during the winter of 1950/51.

839 WOLBERS, Harry Lawrence. *Some Aspects of the Communication of Intentions in Three Great Power Crises: The Out-
break of the Korean War, the Chinese Intervention in Korea, and the Cuban Missile Crisis.* Oxford, 1975 (D.Phil.
in Social Studies). xi, 323p.

Relations with Latin America

840 SIBECK, Gary Page. *Brazil's Independent Foreign Policy.*
Southern California, 1971 (Ph.D. in Latin American Studies). 300p. DAI 33, no.7 (Jan. 1973): 3734-35-A; UM
73-774. Includes Brazilian policy towards China.

841 CHENG, Ying-hsiang [Mme. Y.-h. CADART]. *Idylle sino-cu-
baine, brouille sino-soviétique.* [French: The Sino-Cuban
Romance and the Sino-Soviet Split.] Paris VII, 1973 (Doctorat de 3e cycle). Published as Idylle...sino-soviétique
(Paris: Armand Colin, 1973. 311p. [Fondation Nationale
des Sciences Politiques, Travaux et recherches de science
politique, 24]).

842 SUK, Chin Ha. *Chinese and Soviet Interests in Chile
(1949-Present): A Comparative Study.* George Washington,
1973 (Ph.D. in History). 361p. DAI 34, no.9 (Mar. 1974):
6083-A; UM 74-5127.

843 RATLIFF, William Elmore. *The Chinese Communist Domestic
United Front and Its Application to Latin America, 1921-
1971.* Washington (Seattle), 1974 (Ph.D. in History).
263p. DAI 36, no.6 (Dec. 1975): 3937-A; UM 75-28,424.

844   TRETIAK, Daniel. *Perspectives on Cuba's Relations with the Communist System: The Politics of a Communist Independent, 1959-1969*. Stanford, 1974 (Ph.D. in Political Science). 355p. DAI 35, no.3 (Sept. 1974): 1733-A; UM 74-20,245. On Cuba's interactions with the People's Republic of China.

Relations with South Asia

See also entry 791 and—within the Appendix—the section entitled "International Economic and Political Relations (since 1949)" (pp. 239-42).

845   HOFFMANN, Steven Andrew. *The China Decisions of the Indian Government, 1959-1962: A Social-Psychological Interpretation*. Pennsylvania, 1971 (Ph.D. in Political Science). 926p. DAI 32, no.12 (June 1972): 7067-A; UM 72-17,367.

846   RAJPUT, Mohammad Akram. *An Analysis of the Foreign Policy of Pakistan toward India, Communist China, the Soviet Union, and the United States, 1954-1968*. Minnesota, 1971 (Ph.D. in International Relations). 168p. DAI 32, no.8 (Feb. 1972): 4695-96-A; UM 72-5571.

847   SEN GUPTA, Bhabani. *The Fulcrum of Asia*. City University of New York, 1971 (Ph.D. in Political Science). 389p. DAI 32, no.6 (Dec. 1971): 3401-A; UM 72-1009. Examines relations among China, India, Pakistan, and the U.S.S.R.

848   TRIVEDI, Ram Naresh. *The Sino-Indian Border Dispute and Its Impact on Indo-Pakistan Relations 1959 to 1962*. Magadh, 1971 (D.Litt.).

849   AHMAD, Bashir. *The Politics of the Major Powers toward the Kashmir Dispute: 1947-1965*. Nebraska, 1972 (Ph.D. in Political Science). 329p. DAI 33, no.5 (Nov. 1972): 2461-A; UM 72-27,376. Includes consideration of the People's Republic of China as one of the major powers.

850   BERT, Wayne Eugene. *Mobilization Politics, Revolutionary Ideology, and Chinese Foreign Policy in South and Southeast Asia*. Kansas, 1972 (Ph.D. in Political Science). 395p. DAI 33, no.11 (May 1973): 6425-26-A; UM 73-11,854. On Chinese policy towards Burma, India, Indonesia and Pakistan during the periods of the Great Leap Forward and the Cultural Revolution.

851   BOULNOIS, Lucette. *Les échanges entre le Népal et la Chine et leurs implications socio-économiques au Népal,*

depuis 1950. [French: Barter Trade between Nepal and China since 1950 and Its Socioeconomic Implications for Nepal.] Paris I (Panthéon-Sorbonne), 1972 (Doctorat de 3e cycle ès études extrême-orientales). ii, 394p. A copy is available at the Bibliothèque de la Sorbonne.

852   FISHER, James F. *Trans-Himalayan Traders: Economy, Society, and Culture in Northwest Nepal.* Chicago, 1972 (Ph.D. in Anthropology). 221p. Order copies from the Photoduplication Department, Joseph Regenstein Library, University of Chicago. Deals in part with their trading ties with Tibet.

853   HAQ, A. K. M. Azizul. *Pakistan's External Relations.* Nottingham, 1972 (Ph.D. in Politics). xviii, 365p. Deals extensively with Pakistan's relations with the People's Republic of China.

854   HOMAYOUN, Assad. *Pakistan-China Relations up to 1970.* George Washington, 1972 (Ph.D. in Political Science). 214p. DAI 33, no.11 (May 1973): 6428-A; UM 73-4009.

855   LIM, Heng Cheah. *The Foreign Policy of the Chinese People's Republic toward Pakistan, 1958-1969.* Queen's University at Kingston, 1972 (Ph.D. in Political Studies). vii, 428p. Order copies from the Canadian Theses Division, National Library of Canada at Ottawa; available only in microfilm format, film no.11709, @ $3.50.

856   LU, Chih-hung. *A Border Problem between China and India.* Tennessee, 1972 (Ph.D. in Political Science). 201p. DAI 33, no.11 (May 1973): 6428-29-A; UM 73-12,420. Covers both the Ch'ing period and the 20th century.

857   SANDHU, Bhim Singh. *The Sino-Indian War of 1962: A Framework and Case Study of International Conflict Resolution.* Missouri, 1972 (Ph.D. in Political Science). 427p. DAI 33, no.9 (Mar. 1973): 5263-64-A; UM 73-7084.

858   SHOW, Kuo-kong. *Communist China's Foreign Policy toward the Non-Aligned States with Special Reference to India and Burma, 1949-1962.* Pennsylvania, 1972 (Ph.D. in International Relations). 348p. DAI 33, no.7 (Jan. 1973): 3744-45-A; UM 73-1448.

859   MALLA, Shashi. *Die Aussenpolitik des Königreichs Nepal und ihre innerstaatlichen Voraussetzungen. Eine Analyse hinsichtlich der historischen Entwicklung und der Himalaya-Mächtekonstellation der Gegenwart.* [German: The Foreign Policy of the Kingdom of Nepal and Its Domestic Bases: An Analysis with Regard to Its Historical Development and the Himalayan Power Constellation of the Present Time.]

München, 1973 (Dr., Philosophische Fakultät). xv, 777p.
Includes Nepal's relations with China.

860 SMITH, Raymond Francis. *Behavior and Structure as Influences upon Violence in the International System, 1946-
1962.* Northwestern, 1973 (Ph.D. in Political Science).
235p. DAI 34, no.6 (Dec. 1973): 3510-11-A; UM 73-30,727.
Includes the Sino-Indian conflict of 1962.

861 VARKEY, Ouseph. *At the Crossroads: The Sino-Indian Border Dispute and the Communist Party of India, 1959-1963.*
Temple, 1973 (Ph.D. in Political Science). 420p. DAI 34,
no.6 (Dec. 1973): 3502-A; UM 73-30,178. Published as At
the Crossroads...1963 (Calcutta: Minerva Associates,
1974. 304p.).

862 COGNACQ, Philippe. *Les influences indiennes et chinoises
au Népal 1950-1970.* [French: Indian and Chinese Influences in Nepal, 1950-1970.] Paris I (Panthéon-Sorbonne),
1974 (Doctorat d'Etat ès sciences politiques).

863 LIAO, Kuang-sheng. *Internal Mobilization and External
Hostility in the People's Republic of China, 1960-1962
and 1967-1969.* Michigan, 1974 (Ph.D. in Political Science). 307p. DAI 35, no.5 (Nov. 1974): 3087-88-A; UM
74-25,251. Studies verbal attacks and mass campaigns
against foreign governments (India in 1960-62; the
U.S.S.R. in 1967-69).

864 TANNEBERGER, Hans-Georg. *Das Verhältnis der Volksrepublik
Chinas zum Völkerrecht unter besonderer Berücksichtigung
der historischen Erfahrungen des Landes mit den sogenann-
ten "Ungleichen Verträgen" seit dem Frieden von Nanking
(1842) und der eigenen Vertragspraxis gegenüber den sechs
asiatischen Staaten (Afghanistan, Birma, Ceylon, Indone-
sien, Nepal, Pakistan).* [German: The Attitude of the People's Republic of China towards International Law with
Particular Regard to the Historical Experiences of a Country with the So-Called "Unequal Treaties" since the Treaty
of Nanking (1842) and Its Own Handling of Agreements with
Six Asian States (Afghanistan, Burma, Ceylon, Indonesia,
Nepal, Pakistan).] Bochum, 1974 (Dr., Abteilung für
Rechtswissenschaft). 351p.

865 JONES, Cecil Beam, Jr. *How the Indian Lok Sabha Handles
Defense Matters: An Institutional Study.* American, 1975
(Ph.D. in International Studies). 340p. DAI 36, no.7
(Jan. 1976): 4731-A; UM 76-813. Includes India's military
defense against China.

866 PANDHER, Rachhpal Singh. *An Analysis of the Indian*

*Foreign Policy in the Post-Nehru Period: A Case Study of
the Bangla Desh Crisis Management.* Howard, 1975 (Ph.D.
in Political Science). 258p. DAI 37, no.7 (Jan. 1977):
4607-A; UM 76-30,123. Includes China's involvement in
the Bangladesh crisis.

867   SKINNER, Richard Alan. *Impact Analysis and the Respon-
sive Stage of Foreign Policy: A Study of the Consequences
of Military Intervention.* South Carolina, 1975 (Ph.D. in
Government and International Studies). 295p. DAI 36, no.
11 (May 1976): 7623-24-A; UM 76-10,511. Includes a study
of the consequences of the Chinese intervention in India
in 1958.

Relations with Southeast Asia

See also entries 850, 858, 864, 1684, and 1685.

868   GRÜNDLER, Ulrich. *Revolutionäre und realpolitische Komponenten in der Aussenpolitik der Volksrepublik China gegenüber den Staaten Kontinental-Südostasiens (1949-1962).*
[German: Revolutionary and Realpolitik Components of the
Foreign Policy of the People's Republic of China vis-à-vis
the Nations of Continental Southeast Asia (1949-1962).]
Freie Universität Berlin, 1971 (Dr., Fachbereich Politische Wissenschaft). Published as Revolutionäre...(1949-
1962) (Berlin, 1971. 224p.).

869   LOVELACE, Daniel Dudley. *"People's War" and Chinese Foreign Policy: Thailand as a Case Study of Overt Insurgent
Support.* Claremont, 1971 (Ph.D. in Government). 259p.
DAI 32, no.2 (Aug. 1971): 1051-A; UM 71-21,647. Published
in part as China and People's War in Thailand, 1964-1969
(Berkeley: Center for Chinese Studies, University of California, 1971. 101p. [China research monographs, 8]).

870   PETTMAN, Ralph Harold. *An Analysis of Theories of "Linkage" in International Relations with Special Reference to
Southeast Asia.* London, 1971 (Ph.D. in Economics, London
School of Economics). 412p. Published in part as China
in Burma's Foreign Policy (Canberra: Australian National
University Press, 1973. 56p. [Contemporary China papers, 7]). Includes case studies of the relationships
maintained by the People's Republic of China with Burma
and with Cambodia.

871   FREEDENBERG, Paul. *The Rhetoric of Vietnam: Reaction to
Adversity.* Chicago, 1972 (Ph.D. in Political Science).
253p. Order copies from the Photoduplication Department,

Joseph Regenstein Library, University of Chicago. Chapter 3 of this study on the rhetoric of the Kennedy and Johnson Administrations examines in depth the theme of Chinese Communist involvement in the Vietnam War.

872 ROGERS, Francis Elmo. *China's Foreign Policy in Indochina, 1949-1966.* Virginia, 1972 (Ph.D. in Foreign Affairs). 263p. DAI 33, no.10 (Apr. 1973): 5807-08-A; UM 73-9806.

873 DAKE, Antonie C. A. *In the Spirit of the Red Banteng: Indonesian Communists between Moscow and Peking, 1959-1965.* Freie Universität Berlin, 1973 (Dr., Philosophische Fakultät). Published as In...1965 (The Hague and Paris: Mouton, 1973. xvi, 479p.).

874 KAO, Kan. *Les relations sino-cambodgiennes (1963-1970).* [French: Sino-Cambodian Relations, 1963-1970.] Paris I (Panthéon-Sorbonne), 1973 (Doctorat de 3ᵉ cycle ès études politiques). 515p. A copy is available at the Bibliothèque de la Sorbonne.

875 MOZINGO, David Paul. *Chinese Policy in Indonesia, 1949-1967.* California (Los Angeles), 1973 (Ph.D. in Political Science). 347p. DAI 34, no.6 (Dec. 1973): 3508-A; UM 73-28,737. Published as Chinese Policy toward Indonesia, 1949-1967 (Ithaca, N.Y.: Cornell University Press, 1976. 303p.).

876 NAGARAJAN, S. *Indonesian Society and Foreign Policy, 1956-1962.* Jawaharlal Nehru, 1973 (Ph.D., School of International Studies). v, 461p. Examines in part Indonesia's relations with the People's Republic of China and the position of the Chinese living within Indonesia.

877 RAMACHANDRAN, K. N. *Sino-Indonesian Relations, 1955-65.* Jawaharlal Nehru, 1973 (Ph.D., School of International Studies). ii, 391p. Focuses on the perceptions, attitudes and tactics of the People's Republic of China.

878 SHAW, Brian Carl Joseph. *China and North Vietnam, 1963-1971.* Australian National, 1973 (Ph.D. in International Relations). 322p.

879 DASSÉ, Martial. *Le problème des minorités ethniques en Asie du sud-est continentale.* [French: The Problem of the Ethnic Minorities in Continental Southeast Asia.] Montpellier I, 1974 (Doctorat d'Etat ès sciences politiques). ix, 360p. Includes a discussion of Chinese policy vis-à-vis various ethnic groups.

880 POZSGAI, Joseph. *Die Rolle der Vereinigten Staaten, der Sowjetunion und der VR China im Vietnam-Konflikt.* [German:

The Role of the United States, the U.S.S.R., and the People's Republic of China in the Vietnam Conflict.] München, 1974 (Dr., Philosophische Fakultät I). Published as Vietnam, wie es wirklich war: Indochina im Kräftefeld der 3 Grossmächte, by Peter Parker, pseud. [i.e., by Joseph Pozsgai] (Bern: Verlag SOI, 1974. 322p.).

881 LOESCHER, Gilburt Damian. *National Liberation War in South Vietnam: The Perceptions and Policies of China and North Vietnam, 1954-1969*. London, 1975 (Ph.D. in International Relations, London School of Economics). 421p. Order copies from the British Library Lending Division, Boston Spa, Yorkshire, order no.D14369/76.

Relations with the United States

See also entry 1688 and the section entitled "The Two Chinas and Foreign Affairs" (pp.111-13). For entries on the American reaction to the involvement of the People's Republic of China in the Korean War and in the Vietnam War, see the sections concerning Chinese relations within East Asia (pp.117-18) and with Southeast Asia (pp.122-24) respectively.

882 GEIB, Peter Jacob. *The Congressional Role in the Formulation of Commercial Legislation toward Communist Countries*. Michigan, 1971 (Ph.D. in Political Science). 457p. DAI 32, no.11 (May 1972): 6507-A; UM 72-14,871. Related publication by the author: East-West Trade and Congressional Party Voting, 1947-1970 (Emporia: Kansas State Teachers College, 1972. 47p. [The Emporia State research studies, vol.21, no.2]). On the trade of the United States, Japan and Western Europe with several Communist countries including the People's Republic of China.

883 CHEN, Chin-yuen. *American Economic Policy toward Communist China, 1950-1970*. Columbia, 1972 (Ph.D. in Business). 240p. DAI 33, no.5 (Nov. 1972): 1922-A; UM 72-28,022.

884 ALLEN, Thomas Harrell. *An Examination of the Communicative Interaction between the United States and the People's Republic of China from January 1969 to February 1972*. Ohio State, 1973 (Ph.D. in Speech Communication). 126p. DAI 34, no.8 (Feb. 1974): 5361-A; UM 74-3108.

885 GILBERT, Jerry Don. *John Foster Dulles' Perceptions of the People's Republic of China: A Study of Belief Systems and Perception in the Analysis of Foreign Policy Decision-Making*. Texas Tech, 1973 (Ph.D. in Political Science). 258p. DAI 35, no.1 (July 1974): 552-A; UM 74-15,288.

886 GROSSCUP, George Charles (III). *Isolationism and American
     Foreign Policy*. Massachusetts, 1973 (Ph.D. in Political
     Science). 231p. DAI 33, no.12 (June 1973): 6998-A; UM
     73-14,643. Includes a case study of China in order to
     help clarify the meaning of isolationism.

887 LYMAN, Corinne. *The Role of the Munich Analogy in Ameri-
     can Foreign Policy since World War II*. Johns Hopkins,
     1973 (Ph.D., School of Advanced International Studies).
     483p. DAI 36, no.11 (May 1976): 7621-A; UM 76-11,220.
     Includes a study of the usefulness of the Munich analogy
     for justifying U.S. opposition to Communist China.

888 ROSS, Rodney Joel. *Senator William E. Jenner: A Study in
     Cold War Isolationism*. Pennsylvania State, 1973 (Ed.D.
     in History). 224p. DAI 35, no.3 (Sept. 1974): 1604-A;
     UM 74-20,960. Includes the Senator's views of Communist
     China during the 1950s.

889 TEDIN, Kent Lyndon. *Parental Influence on the Political
     Attitudes of New Voters*. Iowa, 1973 (Ph.D. in Political
     Science). 154p. DAI 34, no.6 (Dec. 1973): 3501-02-A; UM
     73-30,993. American policy towards the People's Republic
     of China was one of the issues examined in this study of
     political socialization among people in the state of Iowa.

890 VORKINK, LeGrand Stuart. *The Orientation of the American
     Foreign Policy Establishment toward Communism in the
     Third World*. Arizona, 1973 (Ph.D. in Government). 273p.
     DAI 34, no.8 (Feb. 1974): 5287-A; UM 74-2012. Includes
     U.S. perceptions of the threat that the People's Republic
     of China posed to the Third World.

891 LONGLEY, Patricia Tipton. *The Influence of Mass Communi-
     cation upon Attitudes toward Selected Foreign Policy Is-
     sues*. North Carolina, 1975 (Ph.D. in Political Science).
     192p. DAI 36, no.10 (Apr. 1976): 6920-A; UM 76-9263.
     This is a study of American attitudes based on an experi-
     ment involving President Lyndon Johnson's views about in-
     creased trade with the People's Republic of China.

892 SCOTT, Rodger Kent. *Journey into the World: An Analysis
     of the Religious, Artistic, Educational and Political
     Forces That Have Determined the World View of an American*.
     New Mexico, 1975 (Ph.D. in American Studies). 217p. DAI
     37, no.4 (Oct. 1976): 2432-33-A; UM 76-22,162. Includes
     information about this Ph.D. student's visit to the Peo-
     ple's Republic of China on an educational exchange.

893 SUTTER, Robert Goodwin. *Toward Sino-American Reconcilia-
     tion: A Study of Three Cases of the Interaction of the*

CCP Leadership with the United States since the Start of World War II. Harvard, 1975 (Ph.D. in History and East Asian Languages). 468p. Available at the Harvard University Archives, Pusey Library, call no.HU 90.10863. Published as Chinese Foreign Policy after the Cultural Revolution (Boulder, Colo.: Westview Press, 1977 [Westview studies on China and East Asia]) and as China-Watch: Toward Sino-American Reconciliation (Baltimore: Johns Hopkins University Press, 1978). Covers interaction during the periods 1942-45, 1954-57, and 1968-71.

Relations with the U.S.S.R.

See also entries 86, 265, 835, 841, 863, 1683, and 1692.

894 POWERS, David Richard. *Five Issues of Politico-Military Strategy: A Content Analysis of Sino-Soviet Documents, 1960-1963.* Pittsburgh, 1971 (Ph.D. in Political Science). 250p. DAI 32, no.3 (Sept. 1971): 1600-A; UM 71-23,949.

895 KANG, Young-hoon. *The Relationship between the Development of Strategic Nuclear Weapons Systems and Deterrence Doctrine in the Soviet Union and Communist China.* Southern California, 1973 (Ph.D. in Political Science). 408p. DAI 33, no.12 (June 1973): 6999-7000-A; UM 73-14,416.

896 RHEE, Sei Young. *The Impact of the Sino-Soviet Conflict on the Japanese Communist Party, 1961-1968.* Missouri, 1973 (Ph.D. in Political Science). 444p. DAI 35, no.3 (Sept. 1974): 1731-32-A; UM 74-18,623.

897 KONG, Corita Shuk-Sinn. *Communist China's Reaction to Khrushchevism: An Appraisal of the Sino-Soviet Rift.* St. John's, 1974 (Ph.D. in History). 336p. DAI 35, no. 8 (Feb. 1975): 5305-06-A; UM 75-3257.

898 LANE, Richard Reno. *Paradigms of Soviet Foreign Policy.* Southern California, 1974 (Ph.D. in International Relations). 553p. DAI 36, no.3 (Sept. 1975): 1791-A; UM 75-19,022. Includes information on Sino-Soviet relations during the 1960s.

899 SULLIVAN, Eugene Patrick. *Soviet Disarmament Policy 1968-1972.* Notre Dame, 1974 (Ph.D. in Government and International Studies). 265p. DAI 35, no.3 (Sept. 1974): 1732-A; UM 74-20,054. Includes information about Sino-Soviet relations and their impact upon Soviet disarmament policy.

900 CHEN, George Po-chung. *Some Legal Aspects of the Sino-*

Soviet Border Dispute. Southern Illinois, 1975 (Ph.D. in Political Science). 325p. DAI 36, no.2 (Aug. 1975): 1076-77-A; UM 75-16,262.

901 JENNINGS, Richard Milburn. *U.S./Soviet Arms Competition, 1945-1972: Aspects of Its Nature, Control, and Results.* Georgetown, 1975 (Ph.D. in Government). 508p. DAI 37, no.1 (July 1976): 587-A; UM 76-16,321. Includes the impact of the Sino-Soviet arms confrontation in the late 1960s upon Soviet-American arms competition.

902 LIU, Ti-hung. *Die völkerrechtliche Argumentation der Volksrepublik China im chinesisch-sowjetischen Grenzkonflikt.* [German: The Argumentation of the People's Republic of China in the Sino-Soviet Border Conflict, Based on International Law.] Freie Universität Berlin, 1975 (Dr., Fachbereich Rechtswissenschaft). 249p.

Republic of China and Hong Kong

See also entries 753 and 1697 as well as the section dealing with the export economy of the Republic of China and Hong Kong (pp.34-36).

903 BURHANS, Arthur Daniel, Jr. *United States Foreign Policy and Private Foreign Investment: The Nexus of Interdependence.* Hawaii, 1971 (Ph.D. in Political Science). vi, 257p. Order copies from the Interlibrary Loan Department, University of Hawaii Library.

904 THIEL, Elroy Bernard. *The Asian and Pacific Council: Regional Organization in the Context of Regional International Politics.* Maryland, 1971 (Ph.D. in Government and Politics). 267p. DAI 32, no.6 (Dec. 1971): 3402-A; UM 72-637. The Republic of China is covered as one of the nine Council members.

905 BULLARD, Anthony Ray. *Harry S. Truman and the Separation of Powers in Foreign Affairs.* Columbia, 1972 (Ph.D. in Political Science). 321p. DAI 34, no.1 (July 1973): 388-89-A; UM 73-16,188. Includes a case study of Truman's resistance to a congressional mandate calling for closer American relations with Nationalist China.

906 SANFORD, Dan Champ. *The United States in Nationalist Chinese Foreign Policy: The Using and the Keeping of an Ally.* Denver, 1972 (Ph.D. in International Relations). 395p. DAI 35, no.6 (Dec. 1974): 3856-A; UM 74-26,809. Covers the 1950s and the 1960s.

907   KHOONTONG INTARATHAI [INTARATHAI, Khoontong]. *The Impact
      of Direct Private Foreign Investment on the Industriali-
      zation of Thailand.* Illinois, 1974 (Ph.D. in Economics).
      157p. DAI 35, no.1 (July 1974): 52–53–A; UM 74–14,559.
      Includes consideration of Chinese investment in Thailand.

908   SYLVAN, Donald Avery. *Models for Foreign Policy Choice:
      The Case of Foreign Assistance to Third World Nations.*
      Minnesota, 1974 (Ph.D. in Political Science). 210p. DAI
      35, no.12 (June 1975): 7996–97–A; UM 75–12,170. Covers
      assistance to fifteen Asian countries including the Re-
      public of China.

909   PEARCE, David Lee. *United States Military Aid and Reci-
      pient Nation Defense Expenditures: A Quantitative Analy-
      sis.* Syracuse, 1975 (Ph.D. in International Relations).
      219p. DAI 36, no.10 (Apr. 1976): 6939–A; UM 76–7708.
      Includes consideration of the Republic of China.

910   SCHUBERT, James Neal. *The Functional Approach to Peace
      in Asia.* Hawaii, 1975 (Ph.D. in Political Science).
      427p. DAI 36, no.9 (Mar. 1976): 6294–95–A; UM 76–6561.
      Includes Nationalist Chinese participation in regional
      organizations within Asia.

911   SUMITRO, Achmad. *Foreign Investment in the Forest Based
      Sector of Indonesia: Increasing Its Contribution to Indo-
      nesian Development.* Minnesota, 1975 (Ph.D. in Forestry).
      248p. DAI 37, no.1 (July 1976): 10–B; UM 76–14,969. In-
      cludes investment from Hong Kong and the Republic of China.

912   TSAO, Jiun Han. *The Asian Development Bank as a Politi-
      cal System.* Oklahoma, 1975 (Ph.D. in Political Science).
      268p. DAI 35, no.9 (Mar. 1975): 6223–A; UM 75–6561.
      Hong Kong and the Republic of China are among the many
      Asian Development Bank members.

                    LANGUAGE AND LINGUISTICS

                    Classical and Modern Chinese

                 General and Miscellaneous Studies
See also entries 968 and 1699.

913   MEYERSON, Marion Diamond. *An Exploration of Comprehension
      Differences in Time Compressed Japanese, Chinese, Hindi,
      and English Speech.* Illinois, 1971 (Ph.D. in Speech).
      132p. DAI 32, no.10 (Apr. 1972): 6101–B; UM 72–12,298.

914 THOMPSON, Robert McMillan. *A Descriptive Procedure for Coding and Decoding Chinese Ideographs*. Indiana, 1972 (Ph.D. in Linguistics). 168p. DAI 33, no.9 (Mar. 1973): 5159-A; UM 73-6511.

915 BARNES, Miller Dayle. *Language Planning in Mainland China: A Sociolinguistic Study of P'ŭ-t'ūng-huà and P'īn-yīn*. Georgetown, 1974 (Ph.D. in Languages and Linguistics). 384p. DAI 35, no.7 (Jan. 1975): 4473-74-A; UM 75-63. On the national language movement and the Latin letter phonetic system for character annotation.

916 CHEUNG, Hung-nin Samuel. *The Language of the Tun-huang Pien-wen*. California (Berkeley), 1974 (Ph.D. in Oriental Languages). x, 354p. Order copies from the Library Photographic Service, General Library, University of California at Berkeley.

917 ROSENBERG, Marc Stephen. *Counterfactives: A Pragmatic Analysis of Presupposition*. Illinois, 1975 (Ph.D. in Linguistics). 294p. DAI 36, no.5 (Nov. 1975): 2783-A; UM 75-24,394. Includes references to Chinese.

Lexicon

918 LI-REICHARDT, Shuxin. *Zweisilbige "Adjektiv-Verb"-Kombinationen im modernen Chinesischen. Ein Beitrag zum Wortproblem*. [German: Two-Syllable "Adjective-Verb" Combinations in the Modern Chinese Language: A Contribution to the Problem of Words.] Leipzig, 1971 (Dr., Sektion Afrika- und Nahostwissenschaft). iii, 200p.

919 COBLIN, Weldon South, Jr. *An Introductory Study of Textual and Linguistic Problems in Erh-ya*. Washington (Seattle), 1972 (Ph.D. in Asian Languages and Literature). 588p. DAI 33, no.5 (Nov. 1972): 2353-A; UM 72-28,584. Concerned with problems surrounding the origins and nature of the earliest Chinese lexicographical work.

920 HOMINAL, François. *Terminologie mathématique en chinois moderne*. [French: Mathematical Terminology in the Modern Chinese Language.] Paris V (René Descartes), 1973 (Doctorat de 3e cycle en linguistique). 159p. A copy is available at the Bibliothèque de la Sorbonne, library catalogue no. I 2491-4°.

921 BOLTZ, William George. *Studies in Old Chinese Word Families*. California (Berkeley), 1974 (Ph.D. in Oriental Languages). iv, 166p. Order copies from the Library Photographic Service, General Library, University of California.

922   METAILLE, Georges. *La terminologie botanique en chinois moderne.* [French: Botanical Terminology in Modern Chinese.] Paris VII, 1974 (Doctorat de 3e cycle ès études extrême-orientales). A copy is available at the Bibliothèque de la Sorbonne.

923   JEN, Hsiao Hsien. *A Frequency Count of Contemporary Chinese Vocabulary Based on Seven Leading Newspapers.* South Carolina, 1975 (Ph.D. in Education). 161p. DAI 36, no. 11 (May 1976): 7258-A; UM 76-10,462. Jen used newspapers printed in the Republic of China during 1974.

924   PRAPIN MANOMAIVIBOOL [MANOMAIVIBOOL, Prapin]. *A Study of Sino-Thai Lexical Correspondences.* Washington (Seattle), 1975 (Ph.D. in Asian Languages and Literature). 441p. DAI 37, no.2 (Aug. 1976): 945-46-A; UM 76-17,554.

Phonology

See also entry 1702.

925   HSIEH, Hsin-i. *The Development of Middle Chinese Entering Tone in Pekinese.* California (Berkeley), 1971 (Ph.D. in Linguistics). iii, 184p. Order copies from the Library Photographic Service, General Library, University of California at Berkeley.

926   LI, Lin-nei Yeung. *An Instrumental Study of Mandarin and Cantonese Tones.* Australian National, 1971 (Ph.D. in Linguistics). iii, 344p.

927   TING, Ai-chen. *Mandarin Tones in Selected Sentence Environments: An Acoustic Study.* Wisconsin, 1971 (Ph.D. in Linguistics). 196p. DAI 32, no.6 (Dec. 1971): 3287-A; UM 71-25,750.

928   CHEN, Gwang-tsai. *A Comparative Study of Pitch Range of Native Speakers of Midwestern English and Mandarin Chinese: An Acoustic Study.* Wisconsin, 1972 (Ph.D. in Chinese Linguistics). 174p. DAI 33, no.4 (Oct. 1972): 1706-A; UM 72-22,079.

929   CHEN, Matthew. *Nasals and Nasalization in Chinese: Explorations in Phonological Universals.* California (Berkeley), 1972 (Ph.D. in Linguistics). iii, 318p. Order copies from the Library Photographic Service, General Library, University of California at Berkeley.

930   LYOVIN, Anatole. *Comparative Phonology of Mandarin Dialects.* California (Berkeley), 1972 (Ph.D. in Linguistics).

ix, 718p. Order copies from the Library Photographic
Service, General Library, University of California at
Berkeley.

931 MÁRTONFI, Ferenc. *Ji-cing T'ang-kori buddhista szansz-*
krit-kinai szótáránák kinai hangtörténeti tanulságai.
[Hungarian: Chinese Phonological Lessons in the I-ching's
Buddhist Sanskrit-Chinese Vocabulary of the T'ang Period.]
Eötvös Lóránd Tudományegyetem, 1972 (Dr.U. in Chinese).

932 TING, Pang-hsin. *Chinese Phonology of the Wei-Chin Peri-*
od: Reconstruction of the Finals as Reflected in Poetry.
Washington (Seattle), 1972 (Ph.D. in Asian Languages and
Literature). 502p. DAI 33, no.5 (Nov. 1972): 2357-A;
UM 72-28,674.

933 CHEN, Teresa Chin-sha. *A Statistical Study of Mandarin*
Phonology. Stanford, 1974 (Ph.D. in Linguistics). 127p.
DAI 35, no.6 (Dec. 1974): 3711-12-A; UM 74-26,994.

934 LIGHT, Timothy. *Phonological Relativity and Constituent*
Analysis Evidence from Chinese Syllable Types and Tradi-
tional Chinese Analyses. Cornell, 1974 (Ph.D. in Linguistics). 261p. DAI 35, no.7 (Jan. 1975): 4482-83-A; UM
74-29,924.

935 TIPTON, Gary Prior. *A Contrastive Analysis of Mandarin*
and Cantonese Phonologies. Indiana, 1974 (Ph.D. in East
Asian Languages and Literatures). 306p. DAI 35, no.7
(Jan. 1975): 4491-92-A; UM 75-1766.

Syntax and Grammar

See also entry 972 and--within the Appendix--the section entitled "Language and Linguistics" (pp.242-44).

936 CHIN, Tsung. *Tensal Systems of Mandarin Chinese and Eng-*
lish: A Contrastive Study. Georgetown, 1971 (Ph.D. in
Linguistics). 226p. DAI 32, no.11 (May 1972): 6402-A;
UM 72-16,034.

937 LAY, Nancy Duke S. *Grammatical Interference in a Multi-*
lingual Situation. Columbia (Teachers College), 1971
(Ed.D.). 212p. DAI 32, no.2 (Aug. 1971): 821-22-A; UM
71-20,018. Studies students in Hong Kong.

938 LI, Charles Na. *Semantics and the Structure of Compounds*
in Chinese. California (Berkeley), 1971 (Ph.D. in Linguistics). 147p. Order copies from the Library Photographic Service, General Library, University of California
at Berkeley.

939   LI, Frances Catheryn. *Case and Communicative Function in the Use of Ba in Mandarin.* Cornell, 1971 (Ph.D. in Linguistics). 186p. DAI 32, no.12 (June 1972): 6956-A; UM 72-15,419.

940   LIANG, James Chao-ping. *Prepositions, Co-Verbs, or Verbs? A Commentary on Chinese Grammar--Past and Present.* Pennsylvania, 1971 (Ph.D. in Oriental Studies). 264p. DAI 32, no.4 (Oct. 1971): 2078-A; UM 71-26,049.

941   WU, Ch'i-yü. *L'expression du nombre en chinois.* [French: Numerical Expression in Chinese.] Paris VII, 1971 (Doctorat d'Etat).

942   COYAUD, Maurice. *Articulations logiques du discours. Thèse soutenue sur un ensemble de travaux.* [French: Logical Articulations of Language. A Thesis Sustained on the Basis of a Group of Works.] Paris III (Sorbonne-Nouvelle), 1972 (Doctorat d'Etat ès lettres). Coyaud's degree was awarded on the basis of 10 published works including 3 relating to China: (a) Questions de grammaire chinoise (Paris: Centre de linguistique quantitative de la Faculté des sciences de l'Université de Paris, 1969. vi, 95p. [Documents de linguistique quantitative, 3]; (b) "Analyse et classification automatiques en chinois" (T.A. Informations 1, 1968, pp.19-29); and (c) "Coordinative Conjunctions of Contemporary Chinese" (Rapport C.N.R.S. 5, 1968. L.A.D.L.).

943   HSU, Vivian Ling. *Er and Zi Suffixation in Chinese.* Michigan, 1972 (Ph.D. in Far Eastern Languages and Literatures). 241p. DAI 33, no.5 (Nov. 1972): 2354-A; UM 72-29,095.

944   LU, Hsiao-tung. *The Verb-Verb Construction in Mandarin Chinese.* Ohio State, 1972 (Ph.D. in Linguistics). 156p. DAI 33, no.4 (Oct. 1972): 1709-A; UM 72-27,057.

945   SALT, Michael. *Aspects of Noun-Formation in Chinese.* Cambridge, 1972 (Ph.D. in Oriental Studies). 204p.

946   TANG, Ting-chi Charles. *Movement Transformations in Chinese Syntax.* Texas, 1972 (Ph.D. in Linguistics). 262p. DAI 33, no.10 (Apr. 1973): 5711-12-A; UM 73-7653.

947   TENG, Shou-hsin. *A Semantic Study of Transitivity Relations in Chinese.* California (Berkeley), 1972 (Ph.D. in Linguistics). vii, 355p. Order copies from the Library Photographic Service, General Library, University of California at Berkeley. Published as A Semantic...Chinese (Berkeley: University of California Press, 1975. ix, 177p. [University of California publications in linguistics, 80]).

948   RODMAN, Robert David. *The Study of Fuzzy Islands within
      the Framework of Transformational Generative Grammar.*
      California (Los Angeles), 1973 (Ph.D. in Linguistics).
      303p. DAI 34, no.7 (Jan. 1974): 4234-A; UM 73-32,074.
      Includes consideration of Mandarin Chinese.

949   TAKASHIMA, Ken-ichi. *Negatives in the King Wu-ting Bone
      Inscriptions.* Washington (Seattle), 1973 (Ph.D. in Asian
      Languages and Literature). 450p. DAI 34, no.7 (Jan.
      1974): 4227-A; UM 74-841. On oracle bone inscriptions of
      the King Wuting period (ca.14th century B.C.).

950   CHEN, Ching-hsiang Lee. *Interactions between Aspects of
      Noun Phrase Structure and Restrictions on Question Forma-
      tion in Mandarin Chinese.* Illinois, 1974 (Ph.D. in Lin-
      guistics). 213p. DAI 35, no.7 (Jan. 1975): 4475-A; UM
      75-278.

951   WANG, Yu-hsu. *A Study of De in Noun Phrase Structure in
      Mandarin Chinese: A Tagmemic-Case Grammar Analysis.*
      Georgetown, 1974 (Ph.D. in Chinese). 281p. DAI 35, no.4
      (Oct. 1974): 2256-A; UM 74-21,650.

952   DURRANT, Stephen W. *An Examination of Textual and Gram-
      matical Problems in Mo Tzu.* Washington (Seattle), 1975
      (Ph.D. in Asian Languages and Literature). 380p. DAI 37,
      no.2 (Aug. 1976): 975-76-A; UM 76-17,456.

953   LII, Yu-hwei Eunice. *Word Order, Transformation, and Com-
      municative Function in Mandarin Chinese.* Cornell, 1975
      (Ph.D. in Linguistics). 148p. DAI 36, no.10 (Apr. 1976):
      6649-50-A; UM 76-8145.

954   WASHBURN, Lucia Yang. *A Tagmemic-Case Grammar Analysis of
      Mandarin Chinese Clauses.* Georgetown, 1975 (Ph.D. in Lan-
      guages). 348p. DAI 36, no.11 (May 1976): 7396-A; UM
      76-11,665.

Writing System

See also entries 914, 915, 1124, and 1132.

955   MILSKY, Constantin. *Préparation de la réforme de l'écri-
      ture en République populaire de Chine (1949-1954).*
      [French: Preparations for the Reform of the Writing Sys-
      tem in the People's Republic of China, 1949-1954.]
      Paris VII, 1971 (Doctorat de 3e cycle). 574p. Published
      as Préparation...(1949-1954) (Paris: Mouton et Maison des
      Sciences de l'Homme, 1974. 507p. [Matérieux pour l'étude
      de l'Extrême-Orient moderne et contemporain, Travaux 7]).

956   STONE, James Warren. *Writing as a Part of Language: A
      Stratificational Study.* California (Berkeley), 1971
      (Ph.D. in Linguistics). 219p. DAI 36, no.6 (Dec. 1975):
      3641-42-A; UM 75-29,428. Includes consideration of Chi-
      nese orthography.

957   CHOU, Nelson Ling-sun. *A New Alphameric Code for Chinese
      Ideographs: Its Evaluation and Applications.* Chicago,
      1972 (Ph.D., Graduate Library School). 150p. Order cop-
      ies from the Photoduplication Department, Joseph Regen-
      stein Library, University of Chicago.

958   CHEN, John T. S. *Les réformes de l'écriture chinoise.*
      [French: The Reforms in Chinese Writing.] Paris VII, 1974
      (Doctorat d'Université ès lettres). 204p. A copy is
      available at the Bibliothèque de la Sorbonne, library cat-
      alogue no. W Univ 1974(38)-4°.

959   LEIDE, John Edgar. *Classification Development Effected
      from Graphical Hierarchies.* Rutgers, 1975 (Ph.D. in Li-
      brary Science). 98p. DAI 35, no.10 (Apr. 1975):
      6741-42-A; UM 75-8410. Analyzes the graphical structure
      of the Chinese Lesser Seal Characters.

960   WELLISCH, Hans Hanan. *The Conversion of Scripts: Its Na-
      ture, History and Utilization with Particular Reference
      to Bibliographic Control.* Maryland, 1975 (Ph.D. in Infor-
      mation and Library Science). 613p. DAI 36, no.6 (Dec.
      1975): 3190-91-A; UM 75-29,141. Published as The Conver-
      sion of Scripts: Its Nature, History and Utilization (New
      York: John Wiley, 1977). Includes coverage of the Chinese
      script and its Romanization.

Chinese Dialects

See also entries 926, 930, and 1935.

961   CHAN, Yuen Yuen Angela. *A Perceptual Study of Tones in
      Cantonese.* London, 1971 (Ph.D. in Linguistics, Universi-
      ty College). 237p.

962   BROSNAHAN, Irene Teoh. *Interrogative Structures in Amoy
      Chinese: A Transformational Approach.* Georgetown, 1972
      (Ph.D. in Linguistics). 199p. DAI 33, no.11 (May 1973):
      6335-A; UM 73-11,804.

963   CHANG, Yü-hung. *The Hinghwa Dialects of Fukien: A De-
      scriptive Linguistic Study.* Cornell, 1972 (Ph.D. in Lin-
      guistics). 232p. DAI 33, no.3 (Sept. 1972): 1154-A; UM
      72-23,649.

964 KILLINGLEY, Siew Yue. *The Grammatical Hierarchy of Malay-*
     an Cantonese. London, 1972 (Ph.D. in Arts, School of Ori-
     ental and African Studies). 418p.

965 SHERARD, Michael Lewis. *Shanghai Phonology.* Cornell,
     1972 (Ph.D. in Linguistics). 246p. DAI 33, no.9 (Mar.
     1973): 5157-A; UM 73-6669.

966 BAUER, Anton. *Das melanesische und chinesische Pidgineng-*
     lisch; linguistische Kriterien und Probleme. [German:
     Melanesian and Chinese Pidgin English: Linguistic Criteria
     and Problems.] Regensburg, 1973 (Dr., Philosophische Fa-
     kultät). Published as Das melanesische...Probleme (Re-
     gensburg: Carl, 1974. x, 190p. [Sprache und Literatur,
     Bd 8]).

967 CONDAX, Iovanna Delano. *Phonology of Lung-yen Chinese: A*
     Synchronic and Diachronic Analysis of a Kiangsi Dialect
     Based on 3,700 Character Readings and Selected Colloquial
     Forms. Princeton, 1973 (Ph.D. in Linguistics). 178p.
     DAI 34, no.8 (Feb. 1974): 5140-41-A; UM 74-2319.

968 BROWNING, Larry Kent. *The Cantonese Dialect with Special*
     Reference to Contrasts with Mandarin as an Approach to
     Determining Dialect Relatedness. Georgetown, 1974 (Ph.D.
     in Linguistics). 187p. DAI 35, no.6 (Dec. 1974): 3727-A;
     UM 74-26,430.

969 CHOW, Chung-yu Chen. *A Study of the Nanping Dialect of*
     Fukien. Cornell, 1974 (Ph.D. in Linguistics). 182p.
     DAI 35, no.5 (Nov. 1974): 2965-A; UM 74-24,273.

970 LIN, Shuang-fu. *The Grammar of Disjunctive Questions in*
     Taiwanese. North Carolina, 1974 (Ph.D. in Linguistics).
     247p. DAI 35, no.6 (Dec. 1974): 3713-A; UM 74-26,903.

971 SUNG, Margaret Mian Yan. *A Study of Literary and Collo-*
     quial Amoy Chinese. Stanford, 1974 (Ph.D. in Linguistics).
     127p. DAI 34, no.12 (June 1974): 7735-A; UM 74-13,693.

972 YAU, Shun-chiu. *Le système de la négation en cantonais.*
     Appendice: La négation en mandarin. [French: The System
     of Negation in Cantonese, with an Appendix on Negation in
     Mandarin Chinese.] Paris VII, 1974 (Doctorat de 3e cycle
     en linguistique). 268p. A copy is available at the Bib-
     liothèque de la Sorbonne.

Mongolian

See also entry 1701.

973 RÓNA-TAS, András. *Az altáji nyelvrokonság vizsgálatának*

alapjai. A nyelvrokonság elmélete és a csuvas-mongol nyelvviszony. [Hungarian: The Foundations for Research into the Genetic Relationship of the Altaic Languages: The Theory of Linguistic Relationship and the Relation of the Chuvash and Mongol Languages.] Magyar Tudományos Akadémia, 1971 (Doctor of Sciences). 1025p. A copy of the dissertation is in the library of the Hungarian Academy of Sciences (Roosevelt-ter 9, Budapest). Several papers based on the thesis have been published in various European journals.

974 SÁRKÖZI, Alice. *Egy preklasszikus nyelvi emlék, a mongol vajracchedika.* [Hungarian: A Preclassical Linguistic Record: The Mongolian Version of <u>Vajracchedikā</u> (The Diamond Sutra).] Eötvös Lóránd Tudományegyetem, 1971 (Dr.U. in Inner Asian Studies).

975 VIETZE, Hans-Peter. *Theorie und Materialien zur automatischen Verarbeitung mongolischer Sprachdaten.* [German: Theory and Materials for the Automated Processing of Mongolian Linguistic Data.] Humboldt-Universität Berlin, 1972 (Dr., Wiss. Rat.). This dissertation consists of six previously published works: (a) "Eine Definition des mongolischen Wortes" (<u>Zeitschrift für Phonetik, Sprachwissenschaft und Kommunikationsforschung</u>, vol.22, 1969, pp.77-82); (b) "Strukturtheorie des Wortes und seiner Komponenten" (<u>Zeitschrift für Phonetik, Sprachwissenschaft und Kommunikationsforschung</u>, vol.23, 1970, pp.261-90); (c) "Das Problem der Semantikstrukturierung bei einer automatischen monematischen Analyse" (<u>Zeitschrift für Phonetik, Sprachwissenschaft und Kommunikationsforschung</u>, vol.24, 1971, appendix of 42 pages); (d) "Zur automatischen Zerlegung mongolischer Wörter in ihre Moneme" (<u>Osnovnye certy programmy dlja avtomaticeskogo monematiceskogo analiza mongol'skogo slova</u>--volume of collected papers from the 2nd International Congress of Mongolian specialists--9 pages); (e) "Die formale morphologische Struktur des mongolischen Wortes" (<u>Formal'naja morfologiceskaja struktura mongol'skogo slova</u>. Moskva, 1971. 14 pages); and (f) "Zur teilautomatisierten Herstellung eines deutsch-mongolischen Wörterbuches" (<u>Beiträge zur maschinellen Sprachverarbeitung</u>. Berlin: Akademie-Verlag, 1971. 12 pages).

976 DASZCEDEN, Tümenbajaryn. *Liczba imion we współczesnym języku mongolskim.* [Polish: The Number of First Names in the Contemporary Mongolian Language.] Uniwersytet Warszawski, 1973 (Rozprawa doktorska, Inst. Orientalistyczny).

977 SOHN, John Young. *A Study of Grammatical Cases of Korean, Japanese, and Other Major Altaic Languages.* Indiana, 1973 (Ph.D. in Linguistics). 432p. DAI 34, no.7 (Jan. 1974): 4235-36-A; UM 74-421. Includes grammatical cases in Manchu and Mongolian.

Tibetan

See also entry 1700.

978 CIVERA, Marco Bernard. *The Distinctive Phonology of Lhasa Central Tibetan: Results of a Field Trip to Study the Himalayas as an Ethno-Linguis. ic Area.* Georgetown, 1971 (Ph.D. in Linguistics). 196p. DAI 32, no.4 (Oct. 1971): 2076-A; UM 71-25,225.

979 BAUMAN, James John. *Pronouns a: Pronominal Morphology in Tibeto-Burman.* California (Berkeley), 1975 (Ph.D. in Linguistics). 339p. DAI 37, no.1 (July 1976): 262-A; UM 76-15,103.

980 NÄTHER, Volkbert. *Das Gilgit-Fragment Or. 11878A im Britischen Museum zu London; herausgegeben, mit dem tibetischen verglichen und übersetzt.* [German: The Gilgit Fragment Or. 11878A in the British Museum in London: Edited, Compared with the Tibetan, and Translated.] Marburg, 1975 (Dr., Fachbereich Aussereuropäische Sprachen und Kulturen). 105p.

Tocharian, Manchu, and Other Languages in China

See also entries 977, 1704, 1705, 1707, and 1708.

981 MARGGRAF, Wolf-Jügen. *Untersuchungen zum Akzent in Tocharisch B.* [German: Investigations of the Accent in the Tocharian B Language.] Kiel, 1971 (Dr., Philosophische Fakultät). 103p. Tocharian is an Indo-European language that was spoken during the first millennium A.D. by a people dwelling in present-day Sinkiang.

982 GRINSTEAD, Eric D. *Analysis of the Tangut Script.* [With a summary in Danish] Copenhagen, 1972 (Dr., Faculty of Arts). Published as Analysis...Script (Lund: Studentlitteratur, 1972. 376p. + 76 plates [Scandinavian Institute of Asian Studies monograph series, 10]).

983 HÁRDI, Péterné [Kornélia]. *Egy preklasszikus mandzsu szótár a K'ien-lung korból.* [Hungarian: A Preclassical

137

Manchurian Vocabulary from the Ch'ien-lung Era.] Eötvös
Lóránd Tudományegyetem, 1972 (Dr.U. in Inner Asian Studies).

984 ZIMMER, Stefan. *Die Satzstellung des finiten Verbs im
Tocharischen*. [German: The Position of Finite Verbs within the Sentence in the Tocharian Language.] Frankfurt,
1972 (Dr., Fachbereich Ost- und Aussereuropäische Sprach-
und Kulturwissenschaft). Published as Die Satzstellung...
Tocharischen (The Hague: Mouton, 1976. xv, 107p. [Janua
linguarum: Ser. practica; 238]).

985 KIYOSE, Gisaburo Norikura. *A Study of the Jurchen Language and Script in the* Hua-yi i-yü*, with Special Reference to the Problem of Its Decipherment*. Indiana, 1973
(Ph.D. in Uralic and Altaic Studies). 310p. DAI 34, no.
4 (Oct. 1973): 1884-A; UM 73-23,019. Examines a Ming period work dealing with the language of the tribes who
founded the Chin dynasty in the early 12th century.

986 LI, Paul Jen-kuei. *Rukai Structure*. Hawaii, 1973 (Ph.D.
in Linguistics). 316p. DAI 34, no.6 (Dec. 1973): 3375-A;
UM 73-28,803. Published as Rukai Structure (Taipei: Institute of History and Philology, Academia Sinica, 1973.
xi, 305, 6p. [Special publications--Institute of History
and Philology, Academia Sinica, 64]). Provides a genera-
tive description of the structure of an Austronesian language spoken in Taiwan.

987 OSHIKA, Beatrice Reyes Teodoro. *The Relationship of Kam-
Sui-Mak to Tai*. Michigan, 1973 (Ph.D. in Linguistics).
164p. DAI 35, no.1 (July 1974): 434-35-A; UM 74-15,822.
On the Kam-Sui-Mak languages of southern China and several
dialects of Thailand.

988 FUTAKY, István. *Tungusische Lehnwörter des Ostjakischen*.
[German: Tungus Loanwords in the Ostiak Language.] Göttingen, 1974 (Habilitationsschrift, Philosophische Fakultät). Published as Tungusische...Ostjakischen (Wiesbaden:
Harrassowitz, 1975. 95p. [Veröffentlichungen der Socie-
tas Uralo-Altaica; Bd.10]). The Tungus inhabit present-
day Manchuria and eastern Siberia.

989 SCHMIDT, Klaus T. *Die Gebrauchsweisen des Mediums im Tocharischen*. [German: The Ways of Using the Middle Voice
in Tocharian.] Göttingen, 1974 (Dr., Philosophische Fakultät). xviii, 562p.

990 TOU, Da Rouin Maria Chiu. *Tonologie du Min-Nan*. [French:
The Tonology of Min-Nan.] Paris III (Sorbonne-Nouvelle),
1974 (Doctorat de 3e cycle en phonétique). v, 257p.
A copy is available at the Bibliothèque de la Sorbonne.

991 DELL, François. *La langue Bai, phonologie et lexique.*
     [French: The Pai Language: Phonology and Lexicon.] Par-
     is VII, 1975 (Doctorat de 3e en linguistique). vii, 247p.
     A copy is available at the Bibliothèque de la Sorbonne,
     library catalogue no.I 3457-4°. On a language spoken in
     southwestern China.

992 TSUCHIDA, Shigeru. *Reconstruction of Proto-Tsouic Pho-
     nology.* Yale, 1975 (Ph.D. in Linguistics). 361p. DAI
     36, no.5 (Nov. 1975): 2785-A; UM 75-24,608. Proto-Tsouic
     is the last proto-language from which three Austronesian
     languages spoken in central Taiwan developed.

LAW AND THE JUDICIAL SYSTEM

See also entries 818, 1192, and 1588, as well as the section--
within the Appendix--entitled "Law and the Judicial System"
(pp.244-45).

993 LI, Victor Hao. *Law and Social Order in the People's Re-
     public of China.* Harvard, 1971 (S.J.D.). ii, 305p.
     Available at the Harvard University Law School library,
     call no.CHIN-PR 903.LI.

994 SCHEU, Henning. *Das Völkerrecht in den Beziehungen Chinas
     zu den europäischen Seemächten und zu Russland. Ein Bei-
     trag zur Geschichte des Völkerrechts.* [German: Interna-
     tional Law as Practiced in China's Relations with the Eu-
     ropean Naval Powers and with Russia: A Contribution to the
     History of International Law.] Frankfurt, 1971 (Dr.,
     Rechtswissenschaftliche Fakultät).   Published as Das
     Völkerrecht...Völkerrechts (Frankfurt a.M., 1971. 371p.).

995 TOMSON, Edgar. *Das Staatsangehörigkeitsrecht der ostasi-
     atischen Staaten China, Japan, Korea, Mongolei.* [German:
     The Citizenship Laws of the East Asian Nations: China,
     Japan, Korea, and Mongolia.] Hamburg, 1971 (Dr.). Pub-
     lished as Das Staatsangehörigkeitsrecht...Mongolei (Frank-
     furt a.M.: Metzner, 1971. 296p.).

996 CHAO, Shou-po. *Comparative Aspects of Conflict of Laws
     in Domestic Relations.* Illinois, 1972 (J.S.D.). 405p.
     DAI 33, no.10 (Apr. 1973): 5756-A; UM 73-9900. Compares
     laws in the Republic of China, western Europe, and the
     United States.

997 CHEN, Charng-ven. *China and the Law of Consular Rela-
     tions.* Harvard, 1972 (S.J.D.). xxv, 528p. Available at

the Harvard University Law School library, call no.
141.5105.

998 CHEN, Kang-shen. *Die Gewerkschaften als Körperschaften
des öffentlichen Rechts. Eine Untersuchung über die
Rechtsstellung der Gewerkschaften in der Republik China
und in den Entwicklungsländern.* [German: The Labor
Unions as Corporations in Public Law: An Investigation
of the Legal Position of the Labor Unions in the Republic of China and in the Developing Nations.] Mannheim,
1972 (Dr., Fakultät für Rechtswissenschaft). Published
as Die Gewerkschaften...Entwicklungsländern (Mannheim,
1973. ix, 183p.).

999 BURNS, Ian Robert. *Private Law in Traditional China
(Sung Dynasty): Using as a Main Source of Information
the Work Ming-kung shu-p'an ch'ing-ming chi.* Oxford,
1973 (D.Phil. in Oriental Studies). 418p. Systematical-
ly analyzes the rights and duties surrounding "family
property".

1000 CH'EN, Paul Heng-chao. *Chih-yüan hsin-ko: The Yüan Code
of 1291 as Reconstructed and a Survey of Yüan Legal Institutions.* Harvard, 1973 (Ph.D. in East Asian Languages
and Civilizations). cxci, 159p. Available at the Harvard University Archives, Pusey Library, call no.
HU 90.10325.20.

1001 LEE, Shane Rong. *The Legal System and Political Development in Communist China, 1949-1969.* North Texas State,
1973 (Ph.D. in Political Science). 247p. DAI 34, no.8
(Feb. 1974): 5269-70-A; UM 74-4044.

1002 LIAW, Yih-nan. *Der öffentliche Einfluss auf das Unter-
nehmen und die Rechtsform des Unternehmens. Rechtsver-
gleichende Darstellung zwischen Deutschland und Taiwan.*
[German: Public Influence on Business Enterprises and
the Legal Form of Business Enterprises: A Comparison of
German and Taiwanese Law.] Tübingen, 1973 (Dr., Fachbereich Rechtswissenschaft). Published as Der öffentliche
...Taiwan (Tübingen, 1973. ix, 271p.).

1003 BRADY, James Peter. *Popular Justice: Conflict and Community in the Chinese Legal System (200 B.C.-1974).* California (Berkeley), 1974 (D.Crim.). v, 267p. Order copies from the Library Photographic Service, General Library, University of California at Berkeley.

1004 BROCKMAN, Rosser Holliday. *Customary Contract Law in
Late Traditional Taiwan.* Harvard, 1974 (Ph.D. in History
and East Asian Languages). ii, 223p. Available at the

Harvard University Archives, Pusey Library, call no.
HU 90.10505.10.

1005 SCHMOLLER, Bernd. *Rechtsfälle der Nördlichen Sung-Zeit,
betrachtet nach den Eingaben des Richters und Staats-
mannes Bao Zheng (999-1062)*. [German: Law Cases of the
Northern Sung Period as Seen in the Presentations of the
Judge and Statesman Pao Chang.] Hamburg, 1974? (Dr.,
Seminar für Sprache und Kultur Chinas).

1006 HUANG, Thomas Weishing. *Law and Economic Development in
Modern China*. Harvard, 1975 (S.J.D. in Comparative Law).
v, 308p. Available at the Harvard University Law School
library, call no.CHIN-PR 971.HUA.

1007 LEE, Bernice June. *The Change in the Legal Status of
Chinese Women in Civil Matters from Traditional Law to
the Republican Civil Code*. Sydney, 1975 (Ph.D. in Oriental Studies). iv, 419p. For copies, contact the
Fisher Library, University of Sydney, Sydney, Australia.

LIBRARIES

See also entries 959, 960, and 1719.

1008 PROETT, Polly-Ann Brumley. *A History of Libraries in
the People's Republic of China, Including Some Aspects
of College and University Library Development, 1949-1974*.
George Washington, 1974 (Ph.D. in Education). 231p.
DAI 35, no.4 (Oct. 1974): 1880-81-A; UM 74-23,497.

1009 ROTHACKER, John Michael. *The Role of the Library in the
Non-Western Studies Programs in Three Liberal Arts Colleges in Indiana*. Indiana, 1975 (Ph.D. in Library Science). 350p. DAI 36, no.5 (Nov. 1975): 2469-A; UM
75-23,499. Focuses on library collections for East Asian
Studies at Earlham and Wabash Colleges and for Asian
Studies at Marian College.

LITERATURE

General and Miscellaneous Studies

See also entries 443, 490, 1721, 1722, and 1726.

1010 COMPTON, Robert William. *A Study of the Translations of
Lin Shu, 1852-1924*. Stanford, 1971 (Ph.D. in Asian

Languages). 581p. DAI 32, no.10 (Apr. 1972): 5779-80-A; UM 72-11,525. On Lin's translation of many works of Western fiction into classical Chinese.

1011 DOERINGER, Franklin Melvin. *Yang Hsiung and His Formulation of a Classicism*. Columbia, 1971 (Ph.D. in East Asian Languages and Cultures). 329p. DAI 32, no.9 (Mar. 1972): 5178-A; UM 72-10,428. Yang Hsiung (53 B.C.-18 A.D.) was a writer and savant who formulated a rudimentary Confucian literary classicism.

1012 EOYANG, Eugene Chen. *Word of Mouth: Oral Storytelling in the Pien-wen*. Indiana, 1971 (Ph.D. in Comparative Literature). 357p. DAI 32, no.8 (Feb. 1972): 4560-A; UM 72-6773. Based on 8th-10th century manuscripts found at Tun-huang.

1013 PERLMUTTER, Ruth. *Arthur Waley and His Place in the Modern Movement between the Two Wars*. Pennsylvania, 1971 (Ph.D. in English). 406p. DAI 32, no.4 (Oct. 1971): 2100-A; UM 71-26,070. Focuses on this English writer's work with Chinese and Japanese literature during the 1920s and 1930s.

1014 YOUNG, Conrad Chün-shih. *The Morphology of Chinese Folk Stories Derived from Shadow Plays of Taiwan*. California (Los Angeles), 1971 (Ph.D. in Anthropology). 961p. DAI 32, no.2 (Aug. 1971): 688-B; UM 71-21,344.

1015 LU, Alexander Ya-li. *Political Control of Literature in Communist China, 1949-1966*. Indiana, 1972 (Ph.D. in Political Science). 481p. DAI 33, no.5 (Nov. 1972): 2450-A; UM 72-30,428.

1016 PEN, Yu Ho-fang. *Spiegelungen von Elementen des sozialen und kulturellen Lebens in chinesischen Volkserzählungen*. [German: Reflections of Elements of Social and Cultural Life in Chinese Folk Tales.] Marburg, 1972 (Dr., Fachbereich Gesellschaftswissenschaft). 288p.

1017 WEST, Stephen Harry. *Studies in Chin Dynasty (1115-1234) Literature*. Michigan, 1972 (Ph.D. in Far Eastern Languages and Literatures). 294p. DAI 33, no.11 (May 1973): 6379-A; UM 73-11,297. Focuses on drama and poetry.

1018 CHAI, Marie. *Heroic Values in Ancient and Mediaeval China and England*. California (Berkeley), 1973 (Ph.D. in Comparative Literature). iii, 473p. Order copies from the Library Photographic Service, General Library, University of California at Berkeley.

1019 LIANG, I-cheng. *Hsü Wei (1521-1593): His Life and Literary Works*. Ohio State, 1973 (Ph.D. in East Asian

Languages and Literatures). 217p. DAI 34, no.8 (Feb. 1974): 5109-A; UM 74-3231. Published as Hsü Wei ti wen hsüeh yü i shu (Taipei: I Wen yin shu kuan, 1976. 378p.). On Hsü Wei's prose, poetry, plays and literary theory.

1020 PICKOWICZ, Paul Gene. *Ch'ü Ch'iu-pai and the Origins of Marxist Literary Criticism in China*. Wisconsin, 1973 (Ph.D. in History). 458p. DAI 34, no.10 (Apr. 1974): 6572-A; UM 74-3546. Focuses on Ch'ü's activities during the 1920s and 1930s as a Marxist literary critic and theoretician.

1021 HSIEH, Chen-ooi Chin. *Evolution of the Theme of Tou O Yüan*. Ohio State, 1974 (Ph.D. in East Asian Languages and Literatures). 162p. DAI 35, no.8 (Feb. 1975): 5349-A; UM 75-3101. Studies the evolution of the story of Tou O in literature and drama from the Han dynasty to the twentieth century.

1022 SCHOLZ, Alexander Georg. *Chinesische Stoffe und Motive in der populären mongolischen Literatur gegen Ende des 19. Jahrhunderts*. [German: Chinese Subjects and Motifs in Popular Mongolian Literature towards the End of the 19th Century.] Bonn, 1975 (Dr., Philosophische Fakultät). 265p.

Drama

Early to 1800

See also entry 1729.

1023 FAUROT, Jeannette Louise. *Four Cries of a Gibbon: A Tsa-chü Cycle by the Ming Dramatist Hsu Wei (1521-1593)*. California (Berkeley), 1972 (Ph.D. in Oriental Languages). ii, 218p. Order copies from the Library Photographic Service, General Library, University of California at Berkeley. On the drama Ssu sheng yüan.

1024 HAYDEN, George Allen. *The Judge Pao Plays of the Yuan Dynasty*. Stanford, 1972 (Ph.D. in Asian Languages). 461p. DAI 32, no.12 (June 1972): 6930-A; UM 72-16,724. Published as Crime and Punishment in Medieval Chinese Drama: Three Judge Pao Plays (Cambridge, Mass.: East Asian Research Center, Harvard University, 1977. [Harvard East Asian monographs, 82]).

1025 ŻBIKOWSKI, Tadeusz. *Early Nan-hsi Plays of the Southern Sung Period*. Uniwersytet Warszawski, 1973 (Rozprawa

habilitacyjna, Wydz. Filologii Obcych). Published as
Early...Period (Warszawa: Wydawnictwa Uniwersytetu Warszawskiego, 1974. 194p.).

1026   LEUNG, Kai-cheong. *Hsü Wei as Dramatic Critic: An Anno-
tated Translation of the Nan-tz'u Hsü-lu, Account of
Southern Drama.* California (Berkeley), 1974 (Ph.D. in
Oriental Languages). viii, 306p. Order copies from the
Library Photographic Service, General Library, University
of California at Berkeley.

1027   CAVANAUGH, Jerome Thomas. *The Dramatic Works of the Yüan
Dynasty Playwright Pai P'u.* Stanford, 1975 (Ph.D. in
Asian Languages). 294p. DAI 36, no.4 (Oct. 1975):
2210-11-A; UM 75-21,852.

1028   CHEN, Catherine Wang. *The Art of Satire in the Han-tan
meng chi.* Minnesota, 1975 (Ph.D. in Chinese). 156p.
DAI 36, no.7 (Jan. 1976): 4500-01-A; UM 76-433. On a
play by T'ang Hsien-tsu (1550-1616).

1029   STRASSBERG, Richard Eric. *The Peach Blossom Fan: Person-
al Cultivation in a Chinese Drama.* Princeton, 1975
(Ph.D. in East Asian Studies). 362p. DAI 37, no.2
(Aug. 1976): 976-A; UM 76-18,245. On T'ao hua Shan by
K'ung Shang-jen (1648-1718).

Modern and Contemporary Drama

1030   YEN, Joseph Chen-ying. *Two Modern Chinese Dramas Translated into English: A Stormy Night Visitor by Chang Yung-
hsiang and As Eternal as Heaven and Earth by Wu Jo Including an Introduction to Modern Chinese Drama.* Brigham Young, 1973 (Ph.D. in Dramatic Arts). 259p. DAI 34,
no.8 (Feb. 1974): 5033-A; UM 73-31,200. On Feng yu ku
jen lai and Tien chang ti chiu, dramas by two contemporary playwrights in the Republic of China.

1031   TAI, Yih-jian. *The Contemporary Chinese Theater and Soviet Influence, 1919-1960.* Southern Illinois, 1974
(Ph.D. in Speech). 203p. DAI 35, no.12 (June 1975):
8066-A; UM 75-13,284. Traces the impact of Soviet dra-
matical production and theories upon modern Chinese drama as revealed in acting, directing, designing, and
playwrighting.

Poetry

Early to 600 A.D.

See also entries 932 and 1724.

1032 KUO, Ta-hsia. *A Study of Metre in Chinese Poetry*. Wisconsin, 1971 (Ph.D. in East Asian Languages and Literature). 197p. DAI 32, no.6 (Dec. 1971): 3257-A; UM 71-23,311.

1033 PAPER, Jordan David. *The Life and Thought of Fu Hsüan (A.D. 217-278)*. Wisconsin, 1971 (Ph.D. in Chinese). 296p. DAI 32, no.1 (July 1971): 339-A; UM 71-14,159. On the philosophical work (the Fu tzu) and poetry of this Confucian official.

1034 SCHULTE, Wilfried. *Ts'ao P'i (187-226)*. *Leben und Dichtungen*. [German: Ts'ao P'i (187-226 A.D.): His Life and Poems.] Bonn, 1971 (Dr., Philosophische Fakultät). Published as Ts'ao P'i...Dictungen (Bonn, 1973. 228p.).

1035 WANG, Ching-hsien. *Shih Ching: Formulaic Language and Mode of Creation*. California (Berkeley), 1971 (Ph.D. in Comparative Literature). 233p. DAI 33, no.4 (Oct. 1972): 1704-05-A; UM 72-22,503. On the "Classic of Songs," a collection of 305 poems dating from the 10th to the 7th century B.C.

1036 CHAN, Ping-leung. *Ch'u tz'ŭ and Shamanism in Ancient China*. Ohio State, 1972 (Ph.D. in East Asian Languages and Literatures). 263p. DAI 33, no.4 (Oct. 1972): 1703-A; UM 72-26,989. The Ch'u tzu, or Elegies of Ch'u, is an important Chou period poetic work.

1037 JUHL, Robert Alvin. *A Survey of the Rhyming of Poets from the Wei Dynasty into the Early T'ang*. Wisconsin, 1972 (Ph.D. in Chinese). 484p. DAI 33, no.7 (Jan. 1973): 3619-A; UM 72-23,745.

1038 MARNEY, John. *Emperor Chien-wen of Liang (503-551): His Life and Literature*. Wisconsin, 1972 (Ph.D. in East Asian Languages and Literatures). 342p. DAI 32, no.12 (June 1972): 6950-A; UM 72-13,983. Published as Liang Chien-wen Ti (Boston: Twayne Publishers, 1976. 221p. [Twayne's world author series; TWAS 374: China]). Focuses on his activities as a government official and as a poet.

1039 HSIEH, Sheau-mann. *The Folk Songs of the Southern Dynasties (318-589 A.D.)*. California (Los Angeles), 1973 (Ph.D. in Oriental Languages). 147p. DAI 34, no.11

(May 1974): 7209-10-A; UM 74-11,537. On folk songs found in chüan 44-49 of the Yüeh-fu shih-chi.

1040 MATTOS, Gilbert Louis. *The Stone Drums of Ch'in.* Washington (Seattle), 1973 (Ph.D. in Asian Languages and Literatures). 685p. DAI 35, no.3 (Sept. 1974): 1629-30-A; UM 74-19,119. Studies the 5th century B.C. poems engraved on the ten so-called Stone Drums.

1041 SANDERS, T'ao-t'ao. *The Balladic Tradition in Yüeh Fu.* Oxford, 1973 (D.Phil. in Oriental Studies). 352p. Yüeh fu are five-syllable line folksongs popular during the Han Dynasty.

1042 WESTBROOK, Francis Abeken. *Landscape Description in the Lyric Poetry and "Fuh on Dwelling in the Mountains" of Shieh Ling-yuun.* Yale, 1973 (Ph.D. in East and South Asian Languages and Literatures). 353p. DAI 34, no.2 (Aug. 1973): 743-44-A; UM 73-16,410. On the writings of Hsieh Ling-yün (385-433 A.D.).

1043 WILLIAMS, Gary Shelton. *A Study of the Oral Nature of the Han Yüeh-fu.* Washington (Seattle), 1973 (Ph.D. in Asian Languages and Literatures). 267p. DAI 34, no.8 (Feb. 1974): 5129-A; UM 74-2238. Analyzes these Han period poems in terms of stylistic devices, formulaic units, and figurative language.

1044 GRAHAM, William Thurmond. *Yü Hsin's "Lament for the South".* Harvard, 1974 (Ph.D. in East Asian Languages and Civilizations). lviii, 265p. Available at the Harvard University Archives, Pusey Library, call no.HU 90.10552.20. On the Ai Chiang-nan fu of Yü Hsin (513-581).

1045 FUSEK, Lois McKim. *The Poetry of Ts'áo P'i (187-226).* Yale, 1975 (Ph.D. in East Asian Languages and Literatures). 322p. DAI 36, no.5 (Nov. 1975): 2832-A; UM 75-24,533.

1046 TAM, Koo-yin. *The Use of Poetry in Tso-chuan: An Analysis of the "Fu-Shih" Practice.* Washington (Seattle), 1975 (Ph.D. in Asian Languages and Literature). 352p. DAI 37, no.2 (Aug. 1976): 976-A; UM 76-17,654.

600-1000 A.D.

See also entries 1032 and 1037.

1047 MILLER, James Whipple. *The Poetry of Meng Hao-jan: Translations and Critical Introduction for the Western Reader.*

Princeton, 1972 (Ph.D. in Comparative Literature). 209p.
DAI 34, no.2 (Aug. 1973): 736-A; UM 73-18,770. Meng
lived between 689 and 740 A.D.

1048 OWEN, Stephen. *The Poetry of Meng Chiao (751-814) and
Han Yü (768-824): A Study of a Chinese Poetic Reform.*
Yale, 1972 (Ph.D. in East Asian Languages and Litera-
tures). 609p. DAI 34, no.1 (July 1973): 283-A; UM
73-16,373. Published as The Poetry of Meng Chiao and
Han Yü (New Haven: Yale University Press, 1975. x, 294p.).

1049 WALLS, Jan Wilson. *The Poetry of Yü Hsüan-chi: A Translation, Annotation, Commentary, and Critique.* Indiana,
1972 (Ph.D. in East Asian Languages and Literatures).
409p. DAI 33, no.6 (Dec. 1972): 2914-A; UM 72-30,458.

1050 WONG, Yoon-wah. *Ssu-K'ung T'u: The Man and His Theory
of Poetry.* Wisconsin, 1972 (Ph.D. in Chinese). 253p.
DAI 33, no.8 (Feb. 1973): 4377-A; UM 72-31,559. Published as Ssu-k'ung T'u: A Poet-Critic of the T'ang (Hong
Kong: Chinese University of Hong Kong, 1976. ix, 68p.).

1051 FISH, Michael Bennett. *Mythological Themes in the Poetry
of Li Ho (791-817).* Indiana, 1973 (Ph.D. in East Asian
Languages and Literatures). 276p. DAI 34, no.10 (Apr.
1974): 6589-A; UM 74-9423.

1052 KUBIN, Wolfgang. *Das lyrische Werk des Tu Mu (803-852).
Versuch einer Deutung.* [German: The Lyric Work of Tu Mu
(803-852): An Interpretive Essay.] Bochum, 1973 (Dr.,
Abteilung für Philologie). Published as Das lyrische...
Deutung (Wiesbaden: Harrassowitz, 1976. ix, 261p. [Ver-
öffentlichungen des Ostasien-Instituts der Ruhr-Universität Bodhum; Bd.19]).

1053 LIU, Stephen Shu-ning. *The Lyrics of Li Yu: A Translation, Analysis and Commentary.* North Dakota, 1973 (Ph.D.,
English Dept.). 151p. DAI 34, no.8 (Feb. 1974): 5109-A;
UM 74-4154. On the poetry of the last king of the Southern T'ang dynasty (938-978).

1054 McLEOD, Russell Edward. *The Poetry of Meng Chiao in the
Chinese Baroque Tradition.* Stanford, 1973 (Ph.D. in
Asian Languages). vii, 173p. Available on interlibrary
loan from the library at Stanford University, call no.
3781.1973M. Not currently available from University Microfilms International. This is a study of Meng Chiao
(751-814 A.D.), an important T'ang period poet.

1055 HERBERT, Penelope Ann. *The Life and Works of Chang Chiu-
ling.* Cambridge, 1974 (Ph.D. in Chinese). 368p. On a
poet and statesman who lived from 678 to 740 A.D.

1056   RUPPENTHAL, Stephen Hal. *The Transmission of Buddhism in
       the Poetry of Han Shan*. California (Berkeley), 1974
       (Ph.D. in Comparative Literature). xiii, 229p. Order
       copies from the Library Photographic Service, General Li-
       brary, University of California at Berkeley. Includes
       an analysis of Cold Mountain as a symbol for public sal-
       vation in this 7th century poet's writings.

1057   TU, Kuo-ch'ing. *The Poetry of Li Ho (790-816): A Criti-
       cal Study*. Stanford, 1974 (Ph.D. in Asian Languages).
       317p. DAI 35, no.9 (Mar. 1975): 6113-14-A; UM 75-6937.

1058   BOYCE, Conal. *Rhythm and Meter of Tsyr in Performance*.
       Harvard, 1975 (Ph.D. in East Asian Languages and Civili-
       zations). 424p. Available at the Harvard University Ar-
       chives, Pusey Library, call no.HU 90.10910.20. About
       tz'u (tsyr), a type of song lyric which evolved into po-
       etry during the T'ang period.

1059   HARTMAN, Charles Matthew. *Language and Allusion in the
       Poetry of Han Yü: The "Autumn Sentiments"*. Indiana, 1975
       (Ph.D. in East Asian Languages and Literatures). 247p.
       DAI 36, no.2 (Aug. 1975): 897-A; UM 75-17,016. On the
       Ch'iu huai of Han Yü (768-824).

1060   HO, Man-wui. *Ch'en Tzǔ-Ang (A.D. 661-702), Innovator in
       T'ang Poetry*. London, 1975 (Ph.D. in Arts, School of
       Oriental and African Studies). 238p. Order copies from
       the British Library Lending Division, Boston Spa, York-
       shire, order no.D13601/75.

1061   WAGNER, Marsha Lynn. *The Art of Wang Wei's Poetry*. Cal-
       ifornia (Berkeley), 1975 (Ph.D. in Comparative Litera-
       ture). 282p. DAI 37, no.1 (July 1976): 322-A;
       UM 76-15,409.

                              1000-1800

See also entries 57, 1032, and 1725.

1062   BIEG, Lutz. *Huang T'ing-chien (1045-1105). Leben und
       Dichtung*. [German: Huang T'ing-chien (1045-1105): His
       Life and Poetry.] Heidelberg, 1971 (Dr., Philosophische
       Fakultät). iv, 404p. Published in Darmstadt by J. G.
       Bläschke Verlag, 1975.

1063   CHAVES, Jonathan. *Mei Yao-ch'en (1002-1060) and the De-
       velopment of Early Sung Poetry*. Columbia, 1971 (Ph.D. in
       East Asian Languages and Cultures). 364p. DAI 32, no.6
       (Dec. 1971): 3277-A; UM 72-1288. Published as Mei Yao-ch'er

...Poetry (New York: Columbia University Press, 1976. viii, 254p. [Studies in oriental culture, 13]).

1064 CHEN, Chantal. *Les poèmes Ci de Li Qing-Chao, 1081-après 1141*. [French: The Shih Poetry of Li Ch'ing-chao (1081-after 1141).] Paris VIII (Paris-Vincennes), 1972 (Doctorat de 3ᵉ cycle en chinois). 258p. A copy is available at the Bibliothèque de la Sorbonne.

1065 LIN, Shuen-fu. *A Structural Study of Chiang K'uei's Songs*. Princeton, 1972 (Ph.D. in East Asian Studies). 188p. DAI 33, no.10 (Apr. 1973): 5698-99-A; UM 73-9624. Studies the tz'u of the poet Chiang K'uei (1155-1221).

1066 YUH, Liou-yi Isabella. *Liu Yung, Su Shih, and Some Aspects of the Development of Early Tz'u Poetry*. Washington (Seattle), 1972 (Ph.D. in Asian Languages and Literature). 307p. DAI 33, no.1 (July 1972): 293-94-A; UM 72-20,903.

1067 JOSEPHS, Hilary Kromelow. *The Tz'u of Ch'in Kuan (1049-1100)*. Harvard, 1973 (Ph.D. in East Asian Languages and Civilizations). iv, 279p. Available at the Harvard University Archives, Pusey Library, call no.HU 90.10568.20.

1068 WU, Shu-shen Huang. *Chang K'o-chiu, a Yüan San-chü Poet*. Washington (Seattle), 1973 (Ph.D. in Asian Languages and Literature). 260p. DAI 34, no.5 (Nov. 1973): 2585-A; UM 73-27,696.

1069 CROWN, Elleanor Hazel. *The Yüan Dynasty Lyric Suite (San-T'ao): Its Macro-Structure, Content, and Some Comparisons with Other Ch'ü Forms*. Michigan, 1974 (Ph.D. in Far Eastern Languages and Literatures). 315p. DAI 35, no.11 (May 1975): 7252-A; UM 75-10,155.

1070 GINSBERG, Stanley Mervyn. *Alienation and Reconciliation of a Chinese Poet: The Huangzhou Exile of Su Shi*. Wisconsin, 1974 (Ph.D. in Chinese). 301p. DAI 35, no.9 (Mar. 1975): 6096-97-A; UM 74-26,495. On this literary scholar-official's experiences between 1080 and 1084.

1071 DUKE, Michael Sherman. *The Life and Work of Lu You (1125-1210)*. California (Berkeley), 1975 (Ph.D. in Oriental Languages). 435p. DAI 37, no.1 (July 1976): 320-A; UM 76-15,165. Published as Lu You (Boston: Twayne Publishers, 1977. 180p. [Twayne's world author series; TWAS: 427: China]). On a patriotic Southern Sung poet.

1072 RADTKE, Kurt Werner. *Yuan Sanqu: A Study of the Prosody and Structure of Xiaoling Contained in the Sanqu Anthology Yangchun baixue Compiled by Yang Chaoying*. Australian

National, 1975 (Ph.D. in Chinese). 522p. DAI 36, no.9
(Mar. 1976): 6072-A; UM 76-6039. On Yüan dynasty songs.

1073 SCHMIDT, Jerry Dean. *The Poetry of Yang Wan-li*. British
Columbia, 1975 (Ph.D. in Asian Studies). vi, 453p. vi,
453p. DAI 36, no.12 (June 1976): 8067-68-A; Order copies
directly from the Canadian Theses Division, National Library of Canada at Ottawa; available only in microfiche
format, fiche no.25985, @ $5.00. On an outstanding shih
poet who lived from 1127 to 1206.

1074 TANG SHANG, Lily. *The Four Dreams of T'ang Hsien-Tsu*.
Hamburg, 1975 (Dr., Fachbereich Orientalistik). 115p.
On the Lin-chuan ssu meng, a collection of four volumes
of poetry by a late Ming author (1550-1616).

Modern and Contemporary Poetry

1075 CHENG, Chi-hsien. *Eau morte: l'oeuvre poétique de Wen
Yi-duo (1899-1946)*. [French: Dead Water: The Poetical
Works of Wen I-to (1899-1946).] Paris VII, 1971 (Doctorat de 3ᵉ cycle). A copy is available at the Bibliothèque
de la Sorbonne.

1076 ODELL, Ling-chung. *Kenneth Rexroth and Chinese Poetry:
Translation, Imitation, and Adaptation*. Wisconsin, 1972
(Ph.D. in Comparative Literature). 297p. DAI 33, no.5
(Nov. 1972): 2338-A; UM 72-23,066.

1077 CHEUNG, Dominic C. N. *Feng Chih: A Study of the Ascent
and Decline of His Lyricism (1920-1959)*. Washington (Seattle), 1973 (Ph.D. in Comparative Literature). 229p.
DAI 35, no.1 (July 1974): 395-96-A; UM 75-15,563

1078 LEUNG, Gaylord Kai-loh. *Hsü Chih-mo: A Literary Biography*. London, 1973 (Ph.D. in Arts, School of Oriental and
African Studies). 390p. A Study of an important poet
(1896-1931).

Prose and Fiction

Early to 1800

See also entry 1419.

1079 MA, Yau-woon. *The Pāo-kūng Tradition in Chinese Popular
Literature*. Yale, 1971 (Ph.D. in East and Southeast
Asian Languages and Literatures). 357p. DAI 32, no.5

(Nov. 1971): 2660-61-A; UM 71-28,912. Traces the development of the tradition from the historical person, who
flourished in the Northern Sung Dynasty, through Ch'ing
period fiction.

1080 YANG, Winston Lih-yeu. *The Use of the San-kuo chih as a
Source of the San-kuo-chih yen-i*. Stanford, 1971 (Ph.D.
in Asian Languages). 387p. DAI 32, no.3 (Sept. 1971):
1537-A; UM 71-23,573. On The Chronicle of the Three
Kingdoms by Ch'en Shou (233-297 A.D.) as used in a Ming
period historical novel.

1081 YEN, Alsace Chun-chiang. *Demon Tales in Early Vernacular
Chinese: A Folkloristic View*. Harvard, 1971 (Ph.D. in
Middle Eastern Studies and Far Eastern Languages). viii,
346p. Available at the Harvard University Archives, Pusey Library, call no.HU 90.10097.12.

1082 BAUS, Wolf. *Das P'ai-an ching-ch'i des Ling Meng-ch'u.
Ein Beitrag zur Analyse umgangssprachlicher Novellen der
Ming-Zeit*. [German: The P'ai an ching ch'i of Ling Meng-
ch'u: A Contribution to the Analysis of Ming Period Nov-
els Written in the Vernacular Language.] Erlangen-Nürn-
berg, 1972 (Dr., Philosophische Fakultät). Published as
Das P'ai-an ching-ch'i...Ming-Zeit (Bern & Frankfurt:
Lang, 1974. iii, 357p. [Würzburger Sino-Japonica, 3]).

1083 CRAWFORD, William Bruce. *Beyond the Garden Wall: A Critical Study of Three Ts'ai-tzu chia-jen Novels*. Indiana,
1972 (Ph.D. in East Asian Languages and Literatures).
226p. DAI 33, no.8 (Feb. 1973): 4337-A; UM 73-2701.
On three anonymous 17th century novels which relate the
courtship and marriage of men of genius (ts'ai-tzu) and
women of beauty (chia-jen).

1084 FASTENAU, Frauke. *Die Figuren des Chin P'ing Mei und des
Yü Huan Chi. Versuch einer Theorie des chinesischen Sit-
tenromans*. [German: The Characters of Chin p'ing mei
and Yü huan chi: An Attempt at a Theory of the Chinese
Novel of Manners.] München, 1972 (Dr., Philosophische
Fakultät). Published as Die Figuren...Sittenromans (München, 1971. 170, iv, 81p.).

1085 FU, James Shu-shien. *The Mythic and Comic Aspects in
Hsi-yu chi: A Quest for Parallels*. Indiana, 1972 (Ph.D.
in Comparative Literature). 210p. DAI 33, no.10 (Apr.
1973): 5677-A; UM 73-9761. On a work by Wu Ch'eng-en
(ca.1500-ca.1582).

1086 TÖPELMANN, Cornelia. *Shan-ko von Feng Meng-lung. Eine
Volksliedersammlung aus der Ming-Zeit*. [German: The

Shan-ko of Feng Meng-lung: A Collection of Folk Songs
from the Ming Period.] München, 1972 (Dr., Philosophische Fakultät). Published as Shan-ko...Ming-Zeit (Wiesbaden: Steiner, 1973. 491p. [Münchener ostasiatische
Studien, Bd.9]). Feng Meng-lung (1574-1646) compiled
collections of short stories written in the vernacular
language.

1087 BRANDAUER, Frederick Paul. *A Critical Study of the Hsi-
yu pu*. Stanford, 1973 (Ph.D. in Asian Languages). 442p.
DAI 34, no.3 (Sept. 1973): 1233-A; UM 73-20,464. On a
late Ming vernacular novel by Tung Yüeh written as a supplement to Wu Ch'eng-en's novel Hsi-yu chi.

1088 HEGEL, Robert Earl. *Sui T'ang yen-i: The Sources and
Narrative Techniques of a Traditional Chinese Novel*.
Columbia, 1973 (Ph.D. in East Asian Languages and Cultures). 396p. DAI 34, no.6 (Dec. 1973): 3365-A; UM
73-28,472. On a traditional historical romance concerning the period 570-770 compiled by Ch'u Jen-huo (fl.1681).

1089 HUEY, Talbott Wistar. *Anti-Orthodox Styles and the Charismatic Tradition in China as Revealed in Three Popular
Novels*. Massachusetts Institute of Technology, 1973
(Ph.D. in Political Science). 246p. Order copies from
the Microreproduction Laboratory, Massachusetts Institute of Technology.

1090 PLAKS, Andrew Henry. *Archetype and Allegory in the Hung-
lou Meng*. Princeton, 1973 (Ph.D. in East Asian Studies).
275p. DAI 34, no.8 (Feb. 1974): 5119-A; UM 74-2354.
Published as Archetype and Allegory in the Dream of the
Red Chamber (Princeton: Princeton University Press,
1976. viii, 246p.). On a major Ch'ing period novel's
structural patterns of bipolar alternation and cyclical
periodicity.

1091 CH'EN, Toyoko Yoshida. *Women in Confucian Society: A
Study of Three T'an-tz'u Narratives*. Columbia, 1974
(Ph.D. in East Asian Languages and Cultures). 351p. DAI
35, no.10 (Apr. 1975): 6659-A; UM 75-7481. On three
Ch'ing period works: Tao Chen-huai's T'ien yü hua, Ch'en
Tuan-sheng and Liang Ch'u-sheng's Tsai sheng yüan, and
Ch'iu Hsin-ju's Pi sheng hua.

1092 DeWOSKIN, Kenneth Joel. *The Sou-shen-chi and the Chih-
kuai Tradition: A Bibliographic and Generic Study*. Columbia, 1974 (Ph.D. in East Asian Languages and Cultures).
351p. DAI 35, no.7 (Jan. 1975): 4466-67-A; UM 74-28,487.
The Sou shen chi, by Kan Pao (fl.317-322), is regarded
as a major ancestor of Chinese fiction.

1093   FOSTER, Lawrence Chapin. *The Shih-i chi and Its Rela-*
       tionship to the Genre Known as Chih-kuai hsiao-shuo.
       Washington (Seattle), 1974 (Ph.D. in Asian Languages and
       Literature). 422p. DAI 35, no.8 (Feb. 1975): 5342-A;
       UM 75-3979. On the Shih-i chi by Wang Chia (died ca.
       386 A.D.) and on a genre of prose literature that flour-
       ished during the Six Dynasties period.

1094   HUNG, Ming-shui. *Yüan Hung-tao and the Late Ming Liter-*
       ary and Intellectual Movement. Wisconsin, 1974 (Ph.D.
       in East Asian Languages and Literature). 338p. DAI 36,
       no.1 (July 1975): 273-74-A; UM 75-9978. Traces the rise
       of the Kung-an romantic movement through one of its cen-
       tral figures.

1095   IDEMA, Wilt Lukas. *Chinese Vernacular Fiction: The For-*
       mative Period. Leiden, 1974 (Dr.). Published as Chinese
       ...Period (Leiden: Brill, 1974. lxiv, 146p. [Sinica
       leidensia, 13]). Focuses on storytelling and the short
       story during the Ming period.

1096   KARABAŞ, Seyfi. *Structure and Function in the Dede Kor-*
       kut Narratives. California (Los Angeles), 1974 (Ph.D.
       in Comparative Literature). 490p. DAI 35, no.8 (Feb.
       1975): 5349-50-A; UM 75-1984. Analyzes a ninth century
       anonymous collection of Oghuz Turkish literature (from
       a period when Turkish tribes inhabited present-day Sin-
       kiang).

1097   KERN, Jean Ellen. *The Individual and Society in the Chi-*
       nese Colloquial Short Story: The Chin-ku ch'i-kuan. In-
       diana, 1974 (Ph.D. in East Asian Languages and Litera-
       tures). 236p. DAI 34, no.12 (June 1974): 7708-09-A;
       UM 73-13,526. On a late Ming anthology of 40 colloquial
       short stories drawn from Feng Meng-lung's San-yen and
       Ling Meng-ch'u's Erh-p'ai collections.

1098   LEVY, André. *Le conte en langue vulgaire du XVIIe siècle:*
       vogue et declin d'un genre narratif de la littérature
       chinoise. [French: The Vernacular Story of the 17th
       Century: The Vogue for and Decline of a Narrative Genre
       in Chinese Literature.] Paris VII, 1974 (Doctorat d'Etat
       ès études extrême-orientales). A copy is available at
       the Bibliothèque de la Sorbonne. Published as Le conte
       ...chinoise (Lille: Service de reproduction des thèses
       de l'Université de Lille III, 1974. iii, 612p.).

1099   WONG, Kam-ming. *The Narrative Art of Red Chamber Dream*
       (Húng-lóu mèng). Cornell, 1974 (Ph.D. in Chinese Liter-
       ature). 317p. DAI 35, no.2 (Aug. 1974): 1069-70-A; UM
       74-17,657.

1100   GJERTSON, Donald Edward. *A Study and Translation of the*
       Ming-pao chi: A T'ang Dynasty Collection of Buddhist
       Tales. Stanford, 1975 (Ph.D. in Asian Languages). 476p.
       DAI 36, no.9 (Mar. 1976): 6106-A; UM 76-5736. On a col-
       lection of Buddhist-centered miracle tales (compiled by
       T'ang Lin) that is regarded as part of an important genre
       of narrative prose.

1101   WONG, Meng-voon. *Sung-Yüan Vernacular Fiction and Its*
       Conceptual and Stylistic Characteristics. Washington
       (Seattle), 1975 (Ph.D. in Asian Languages and Litera-
       ture). 372p. DAI 37, no.5 (Nov. 1976): 2846-A; UM
       76-17,689.

1102   WONG, Timothy Chung-tai. *Satire and the Polemics of the*
       Criticism of Chinese Fiction: A Study of the Ju-lin wai-
       shih. Stanford, 1975 (Ph.D. in Asian Languages). 348p.
       DAI 36, no.9 (Mar. 1976): 6107-A; UM 76-5829. On a novel
       by Wu Ching-tzu (1701-1754).

                  Modern and Contemporary Prose and Fiction

See also entries 1720 and 1723.

1103   ALBER, Charles Julius. *Soviet Criticism of Lu Hsün*
       (1881-1936). Indiana, 1971 (Ph.D. in East Asian Langua-
       ges and Literatures). 399p. DAI 32, no.5 (Nov. 1971):
       2670-A; UM 71-29,553.

1104   LYELL, William A. *The Short Story Theatre of Lu Hsun*.
       Chicago, 1971 (Ph.D. in Far Eastern Languages and Civili-
       zations). 629p. Order copies from the Photoduplication
       Department, Joseph Regenstein Library, University of Chi-
       cago. Published as Lu Hsün's Vision of Reality (Berke-
       ley: University of California Press, 1976. x, 355p.).

1105   PETERS, Irma. *Zur ideologischen Entwicklung des chine-*
       sischen Schriftstellers Lu Xun (1881-1936). Eine Unter-
       suchung anhand seiner künstlerischen Publizistik. [Ger-
       man: On the Ideological Development of the Chinese Author
       Lu Hsün (1881-1936): An Investigation Based on His Artis-
       tic Published Works.] Humboldt-Universität Berlin, 1971
       (Dr., Gesellschaftswissenschaftliche Fakultät). vii,
       181p.

1106   TUNG, Constantine Pao-chung. *The Search for Order and*
       Form: The Crescent Moon Society and the Literary Movement
       of Modern China, 1928-1933. Claremont, 1971 (Ph.D. in
       Asian Studies). 272p. DAI 32, no.3 (Sept. 1971): 1534-A;
       UM 71-21,684.

1107 CHARBONNIER, Jean. *Lu Xun et la libération de l'homme.*
[French: Lu Hsün and the Liberation of Man.] Paris VII,
1972 (Doctorat de 3e cycle ès études extrême-orientales).
450p. A copy is available at the Bibliothèque de la Sorbonne, library catalogue no. I 2235-4°.

1108 HENJES, Irmtraud. *Antifeudale und antiimperialistische
Aspekte des künstlerischen Schaffens von Cao Yu, Tian Han
und Lao She. Dargestellt anhand ihrer dramatischen Werke
aus der Zeit des Widerstands gegen die japanische Aggression (1931-1945) in China.* [German: Anti-feudal and
Anti-imperialist Aspects of the Artistic Works of Kao Yu,
T'ien Han and Lao She. Demonstrated on the Basis of
Their Dramatic Works from the Time of the Resistance to
Japanese Aggression (1931-1945) in China.] Humboldt-Universität Berlin, 1972 (Dr., Gesellschaftswissenschaft-
liche Fakultät). x, 186p.

1109 HSÜ, Raymond Shih-wen. *The Vocabulary of Lu Hsün: A
Stylistic Study.* Cambridge, 1972 (Ph.D. in Oriental
Studies). xii, 575p.

1110 LI, Peter. *Tseng P'u: The Literary Journey of a Chinese
Writer (1872-1935).* Chicago, 1972 (Ph.D. in Far Eastern
Languages and Civilizations). 255p. Order copies from
the Photoduplication Department, Joseph Regenstein Library, University of Chicago.

1111 ROSS, Timothy Arrowsmith. *Chiang Kuei: A Chinese Writer
in His Time.* Iowa, 1972 (Ph.D. in History). 273p. DAI
33, no.4 (Oct. 1972): 1659-A; UM 72-26,728. Published
as Chiang Kuei (New York: Twayne Publishers, 1974. 161p.
[Twayne's world authors series, TWAS 320]). On a 20th
century novelist.

1112 RUH, Christel. *Das Kuan-ch'ang hsien-hsing chi. Ein
Beispiel für den politischen Roman der ausgehenden Ch'ing-
Zeit (Versuch einer Analyse der Idee und Struktur der Kapitel 1-30 und 60 des Werkes).* [German: The Kuan ch'ang
hsien hsing chi: An Example of the Political Novel of
the Late Ch'ing Period (Attempt at an Analysis of the
Idea and Structure of Chapters 1-30 and 60 of the Work).
Würzburg, 1972 (Dr., Philosophische Fakultät). Published
as Das Kuan-ch'ang...Werkes (Bern & Frankfurt a.M.: Lang,
1974. iv, 275p. [Würzburger Sino-Japonica; Bd.2]).
On a novel by Li Pao-chia (1867-1906).

1113 DIETSCH, Klaus Andreas. *Der Weg der sozialistischen Literatur in China nach 1949. Dargestellt an den Kritiken
der Theorien von Feng Hsüeh-feng, Hu Feng und Chou Yang.*
[German: The Path of Socialist Literature in China after

1949: Shown in the Critiques of the Theories of Feng
Hsüeh-feng, Hu Feng and Chou Yang.] München, 1973 (Dr.,
Philosophische Fakultät). xxv, 216p.

1114   HUNTER, Neale James. *The Chinese League of Left-Wing
Writers, Shanghai 1930-1936*. Australian National, 1973
(Ph.D. in Far Eastern History). ii, 386p.

1115   BISSAT, Violette. *Ye Sheng-t'ao: étude sur un intellec-
tuel chinois*. [French: Yeh Sheng-t'ao: A Study of a
Chinese Intellectual.] Paris VII, 1974 (Doctorat de 3e
cycle en histoire). A copy is available at the Bibliothèque de la Sorbonne. On Yeh Sheng-t'ao, the pseudonym
of the author Yeh Shao-chün (1893-).

1116   CHANG, Randall Oliver. *Yü Ta-fu (1896-1945): The Alienated Artist in Modern Chinese Literature*. Claremont,
1974 (Ph.D. in Asian Studies). 187p. DAI 35, no.1 (July
1974): 442-A; UM 74-14,880.

1117   GOLDBLATT, Howard Charles. *A Literary Biography of Hsiao
Hung (1911-1942)*. Indiana, 1974 (Ph.D. in East Asian
Languages and Literatures). 331p. DAI 35, no.10 (Apr.
1975): 6711-A; UM 75-8980. Published as Hsiao Hung (Boston: Twayne Publishers, 1976. 161p. [Twayne's world
author series; TWAS 386: China]).

1118   MÄDING, Klaus. *Massenhaft verbreitete Literatur in einer
Gesellschaft mit hohen soziopsychischen Belastungen;
eine systematische Analyse des Orientierungsangebots in
chinesischen Romanen und Kurzgeschichten aus Hongkong
(1964-1968)*. [German: Mass Circulation Literature in a
Society with High Socio-psychological Stresses: A System-
atic Analysis of the Orientation Offered in Chinese Novels and Short Stories from Hong Kong (1964-1968).] Marburg, 1974 (Dr., Fachbereich Gesellschaftswissenschaft).
Published as Massenhaft...1968 (Wiesbaden: Harrassowitz,
1975. 227p. [Schriften des Instituts für Asienkunde in
Hamburg; Bd.41]).

1119   DUVAL, Jean R. *Les aventures révélatrices d'un Dandy
amoureux: étude d'un roman en dialecte "wu" de la fin de
l'époque Qing, La Tortue à neuf queues, de Zhang Chunfan*.
[French: The Revealing Adventures of a Romantic Dandy:
Study of a Novel in the Wu Dialect from the End of the
Ch'ing Period, Chiu wei kuei (The Turtle with Nine Tails)
by Chang Ch'un-fan.] Paris III (Sorbonne-Nouvelle), 1975
(Doctorat de 3e cycle ès études orientales). vi, 135,
xlvi p.

1120   HOLOCH, Donald. *A Bourgeois View of the State: Li Bo-
yuan's Novel The Bureaucrats*. Cornell, 1975 (Ph.D. in

Chinese Literature).   315p.   DAI 36, no.10 (Apr. 1976):
6694-A; UM 76-8167.   On the novel <u>Kuan ch'ang hsien hsing
chi</u> by Li Po-yüan (Li Pao-chia, 1867-1906).

1121   SELIS, David Joel. *Yeh Shao-chün: A Critical Study of
His Fiction, 1919-1944.* Indiana, 1975 (Ph.D. in East
Asian Languages and Literatures). 325p. DAI 36, no.5
(Nov. 1975): 2832-33-A; UM 75-23,506.

1122   TSAI, Mei-hsi. *The Construction of Positive Types in
Contemporary Chinese Fiction.* California (Berkeley),
1975 (Ph.D. in Comparative Literature). 274p. DAI 37,
no.1 (July 1976): 287-A; UM 76-15,398.

MASS COMMUNICATIONS AND JOURNALISM

See also entries 276, 586, 602, 798, 1142, and 1727.

1123   KOSCHWITZ, Hansjürgen. *Pressepolitik und Parteijournal-
ismus in der UdSSR und der Volksrepublik China.* [German:
Press Policies and Party Journalism in the U.S.S.R. and
the People's Republic of China.] Göttingen, 1971 (Habilitationsschrift, Wirtschaftlich- und sozialwissenschaftliche Fakultät). Published as <u>Pressepolitik...China</u>
(Düsseldorf: Bertelsmann Universitätsverlag, 1971. 304p.).

1124   YANG, Shou-jung. *A Readability Formula for Chinese Language.* Wisconsin, 1971 (Ph.D. in Mass Communication).
116p. DAI 31, no.12 (June 1971): 6536-A; UM 71-12,723.
Yang sought to develop a formula applicable to problems
of education and mass communication in the Republic of
China.

1125   WEI, Kwang-cheng. *Analyse des Zeitungswesens der Republik China von 1949 bis zur Gegenwart in Taiwan.* [German:
An Analysis of the Press of the Republic of China from
1949 to the Present Time in Taiwan.] Salzburg, 1972
(Dr., Philosophische Fakultät). 151p.

1126   KING, James Calvin. *A Survey and Analysis of the Major
International Evangelical Short Wave Broadcasters: Trans
World Radio, HCJB and the Far East Broadcasting Company.*
Michigan, 1973 (Ph.D. in Speech). 325p. DAI 35, no.1
(July 1974): 611-12-A; UM 74-15,778. Operating out of
the Philippines and the Ryukyus, the Far East Broadcast-
ing Company broadcasts throughout much of Asia including
the People's Republic of China and the Republic of China.

1127   LIU, Han-chin. *Media Use, Academic Performance, and*

Social-Demographic Background: A Study of Taiwanese Children. Minnesota, 1973 (Ph.D. in Mass Communication). 145p. DAI 34, no.7 (Jan. 1974): 3994-A; UM 74-720.

1128 FOLLATH, Erich. *Ein internationaler Vergleich von Rundfunksystemen. Die Interdependenz von Rundfunkpolitik und Gesamtpolitik in Grossbritannien, Frankreich, der Sowjetunion, der VR China und Indien.* [German: An International Comparison of Radio Broadcasting Systems: The Interdependence of Broadcasting Policy and General Policy in Great Britain, France, the U.S.S.R., the People's Republic of China, and India.] Hohenheim, 1974 (Dr., Fachbereich Wirtschafts- und Sozialwissenschaft). 422p.

1129 WEAVER, David Hugh. *The Press and Government Control: International Patterns of Development from 1950 to 1966.* North Carolina, 1974 (Ph.D. in Journalism). 272p. DAI 35, no.8 (Feb. 1975): 5442-A; UM 75-4884. Includes coverage of the Republic of China and the People's Republic of China.

1130 HUR, Kyoon. *A Cross-National Study of Satellite Communication.* Oregon, 1975 (Ph.D. in Speech). 280p. DAI 36, no.7 (Jan. 1976): 4106-A; UM 76-934. Covers many countries including the People's Republic of China, the Republic of China, and the Mongolian People's Republic.

1131 LEE, Kam-Hon. *Promotion of Breast Feeding: A Persuasive Communication Approach.* Northwestern, 1975 (Ph.D. in Management). 295p. DAI 36, no.7 (Jan. 1976): 4722-23-A; UM 75-29,691. Based on research undertaken in Hong Kong, this is a study in the area of social marketing and communication theory.

1132 TARANTINO, Anthony George. *Chinese Media of Communication: Their History and Political Impact in Respect to Western Developments.* California (Irvine), 1975 (Ph.D. in Comparative Culture). 202p. DAI 36, no.12 (June 1976): 7716-17-A; UM 76-13,857. Focuses on the reform of the written language and the impact of mass phonetic literacy during the twentieth century.

MUSIC

See also entries 123, 1072, and 1261 as well as the section-- within the Appendix--on music (pp.246-47).

1133 BLUM, Martine. *Vertus et méfaits de la musique: La "Dissertation sur la musique" de Jouan Tsi; traduction et*

commentaire. [French: Virtues and Harmful Effects of
Music: Juan Chi's Dissertation on Music. A Translation
and Commentary.] Paris VII, 1971 (Doctorat de 3e cycle
ès études extrême-orientales). 220p.

1134 KING, Carl Darlington. *The Conservation of Melodic Pitch
Patterns by Elementary School Children as Determined by
Ancient Chinese Music.* Ohio State, 1972 (Ph.D. in Music).
265p. DAI 33, no.8 (Feb. 1973): 4455-56-A; UM 73-2039.

1135 FOO, Timothy Wo-ping. *Survey Appraisal of Secondary
School Music in Hong Kong.* Oregon, 1973 (D.M.A.). 130p.
DAI 34, no.9 (Mar. 1974): 6021-A; UM 74-6827.

1136 HELFFER, Mireille. *Les chants dans l'épopée tibétaine
de Ge-sar, d'après le livre de "La course de cheval"
(Rta-rgyug), version chantée par Blo-bzan bstan-'jin.*
[French: The Songs in the Tibetan Epic of Ge-sar According to the Book The Horse Race: A Version Sung by Blo-
bzan bstan-'jin.] Paris IV (Paris-Sorbonne), 1973 (Doctorat de 3e cycle en ethnomusicologie). 502 + vi, 247p.
A copy is available at the Bibliothèque de la Sorbonne.

1137 HSÜEH, Robert Chung Ming. *Zur musikwissenschaftlichen
Bedeutung Dschu Dsai-yüs. (Dem Erfinder der gleichschwe-
benden Temperatur des Zwölftonsystems.)* [German: On the
Musicological Importance of Chu Tsai-yü: Dedicated to the
Inventor of the Equal Temperament of the Twelve-Note
System.] Wien, 1973 (Dr., Philosophische Fakultät).
ii, 231p.

1138 LIANG, Ming-yueh. *The Art of Yin-Jou Techniques for the
Seven-Stringed Zither.* California (Los Angeles), 1973
(Ph.D. in Music). 334p. DAI 34, no.11 (May 1974):
7269-A; UM 74-11,544.

1139 RAULT, Lucie. *La cithare zhēng: ses origines, ses fonc-
tions sociales et sa diffusion en Extrême-Orient.*
[French: The Chinese Zither Known as the Cheng: Its Origins, Its Social Functions, and Its Diffusion in the Far
East.] Paris X (Paris-Nanterre), 1973 (Doctorat de 3^e
cycle en ethnologie). viii, 520p. + 105 plates. A copy
is available at the Bibliothèque de la Sorbonne.

1140 STEVENS, Catherine. *Peking Drumsinging.* Harvard, 1973
(Ph.D. in East Asian Languages and Civilizations). 300p.
+ a tape which is available only from the author. DAI
36, no.4 (Oct. 1975): 2346-A; UM 75-21,457. Discusses
the development of Peking drumsinging (ching yün ta ku),
a performed popular narrative indigenous to northern China, between 1910 and 1950. [Note: The dissertation is
also available at the Harvard University Archives.]

1141   YANG, Schuman Chuo. *Twentieth-Century Chinese Solo
Songs: A Historical and Analytical Study of Selected Chinese Solo Songs Composed or Arranged by Chinese Composers
from the 1920's to the Present*. George Peabody College
for Teachers, 1973 (Ph.D. in Music). 500p. DAI 34, no.
8 (Feb. 1974): 5238-A; UM 74-4638.

1142   CHENG, Philip Hui-ho. *The Function of Chinese Opera in
Social Control and Change*. Southern Illinois, 1974
(Ph.D., School of Journalism). 151p. DAI 35, no.12
(June 1975): 7933-34-A; UM 75-13,266. On the structure
and function of Peking opera as an effective communication medium of social control and change under the Chinese Communists.

1143   HO, Ting. *Journey to the Mountain of Clouds*. Rochester,
1974 (Ph.D. in Composition, Eastman School of Music).
55p. DAI 35, no.4 (Oct. 1974): 2320-21-A; UM 74-21,524.
This is original music for a ballet based on a Chinese
parable.

1144   CHENG, Shui-cheng. *Les techniques instrumentales du Pipa
chinois, et les études à titre comparatif, celles des
luths piriformes dans les pays d'Extrême-Orient: biwa japonais, pipa coréen et tyba vietnamien.* [French: The
Instrumental Techniques of the Chinese Pipa and Studies,
for Reasons of Comparison, of the Pyriform Lutes in the
Countries of the Far East: Japanese Biwa, Korean Pipa,
and Vietnamese Tyba.] Paris IV (Paris-Sorbonne), 1975
(Doctorat de 3e cycle en musicologie). 299p. A copy is
available at the Bibliothèque de la Sorbonne, library
catalogue no. I 3610-4°.

1145   CHO, Gene Jinsiong. *Some Non-Chinese Elements in the Ancient Japanese Music: An Analytical-Comparative Study*.
Northwestern, 1975 (Ph.D. in Music). 236p. DAI 36, no.
7 (Jan. 1976): 4094-A; UM 75-29,600. This comparison of
ancient Chinese and Japanese music includes an examination of Chinese songs contained in Sonq Dynasty Sources
and Their Interpretation by Rulan Chao Pian (1967).

1146   WOLPERT, Rembrandt Friedrich. *Lute Music and Tablatures
of the T'ang Period*. Cambridge, 1975 (Ph.D. in Oriental
Studies). 382p.

OVERSEAS CHINESE COMMUNITIES

General and Miscellaneous Studies

See also entries 519 and 1764.

1147 CHANG, Ching-fong. *Die wirtschaftliche Rolle der Aus-landschinesen.* [German: The Economic Role of the Overseas Chinese.] München, 1971 (Dr., Staatswirtschaftliche Fakultät). Published as Die wirtschaftliche...Auslandschinesen (München, 1971. vi, 247p.).

1148 HANNUM, Ellwood Brown. *The Transvaal Labor Ordinance and Its Impact on British Politics 1904-1906.* South Carolina, 1972 (Ph.D. in History). 484p. DAI 33, no.9 (Mar. 1973): 5088-A; UM 72-25,909. Focuses on the controversial issue of importing indentured Chinese laborers into South Africa.

1149 WATSON, James Lee. *A Chinese Emigrant Community: The Man Lineage in Hong Kong and London.* California (Berkeley), 1972 (Ph.D. in Anthropology). 336p. DAI 33, no.5 (Nov. 1972): 1907-B; UM 72-27,149. Published as Emigration and the Chinese Lineage: The Mans in Hong Kong and London (Berkeley: University of California Press, 1975. xiii, 242p.). "Man" refers to the common surname of the emigrants.

1150 CAPDEVILLE, Christian Georges. *Influence du milieu sur la schizophrénie chez les Chinois à la Réunion.* [French: The Influence of the Environment on Schizophrenia among the Chinese on the Island of Réunion.] Montpellier I, 1973 (Doctorat d'Etat en médecine).

1151 GRIFFIN, Nicholas John. *The Use of Chinese Labour by the British Army, 1916-1920: The "Raw Importation," Its Scope and Problems.* Oklahoma, 1973 (Ph.D. in History). 286p. DAI 34, no.4 (Oct. 1973): 1822-A; UM 73-23,922. On the 100,000 Chinese (mostly from Shantung) who worked for the British armies in Europe during World War I.

1152 ALVAREZ, Gabriel C. *Permanent Migration and Some Structural Correlates: A Comparative Analysis of Recent International Migration.* Chicago, 1975 (Ph.D. in Sociology). viii, 206p. DAI 36, no.7 (Jan. 1976): 4789-A; Order copies from the Photoduplication Department, Joseph Regenstein Library, University of Chicago. Includes consideration of migration from Hong Kong and the Republic of China.

Chinese Communities in Australasia

See also entry 1742.

1153 CHOI, Ching-yan. *Chinese Migration and Settlement in
      Australia, with Special Reference to the Chinese in Mel-
      bourne.* Australian National, 1971 (Ph.D. in Demography).
      xviii, 363p. Published as Chinese Migration and Settle-
      ment in Australia (Sydney: Sydney University Press,
      1975. 129p.).

1154 GREIF, Stuart William. *The Historical, Social, and Po-
      litical Development of the Chinese of New Zealand.* Cal-
      ifornia (Berkeley), 1972 (Ph.D. in Political Science).
      338p. Order copies from the Library Photographic Ser-
      vice, General Library, University of California at Berke-
      ley.

1155 PRESTON, Noel William. *An Ethical Analysis of Austra-
      lian Policies in Development Partnership and Immigration
      Restriction.* Boston University, 1972 (Th.D. in Sociology
      of Religion and Social Ethics). 360p. DAI 33, no.5
      (Nov. 1972): 2485-86-A; UM 72-27,998. Includes some in-
      formation about Australian relations with the People's
      Republic of China as well as about the immigration of
      Chinese into Australia.

1156 WU, David Yen-ho. *An Ethnic Minority: The Adaptation of
      Chinese in Papua New Guinea.* Australian National, 1974
      (Ph.D. in Anthropology). 380, xii p. + 26 plates.

Chinese Communities in Canada

See also entry 1763.

1157 AVERY, Donald Howard. *Canadian Immigration Policy and
      the Alien Question, 1896-1919: The Anglo-Canadian Per-
      spective.* Western Ontario, 1973 (Ph.D. in History). vi,
      1-372p.; viii, 373-653p. (2 vols.). DAI 34, no.4 (Oct.
      1973): 1806-07-A; Order copies directly from the Canadian
      Theses Division, National Library of Canada at Ottawa;
      available only in microfiche format, fiche no.20475, @
      $2.00. The question of Chinese immigration to Canada
      is discussed within the dissertation.

1158 WARD, William Peter. *White Canada Forever: British Co-
      lumbia's Response to Orientals, 1858-1914.* Queen's Uni-
      versity at Kingston, 1973 (Ph.D. in History). vii, 292p.
      Order copies directly from the Canadian Theses Division,

National Library of Canada at Ottawa; available only in microfiche format, fiche no.21172, @ $2.00. This is a study of the animosity which British Columbians harbored toward the Chinese and Japanese immigrants.

1159   CON, Ronald Jonathan. *Government and Ethnic Minority Groups: A Case Study of the Relationships between Federal Adult-Oriented Programs and Citizen Organizations of the Chinese in Canada.* Boston University, 1974 (Ed.D. in Adult Education). 175p. DAI 35, no.3 (Sept. 1974): 1413-14-A; UM 74-20,425. Focuses on the Chinese community of Vancouver, British Columbia.

1160   HOE, Ban Seng. *Structural Changes of Two Chinese Communities in Alberta, Canada.* Vanderbilt, 1974 (Ph.D. in Sociology). 410p. DAI 35, no.8 (Feb. 1975): 5530-A; UM 75-1137.

1161   PALMER, Howard Delbert. *Nativism and Ethnic Tolerance in Alberta: 1920-1972.* York, 1974 (Ph.D. in History). 476p. DAI 36, no.10 (Apr. 1976): 6876-77-A; Order copies directly from the Canadian Theses Division, National Library of Canada at Ottawa; available only in microfiche format. Related publication by the author: Land of the Second Chance: A History of Ethnic Groups in Southern Alberta (Alberta: Lethbridge Herald, 1972. 287p.). Includes Canadian attitudes towards the Chinese who were living in the province of Alberta.

Chinese Communities in Latin America

See also entries 519 and 1752.

1162   DAMBOURGES JACQUES, Leo Michael. *The Anti-Chinese Campaigns in Sonora, Mexico, 1900-1931.* Arizona, 1974 (Ph.D. in History). 342p. DAI 35, no.11 (May 1975): 7220-A; UM 75-11,469.

1163   HELLY, Denise. *Histoire des gens sans histoire: les Chinois de Macao à Cuba. Travail sous contrat et communauté raciale dans une société esclavagiste.* [French: History of a People without History: The Chinese from Macao in Cuba. Contract Labor and Racial Community in a Slave Society.] Paris V (René Descartes), 1975 (Doctorat de 3e cycle en ethnologie). iii, 399 + 199p. (2 vols.). A copy is available at the Bibliothèque de la Sorbonne, library catalogue no. I 3477(1-2)-4°.

1164   KALM, Florence. *The Dispersive and Reintegrating Nature*

*of Population Segments of a Third World Society: Aruba,
Netherlands Antilles.* City University of New York, 1975
(Ph.D. in Anthropology). 269p. DAI 35, no.10 (Apr.
1975): 6289-A; UM 75-9061. Includes a detailed discussion of the resident Chinese.

1165 MEAGHER, Arnold Joseph. *The Introduction of Chinese Laborers to Latin America: The "Coolie Trade", 1847-1874.*
California (Davis), 1975 (Ph.D. in History). 503p. DAI
36, no.7 (Jan. 1976): 4703-A; UM 76-1797.

Chinese Communities in Southeast Asia

Indonesia and the Philippines

See also entry 1751.

1166 OMOHUNDRO, John Thomas. *The Chinese Merchant Community
of Iloilo City, Philippines.* Michigan, 1974 (Ph.D. in
Anthropology). 388p. DAI 35, no.5 (Nov. 1974): 2449-A;
UM 74-25,285.

1167 SURYADINATA, Leo. *Indigenous Indonesians, the Chinese
Minority and China: A Study of Perceptions and Policies.*
American, 1975 (Ph.D. in International Studies). 313p.
DAI 36, no.7 (Jan. 1976): 4747-A; UM 76-818. Related
publication by the author: Peranakan Chinese Politics in
Java, 1917-42 (Singapore: Institute of Southeast Asian
Studies, 1976. 184p.).

Malaysia

This section includes North Borneo (Sabah), Sarawak, and pre-
1963 Malaya. *See also* entry 1412.

1168 BHARGAVA, Janki Vallabh. *Nationalism and Communism in
Malaya.* Saugar, 1971 (Ph.D. in Political Science).
viii, 329, xix p. For copies, write to the Jawaharlal
Nehru Library, University of Saugar, Gour Nagar, Sagar
M.P. 470 003, India. This dissertation includes infor-
mation about the Chinese in Malaya.

1169 BOCK, John Charles. *Education and Nation-Building in Malaysia: A Study of Institutional Effects in Thirty-Four
Secondary Schools.* Stanford, 1971 (Ph.D. in Education).
479p. DAI 32, no.2 (Aug. 1971): 1101-A; UM 71-19,653.
Related publication by the author: Educational Sponsorship

by Ethnicity: A Preliminary Analysis of the West Malaysian Experience. By Yoshimitsu Takei, John C. Bock and
Bruce Saunders (Athens: Ohio University, Center for International Studies, 1973. vii, 37p. [Papers in international studies: Southeast Asia series, 28]). Bock
deals explicit with the Chinese and other ethnic groups.

1170 HAN, Sin Fong. *A Study of the Occupational Patterns and
Social Interaction of Overseas Chinese in Sabah, Malaysia.* Michigan, 1971 (Ph.D. in Geography). 307p. DAI
32, no.7 (Jan. 1972): 4002-B; UM 72-4891.

1171 HUMPHREY, John Weldon. *Population Resettlement in Malaya.*
Northwestern, 1971 (Ph.D. in Geography). 408p. DAI 32,
no.6 (Dec. 1971): 3431-B; UM 71-30,838. Focuses on the
resettlement of the so-called Chinese "squatters" during
the 1950s.

1172 TAKEI, Yoshimitsu. *Ethnic Sponsorship in Education: A
Case Study of Malaysia.* California (Berkeley), 1971
(Ph.D. in Education). ix, 230p. Order copies from the
Library Photographic Service, General Library, University
of California. Related publication by the author: Educational Sponsorship by Ethnicity: A Preliminary Analysis
of the West Malaysian Experience. By Yoshimitsu Takei,
John C. Bock and Bruce Saunders (Athens: Ohio University,
Center for International Studies, 1973. vii, 37p. [Pa-
pers in international studies: Southeast Asia series,
28]).

1173 DIXON, Gale. *Rural Settlement in Sarawak.* Oregon, 1972
(Ph.D. in Geography). 310p. DAI 33, no.9 (Mar. 1973):
4332-B; UM 73-7880. Includes information about the contemporary activities of Chinese businessmen and farmers.

1174 DOBBS, Jack Percival Baker. *Music in the Multi-Racial
Society of West Malaysia.* London, 1972 (Ph.D. in Arts,
School of Oriental and African Studies). 589p.

1175 HIRSCHMAN, Charles. *Ethnic Stratification in West Malaysia.* Wisconsin, 1972 (Ph.D. in Sociology). 278p. DAI
33, no.8 (Feb. 1973): 4562-A; UM 72-29,494. Published
as Ethnic and Social Stratification in Peninsular Malaysia (Washington, D.C.: American Sociological Association,
1975. x, 115p. [The Arnold and Caroline Rose monograph
series in sociology]). Deals in part with the Chinese
in Malaysia.

1176 ISSALYS, Pierre Francois. *Ethnic Pluralism and Public
Law in Selected Commonwealth Countries.* London, 1972
(Ph.D. in Laws, London School of Economics). 522p.

Contains case studies of Malaysia and Mauritius with
their Chinese inhabitants.

1177 STARR, Paul Douglas Marshall. *Status Consistency and
Marginality: A Study of Self and Society in Malaysia.*
California (Santa Barbara), 1972 (Ph.D. in Sociology).
237p. DAI 33, no.10 (Apr. 1973): 5845-46-A; UM 73-8108.
Deals in part with Malaysian Chinese secondary school
students.

1178 STROEBE, Margaret Susan. *The Development of Equivalence
Judgements in Malaysian Children.* Bristol, 1972 (Ph.D.
in Psychology). xiii, 423p. Deals in part with Chinese
school children in Malaysia.

1179 FIDLER, Richard Calvin. *Kanowit: An Overseas Chinese
Community in Borneo.* Pennsylvania, 1973 (Ph.D. in An-
thropology). 361p. DAI 34, no.4 (Oct. 1973): 1346-47-B;
UM 73-24,143.

1180 HORNER, Layton. *Japanese Military Administration in Malaya and the Philippines.* Arizona, 1973 (Ph.D. in History). 322p. DAI 34, no.3 (Sept. 1973): 1209-A; UM
73-20,637. Deals in part with the treatment and the response of the Malayan Chinese to Japanese wartime administration.

1181 KHOO, Kay-kim. *The Beginnings of Political Extremism in
Malaya, 1915-1935.* Malaya, 1973 (Ph.D. in History).
viii, 369p. Includes consideration of extremist politics
among the Chinese.

1182 LO-LIM, Miriam Kui Kiaw. *Inter-Cultural Spatial Perception: The Case of Malaya.* Western Ontario, 1973 (Ph.D.
in Geography). xii, 230p. DAI 35, no.2 (Aug. 1974):
976-A; Order copies directly from the Canadian Theses
Division, National Library of Canada at Ottawa; available
only in microfilm format, film no.16611, @ $2.50. This
dissertation analyzes the cross-cultural relationships
of the Malays, Chinese and Indians.

1183 LOCKARD, Craig Alan. *The Southeast Asian Town in Historical Perspective: A Social History of Kuching, Malaysia,
1820-1970.* Wisconsin, 1973 (Ph.D. in History). 727p.
DAI 34, no.12 (June 1974): 7682-83-A; UM 74-9009. Includes the city's important Chinese community.

1184 OSMAN BIN MOHAMED [MOHAMED, Osman Bin]. *Education and
Social Integration in Malaya.* Nebraska, 1973 (Ph.D. in
History and Philosophy of Education). 208p. DAI 34, no.
5 (Nov. 1973): 2463-A; UM 73-25,466. Deals in part with
the Malaysian Chinese.

1185   CHU, Chi-hung. *Minority Representation in the Malaysian Legislature*. Kentucky, 1974 (Ph.D. in Political Science). 278p. DAI 36, no.3 (Sept. 1975): 1769-A; UM 75-18,467. Includes representation of the Chinese.

1186   GROVE, David John W. *A Cross-National Analysis of Two Theoretical Approaches toward the Politics of Ethnic and Race Relations*. Oregon, 1974 (Ph.D. in Political Science). 143p. DAI 35, no.8 (Feb. 1975): 5497-A; UM 75-4511. Published in part as The Race vs. Ethnic Debate: A Cross-National Analysis of Two Theoretical Approaches (Denver: University of Denver, 1974. 44p. [Studies in race and nations; vol.5, no.4]). Includes a study of the Chinese in Malaysia.

1187   GARDNER, Stuart William. *Ethnicity and Work: Occupational Distribution in an Urban Multi-Ethnic Setting--George Town, Penang, West Malaysia*. California (Berkeley), 1975 (Ph.D. in Sociology). 279p. DAI 36, no.10 (Apr. 1976): 7000-A; UM 76-9024. Includes the Chinese in Malaysia.

1188   KINNEY, W. P. *Aspects of Malayan Economic Development, 1900-1940*. London, 1975 (Ph.D. in Economics, School of Oriental and African Studies). 369p. Order copies from the British Library Lending Division, Boston Spa, Yorkshire, order no.D14366/76. Includes the Chinese in Malaya.

1189   RAGHAVAN, Rabeendran. *A Study of the Political Attitudes of Students from the University of Malaya*. Rutgers, 1975 (Ph.D. in Political Science). 456p. DAI 36, no.10 (Apr. 1976): 6924-A; UM 76-7326. Includes the Chinese student body at the University of Malaya.

1190   STRAUCH, Judith Vivian. *Sanchun, Malaysia: Local-Level Politics in a Rural Chinese Town*. Stanford, 1975 (Ph.D. in Anthropology). 299p. DAI 36, no.4 (Oct. 1975): 2299-A; UM 75-21,902.

1191   WANG, Bee-Lan Chan. *An Inter-Ethnic Comparison of Educational Selection, Achievement, and Decision-Making among Fifth-Form Students in West Malaysia*. Chicago, 1975 (Ph.D. in Education). 422p. DAI 36, no.7 (Jan. 1976): 4130-A; Order copies from the Photoduplication Department, Joseph Regenstein Library, University of Chicago. Includes information about the Chinese in Malaysia.

Singapore

See also entry 1749 and--within the Appendix--the section entitled "Overseas Chinese Communities" (pp.247-51).

1192 McBRIDE, John Douglas. *Law in the Pluralistic State: Malay and Chinese Law in the Pluralistic State of Singapore.* Southern Illinois, 1971 (Ph.D. in Anthropology). 146p. DAI 32, no.9 (Mar. 1972): 4993-B; UM 72-10,267.

1193 MURRAY, Douglas Patterson. *Multilanguage Education and Bilingualism: The Formation of Social Brokers in Singapore.* Stanford, 1971 (Ph.D. in Education). 419p. DAI 32, no.10 (Apr. 1972): 5475-76-A; UM 72-11,627.

1194 BELL, David Scott. *Unity in Diversity: Education and Political Integration in an Ethnically Pluralistic Society.* Indiana, 1972 (Ph.D. in Political Science). 659p. DAI 32, no.12 (June 1972): 7050-A; UM 72-18,526. Focuses on Singapore.

1195 BUSCH, Peter Alan. *Political Unity and Ethnic Diversity: A Case Study of Singapore.* Yale, 1972 (Ph.D. in Political Science). 446p. DAI 33, no.5 (Nov. 1972): 2439-A; UM 72-29,523. Published as Legitimacy and Ethnicity: A Case Study of Singapore (Lexington, Mass.: Lexington Books, 1974. xv, 157p.). Deals extensively with the Chinese in Singapore.

1196 FUNG, Wye-Poh. *Acute Alcoholic Hepatitis: A Prospective Clinicopathological Study of 50 Cases.* Singapore, 1972 (M.D.). 138p. Many of the patients were ethnic Chinese in Singapore.

1197 AHMAD, Zahoor. *Analysis of the Effects of Changes in Administrative Policies of the Singapore Ministry of Education on the Operation of the Singapore School System 1960-1972.* Kansas, 1973 (Ph.D. in Administration, Foundations and Higher Education). 206p. DAI 34, no.12 (June 1974): 7477-78-A; UM 74-12,515. Includes education for the ethnic Chinese citizens of Singapore.

1198 DAVIDI, Aharon. *Some Cultural Changes in the Chinese Minority Communities in Southeast Asia: A Study in Political Geography with Special Reference to Singapore.* London, 1973 (Ph.D. in Science, School of Oriental and African Studies). 488p.

1199 LEE, Poh Ping. *Chinese Society in Nineteenth- and Early Twentieth-Century Singapore: A Socioeconomic Analysis.* Cornell, 1974 (Ph.D. in Government). 269p. DAI 35, no. 7 (Jan. 1975): 4739-A; UM 74-17,117.

1200 BEAULIEU, Peter Dennis. *Singapore: A Case Study of Communalism and Economic Development*. Washington (Seattle), 1975 (Ph.D. in Urban Planning). 354p. DAI 37, no.2 (Aug. 1976): 1265-A; UM 76-17,396. Includes the ethnic Chinese of Singapore.

1201 JUVE, Richard G. *Education as an Integrating Force in Singapore, a Multi-Cultural Society*. Rutgers, 1975 (Ph.D. in Education). 459p. DAI 36, no.9 (Mar. 1976): 5694-95-A; UM 76-1116.

1202 WILSON, Harold Edmund. *Educational Policies in a Changing Society: Singapore, 1918-1959*. British Columbia, 1975 (Ph.D. in History). ix, 410p. DAI 36, no.7 (Jan. 1976): 4693-A; Order copies directly from the Canadian Theses Division, National Library of Canada at Ottawa; available only in microfiche format, fiche no.25307, @ $5.00. Related publication by the author: Educational Policy and Performance in Singapore, 1942-1945 (Singapore: Institute of Southeast Asian Studies, 1973. 28p. [Occasional paper, 16]). Includes the impact of these policies upon the Chinese-run schools in Singapore.

Thailand

1203 MAXWELL, William Edgar. *Modernization and Mobility into the Elites among Medical Students in Thailand*. California (Los Angeles), 1971 (Ph.D. in Sociology). 365p. DAI 34, no.7 (Jan. 1974): 4436-A; UM 71-23,022. Half of the students are ethnically Chinese.

1204 JIRAWAT WONGSWADIWAT [WONGSWADIWAT, Jirawat]. *The Psychological Assimilation of Chinese University Students in Thailand*. Illinois, 1973 (Ph.D. in Educational Psychology). 289p. DAI 34, no.12 (June 1974): 7602-03-A; UM 74-12,257.

1205 TOBIAS, Stephen Frederic. *Chinese Religion in a Thai Market Town*. Chicago, 1973 (Ph.D. in Anthropology). vi, 286p. Order copies from the Photoduplication Department, Joseph Regenstein Library, University of Chicago.

1206 AMARA BHUMIRATANA [BHUMIRATANA, Amara]. *Industrialization and Social Change in Thailand*. Washington (Seattle), 1974 (Ph.D. in Anthropology). 291p. DAI 35, no.7 (Jan. 1975): 3950-51-A; UM 74-29,374. Includes information about the increased assimilation of the ethnically Chinese residents of Chonburi town (southeast of Bangkok) into Thai society.

Chinese Communities in the United States

Chinese Americans during the 1800s

See also the section within the Appendix entitled "Overseas Chinese Communities" (pp.247-51).

1207   JANISCH, Hudson Noel. *The Chinese, the Courts, and the Constitution: A Study of the Legal Issues Raised by Chinese Immigration to the United States 1850-1902*. Chicago, 1971 (J.S.D.). 1166p. Available at the University of Chicago Law Library.

1208   LEONARD, Stephen J. *Denver's Foreign Born Immigrants, 1859-1900*. Claremont, 1971 (Ph.D. in Education). 271p. DAI 32, no.5 (Nov. 1971): 2609-A; UM 71-29,641. Includes the Chinese and Japanese residents of this Colorado city.

1209   ZO, Kil Young. *Chinese Emigration into the United States, 1850-1880*. Columbia, 1971 (Ph.D. in History). 231p. DAI 32, no.3 (Sept. 1971): 1461-A; UM 71-23,639.

1210   SALZMANN, Werner. *Die Einwanderung der Chinesen nach Kalifornien*. [German: The Immigration of the Chinese to California.] Zürich, 1972 (Dr. der Wirtschaftswissenschaft). xiv, 140p.

1211   SHUMSKY, Neil Larry. *Tar Salt and Nob Hill: A Social History of Industrial San Francisco during the 1870's*. California (Berkeley), 1972 (Ph.D. in History). iv, 351p. Order copies from the Library Photographic Service, General Library, University of California at Berkeley. Chapter 6 includes material on the Chinese in San Francisco and on the widespread animosity towards them.

1212   BEJA, Jean-Philippe. *La communauté chinoise de San Francisco au XIXème siècle: étude historique*. [French: The Chinese Community of San Francisco during the Nineteenth Century: An Historical Study.] Paris VII, 1973 (Doctorat de 3ᵉ cycle). viii, 274p. A copy is available at the Bibliothèque de la Sorbonne, library catalogue no. I 2697-4°.

1213   HELLWIG, David John. *The Afro-American and the Immigrant, 1880-1930: A Study of Black African Thought*. Syracuse, 1973 (Ph.D. in History). 298p. DAI 34, no.11 (May 1974): 7151-A; UM 74-10,146. Includes studies of Afro-American attitudes towards the Chinese and the Japanese in the United States.

1214   ORSI, Richard J. *Selling the Golden State: A Study of Boosterism in 19th Century California*. Wisconsin, 1973

(Ph.D. in History). 729p. DAI 34, no.2 (Aug. 1973): 708-09-A; UM 73-15,983. Includes information about anti-Chinese sentiment in California.

1215 ROTH, Arnold. *The California State Supreme Court, 1860-1879: A Legal History.* Southern California, 1973 (Ph.D.). 335p. DAI 33, no.9 (Mar. 1973): 5104-A; UM 73-7262. Includes information about the Chinese in California.

1216 SHANKS, Ronald Duane. *Race and Ethnic Relations: A Modernization and Stratification Perspective, 1876-1896.* California (Irvine), 1973 (Ph.D. in History). 422p. DAI 34, no.12 (June 1974): 7689-90-A; UM 74-13,836. Includes racial and ethnic relations in the American Far West, focusing on the Chinese in California.

1217 BECK, Nicholas Patrick. *The Other Children: Minority Education in California Public Schools from Statehood to 1890.* California (Los Angeles), 1975 (Ed.D.). 216p. DAI 36, no.5 (Nov. 1975): 2681-A; UM 75-22,604. Includes the educational history of the Chinese in California.

1218 ERIE, Steven Philip. *The Development of Class and Ethnic Politics in San Francisco 1870-1910: A Critique of the Pluralist Interpretation.* California (Los Angeles), 1975 (Ph.D. in Political Science). 515p. DAI 36, no.5 (Nov. 1975): 3084-85-A; UM 75-25,195. Includes information about the Chinese and about anti-Chinese sentiment.

Chinese Americans since 1900

--General and Miscellaneous Studies--

See also entries 68 and 1757, as well as the section entitled "Chinese Students at Foreign Universities" (pp.48-51).

1219 DUNN, Lynn Pratt. *An Ethnic Studies Guide and Sourcebook.* Illinois, 1972 (Ph.D. in English). 650p. DAI 34, no.2 (Aug. 1973): 766-A; UM 73-17,190. Published as four individual ethnic guides, among them one entitled <u>Asian Americans: A Study Guide and Sourcebook</u> (San Francisco: R and E Research Associates, 1975. x, 111p.).

1220 LAMARCHE, Reverend Maurice Marcel, S.J. *The Topic-Comment Pattern in the Development of English among some Chinese Children Living in the United States.* Georgetown, 1972 (Ph.D. in Linguistics). 400p. DAI 33, no.3 (Sept. 1972): 1156-A; UM 72-23,400.

1221 MAXEY, Alva B. *A Probe into the Dimensionality of Racial and Ethnic Stereotyping.* Saskatchewan, 1972 (Ph.D.). 207p. DAI 33, no.6 (Dec. 1972): 3038-A; UM 72-31,371. Includes the Chinese as one of several groups in this experimental study.

1222 CHOW, Willard Tim. *The Reemergence of an Inner City: The Pivot of Chinese Settlement in the East Bay Region of the San Francisco Bay Area.* California (Berkeley), 1974 (Ph.D. in Geography). ix, 344p. Order copies from the Library Photographic Service, General Library, University of California at Berkeley.

1223 DAY, Horace Talmage, Jr. *A Study of Political Opportunity Structure: Political Opportunity in Hawaii, 1926-1966.* Hawaii, 1974 (Ph.D. in Political Science). 628p. DAI 35, no.11 (May 1975): 7361-A; UM 75-5035. Includes information about the Chinese Americans in Hawaii.

1224 KWONG, Victor Kwonglee. *Some Negro and Chinese Comparisons: Recommendations for Adult Education.* Arizona State, 1974 (Ph.D. in Education). 236p. DAI 34, no.11 (May 1974): 6933-A; UM 74-9888. Focuses on the Blacks and the Chinese in the San Francisco Bay area and recommends educational programs designed to eliminate racial prejudice and discrimination.

1225 WU, Frances Yu-tsing. *Mandarin-Speaking Aged Chinese in the Los Angeles Area: Needs and Services.* Southern California, 1974 (D.S.W.). 271p. DAI 35, no.4 (Oct. 1974): 2401-02-A; UM 74-21,518.

1226 BHATIA, Anand Ranjan. *Differences in Training Needs of First-Level Supervisors Born and Raised in Families of Caucasian, Negro, Mexican, and Asian Descent Working in Public Utility Companies in Southern California.* Southern California, 1975 (D.B.A.). iii, 278p. DAI 37, no.3 (Sept. 1976): 1663-64-A; Order copies directly from the University of Southern California library. This study includes consideration of Chinese Americans.

1227 CHIU, Peter Yee-Chew. *Proposed Improvements for the Solid Waste Management System in San Francisco's Chinatown.* California (Berkeley), 1975 (Dr.P.H.). xiii, 242p. Order copies from the Library Photographic Service, General Library, University of California at Berkeley.

1228 LEE, Kyung. *Far Eastern Cultures in California: An Inquiry into Landscape Effects.* California (Los Angeles), 1975 (Ph.D. in Geography). 267p. DAI 36, no.5 (Nov. 1975): 3126-A; UM 75-22,643. Analyzes the geographical impact of the Chinese, Japanese and Koreans living in California on the contemporary California landscape.

1229   LOUIE, Theresa Ts'ung-tz'u. *The Pragmatic Context: A Chinese-American Example of Defining and Managing Illness*. California (San Francisco), 1975 (D.N.S.). 375p. DAI 38, no.1 (July 1977): 140-41-B; UM 77-13,872. Focuses on San Francisco's Chinatown.

1230   MIYA, Mildred. *The Metaphor of Ethnic Experience: A Teaching Dissertation*. Utah, 1975 (Ph.D. in English). 286p. DAI 36, no.9 (Mar. 1976): 6086-87-A; UM 76-5677. Includes a study of Chinese Americans.

1231   ODO, Carol. *Phonological Processes in the English Dialect of Hawaii*. Hawaii, 1975 (Ph.D. in Linguistics). v, 128p. Order copies from the Interlibrary Loan Department, University of Hawaii Library. Deals in part with the Chinese living in Hawaii.

 --Anthropological, Psychological, and Sociological Aspects--

See also entries 1736, 1741, 1753, and 1756.

1232   HIRATA, Lucie Cheng. *Immigrant Integration in a Polyethnic Society*. Hawaii, 1971 (Ph.D. in Sociology). ix, 182p. Order copies from the Interlibrary Loan Department, University of Hawaii Library. Includes coverage of Chinese immigrants to the Hawaiian Islands.

1233   SMITH, Jacqueline Marie. *Planning for Homeless Children: A Study of Chinese Girls Adopted into American Families*. Harvard, 1971 (Ed.D.). ii, 259p. Available at the Harvard University Archives, Pusey Library, call no. HU 90.10065.5.

1234   WEISS, Melford Stephen. *Conflict and Compromise: The Social Organization of a Chinese Community in America*. Michigan State, 1971 (Ph.D. in Anthropology). 435p. DAI 32, no.6 (Dec. 1971): 3137-B; UM 71-31,331. Published as Valley City: A Chinese Community in America (Cambridge, Mass.: Schenkman Publishing Company, 1974. xvii, 269p.). Focuses on the Chinese community of Sacramento, California.

1235   YOUNG, Nancy Foon. *The Development of Achievement Oriented Behavior among the Chinese of Hawaii*. Hawaii, 1971 (Ph.D. in Anthropology). vii, 273p. Order copies from the Interlibrary Loan Department, University of Hawaii Library.

1236   BIERBRYER, Bruce. *Conceptual Tempo, Sex, and Creative Thinking*. Yeshiva, 1972 (Ph.D in Educational Psychology).

173

134p. DAI 33, no.11 (May 1973): 6168-A; UM 73-11,983.
Based on a study of Chinese American children.

1237 CASE, Theo Marshall. *A Cross-Cultural Study of Personal Space in the Family*. Hawaii, 1972 (Ph.D. in Educational Psychology). 134p. DAI 33, no.6 (Dec. 1972): 2759-A; UM 72-31,051. Compares Chinese, Japanese, Filipino, and Caucasian residents of the Hawaiian Islands.

1238 KUO, Eddie Chen-yu. *Bilingual Socialization of Preschool Chinese Children in the Twin Cities Area*. Minnesota, 1972 (Ph.D. in Sociology). 197p. DAI 33, no.10 (Apr. 1973): 5840-A; UM 73-10,594. On the Chinese living in Minneapolis and St. Paul, Minnesota.

1239 KUYKENDALL, Kenneth Lee. *Acculturative Change in Family Structure among Chinese-Americans*. Colorado, 1972 (Ph.D. in Anthropology). 230p. DAI 34, no.3 (Sept. 1973): 965-66-B; UM 73-18,577. On Chinese Americans living in central California.

1240 LEIFER, Anna. *Ethnic Patterns in Cognitive Tasks*. Yeshiva, 1972 (Ph.D. in Educational Psychology). 143p. DAI 33, no.3 (Sept. 1972): 1270-71-B; UM 72-23,578. Compares Chinese, Italian, Black, and Puerto Rican children living in New York.

1241 HARKNESS, Ellen Gail. *Culture and Role of Chinese Health Professionals with Multi-Ethnic Clients*. Arizona, 1973 (Ph.D. in Anthropology). 280p. DAI 34, no.6 (Dec. 1973): 2428-B; UM 73-28,794. On second generation Chinese Americans living in Tucson, Arizona.

1242 KANG, Shin-Pyo. *The East Asian Culture and Its Transformation in the West: A Cognitive Approach to Changing World View among East Asian Americans in Hawaii*. Hawaii, 1973 (Ph.D. in Anthropology). 283p. DAI 34, no.6 (Dec. 1973): 2429-B; UM 73-28,800. Studies the Chinese, Japanese and Koreans living in the Hawaiian Islands.

1243 LAW, Timothy Tinman. *Differential Child-Rearing Attitudes and Practices of Chinese-American Mothers*. Claremont, 1973 (Ph.D. in Education). 155p. DAI 34, no.7 (Jan. 1974): 4406-A; UM 74-967.

1244 PETERSON, Susan Blackmore. *Decisions in a Market: A Study of the Honolulu Fish Auction*. Hawaii, 1973 (Ph.D. in Anthropology). 294p. DAI 35, no.2 (Aug. 1974): 640-A; UM 74-17,216. Studies the variety of ethnic groups within the community, among them the Chinese Americans.

1245   STEIN, David Joel. *The Phenomenology of Resettlement:*
        An Exploration into the Experiences of Chinese Immigrants
        in San Francisco. California School of Professional Psy-
        chology (San Francisco), 1973 (Ph.D.). 362p. DAI 34,
        no.7 (Jan. 1974): 3476-77-B; UM 73-31,512.

1246   HO, Kuo-hsiung. *Exploratory Study of Spatial Dimension-*
        ality across Two Ethnic Groups. Maryland, 1974 (Ph.D.
        in Education). 119p. DAI 36, no.2 (Aug. 1975): 781-A;
        UM 75-18,104. Includes consideration of East Asian ele-
        mentary school children living within Baltimore County
        in the state of Maryland.

1247   JUNG, Marshall. *Organizational Performance in an Ameri-*
        can Chinatown: An Analysis of the Criteria Utilized by
        Organizations in Philadelphia's Chinatown to Assess Their
        Performance. Pennsylvania, 1974 (D.S.W.). 395p. DAI
        35, no.4 (Oct. 1974): 2398-A; UM 74-23,033.

1248   LAWITZKE, Dick Bruce. *A Comparison of Selected Person-*
        ality Characteristics of Five Ethnic Groups as Measured
        by the Mann Inventory. Michigan State, 1974 (Ph.D. in
        Secondary Education and Curriculum). 309p. DAI 35, no.
        9 (Mar. 1975): 5784-A; UM 75-7192. Includes Asian Ameri-
        cans as one of the ethnic groups.

1249   NOBLE, Vicente N. *Client Perceptions of the Counseling*
        Process in a Multi-Cultural Population. Claremont, 1974
        (Ph.D. in Education). 210p. DAI 35, no.4 (Oct. 1974):
        1985-A; UM 74-14,888. Includes coverage of Asian Ameri-
        can students living in the Los Angeles, California metro-
        politan area.

1250   TAKATA, Glenn. *An Examination of Cultural Differences*
        in the Use of English Mood Words: A Multidimensional
        Scaling Analysis. Northwestern, 1974 (Ph.D. in Psycholo-
        gy). 147p. DAI 35, no.10 (Apr. 1975): 5094-B; UM
        75-8001. Takata's subjects consisted of Chinese, Cauca-
        sians, Filipinos, native Hawaiians, and Japanese living
        in the Hawaiian Islands.

1251   BROWN, John Amos. *Voluntary Associations among Ethnic*
        Minority Groups in Detroit, Michigan: A Comparative
        Study. California (Berkeley), 1975 (D.S.W.). 238p.
        DAI 37, no.1 (July 1976): 606-A; UM 76-15,085. Includes
        information about the Chinese mutual aid groups in De-
        troit during the early 1900s.

1252   COLE, Joan Hays. *Institutional Racism in a Community*
        Mental Health Center. Wright Institute, 1975 (Ph.D. in
        Social-Clinical Psychology). 314p. DAI 36, no.4 (Oct.

1975): 2455-56-A; UM 75-22,537. Includes diagnoses of emotional disorders and treatment of Asian Americans.

1253 HOMMA-TRUE, Reiko. *Mental Health Needs and Alternatives in a Chinese American Community*. California School of Professional Psychology, 1975 (Ph.D.). 123p. DAI 36, no.6 (Dec. 1975): 2723-24-B; UM 75-28,719. Focuses on Oakland, California.

1254 JEDLICKA, Davor. *Ethnic Serial Marriages in Hawaii: Application of a Sequential Preference Model*. Hawaii, 1975 (Ph.D. in Sociology). vii, 128p. Order copies from the Interlibrary Loan Department, University of Hawaii Library. On the Chinese, Filipinos, Japanese and Koreans living in the Hawaiian Islands.

1255 KUO, Chia-ling. *Voluntary Associations and Social Change in New York Chinatown*. New York, 1975 (Ph.D. in Anthropology). 225p. DAI 36, no.11 (May 1976): 7502-A; UM 76-10,188. Published as Social and Political Change in New York's Chinatown: The Role of Voluntary Associations (New York: Praeger, 1977. xxix, 160p. [Praeger special studies in U.S. economic, social, and political issues]).

1256 LEON, Joseph James. *A Test of the Milton M. Gordon Ethclass Hypotheses on Samples of Public High School Youth in Hawaii*. Hawaii, 1975 (Ph.D. in Sociology). xiv, 230p. Order copies from the Interlibrary Loan Department, University of Hawaii Library. Deals in part with Chinese living in Hawaii.

1257 LEUNG, Eric Kwok-wing. *A Sociological Study of the Chinese Language Schools in the San Francisco Bay Area*. Missouri, 1975 (Ph.D. in Sociology). 144p. DAI 36, no. 7 (Jan. 1976): 4317-18-A; UM 76-1030.

1258 LI, Peter Sing-Sang. *Occupational Mobility and Kinship Assistance: A Study of Chinese Immigrants in Chicago*. Northwestern, 1975 (Ph.D. in Sociology). 250p. DAI 36, no.11 (May 1976): 7655-A; UM 76-11,907.

--Cultural and Religious Aspects--

1259 LEE, Marjorie. *Cultural Pluralism and American Textbooks: A Study of the Chinese Immigrants in Oregon*. Oregon, 1972 (Ph.D. in Curriculum and Instruction). 73p. DAI 33, no.9 (Mar. 1973): 4682-83-A; UM 73-7922.

1260 HEATH, Harris McDonald. *Teaching Minority Literature: A Study of Minority Literature Content in the American*

Literature Course in the Secondary Schools of South Carolina, 1973-74. Duke, 1974 (Ph.D. in Education). 139p.
DAI 35, no.9 (Mar. 1975): 6005-A; UM 75-6771. Includes
coverage of Asian Americans.

1261   OKIMOTO, Ray Ichiro. Folk Music of the Dominant Immigrant Cultures of Hawaii as Resource for Junior High
School General Music. George Peabody College for Teachers, 1974 (Ed.D. in Music). 171p. DAI 35, no.7 (Jan.
1975): 4597-A; UM 74-29,149. Includes Chinese music.

1262   OWYANG, Gregory Robert. The Chinese Church and the Amer-
ican-Born Chinese: An Exploration of the Issues and Problems Involved in Reaching and Serving Them. Fuller Theological Seminary, 1974 (D.Miss.). 183p. For copies,
write to the McAlister Library, Fuller Theological Seminary, Pasadena, California.

1263   YU, Danny Kwok Leung. A Study of Church Unity among Chinese-American Churches. Fuller Theological Seminary,
1975 (D.Min.). 194p. For copies, write to the McAlister
Library, Fuller Theological Seminary, Pasadena, California.

--Economic Aspects--

See also entry 1762.

1264   FEARIS, Donald Friend. The California Farm Workers, 1930-
1942. California (Davis), 1971 (Ph.D. in History).
328p. DAI 32, no.9 (Mar. 1972): 5146-A; UM 72-9891.
Includes Chinese American laborers.

1265   CHI, Peter Shen-kuo. Inter- and Intra-Group Income
Equalities of Racial and Ethnic Groups in the United
States. Brown, 1972 (Ph.D. in Sociology). 225p. DAI
33, no.8 (Feb. 1973): 4560-61-A; UM 73-2248. Includes
Chinese Americans.

1266   NASH, Robert Alan. The Chinese Shrimp Fishery in California. California (Los Angeles), 1973 (Ph.D. in Geography). 361p. DAI 34, no.6 (Dec. 1973): 2697-B; UM
73-28,742.

1267   WONG, Bernard. Patronage, Brokerage, Entrepreneurship
and the Chinese Community of New York. Wisconsin, 1974
(Ph.D. in Anthropology). 350p. DAI 35, no.10 (Apr.
1975): 6294-95-A; UM 74-30,135.

1268   WONG, Harold H. The Relative Economic Status of Chinese,
Japanese, Black, and White Men in California. California

(Berkeley), 1974 (Ph.D. in Economics). 205p. DAI 35, no.10 (Apr. 1975): 6326-27-A; UM 75-8037. Published as The Relative...California (Berkeley: the author; Springfield, Va.: available from the National Technical Information Service, 1974. xix, 186p.).

1269 YOUNG, Jared Jack. *Discrimination, Income, Human Capital Investment, and Asian-Americans.* Southern California, 1974 (Ph.D. in Economics). 174p. DAI 35, no.2 (Aug. 1974): 681-82-A; UM 74-17,389. Focuses on the Asian American response to economic discrimination.

1270 MOAYED-DADKHAH, Kamran. *Economics of Migration: International Migration of Professionals to the United States.* Indiana, 1975 (Ph.D. in Economics). 123p. DAI 36, no.8 (Feb. 1976): 5416-A; UM 76-2866. Includes the migration of professionals from Hong Kong, the Republic of China, and the Chinese mainland.

--Educational Aspects--

1271 PRANZO, Mary Louise. *Studies in Production Relationships in Secondary Education for Minority Groups in the United States.* Pittsburgh, 1971 (Ph.D. in Economics). 141p. DAI 32, no.9 (Mar. 1972): 4794-A; UM 72-7876. Includes consideration of Asian Americans.

1272 REED, Rodney Joseph. *Ethnicity, Social Class, and Out-of-School Educational Opportunity.* California (Berkeley), 1971 (Ph.D. in Education). iii, 179p. Order copies from the Library Photographic Service, General Library, University of California at Berkeley. Reed's research focused on the San Francisco Bay area and included coverage of Chinese Americans living there.

1273 TANG, Benita Siu Tankiong. *A Psycholinguistic Study of the Relationships between Children's Ethnic-Linguistic Attitudes and the Effectiveness of Methods Used in Second-Language Reading Instruction.* Stanford, 1971 (Ph.D. in Education). 159p. DAI 32, no.10 (Apr. 1972): 5624-25-A; UM 72-11,678. The subjects were 106 Cantonese-speaking school children living in San Francisco.

1274 AMPARAN, Robert L. *Teacher and Pupil: Ethnicity as an Independent Variate in Grading Patterns.* California (Berkeley), 1972 (Ph.D. in Education). viii, 143p. Order copies from the Library Photographic Service, General Library, University of California at Berkeley. Amparan's thesis includes Asian Americans living in California.

1275 DUNN, Melvin Baird. *Characteristics and Prediction of Success of Minority Students in Arizona Community Colleges*. Arizona State, 1972 (Ph.D. in Educational Administration and Supervision). 111p. DAI 33, no.3 (Sept. 1972): 967-68-A; UM 72-23,159. Includes coverage of Asian Americans.

1276 GRIFFIN, John Chaney. *A Prediction Study of First Year College Performance of High School Graduates by Sex and Ethnic Background*. Wyoming, 1972 (Ed.D. in Guidance). 128p. DAI 33, no.12 (June 1973): 6664-65-A; UM 73-14,273. Includes coverage of Asian Americans.

1277 McARDLE, H. Roy. *Work Values of Hawaii Public High School Seniors*. New Mexico, 1972 (Ed.D. in Guidance and Special Education). 253p. DAI 33, no.7 (Jan. 1973): 3297-98-A; UM 73-1544. Includes Asian American students.

1278 SIU, Ping-kee. *Relationships between Motivational Patterns and Academic Achievement in Chinese and Puerto Rican Second- and Third-Grade Students*. Fordham, 1972 (Ph.D. in Education). 126p. DAI 33, no.7 (Jan. 1973): 3407-A; UM 73-1519. On Chinese students in New York City.

1279 HOLOWENZAK, Stephen Paul. *The Analyses of Selected Family Background, Achievement, and Area of Residence-School: Factors Influencing Differences in the Educational Plans and Desires of Twelfth Grade Males and Females from Six Ethnic Groups*. Catholic University of America, 1973 (Ph.D. in Education). 290p. DAI 34, no.11 (May 1974): 7045-A; UM 74-9896. Asian Americans throughout the United States were included in this study.

1280 TRIBBLE, Gloria Dean. *An Evaluation of Basal Readers Currently Being Used by Students of Appalachian, American Indian, Negro, Oriental or Spanish-American Background in the State of Ohio*. Akron, 1973 (Ph.D. in Elementary Education). 231p. DAI 34, no.10 (Apr. 1974): 6373-74-A; UM 74-9775.

1281 CIRINCIONE-COLES, Kathryn. *Correlates of Culture-Conflict in School*. California (Berkeley), 1974 (Ph.D. in Education). iii, 75p. Order copies from the Library Photographic Service, General Library, University of California at Berkeley. This thesis studies the conflict between home and school values among members of five ethnic groups, among them Asian Americans.

1282 DULAY, Heidi Caroline. *Aspects of Child Second Language Acquisitions*. Harvard, 1974 (Ed.D.). 157p. DAI 36, no. 6 (Dec. 1975): 3632-33-A; UM 75-16,859. Based in part

on a study of Chinese-speaking children in the United
States who were learning English.

1283   JONES, Albert Lee. *A Survey of Counseling/Psychotherapy
of Minority Students in Three Inner-City High Schools in
Seattle, Washington.* Washington (Seattle), 1974 (Ph.D.
in Education). 133p. DAI 35, no.8 (Feb. 1975):
5122-23-A; UM 75-4000. Includes Chinese American students in Seattle.

1284   LAMB, Richard Ray. *Concurrent Validity of the American
College Testing Interest Inventory for Minority Group
Members.* Iowa, 1974 (Ph.D. in Education). 144p. DAI
35, no.7 (Jan. 1975): 4161-A; UM 75-1216. Includes coverage of Asian Americans.

1285   TOU, Louis Aloysius. *A Study of Work Value Orientations
of Chinese-American and White-American Students of the
7th and 8th Grades in Catholic Elementary Schools.* Catholic University of America, 1974 (Ph.D. in Education).
140p. DAI 35, no.2 (Aug. 1974): 831-A; UM 74-17,070.

1286   BOARDMAN, Anthony Edward. *Simultaneous Equation Models
of the Education Process.* Carnegie-Mellon, 1975 (Ph.D.
in Urban and Public Affairs). 459p. DAI 36, no.5 (Nov.
1975): 2495-A; UM 75-21,776. Includes information about
Asian Americans.

1287   CRISCO, James Jeffrey. *The Prediction of Academic Performance for Minority Engineering Students from Selected
Achievement-Proficiency, Personality, Cognitive Style,
and Demographic Variables.* Marquette, 1975 (Ph.D. in
Educational Psychology). 155p. DAI 36, no.10 (Apr.
1976): 6545-A; UM 76-8634. The subjects included several
Asian Americans.

1288   INN, Kalei. *Ethnic Mix in Elementary Classrooms, Chinese-American Ethnic Self-Esteem, and Sense of Marginality.* Stanford, 1975 (Ph.D. in Education). 187p. DAI
36, no.6 (Dec. 1975): 4074-A; UM 75-25,548.

1289   LUM, Philip Albert. *The Chinese Freedom Schools of San
Francisco: A Case Study of the Social Limits of Political System Support.* California (Berkeley), 1975 (Ph.D.
in Education). 201p. DAI 36, no.4 (Oct. 1975):
1957-58-A; UM 75-22,484.

--The Chinese American Image in Literature--

See also entry 1745.

1290   LOCHHEAD, Donald George. *An Examination of the*

*Presentation of Non-Anglo Saxon Ethnic Groups in High
School Literature Anthologies*. Utah, 1971 (Ph.D. in Educational Administration). 130p. DAI 32, no.6 (Dec.
1971): 3006-A; UM 72-494. Includes Asian Americans.

1291 McKAY, Ralph Yarrelle. *A Comparative Study of the Character Representation of California's Dominant Minority
Groups in the Officially Adopted California Reading Textbooks of the 1950's, 1960's, and 1970's*. University of
the Pacific, 1971 (Ed.D.). 272p. DAI 32, no.5 (Nov.
1971): 2405-A; UM 71-28,076. Includes the Chinese.

1292 MORGAN, Betty M. *An Investigation of Children's Books
Containing Characters from Selected Minority Groups Based
on Specific Criteria*. Southern Illinois, 1973 (Ph.D. in
Education). 306p. DAI 34, no.10 (Apr. 1974): 6364-A;
UM 74-6232. Includes Chinese Americans as depicted in
books written for elementary school children since 1945.

1293 WILLEY, Michael Lee. *The Debt to Minority Literature:
Images of Change and Action in Recent White Literature*.
Nebraska, 1973 (Ph.D. in English). 202p. DAI 34, no.12
(June 1974): 7792-93-A; UM 74-13,032. One chapter covers
Asian American literature.

1294 MARTIN, Joan Marie. *American Literature: Towards a Re-
definition*. Michigan, 1975 (A.D. in English Language
and Literature). 148p. DAI 36, no.10 (Apr. 1976):
6687-A; UM 76-9318. Includes consideration of Chinese
American literary contributions and of Chinese American
stereotypes in American literature.

1295 ROBERTS, Charles Edward. *The Racial Attitudes of American Best-Selling Novelists, 1895-1915*. Oregon, 1975
(Ph.D. in History). 630p. DAI 36, no.7 (Jan. 1976):
4681-A; UM 76-967. Includes coverage of Caucasian attitudes towards the Chinese in the United States.

OVERSEAS TIBETAN COMMUNITIES

1296 OTT-MARTI, Anna Elisabeth. *Tibeter in der Schweiz. Kul-
turelle Verhaltensweisen im Wandel*. [German: Tibetans
in Switzerland: Changes in Cultural Behavior.] Zürich,
1971 (Dr., Philosophische Fakultät I). Published as Tibeter...Wandel (Erlenbach-Zürich: Eugen Rentch, 1971.
190p.).

1297 PAWSON, Ivan Guy. *The Growth and Development of High Al-
titude Children with Special Emphasis on Populations of*

181

Tibetan Origin in Nepal. Pennsylvania State, 1974 (Ph.D.
in Anthropology). 182p. DAI 36, no.3 (Sept. 1975):
1627-A; UM 75-19,918.

1298 CORLIN, Claes. *The Nation in Your Mind: Continuity and
Change among Tibetan Refugees in Nepal.* Göteborg, 1975
(Akad. avh.). iii, 161p.

POLITICS AND GOVERNMENT

(since 1949)

General and Miscellaneous Studies

See also entries 1421 and 1649.

1299 MIGDAL, Joel. *Peasants in a Shrinking World: The Socio-
Economic Basis of Political Change.* Harvard, 1972 (Ph.D.
in Political Science). iv, 458p. Available at the Harvard University Archives, Pusey Library, call no.
HU 90.10201.5. Published as Peasants, Politics, and Revolution: Pressures toward Political and Social Change in
the Third World (Princeton: Princeton University Press,
1975. x, 300p.). Includes coverage of peasant communities in pre-1949 China, the People's Republic of China,
Hong Kong, and the Republic of China.

1300 NÄTH, Marie-Luise. *Chinas Weg in die Weltpolitik. Die
nationalen und aussenpolitischen Konzeptionen Sun Yat-
sens, Chiang Kai-sheks und Mao Tse-tungs.* [German: China's Course in World Politics: The National and International Concepts of Sun Yat-sen, Chiang Kai-shek and Mao
Tse-tung.] Freie Universität Berlin, 1972 (Dr., Fachbereich Politische Wissenschaft). Published as Chinas...
Mao Tse-tungs (Berlin: de Gruyter, 1976. viii, 259p.
[Beiträge zur auswärtigen und internationalen Politik;
Bd.7]).

1301 OLSEN, Edward Allan. *East Asia and the Ecological Perspectives on the Roots of Power of H. and M. Sprout: An
Inquiry into the Nature of Power and the Power of Nature
in East Asian Political Culture.* American, 1974 (Ph.D.
in International Studies). 585p. DAI 35, no.5 (Nov.
1974): 3088-89-A; UM 74-21,705. Assesses the geopoliti-
cal writings of Harold and Margaret Sprout and the utility of a Western conceptual framework in the East Asian
context.

1302 CARIÑO, Feliciano Vergara. *Theology, Modernization and*

Ideological Politics: A Study in Christian Participation in Contemporary Asian Politics. Princeton Theological Seminary, 1975 (Ph.D. in Ecumenics). 511p. DAI 36, no. 4 (Oct. 1975): 2284-A; UM 75-23,156. Includes an historical case study of modern Chinese politics as well as information about Christian participation in contemporary Chinese social and political life.

1303   HANIFF, Ghulam Mohammed. *Political and Economic Dimensions of Social Policy: A Cross-National Analysis.* Case Western Reserve, 1975 (Ph.D. in Political Science). 280p. DAI 36, no.6 (Dec. 1975): 3982-83-A; UM 75-27,919. Based on data from 125 countries including China.

Mongolian People's Republic

Note: For studies of political developments in Inner Mongolia, *see* entries 1351 and 1373.

1304   KOJŁO, Stefan. *Etapy przemian rewolucyjnych w Mongolii na drodze rozwoju do socjalizmu.* [Polish: Stages of Revolutionary Change in Mongolia while on the Road to Socialism.] Wyższa Szkoła Nauk Społecznych przy KC PZPR w Warszawie, 1973 (Rozprawa doktorska, Wydz. Nauk Społecznych).

People's Republic of China

General and Miscellaneous Studies

See also entries 179, 180, 371, 665, 813, 1001, 1533, 1767, and 1768, as well as the sections entitled "Politics and Education" (pp.41-42) and "Sociology--People's Republic of China" (p.219).

1305   HART, Thomas G. *The Dynamics of Revolution: A Cybernetic Theory of the Dynamics of Modern Social Revolution with a Study of Ideological Change and Organizational Dynamics in the Chinese Revolution.* Stockholm, 1971 (Akad.avh.). Published as The Dynamics...Revolution (Stockholm: Statsvetenskapliga institutionen, Stockholms universitet, 1971. xiii, 203p. [Stockholm studies in politics, 1]).

1306   MENDES, Richard Gerald. *The Role of Intermediate Organizations in a Totalitarian Society: The Case of Communist*

China 1949-1964. Michigan State, 1971 (Ph.D. in Political Science). 247p. DAI 32, no.12 (June 1972): 7059-A; UM 72-16,479.

1307   CHO, Jaekwan. *A Comparative Analysis of the Communist Cadre System.* California (Berkeley), 1972 (Ph.D. in Political Science). iii, 268p. Order copies from the Library Photographic Service, General Library, University of California at Berkeley. Cho's thesis compares the People's Republic of China and North Korea.

1308   GROW, Roy Franklin. *The Politics of Industrial Development in China and the Soviet Union: Organizational Strategy as a Linkage between National and World Politics.* Michigan, 1973 (Ph.D. in Political Science). 517p. DAI 34, no.4 (Oct. 1973): 1982-83-A; UM 73-24,578. Focuses on the period 1953-1955.

1309   WHITE, Lynn Townsend (III). *Policies and Careers in Communist China.* California (Berkeley), 1973 (Ph.D. in Political Science). v, 488p. Order copies from the Library Photographic Service, General Library, University of California at Berkeley.

1310   KRAUS, Richard Curt. *The Evolving Concept of Class in Post-Liberation China.* Columbia, 1974 (Ph.D. in Political Science). 377p. DAI 35, no.12 (June 1975): 7979-A; UM 75-12,321.

1311   BUCHHOLZ, Jochen Bernhard. *Selbstbestimmung der Arbeitnehmer im Sozialismus? Eine vergleichende Untersuchung der Stellung und der Einflussmöglichkeiten der Werktätigen in den sozialistischen Systemen der Volksrepublik China und der Deutschen Demokratischen Republik.* [German: Self-Determination of Employees in Socialism? A Comparative Investigation of the Position and the Powers of Influence of the Workers in the Socialist Systems of the People's Republic of China and the German Democratic Republic.] Bonn, 1975 (Dr., Rechts- und Staatswissenschaftliche Fakultät). 422p. DAI 37, no.3 (Spring 1977): Vol.C--entry no.1/3650c.

1312   HAMRIN, Carol Lee. *Alternatives within Chinese Marxism 1955-1965: Yang Hsien-chen's Theory of Dialectics.* Wisconsin, 1975 (Ph.D. in History). 528p. DAI 36, no.9 (Mar. 1976): 6252-53-A; UM 75-28,009.

1313   LEE, Hwasoo. *A Comparative Study of Economic, Social and Political Conditions for Political Violence from the Perspectives Revolution: China, Japan and Korea.* Oregon, 1975 (Ph.D. in Political Science). 289p. DAI 36, no.7

(Jan. 1976): 4732-33-A; UM 76-942. Seeks to explain the "Communist Revolution in China".

1314 LIU, Peter Han-shan. *A Comparative Study of the Development of Specialist Groups in Communist China with Those in the Soviet Union.* Southern Illinois, 1975 (Ph.D. in Government). 222p. DAI 36, no.8 (Feb. 1976): 5515-A; UM 76-3326. Compares the military and the economists.

1315 McDOWELL, Samuel Garrett. *"Cultural Aggression" versus "Patriotism": Some Chinese Definitions and Remedies.* California (Berkeley), 1975 (Ph.D. in Political Science). 486p. DAI 37, no.1 (July 1976): 573-A; UM 76-15,299. Focuses on the People's Republic of China between 1949 and 1970.

1316 OGDEN, Suzanne Peckham. *Chinese Concepts of the Nation, State, and Sovereignty.* Brown, 1975 (Ph.D. in Political Science). 366p. DAI 37, no.1 (July 1976): 588-89-A; UM 76-15,683. Focuses on Communist Chinese perceptions and attitudes.

The Armed Forces

See also entry 1314.

1317 WANG, James C. F. *The People's Liberation Army in Communist China's Political Development: A Contingency Analysis of the Military's Perception and Verbal Symbolization during the Cultural Revolution, 1966-1969.* Hawaii, 1971 (Ph.D. in Political Science). 292p. DAI 32, no.9 (Mar. 1972): 5325-26-A; UM 72-10,161.

1318 CLARK, Sharon Waite. *History of the Political Organization of the Chinese People's Liberation Army: Organizational Conflict and Charismatic Change.* North Carolina, 1972 (Ph.D. in Political Science). 139p. DAI 33, no.3 (Sept. 1972): 1203-04-A; UM 72-24,775.

1319 NELSEN, Harvey Walter. *An Organizational History of the Chinese People's Liberation Army: 1966-1969.* George Washington, 1972 (Ph.D. in History). 291p. DAI 33, no. 5 (Nov. 1972): 2300-A; UM 72-25,060. Published as The Chinese Military System: An Organizational Study of the People's Liberation Army (Boulder, Colo.: Westview Press, 1977. xiv, 266p. [Westview special studies on China and East Asia]).

1320 RIGDON, Susan Marie. *The Chinese Military Ethic.* Illinois, 1972 (Ph.D. in Political Science). 162p. DAI 32,

no.10 (Apr. 1972): 5871-A; UM 72-12,354. Discusses the
impact of a unified military doctrine (based on the Chinese Communist revolutionary war-base area strategy) on
the extant political orthodoxy in China.

1321   CHANG, Pao-min. *Politics of the Chinese Red Army: A
Study of the Political Work System of the PLA, 1928-1972.*
Brown, 1974 (Ph.D. in Political Science). 293p. DAI 35,
no.11 (May 1975): 7359-A; UM 75-9132.

1322   JORDAN, James Douglas. *Evolution of a People's Army in
the People's Republic of China.* American, 1975 (Ph.D.
in International Studies). 321p. DAI 36, no.3 (Sept.
1975): 1788-A; UM 75-18,325. Covers the period from
1927 through the early 1970s.

1323   LEE, Luke Wen-yuen. *Role of the Military in Mainland
China's Power Struggles: 1966-1969.* Idaho, 1975 (Ph.D.
in Political Science). 179p. DAI 36, no.9 (Mar. 1976):
6282-A; UM 76-4960.

The Cultural Revolution

See also entries 267, 270, 271, 1317, 1319, and 1323.

1324   CHIOU, Chwei Liang. *Ideology and Political Power in Mao
Tse-tung's Cultural Revolution, 1965-1968.* California
(Riverside), 1971 (Ph.D. in Political Science). 220p.
DAI 32, no.4 (Oct. 1971): 2149-A; UM 71-27,073. Pub-
lished as Maoism in Action: The Cultural Revolution (St.
Lucia: University of Queensland Press; New York: Crane,
Russak, 1974. x, 176p.]).

1325   DITTMER, Lowell. *Liu Shao-ch'i and the Chinese Cultural
Revolution.* Chicago, 1971 (Ph.D. in Political Science).
420p. Order copies from the Photoduplication Department,
Joseph Regenstein Library, University of Chicago. Published as Liu Shao-ch'i and the Chinese Cultural Revolution: The Politics of Mass Criticism (Berkeley: University of California Press, 1974. xiv, 386p.).

1326   HEASLET, Juliana Pennington. *The Cultural Revolution,
1966-1969: The Failure of Mao's Revolution in China.*
Colorado, 1971 (Ph.D. in History). 233p. DAI 32, no.7
(Jan. 1972): 3922-A; UM 72-3660.

1327   HOFFMANN, Rainer. *Entmaoisierung in China; zur Vorge-
schichte der Kulturrevolution.* [German: "De-Maoization"
in China: Towards the Antecedents of the Cultural Revolution.] Freiburg i.B., 1972 (Dr., Philosophische

Fakultät). Published as Entmaoisierung...Kulturrevolution (München: Weltforum-Verlag, 1972. 239p. [Studien zur Entwicklung und Politik, 1]).

1328 BAUMGART, Wiesław Marek. *Rewolucja kulturalna w ChRL w opinii piśmiennictwa amerykańskiego, angielskiego i zachodnioniemieckiego.* [Polish: The Cultural Revolution in the People's Republic of China as Seen in American, British and West German Literature.] Uniwersytet im. A. Mickiewicza w Poznaniu, 1973 (Rozprawa doktorska, Wydz. Filozofino-Historyczny).

1329 DOYLE, Jean Louise. *Conflict Management in the Chinese Cultural Revolution: A Case Study in Political Change.* Boston University, 1973 (Ph.D. in Political Science). 315p. DAI 34, no.4 (Oct. 1973): 1981-A; UM 73-23,476.

1330 GERONIMI, Francis. *La Révolution culturelle dans la province de Szechwan.* [French: The Cultural Revolution in the Province of Szechwan.] Paris I (Panthéon-Sorbonne), 1973 (Doctorat de 3e cycle ès études politiques). 236p. A copy is available at the Bibliothèque de la Sorbonne.

1331 KURIYAMA, Yoshihiro. *Political Leadership and Students in China (1966-1968) and France (1968).* California (Berkeley), 1973 (Ph.D. in History). 273p. DAI 34, no. 9 (Mar. 1974): 5874-A; UM 74-7516.

1332 LEE, Hong Yung. *The Political Mobilization of the Red Guards and Revolutionary Rebels in the Cultural Revolution.* Chicago, 1973 (Ph.D. in Political Science). 657p. Order copies from the Photoduplication Department, Joseph Regenstein Library, University of Chicago.

1333 EYUBOGLU, Ercan. *Idéologie et appareils idéologiques d'état dans la Révolution culturelle en Chine.* [French: Ideology and Ideological Apparatus of the State during the Cultural Revolution in China.] Paris I (Panthéon-Sorbonne), 1974 (Doctorat d'Etat en droit).

1334 KATO, Hiroki. *The Red Guard Movement (May, 1966 - January, 1967): A Case of a Student Movement in China.* Chicago, 1974 (Ph.D. in Political Science). iv, 150p. Order copies from the Photoduplication Department, Joseph Regenstein Library, University of Chicago.

1335 LEMÉE, Herve. *Recherche sur les conséquences de la Révolution culturelle sur le gouvernement et l'administration de la Chine populaire.* [French: An Investigation into the Consequences of the Cultural Revolution for the Government and the Administration of the People's Republic of China.] Paris I (Panthéon-Sorbonne), 1974 (Doctorat d'Etat en droit).

1336   RADDOCK, David Miles. *Origins of the Political Behav-*
       ior of Chinese Adolescents: The Case of the Beginnings
       of the Cultural Revolution in Canton. Columbia, 1974
       (Ph.D. in Political Science). 340p. DAI 35, no.2
       (Aug. 1974): 1186-87-A; UM 74-18,449.

1337   TSAO, James Jhy-yuan. *Chinese Communist Cultural Revo-*
       lution: An Analytical Reappraisal from the Historical
       Point of View. American, 1974 (Ph.D. in International
       Studies). 359p. DAI 35, no.4 (Oct. 1974): 2201-02-A;
       UM 74-22,279.

1338   WAGEMANN, Mildred Lina Ellen. *The Changing Image of*
       Mao Tse-tung: Leadership Image and Social Structure.
       Cornell, 1974 (Ph.D. in Development Psychology). 175p.
       DAI 35, no.6 (Dec. 1974): 3904-A; UM 74-26,330. Exam-
       ines Mao's position and image during the Cultural Revo-
       lution in the context of structural changes in progress
       since 1949.

1339   MARTIN, Charles Michael. *Red Guards and Political In-*
       stitutions: A Study of Peking and Canton. Harvard,
       1975 (Ph.D. in Political Science). 525p. Available at
       the Harvard University Archives, Pusey Library, call
       no.HU 90.10804.10.

1340   ZOULIM, Seddik. *Contribution à l'étude de la culture*
       et de l'éducation socialistes. L'Expérience chinoise
       de la "Révolution culturelle". [French: Contribution
       to the Study of Socialist Culture and Education: The
       Chinese Experience of the "Cultural Revolution".]
       Paris V (Réne Descartes), 1975 (Doctorat de 3e cycle
       en psychologie). v, 232p. A copy is available at the
       Bibliothèque de la Sorbonne, library catalogue no.I
       3144-4°.

                    Local and Regional Politics
See also entries 1330 and 1339.

1341   CHAMBERLAIN, Heath Brosius. *Transition and Consolida-*
       tion in Urban China: A Study of Leaders and Organiza-
       tions in Three Cities, 1949-1953. Stanford, 1971 (Ph.D.
       in Political Science). 421p. DAI 32, no.8 (Feb. 1972):
       4672-73-A; UM 72-5895. On Canton, Shanghai and Tientsin.

1342   FALKENHEIM, Victor Carl. *Provincial Administration in*
       Fukien: 1949-1966. Columbia, 1972 (Ph.D. in Political
       Science). 396p. DAI 33, no.2 (Aug. 1972): 810-A;
       UM 72-20,035.

1343 LI, Karl Goh-jou. *The Commune System: A Study of the Chinese Political System.* Maryland, 1972 (Ph.D. in Government and Politics). 303p. DAI 34, no.1 (July 1973): 381-A; UM 73-17,041. On the political development of the commune system and its place in Chinese political culture.

1344 LIEBERTHAL, Kenneth Guy. *Reconstruction and Revolution in a Chinese City: The Case of Tientsin, 1949-1953.* Columbia, 1972 (Ph.D. in Political Science). 566p. DAI 37, no.1 (July 1976): 570-71-A; UM 76-15,562.

1345 WU, Hung-sen. *The Political Functions of the Chinese People's Communes.* Idaho, 1972 (Ph.D. in Political Science). 263p. DAI 34, no.1 (July 1973): 386-87-A; UM 73-15,742.

1346 CARDARONELLA, Gary Leonce. *Buduan geming: The Politics of Revolutionary Institutionalization in Rural China, 1955-1960.* Virginia, 1973 (Ph.D. in Government). 327p. DAI 34, no.4 (Oct. 1973): 1980-A; UM 73-24,984. Analyzes and interprets the theory and practice of "uninterrupted revolution".

1347 HUEY, Alison Baker. *The Consolidation of Central Control in Szechuan, 1950-1954.* George Washington, 1974 (Ph.D. in History). 203p. DAI 35, no.5 (Nov. 1974): 2902-A; UM 74-22,257.

1348 PINKELE, Carl Frederic. *Local Government and Politics in the People's Republic of China: 1949-1952.* New School for Social Research, 1974 (Ph.D. in Political Science). 247p. DAI 35, no.6 (Dec. 1974): 3841-A; UM 74-26,969.

1349 SHUE, Vivienne Bland. *Transforming China's Peasant Villages: Rural Political and Economic Organization, 1949-1956.* Harvard, 1975 (Ph.D. in Political Science). 526p. Available at the Harvard University Archives, Pusey Library, call no.HU 90.10853.

1350 SOLINGER, Dorothy Jane. *Regional Government and Political Integration: The Case of Southwest China, 1949-1954.* Stanford, 1975 (Ph.D. in Political Science). 386p. DAI 35, no.12 (June 1975): 7988-A; UM 75-13,602 Published as Regional Government and Political Integration in Southwest China, 1949-1954: A Case Study (Berkeley: University of California Press, 1977. ix, 291p.).

1351 SOONG, James Chu-yul. *An Elite Perspective on Developmental Crisis: China's Experiences in Inner Mongolia.*

Georgetown, 1975 (Ph.D. in Government). 546p. DAI 36,
no.5 (Nov. 1975): 3100-A; UM 72-24,486.

1352   THURSTON, Anne Fritter. *Authority and Legitimacy in
Post-Revolution Rural Kwangtung: The Case of the People's
Communes.* California (Berkeley), 1975 (Ph.D. in Polit-
ical Science). 597p. DAI 37, no.1 (July 1976): 581-A;
UM 76-15,394.

National Politics

1353   MOODY, Peter Richard, Jr. *The Politics of the Eighth
Central Committee of the Communist Party of China.*
Yale, 1971 (Ph.D. in Political Science). 447p. DAI 32,
no.5 (Nov. 1971): 2761-A; UM 71-29,707. Published as
The Politics...China (Hamden, Conn.: Shoe String Press,
1973. xi, 346p.).

1354   TEIWES, Frederick Carl. *Rectification Campaigns and
Purges in Communist China, 1950-1961.* Columbia, 1971
(Ph.D. in Political Science). 620p. DAI 33, no.1
(July 1972): 376-A; UM 72-19,167. Published as (1)
Provincial Party Personnel in Mainland China, 1956-
1966 (New York: East Asian Institute, Columbia Univer-
sity, 1967. vi, 114p.) and (2) Provincial Leadership in
China: The Cultural Revolution and Its Aftermath (Ithaca,
N.Y.: China-Japan Program, Cornell University, 1974.
165p. [Cornell University East Asia papers, 4]).

1355   THEERAVITAYA, Khien. *The Hsia-fang System: Bureacracy
and Nation-Building in Communist China, 1957-1969.*
Washington (Seattle), 1971 (Ph.D. in Political Science).
339p. DAI 32, no.5 (Nov. 1971): 2766-A; UM 71-28,483.
The hsia-fang program seeks to integrate social values
and economic roles and to create a classless and state-
less society based on productive work.

1356   AHN, Byung-joon. *Ideology, Policy, and Power in Chinese Politics and the Evolution of the Cultural Revolution, 1959-1965.* Columbia, 1972 (Ph.D. in Political
Science). 540p. DAI 33, no.1 (July 1972): 365-66-A;
UM 72-19,096. Published as Chinese Politics and the
Cultural Revolution: Dynamics of Policy Processes
(Seattle: University of Washington Press, 1976. xi,
392p. [Publications on Asia of the Institute for Comparative and Foreign Area Studies, 30]).

1357   KAO, George Chi-tsing. *Theory and Practice of Personnel Management in the State Administrative System of*

Communist China. Tennessee, 1972 (Ph.D. in Political
Science). 342p. DAI 33, no.2 (Aug. 1972): 811-A; UM
72-21,357.

1358 OJHA, Ellen Frost. *State Power and Bureaucracy in Communist China, 1949-1957.* Harvard, 1972 (Ph.D. in Government). xiii, 359p. Available at the Harvard University Archives, Pusey Library, call no.HU 90.10224.15.

1359 SAMELSON, Louis. *Peasant Politicization: Compliance
and Activism in Rural China.* Illinois, 1972 (Ph.D. in
Political Science). 426p. DAI 34, no.2 (Aug. 1973):
840-41-A; UM 73-17,396. Examines internal political
programs of the People's Republic of China and their
relevance for the modernization of a peasant-based,
tradition-oriented society.

1360 TANAKA, Kyoko. *Mass Mobilization: The Chinese Communist Party and the Peasants.* Australian Nation
(Ph.D. in International Relations). 358p.

1361 BENNETT, Gordon Anderson. *Activists and Professionals:
China's Revolution in Bureaucracy 1959-1965, A Case
Study of the Finance-Trade System.* Wisconsin, 1973
(Ph.D. in Political Science). 375p. DAI 34, no.3
(Sept. 1973): 1326-A; UM 73-19,290. Related publica-
tion by the author: Yundong: Mass Campaigns in Chinese
Communist Leadership (Berkeley: Center for Chinese
Studies, University of California, 1976. 133p. [China
research monographs, 12]).

1362 CELL, Charles Preston. *Making the Revolution Work:
Mass Mobilization Campaigns in the People's Republic
of China.* Michigan, 1973 (Ph.D. in Sociology). 317p.
DAI 34, no.8 (Feb. 1974): 5360-A; UM 74-3595. Published
as Revolution at Work: Mobilization Campaigns in China
(New York: Academic Press, 1977. xxi, 221p. [Studies
in social discontinuity]).

1363 STAVIS, Benedict Rudy. *Political Dimensions of the
Technical Transformation of Agriculture in China.* Columbia, 1973 (Ph.D. in Political Science). 382p. DAI
34, no.5 (Nov. 1973): 2729-A; UM 73-26,640. Published
as China's Green Revolution (Ithaca, N.Y.: China-Japan
Program, Cornell University, 1974. 54p. Cornell University East Asia papers, 2) and as Making Green Revolution: The Politics of Agricultural Development in
China (Ithaca, N.Y.: Cornell University, 1974. 274p.
[Rural Development Committee, monograph no.1]).

1364 TAI, Dwan-liang. *Chiang Ch'ing: The Emergence of a*

Revolutionary Political Leader. George Washington, 1973 (Ph.D. in Political Science). 283p. DAI 34, no.5 (Nov. 1973): 2730-A; UM 73-25,097. Published as Chiang...Leader (Hicksville, N.Y.: Exposition Press, 1974. xxviii, 222p.).

1365 HARDING, Harry, Jr. *The Organizational Issue in Chinese Politics, 1959-72.* Stanford, 1974 (Ph.D. in Political Science). 491p. DAI 34, no.12 (June 1974): 7836-37-A; UM 74-13,634. Focuses on the Chinese Communist Party and on state bureaucracies.

1366 LEE, Lai-to. *Political Mobilization of Workers in the People's Republic of China, 1949-1965.* California (Santa Barbara), 1974 (Ph.D. in Political Science). x, 320p. Order copies directly from the Department of Special Collections, University of California at Santa Barbara Library.

1367 TANNEBERGER, Hans-Georg. *Grundzüge der Politik gegenüber den Intellektuellen in der Volksrepublik China seit der "Hundert-Blumen-Kampagne".* [German: Characteristics of Policy vis-à-vis the Intellectuals in the People's Republic of China since the "Hundred Flowers" Campaign.] Bochum, 1974 (Dr., Abteilung für Sozialwissenschaft). 146p.

1368 HUH, Kyung-Koo. *Mobilization Patterns in Communist China.* Hawaii, 1975 (Ph.D. in Political Science). viii, 267p. Order copies from the Interlibrary Loan Department, University of Hawaii Library.

1369 LEE, Nan-Shong. *China's Industrial Bureaucracy, 1949-1973.* Chicago, 1975 (Ph.D. in Political Science). vii, 506p. Order copies from the Photoduplication Department, Joseph Regenstein Library, University of Chicago.

1370 PERROLLE, Pierre M. *Politics and the Construction of Chinese Railways, 1950-1974.* Brown, 1975 (Ph.D. in Political Science). 344p. DAI 37, no.1 (July 1976): 575-A; UM 76-15,691. This is a case study in the relationship of central and local (provincial) authorities.

1371 TAVEDIKUL, Prachya Davi. *An Empirical Study of Asian Elite Recruitment: The Chinese Central Committee and the Japanese Cabinet, 1945-1973.* Nebraska, 1974 (Ph.D. in Political Science). 307p. DAI 36, no.12 (June 1976): 8280-81-A; UM 76-13,352. In the case of China, Tavedikul investigates the political elites who hold memberships in the Chinese Communist Party's Central Committee versus those who hold memberships in the Politburo.

Policies towards the National Minorities

See also entries 879, 1351, and 1769.

1372 DEAL, David Michael. *National Minority Policy in South-
      west China 1911-1965.* Washington (Seattle), 1971 (Ph.D.
      in History). 427p. DAI 32, no.8 (Feb. 1972): 4510-11-A;
      UM 72-7334.

1373 HEATON, William Reo, Jr. *The Politics of Minority Na-
      tionalism in Communist China: A Case Study of Inner Mon-
      golia.* California (Berkeley), 1972 (Ph.D. in Political
      Science). x, 469p. Order copies from the Library Photo-
      graphic Service, General Library, University of Califor-
      nia at Berkeley.

1374 DREYER, June Elizabeth Teufel. *Chinese Communist Policy
      toward Indigenous Minority Nationalities: A Study in Na-
      tional Integration.* Harvard, 1973 (Ph.D. in Government
      and Far Eastern Languages). iv, 432p. Available at the
      Harvard University Archives, Pusey Library, call no.HU
      90.10339.10. Published as China's Forty Millions: Minor-
      ity Nationalities and National Integration in the People's
      Republic of China (Cambridge, Mass.: Harvard University
      Press, 1976. 333p. [Harvard East Asian series, 87]).

1375 LEE, Fu-hsiang. *The Turkic-Moslem Problem in Sinkiang:
      A Case Study of the Chinese Communists' National Policy.*
      Rutgers, 1973 (Ph.D. in Political Science). 434p. DAI
      34, no.10 (Apr. 1974): 6717-18-A; UM 74-8801.

Thought of Mao Tse-tung

See also entries 254, 264, 1429, and 1770.

1376 STARR, John Bryan. *Mao Tse-tung's Theory of Continuing
      the Revolution under the Dictatorship of the Proletariat:
      Its Origins, Development, and Practical Implications.*
      California (Berkeley), 1971 (Ph.D. in Political Science).
      iii, 604p. Order copies from the Library Photographic
      Service, General Library, University of California at
      Berkeley. Related publication by the author: Ideology
      and Culture: An Introduction to the Dialectic of Contem-
      porary Chinese Politics (New York: Harper-Row, 1973.
      xiii, 300p. [Harper's comparative government series]).

1377 AUSTIN, Willis. *Mao Tse-tung's Theory of War as an In-
      strument for Social Change.* United States International
      University, 1972 (Ph.D.). 186p. DAI 33, no.3

(Sept. 1972): 1249-A; UM 72-23,484.

1378   CUMMINS, Howard Wallace. *Mao Tse-tung: A Value Analysis.*
Oregon, 1972 (Ph.D. in Political Science). 106p. DAI
33, no.9 (Mar. 1973): 5247-A; UM 73-7876. Related
publication by the author: Mao, Hsiao, Churchill and
Montgomery: Personal Values and Decision Making (Beverly
Hills: Sage Publications, 1973. 63p. [Sage professional
papers in international studies, series no.02-021]).

1379   WHITEHEAD, Raymond Leslie. *A Christian's Inquiry into
the Struggle-Ethic in the Thought of Mao Tse-tung.*
Union Theological Seminary in the City of New York,
1972 (Th.D. in Christian Ethics). 348p. DAI 33, no.11
(May 1973): 6445-46-A; UM 73-7274. Published as Love
and Struggle in Mao's Thought (Maryknoll, N.Y.: Orbis
Books, 1977. xx, 166p.).

1380   MARSHALL, James Allen. *The New Guerrillas: Public Administration in the New Industrial State.* Southern
California, 1973 (Ph.D. in Public Administration).
621p. DAI 34, no.7 (Jan. 1974): 4381-A; UM 73-31,654.
Presents a model for change based in part on an examination of guerrilla warfare and the basic concepts of
Mao Tse-tung.

1381   BRIGGS, Horace Wilkinson (II). *Mao Tse-tung's Revolu-
tionized "New Man": The Route to Power and Communism.*
Fletcher School of Law and Diplomacy, 1974 (Ph.D.).
vi, 1087p. Order copies from the Edwin Ginn Library,
Fletcher School of Law and Diplomacy, Tufts University.

1382   DOUSE, George Hunt. *A Comparative Study of Conflict
Theory.* Maryland, 1974 (Ph.D. in Government and Politics). 341p. DAI 35, no.7 (Jan. 1975): 4652-53-A;
UM 75-1800. Examines the political theory of conflict
of 6 theoreticians including Mao Tse-tung.

1383   GANDARIAS, Jon Daniel. *Division and Unity: The Thought
of Mao Tse-tung.* Columbia, 1974 (Ph.D. in Political
Science). 505p. DAI 35, no.6 (Dec. 1974): 3827-A; UM
74-28,497. Examines Mao's political thought from the
standpoint of its Marxist-Leninist logic and outlook.

1384   BLACK, David Frank. *A Comparative Analysis of the Role
of the Peasantry in Marxist Theories of Social Change.*
Michigan, 1975 (Ph.D. in Political Science). 327p.
DAI 36, no.10 (Apr. 1976): 6910-A; UM 76-9346. Includes Mao Tse-tung's view of the peasantry.

1385   FILSOUFI, Fariborz. *Revisionism and the Contemporary*

Problems in Marxist Philosophy. California (Los Angeles), 1975 (Ph.D. in Sociology). 197p. DAI 36, no.10 (Apr. 1976): 7005-06-A; UM 75-25,196. Deals in part with Maoist thought.

Republic of China

1386   KIM, Kwang-Woong. *Politics, Administration, and National Development*. Hawaii, 1971 (Ph.D. in Political Science). 220p. DAI 33, no.3 (Sept. 1972): 1207-A; UM 72-24,373. A "multimethodological" study of 28 developing countries including the Republic of China.

1387   CHANG, Wen-lung. *A Study of Political Coercion in Urban Taiwan*. Northwestern, 1972 (Ph.D. in Sociology). 151p. DAI 38, no.1 (July 1977): 487-88-A; UM 77-13,836.

1388   LERMAN, Arthur Jay. *Political, Traditional, and Modern Economic Groups, and the Taiwan Provincial Assembly*. Princeton, 1972 (Ph.D. in Political Science). 506p. DAI 33, no.10 (Apr. 1973): 5794-95-A; UM 73-9623.

1389   CHIANG, Jan-kwei. *Perceptions and Patterns of Bureaucratic Behavior in a Municipal Administration*. Michigan, 1973 (Ph.D. in Political Science). 277p. DAI 36, no.2 (Aug. 1975): 1083-A; UM 75-10,358. On the Taipei municipal government.

1390   HEINLEIN, Joseph J., Jr. *Political Warfare: The Chinese Nationalist Model*. American, 1974 (Ph.D. in International Studies). 687p. DAI 35, no.8 (Feb. 1975): 5480-81-A; UM 75-4703. On the political warfare system in the Chinese Nationalist armed forces from its inception in 1924 to the 1970s.

1391   WINCKLER, Edwin Arthur. *The Politics of Regional Development in Northern Taiwan: Case Studies and Organizational Analysis*. Harvard, 1974 (Ph.D. in Political Science). xxiii, 640p. Available at the Harvard University Archives, Pusey Library, call no.HU 90.10690.

1392   JACOBS, Jeffrey Bruce. *Local Politics in Rural Taiwan: A Field Study of Kuan-hsi, Face and Faction in Matsu Township*. Columbia, 1975 (Ph.D. in Political Science). 403p. DAI 36, no.12 (June 1976): 8271-A; UM 76-12,747.

1393   LEE, John Mingsien. *Political Change in Taiwan, 1949-1974: A Study of the Processes of Democratic and Integrative Change with Focus on the Role of Government*. Tennessee, 1974 (Ph.D. in Political Science). 275p.

DAI 36, no.11 (May 1976): 7607-08-A; UM 76-11,064.

1394   SOHN, Yang-Ho. *The Effect of Socioeconomic Develop-
ment and Political Processes on the Public Policy: A
Study of Fifteen Asian Countries.* Mississippi, 1975
(Ph.D. in Political Science). 204p. DAI 36, no.11
(May 1976): 7613-A; UM 76-11,741. The Republic of
China is included.

PSYCHOLOGY AND SOCIAL PSYCHOLOGY

See also the section "Overseas Chinese Communities"
(pp.161-81).

1395   LI, Chen-king Fun Anita. *Parental Attitudes, Test
Anxiety and Achievement Motivation: A Study of Fifth
and Sixth Grade Children.* Hong Kong, 1971 (Ph.D. in
Psychology). 245p. The subjects were residents of
Hong Kong.

1396   LIN, Chen-shan. *An Experimental Study of the Visual
Eidetic Imagery of Chinese School Children.* Hawaii,
1971 (Ph.D. in Educational Psychology). 155p. DAI 33,
no.3 (Sept. 1972): 1025-A; UM 72-24,375. The subjects
were elementary school children in Taipei.

1397   CHAN, Wing-cheung Jimmy. *A Study of the Relation of
Parent-Child Interaction and Certain Psychological Attributes of Adolescents in Hong Kong.* London, 1972
(Ph.D. in Educational Psychology, Institute of Education). 376p.

1398   CHIEN, Maw-fa. *A Comparative Study of Adjustment Problems among American and Chinese College Students.*
Northern Colorado, 1973 (Ed.D. in Psychology, Counseling
and Guidance). 163p. DAI 34, no.5 (Nov. 1973):
2380-81-A; UM 73-26,488. Compares students at the
National Taiwan Normal University and at the University
of Northern Colorado.

1399   HESS-BEHRENS, Betsy. *The Development of the Concept
of Space as Observed in Children's Drawings: A Cross-
National/Cross-Cultural Study (Based on Piaget's Theories).* California (Berkeley), 1973 (Ph.D. in Education). x, 269p. Order copies from the Library Photographic Service, General Library, University of California at Berkeley. Includes school children in Hong
Kong.

1400 HUANG, Lily Chu. *A Cross-Cultural Study of Conformity in Americans and Chinese*. New Mexico, 1973 (Ph.D. in Education). 110p. DAI 34, no.11 (May 1974): 5714-B; UM 74-11,788. Based on studies in Taipei and Albuquerque, New Mexico.

1401 HWANG, Chien-hou. *A Comparative Study of Social Attitudes of Adolescents in Glasgow and in Taipei*. Glasgow, 1973 (Ph.D. in Psychology). vii, 219p.

1402 HUANG, Chin-li. *Career Maturity of American and Chinese Students*. Rochester, 1974 (Ed.D. in Guidance). 293p. DAI 35, no.4 (Oct. 1974): 2133-34-A; UM 74-20,625. Elementary and high school students in Taipei and in Monroe County, New York.

1403 LOW, Daphne Nai-ling. *Dimensions in the Identity Profile of the American Educated Hong Kong Chinese*. Illinois Institute of Technology, 1974 (Ph.D. in Psychology). 167p. DAI 35, no.5 (Nov. 1974): 2408-09-B; UM 74-23,989.

1404 TSENG, Anthony Tsai-pen. *The Biographical Inventory: A Cross-Cultural Study*. [Portions of the text in Chinese]. Utah, 1974 (Ph.D. in Psychology). 169p. DAI 35, no.4 (Oct. 1974): 1960-61-B; UM 74-21,359. Tested the cross-cultural effectiveness of the Alpha Biographical Inventory among Taiwan university students.

1405 CHANG-YU, Wan Ching (Johanna). *The Effect of Controllability of a Task on Children's Performance*. Cornell, 1975 (Ph.D. in Human Development and Family Studies). 112p. DAI 36, no.9 (Mar. 1976): 4750-51-B; UM 76-5910. As part of the author's research project, American children were asked to describe a set of Chinese characters as clearly as possible.

1406 CHEN, Tse-pu. *The Acceptability of Behavioristic and Phenomenological Schools of Counseling Psychology in Chinese Higher Education*. Brigham Young, 1975 (Ed.D. in Educational Psychology). 139p. DAI 36, no.11 (May 1976): 7286-A; UM 76-9827. Deals with the Republic of China.

1407 CHEN, Ying-hau. *A Study of Attitude, Personal Characteristics, and Personality Traits of Outstanding Teachers in Taiwan, the Republic of China*. Northern Colorado, 1975 (Ed.D. in Psychology, Counseling and Guidance). 109p. DAI 36, no.7 (Jan. 1976): 3670-71-B; UM 76-187. Chen's subjects consisted of 223 elementary school teachers.

1408 YEE, Leland Yin. *Classification Behavior: Across Age,
Culture, and Task*. Hawaii, 1975 (Ph.D. in Psychology).
x, 164p. Order copies from the Interlibrary Loan Department, University of Hawaii Library. Studies Chinese culture.

RELIGION AND PHILOSOPHY

General and Miscellaneous Studies

See also entries 3, 4, 19, 52, 113, 124, 391, 952, 1036,
1205, and 1312, as well as the section--within the Appendix--
entitled "Religion and Philosophy" (pp.252-56). For political
philosophy, *also see* the "Thought of Mao Tse-tung" (pp.193-95).

1409 AHERN, Emily Martin. *The Cult of the Dead in Ch'inan,
Taiwan: A Study of Ancestor Worship in a Four-Lineage
Community*. Cornell, 1971 (Ph.D. in Anthropology).
363p. DAI 32, no.12 (June 1972): 6794-95-B; UM 72-15,384.
Published as The Cult of the Dead in a Chinese Village
(Stanford: Stanford University Press, 1973. xiv, 280p.).

1410 FRIMODIG, Frank Victor. *A Philosophical Examination of
Recent Educational Criticism Considering the Possible
Application of Themes in Chinese Philosophy*. Clare-
mont, 1971 (Ph.D. in Education). 151p. DAI 32, no.2
(Aug. 1971): 836-A; UM 71-21,679. Deals with major
philosophical themes in Confucianism, Taoism and Ch'an
Buddhism.

1411 SUN, George Chih-hsin. *Chinese Metaphysics and Whitehead*. Southern Illinois, 1971 (Ph.D. in Philosophy).
241p. DAI 33, no.2 (Aug. 1972): 789-90-A; UM 72-22,491.
Interprets Chinese metaphysics in conceptual terms
worked out by the philosopher Alfred North Whitehead
(1861-1947).

1412 HAGLAND, Åke. *Contact and Conflict: Studies in Con-
temporary Religious Attitudes among Chinese People*.
Lund, 1972 (Fil.dr.). DAI 37, no.2 (Winter 1976/77):
Vol.C--entry no.1/1568c. Published as Contact...People
(Lund: Gleerup, 1972. 248p.). Studies Chinese in the
People's Republic of China and in Penang, Malaysia.

1413 PARK, O'Hyun. *Oriental Ideas in Recent Religious
Thought*. Temple, 1972 (Ph.D. in Religion). 268p.
DAI 33, no.1 (July 1972): 394-A; UM 72-17,709. Published as Oriental...Thought (Lakemont, Ga.: CSA Press,
1974. 206p.). Deals with Confucianism, Taoism, Buddhism and Hinduism.

1414 TATÁR, Mária Magdolna. *A mongol népvallási szövegek prolemái. A hegyek és obók kultusza.* [Hungarian: Problems of the Mongolian Folk-Religious Texts: The Cult of the Mountains and the Obos.] Eötvös Lóránd Tudományegyetem, 1972 (Dr.U. in Inner Asian Studies).

1415 THI ANH TO [TO, Thi Anh]. *Eastern and Western Cultural Values: Conflict or Harmony?* United States International University, 1972 (Ph.D. in Human Behavior). 157p. DAI 33, no.4 (Oct. 1972): 1788-A; UM 72-23,507. Includes Buddhism, Confucianism and Taoism.

1416 WARNER, Robert Stephen. *The Methodology of Max Weber's Comparative Studies.* California (Berkeley), 1972 (Ph.D. in Sociology). ix, 346p. Order copies from the Library Photographic Service, General Library, University of California at Berkeley. Includes Weber's writings about China within this study of his sociology of religion.

1417 WILE, Douglas David. *T'an Ssu-t'ung: His Life and Major Work, the Jên hsüeh.* Wisconsin, 1972 (Ph.D. in East Asian Languages and Literature). 659p. DAI 33, no.7 (Jan. 1973): 3607-A; UM 72-23,769. On an eclectic, late Ch'ing philosopher and reformer.

1418 HUMPHREY, Caroline. *Magical Drawings in the Religion of the Buryat.* Cambridge, 1973 (Ph.D. in Social Anthropology). 408p. On a people of Mongol descent in eastern Siberia.

1419 MARTINSON, Paul Varo. *Pao Order and Redemption: Perspectives on Chinese Religion and Society Based on a Study of the Chin P'ing Mei.* Chicago, 1973 (Ph.D. in History of Religions). viii, 497p. Order copies from the Photoduplication Department, Joseph Regenstein Library, University of Chicago.

1420 MEYER, Jeffrey Frederick. *Peking as a Sacred City.* Chicago, 1973 (Ph.D., Divinity School). iii, 225p. Order copies from the Photoduplication Department, Joseph Regenstein Library, University of Chicago.

1421 PAN, Yun-Tong. *Philosophical Foundations of Chinese Political Ethics.* Massachusetts, 1973 (Ph.D. in Political Science). 193p. DAI 34, no.8 (Feb. 1974): 5273-A; UM 74-2025. Analyzes Confucian, Neo-Confucian, Moist, Taoist, Legalist, Socialist and Communist writings.

1422 BAITY, Philip Chesley. *Religion in a Chinese Town.*

California (Berkeley), 1974 (Ph.D. in Anthropology).
ix, 307p. Order copies from the Library Photographic
Service, General Library, University of California at
Berkeley.

1423 DELABY, Laurence. *Matériaux pour une bibliographie
analytique des ouvrages sur le chamanisme des Tungus et
des peuples apparentés.* [French: Materials for an Analytical Bibliography of the Works on the Shamanism of
the Tungus and Related Peoples.] Paris V (René Descartes), 1974 (Doctorat de 3e cycle ès lettres).

1424 HSUANG, Joseph Ran-Fun. *East-West Cultural Systems: A
Chinese Translation.* California Institute of Asian
Studies, 1974 (Ph.D. in Comparative Philosophy). 240p.
DAI 35, no.5 (Nov. 1974): 3057-A; UM 74-24,547. In-
cludes a summary of the major concepts in Chinese cul-
ture.

1425 HARRELL, Clyde Stevan. *Belief and Unbelief in a Taiwan
Village.* Stanford, 1974 (Ph.D. in Anthropology). 175p.
DAI 35, no.9 (Mar. 1975): 5591-A; UM 75-6860. On a
Hokkien-speaking village.

1426 OEI, Lee Tjiek. *Hu Shih's Philosophy of Man as Influenced by John Dewey's Instrumentalism.* Fordham, 1974
(Ph.D. in Philosophy). 304p. DAI 35, no.3 (Sept. 1974):
1706-07-A; UM 74-19,681.

1427 SEAMAN, Gary Worth. *Temple Organization in a Chinese
Village.* Cornell, 1974 (Ph.D. in Anthropology). 179p.
DAI 35, no.6 (Dec. 1974): 3201-A; UM 74-26,314. On the
historical development of a religious cult in a Chinese
village (with focus on Taiwan).

1428 DENMARK, Ted Howard. *Approaches to Self-Realization in
Adult Education through Meditation.* California (Berkeley), 1975 (Ph.D. in Education). 451p. DAI 37, no.1
(July 1976): 96-A; UM 76-15,158. Deals in part with the
occult philosophy and esoteric psychology of the Tibetan
teacher Djwhal Khul.

1429 NOUMOFF, Samuel Joseph. *The Philosophic Basis of the
Theory of Social Transformation in China.* New York,
1975 (Ph.D. in Politics). 313p. DAI 36, no.6 (Dec.
1975): 3991-92-A; UM 75-28,572. On some of the philosophic assumptions underlying the ideological premises
of Marxism as practiced by the Chinese Communists.

1430 WYCOFF, William Alfred, Jr. *The New Rationalism of
Fung Yu-lan.* Columbia, 1975 (Ph.D. in East Asian Languages and Cultures). 345p. DAI 36, no.6 (Dec. 1975):

3777-A; UM 75-27,475. On the philosophic system propounded by this leading philosopher (1895-) in such
works as Hsin li hsüeh.

Ancient Chinese Religion and Philosophy
(General Studies)

See also entry 34.

1431   BILSKY, Lester James. *The State Religion of Ancient
       China*. Washington (Seattle), 1971 (Ph.D. in History).
       477p. DAI 32, no.5 (Nov. 1971): 2581-82-A; UM 71-28,381.
       Studies the religious ceremonies which comprised State
       worship and their relationships to political practices,
       ca.1100 B.C.-87 B.C.

1432   CHAN, P. *Il rapporto tra Dio e l'uomo nella cultura
       antica cinese*. [Italian: The Relationship between God
       and Man in Ancient Chinese Culture.] Pontificia Uni-
       versitas Urbaniana, 1971.   DAI 37, no.2 (Winter
       1976/77): Vol.C--entry no.1/1590c.

1433   RHIE, Tyong Bok. *Die Problematik des Grundgedankens in
       der alten chinesischen Philosophie*. [German: The Prob-
       lems of the Fundamental Idea in Ancient Chinese Philos-
       ophy.] München, 1971 (Dr., Philosophische Fakultät).
       Published as Die Problematik...Philosophie (München,
       1970. 155p.).

1434   HANSEN, Chad Deloy. *Philosophy of Language and Logic
       in Ancient China*. Michigan, 1972 (Ph.D. in Philosophy).
       175p. DAI 34, no.1 (July 1973): 359-A; UM 73-11,139.
       Covers Confucianism, Taoism and Mohism.

1435   SPROUL, Barbara Chamberlain. *Prolegomena to the Study
       of Creation Myths*. Columbia, 1972 (Ph.D. in Religion).
       357p. DAI 35, no.7 (Jan. 1975): 4687-88-A; UM 74-29,667.
       Includes coverage of China.

1436   HART, James Pinckney, Jr. *The Philosophy of the Chou Yü*.
       Washington (Seattle), 1973 (Ph.D. in Asian Languages
       and Literature). 423p. DAI 34, no.7 (Jan. 1974): 4205-A;
       UM 74-806. The Chou Yü, the first 3 chapters of the
       Kuo Yü, is a series of chronologically arranged speeches
       of political advice or criticism from ca.1000-500 B.C.

1437   DAOR, Dan. *The Yin Wenzi and the Renaissance of Phi-
       losophy in Wei-Jin China*. London, 1974 (Ph.D. in Arts,
       School of Oriental and African Studies). iv, 199p. On
       the Yin Wen-tzu during the 3rd and 4th centuries A.D.

1438   IMBER, Alan. *Kuo Yü: An Early Chinese Text and Its Relationship with the Tso Chuan.* Stockholm, 1975 (Akad. avh.). 357p.

Buddhism

Chinese Buddhism

See also entries 47, 1056, 1100, 1501, and 1772.

1439   OVERMEYER, Daniel Lee. *Folk-Buddhist Sects: A Structure in the History of Chinese Religions.* Chicago, 1971 (Ph.D., Divinity School). 348p. Order copies from the Photoduplication Department, Joseph Regenstein Library, University of Chicago.

1440   CISSELL, Kathryn Ann Adelsperger. *The Pi-ch'iu-ni chuan: Biographies of Famous Nuns from 317-516 C.E.* Wisconsin, 1972 (Ph.D. in East Asian Languages and Literature). 330p. DAI 33, no.9 (Mar. 1973): 5274-A; UM 72-31,668. On a Chinese Buddhist work collected and edited by the monk Pao-ch'ang ca.516 A.D.

1441   DAYE, Douglas Dunsmore. *Metalogical Studies in Sixth Century Buddhist Proto-Metalogic from the Sanskrit and Chinese Texts of the Nyāyapraveśa: Or Unpacking Ordinary Sanskrit.* Wisconsin, 1972 (Ph.D. in Buddhist Studies). 221p. DAI 33, no.8 (Feb. 1973): 4469-70-A; UM 72-31,526.

1442   HELD, Axel. *Der buddhistische Mönch Yen-ts'ung (557-610) und seine Übersetzungstheorie.* [German: The Buddhist Monk Yen-ts'ung (557-610) and His Theory of Translation.] Köln, 1972 (Dr., Philosophische Fakultät). Published as Der buddhistische...Übersetzungstheorie (Köln, 1972. 150p.). On translating the Tripiṭaka.

1443   HUYNH VAN HAI. *T'ai-Hiu (1889-1947) et ses idées concernant la réforme du bouddhisme chinois.* [French: T'ai-Hsü (1889-1947) and His Ideas Regarding the Reform of Chinese Buddhism.] Paris IV (Paris-Sorbonne), 1972 (Doctorat de 3e cycle ès études extrême-orientales). vi, 232p. A copy is available at the Bibliothèque de la Sorbonne, library catalogue no. I 1890-4°.

1444   SCHMIDT-GLINTZER, Helwig. *Das Hung-ming chi, eine Sammlung zur Verbreitung und Erhellung des Buddhismus in China, zusammengestellt in der südlichen Hauptstadt von dem Mönch Shih Seng-yu (445-518) zur Zeit der Herrschaft des Kaisers Wu-ti von Liang.* [German: The Hung

ming chi: A Collection for the Dissemination and Clari-
fication of Buddhism in China, Compiled in the Southern
Capital by the Monk Shih Seng-yu (445-518) during the
Reign of Emperor Wu-ti of Liang.] München, 1972 (Dr.,
Philosophische Fakultät). Published as Das Hung-ming
chi und die Aufnahme des Buddhismus in China (Wiesbaden: Steiner, 1976. viii, 212p. [Münchener ostasiatische Studien; Bd.12]).

1445 CORLESS, Roger Jonathan. *T'an-luan's Commentary on the*
Pure Land Discourse: An Annotated Translation and Soteri-
ological Analysis of the Wang-shêng-lun Chu (T.1819).
Wisconsin, 1973 (Ph.D. in Buddhist Studies). 356p.
DAI 34, no.9 (Mar. 1974): 6093-A; UM 73-27,095. On the
first major work of Chinese Pure Land Buddhism by Shih
T'an-luan (ca.488-554 A.D.).

1446 GREENBLATT, Kristin Yü. *Yün-ch'i Chu-hung: The Career*
of a Ming Buddhist Monk. Columbia, 1973 (Ph.D. in Religion). 445p. DAI 34, no.6 (Dec. 1973): 3526-A; UM
73-29,832.

1447 PAS, Julian Francis, S.T.L. *Shan-tao's Commentary on*
the Amitāyur-Buddhānusmṛti-sūtra. McMaster, 1973 (Ph.D.
in Religion). xvi, 626p. DAI 35, no.8 (Feb. 1975):
5518-A; Order copies directly from the Canadian Theses
Division, National Library of Canada at Ottawa; available
only in microfiche format. Studies this philosopher's
views on Pure Land thought and practice during the 7th
century.

1448 CHENG, Hsueh-li. *An Expository and Critical Study of*
Mādhyamika Philosophy from Chinese Sources. Wisconsin,
1974 (Ph.D. in Philosophy). 335p. DAI 35, no.11 (May
1975): 7346-47-A; UM 75-5925. Based on a study of the
Middle Treatise, the Twelve Gate Treatise, and the
Hundred Treatise.

1449 PAUL, Diana Mary. *A Prolegomena to the Śrīmālādevī sūtra*
and the Tathāgatagarbha Theory: The Role of Women in
Buddhism. Wisconsin, 1974 (Ph.D. in Buddhist Studies).
299p. DAI 35, no.10 (Apr. 1975): 6805-A; UM 74-30,123.
Based on a study of the extant Chinese recensions of
this 2nd-3rd century A.D. text.

1450 BROUGHTON, Jeffrey Lyle. *Kuei-feng Tsung-mi: The Con-*
vergence of Ch'an and the Teachings. Columbia, 1975
(Ph.D. in East Asian Languages and Cultures). 319p.
DAI 36, no.12 (June 1976): 8125-A; UM 76-13,124. On a
9th century Chinese Buddhist exegete and Ch'an master.

1451 CLEARY, Thomas Francis. *Sayings and Doings of Pai-chang*

203

Huai-hai, Ch'an Master of Great Wisdom. Harvard, 1975
(Ph.D. in East Asian Languages and Civilizations). 165p.
Available at the Harvard University Archives, Pusey Li-
brary, call no.HU 90.10728.

1452 EPSTEIN, Ronald B. *The Śuraṅgama-Sūtra with Tripiṭaka
Master Hsüan-hua's Commentary An Elementary Explanation
of Its General Meaning: A Preliminary Study and Partial
Translation.* California (Berkeley), 1975 (Ph.D. in Buddhist Studies). vii, 428p. Order copies from the Library Photographic Service, General Library, University of
California at Berkeley.

1453 GRAHAM, Thomas Edward. *The Reconstruction of Popular
Buddhism in Medieval China Using Selected Pien-wen from
Tun-huang.* Iowa, 1975 (Ph.D. in Religion). 386p. DAI
36, no.4 (Oct. 1975): 2270-71-A; UM 75-23,038.

1454 KIM, T.-J. *A Comparative Study between the Mysticism of
Saint John of the Cross and the Mysticism of the Zen Master, Hui-neng.* Pontificia Universitas Gregoriana [Rome],
1975 (Ph.D.). 212p. DAI 37, no.1 (Autumn 1976): Vol.C
--entry no.1/199c. A reference copy is available at the
Gregorian Library, catalogue no. II.4716.

1455 LAI, Whalen Wai-lun. *The Awakening of Faith in Mahayana
(Ta-ch'eng ch'i-hsin lun): A Study of the Unfolding of
Sinitic Mahayana Motifs.* Harvard, 1975 (Ph.D. in the Study
of Religion). viii, 269p. Available at the Harvard Uni-
versity Archives, Pusey Library, call no.HU 90.10975.10.
Deals with China during the sixth century.

1456 SEAH, Ingram Samuel. *Shan-tao, His Life and Teachings.*
Princeton Theological Seminary, 1975 (Ph.D. in Compara-
tive Religion). 420p. DAI 36, no.4 (Oct. 1975): 2280-A;
UM 75-23,166.

Mongolian and Uighur Buddhism

See also entries 974 and 1462.

1457 MOSES, Larry William. *Revolutionary Mongolia Chooses a
Faith: Lamaism or Leninism.* Indiana, 1972 (Ph.D. in
Uralic and Altaic Studies). 212p. DAI 33, no.6 (Dec.
1972): 2865-A; UM 72-30,435. Studies the eradication of
the Buddhist Church during the 1920s and the 1930s.

1458 TEZCAN, Semih. *Das uigurische Insadi-Sūtra; mit 69 Faks.*
[German: The Uighur Insadi-Sūtra: With 69 Facsimiles.]
Göttingen, 1974 (Dr., Philosophische Fakultät). Published
as Das uigurische Insadi-Sūtra; mit 69 Faks (Berlin: Akademie-Verlag, 1974. 107, lxix p. [Schriften zur Geschichte

und Kultur des Alten Orients; 6: Berliner Turfantexte,
3]).

Tibetan Buddhism

See also the section within the Appendix entitled "Religion
and Philosophy" (pp.252-56).

1459   BERZIN, Alexander. LAM.RIM.MAN.NGAG: A Standard Inter-
       mediate Level Textbook of the Graded Courses to En-
       lightenment: Selected Materials from the Indo-Tibetan
       Mahāyāna Buddhist Textual and Oral Traditions (Sections
       I-4B2B). Harvard, 1972 (Ph.D. in Far Eastern Lan-
       guages and Sanskrit and Indian Studies). xxvi, 436p.
       Available at the Harvard University Archives, Pusey
       Library, call no.HU 90.10109.10

1460   THURMAN, Robert Alexander Farrar. Golden Speech: A
       Portrait of Sumati Kirti, Presenting English Transla-
       tions of the Eloquence-Essences, The Smaller (Complete)
       and the Greater (Chapters I - III). Harvard, 1972
       (Ph.D. in Sanskrit and Indian Studies). iii, 401p.
       Available at the Harvard University Archives, Pusey
       Library, call no.HU 90.10283.5. Tibetan Buddhist tract
       of Sumati Kirti (1357-1420).

1461   VAN TUYL, Charles Don. An Analysis of Chapter Twenty-
       Eight of the Hundred Thousand Songs of Mila-Raspa, a
       Buddhist Poet and Saint of Tibet. Indiana, 1972 (Ph.D.
       in Uralic and Altaic Studies). 175p. DAI 32, no.12
       (June 1972): 6869-A; UM 72-15,933.

1462   FRYE, Stanley Newell. The Sutra of Forty-Two Sections.
       Indiana, 1973 (Ph.D. in Uralic and Altaic Studies).
       363p. DAI 34, no.3 (Sept. 1973): 1240-A; UM 73-19,738.
       A study and translation of this Buddhist work based
       upon an examination of Tibetan and Mongol texts.

1463   HOPKINS, Paul Jeffrey. Meditation on Emptiness. Wis-
       consin, 1973 (Ph.D. in Buddhist Studies). 1165p. DAI
       34, no.7 (Jan. 1974): 4392-93-A; UM 73-21,160. Explains
       the modes of meditation on emptiness in the Prāsangika-
       Mādhyamika system of Buddhist philosophy as interpreted
       by the Gelukpa order of Tibetan Buddhism.

1464   RAY, Reginald Alden. Mandala Symbolism in Tantric
       Buddhism. Chicago, 1973 (Ph.D., Divinity School).
       446p. Order copies from the Photoduplication Depart-
       ment, Joseph Regenstein Library, University of Chicago.
       Includes coverage of Tibet.

1465   EIMER, Helmut R. H. H. *Berichte über das Leben des Dī-pamkaraśrījñāna. Eine Untersuchung der Quellen.* [German: Reports on the Life of Dīpamkaraśrījñāna: An Investigation of the Sources.] Bonn, 1974 (Dr.phil., Indologisches Seminar und Seminar für Sprach- und Kulturwissenschaft Zentralasiens). 350p. Studies the development of a biographical/hagiographical tradition in Tibet. Dīpamkaraśrījñāna is the name given to the 11th century Indo-Tibetan monk and saint Atiśa who established Buddhism as a religion in Tibet.

1466   BARKER, David Read. *Lama Chöpa: A Ritual Text of the Gelugpa Sect in Tibet.* New School for Social Research, 1975 (Ph.D. in Anthropology). 226p. DAI 36, no.5 (Nov. 1975): 2935-A; UM 75-25,442. On the <u>Offerings to the Lama(s)</u>, an important text of Buddhist poetry written by Lobzang Chökyi Gyaltsen, the first Panchen Lama.

1467   CARTIER, Robert Raymond. *Syncretism in a Sanskritic Religion.* Rice, 1975 (Ph.D. in Behavioral Science). 154p. DAI 36, no.4 (Oct. 1975): 2293-A; UM 75-22,001. Focuses on Tibetan Buddhism.

1468   JASTRAM, Judy Ann. *Three Chapters from the <u>Gandavyūha Sūtra</u>: A Critical Edition of the Sanskrit and Tibetan Texts of the Youth Sudhana's Visits to the Bhikṣus Meghaśrī, Sāgaramegha, and Supratiṣṭhita, with English Translation and Commentary.* California (Berkeley), 1975 (Ph.D. in South and Southeast Asian Studies). 442p. DAI 37, no.1 (July 1976): 321-A; UM 76-15,237.

1469   MAXWELL, Natalie. *Great Compassion: The Chief Cause of Bodhisattvas.* Wisconsin, 1975 (Ph.D. in Buddhist Studies). 394p. DAI 36, no.11 (May 1976): 7485-A; UM 76-2495. Focuses on the beliefs of the Tibet Gelug sect founded in the 1400s by Tsong-kha-pa.

1470   ROBINSON, James Burnell. *The Eighty-Four Siddhas.* Wisconsin, 1975 (Ph.D. in Buddhist Studies). 511p. DAI 37, no.1 (July 1976): 403-04-A; UM 76-8607. Contains a translation from the Tibetan of the <u>Caturasiti-siddha-pravrtti</u>, a description of their iconography, analyses of their stories, and lists of their works in the Tibetan canon.

1471   ZIMMERMANN, Heinz. *Die <u>Subhasita-ratna-karandaka-katha</u> (dem Āryaśūra zugeschrieben) und ihre tibetische Übersetzung. Ein Vergleich zur Darlegung der Irrtumsrisiken bei der Auswertung tibetischer Übersetzungen.* [German: The <u>Subhasita-ratna-karandaka-katha</u> (Ascribed to Āryaśūra) and Its Tibetan Translation: A Comparison Showing

the Risks of Error in the Evaluation of Tibetan Transla-
tions.] Basel, 1975 (Dr., Philosophisch-historische
Fakultät). Published as Die Subhasita...Übersetzungen
(Wiesbaden: Harrassowitz, 1975. vi, 273p. [Freiburger
Beiträge zur Indologie, 8]).

Christianity

See also entries 410, 418, 439, 445, 466, 513, 1262, 1263,
1302, 1485, 1555, 1656, and 1774, as well as the sections on
Missions and Missionaries in China during the late Ch'ing period (pp.85-86) and the Republican period (pp.93-94).

1472 CHAO YUN SIA, J. *Nova Methodus Evangelizationis in Si-
      nis*. [Latin: A New Method of Evangelization in China.]
      Pontificia Universitas Urbaniana, 1971. DAI 37, no.2
      (Winter 1976/77): Vol.C--entry no.1/1563c.

1473 NG, Lee-ming. *Christianity and Social Change: The Case
      of China, 1920-1950*. Princeton Theological Seminary,
      1971 (Th.D. in Christianity and Society). 286p. DAI 32,
      no.5 (Nov. 1971): 2790-91-A; UM 71-29,245.

1474 RICHARDSON, William Jerome. *Christianity in Taiwan under
      Japanese Rule, 1895-1945*. St. John's, 1972 (Ph.D. in
      Asian History). 235p. DAI 33, no.2 (Aug. 1972):
      705-06-A; UM 72-21,731.

1475 SILVA, John William. *A Study of the Theology of Church
      Government and the Practice of Church Administration,
      with Special Reference to the Churches in Asia*. Edin-
      burgh, 1972 (Ph.D. in Divinity). xiv, 495, xv p. Hong
      Kong and the Republic of China are among the Asian coun-
      tries covered.

1476 LEUNG, Peter. *The Response of Asian Christians and the
      East African Conference to the Quests of East Asia in
      the Period 1945-1968*. St. Andrews, 1973 (Ph.D. in The-
      ology). 369p. On the response of Christians in Hong
      Kong, the Republic of China, and other countries to the
      problems of nationhood and socio-political dislocation.

1477 HASS, Ilse. *Die protestantische Christenheit in der
      Volksrepublik China und die Chinaberichterstattung in
      der deutschen evangelischen Missionsliteratur*. [German:
      Protestant Christians in the People's Republic of China
      and the Reports about China in the German Evangelical
      Missionary Literature.] Hamburg, 1974 (Dr., Fachbereich
      Evangelische Theologie). Published as Die protestantische

...Missionsliteratur (Hamburg, 1974. xvi, 314p.).

1478   FRED, Morris Aaron. *Ritual as Ideology in an Indigenous Chinese Christian Church*. California (Berkeley), 1975 (Ph.D. in Anthropology). iii, 248p. Order copies from the Library Photographic Service, General Library, University of California at Berkeley.

1479   SPALATIN, C. A. *Matteo Ricci and a Confucian Christianity: A Study Based on Ricci's* Book of 25 Paragraphs. Pontificia Universitas Gregoriana, 1975 (Th.D.). 350p. DAI 37, no.1 (Autumn 1976): Vol.C--entry no.1/286c. A reference copy is available at the Gregorian Library, catalogue number II.4686. An excerpt has been published in Waegwan (Korea), 1975 (101p.).

Confucianism and Neo-Confucianism

See also entries 118, 433, 447, and 1033.

1480   CHAO, Paul Yang-hsiung. *An Examination of the Differences and Similarities of Pragmatism and Confucianism Thought as They Relate to Educational Administration Theory and Practice*. Tennessee, 1971 (Ed.D.). 178p. DAI 32, no.8 (Feb. 1972): 4271-A; UM 72-5421.

1481   CHING, Julia. *To Acquire Wisdom: The "Way" of Wang Yang-ming (1472-1529)*. Australian National, 1971 (Ph.D. in Asian Civilizations). xxvii, 409p. Published as To Acquire...Wang Yang-ming (New York: Columbia University Press, 1976. xxvi, 373p. [Studies in oriental culture, 11] [Oriental monograph series, 16]).

1482   GEDALECIA, David. *Wu Ch'eng: A Neo-Confucian of the Yüan*. Harvard, 1971 (Ph.D. in Far Eastern Languages). 481p. DAI 32, no.6 (Dec. 1971): 3366-A; UM 71-30,156. Also available at the Harvard University Archives, Pusey Library, call no. HU 90.9957.

1483   HSIEH, Shan-yuan. *The Life and Thought of Li Kou (1009-1059)*. Chicago, 1972 (Ph.D. in Far Eastern Languages and Civilizations). 252p. Order copies from the Photoduplication Department, Joseph Regenstein Library, University of Chicago. On a Confucian scholar who opposed the ideas of Mencius.

1484   NAMJOSHI, Suniti Manohar. *Ezra Pound and Reality: A Study of the Metaphysics of the Cantos*. McGill, 1972 (Ph.D. in English). x, 261p. DAI 34, no.2 (Aug. 1973): 785-A; Order copies directly from the Canadian Theses

Division, National Library of Canada at Ottawa; available
only in microfilm format, film no.14518, @ $2.50. Deals
in part with this poet's translations of the writings of
Confucius.

1485 RULE, Paul Anthony. *K'ung-tzu or Confucius? The Jesuit
      Interpretation of Confucianism*. Australian National,
      1972 (Ph.D. in Asian Civilization). viii, 498p. + bib-
      liography.

1486 HSIAO, Hsin-i. *A Study of the Hsiao-ching: With an Em-
      phasis on Its Intellectual Background and Its Problems*.
      Harvard, 1973 (Ph.D. in History and East Asian Languages).
      563p. Available at the Harvard University Archives, Pu-
      sey Library, call no.HU 90.10369.20. On the Classic of
      Filial Piety, one of the thirteen classics that espouses
      Hsün-tzu's form of Confucianism.

1487 MUNGELLO, David Emil. *Leibniz and Confucianism: Failure
      and Future in Ecumenism*. California (Berkeley), 1973
      (Ph.D. in History). 222p. Order copies from the Library
      Photographic Service, General Library, University of Cal-
      ifornia at Berkeley. Published as Leibniz and Confucian-
      ism, the Search for Accord (Honolulu: University Press
      of Hawaii, 1977).

1488 BRAGG, Gerald Ernest. *The Life and Thought of Yen Hsi-
      chai (1635-1704)*. Arizona, 1974 (Ph.D. in Oriental Stud-
      ies). 348p. DAI 35, no.8 (Feb. 1975): 5286-A; UM
      75-4113. Focuses on Yen's Neo-Confucian and Confucian
      views.

1489 CHAO, Stephen Shyong. *Existential Themes in Confucian-
      ism*. De Paul, 1974 (Ph.D. in Philosophy). 199p. DAI
      35, no.5 (Nov. 1974): 3048-49-A; UM 74-23,648.

1490 DAVISON, Joanne Letitia. *The Shaping of a Seventeenth-
      Century Confucian Philospher: The Thought and Environment
      of Li Yung*. Stanford, 1974 (Ph.D. in Asian Languages).
      235p. DAI 35, no.3 (Sept. 1974): 1697-A; UM 74-20,185.

1491 KULLER, Janet Ann Harrington. *Early Confucian Resistance
      to Taoist Thought: A Study of Anti-Taoism in the Hsün
      Tzu*. Chicago, 1974 (Ph.D. in Far Eastern Languages and
      Civilizations). 185p. DAI 36, no.1 (July 1975): 463-A;
      Order copies from the Photoduplication Department, Joseph
      Regenstein Library, University of Chicago.

1492 LIN, Yu-tee. *A Study of Hsuntzu's Philosophy of Educa-
      tion*. Iowa, 1974 (Ph.D. in Education). 124p. DAI 36,
      no.1 (July 1975): 159-60-A; UM 75-13,786.

1493   MIRANDA-GOLLAZ, Eduardo. *Tchoung-Ioung (le juste milieu)
et Wu-Wei (le non-agir) chez Confucius et Lao-Tseu.*
[French: Chung-yung (The Doctrine of the Mean) and Wu-wei
(Non-Action) in the Writings of Confucius and Lao-tzu.]
Caen, 1974 (Doctorat de 3e cycle ès Lettres).

1494   PHAM VAN HIEN, Dominique. *La pensée confucéenne et pla-
tonicienne sur la politique.* [French: Confucian and
Platonic Thought about Politics.] Fribourg, 1974 (Dr.,
Faculté des Lettres). Published as La penseé...poli-
tique (Zürich: Juris-Verlag, 1974. 146p.).

1495   TAIN, Tzey-yueh. *Tung Chung-shu's System of Thought: Its
Sources and Its Influence on Han Scholars.* California
(Los Angeles), 1974 (Ph.D. in Oriental Languages). 314p.
DAI 35, no.8 (Feb. 1975): 5281-A; UM 75-2240. Tung was
an influential 2nd century B.C. "Confucian" scholar and
philosopher.

1496   TAYLOR, Rodney Leon. *The Cultivation of Sagehood as a
Religious Goal in Neo-Confucianism: A Study of Selected
Writings of Kao P'an-lung (1562-1626).* Columbia, 1974
(Ph.D. in Religion). 377p. DAI 35, no.6 (Dec. 1974):
3874-75-A; UM 74-28,538.

1497   PHAM VAN YÊN. *Deux méthodes d'approche du mystère de
Dieu: Confucianisme et Thomas d'Aquin.* [French: Two
Methods for Approaching the Mystery of God: Confucianism
and Thomas Aquinas.] Fribourg, 1975 (Dr., Faculté des
Lettres). 280p.

1498   RAH, Halk Jin. *The Political Relevance of Jen in Early
China and Agape in the Theology of Reinhold Niebuhr.*
Princeton Theological Seminary, 1975 (Ph.D. in Theology).
278p. DAI 36, no.5 (Nov. 1975): 2924-A; UM 75-23,164.
Deals extensively with the writings of Hsün-tzu.

1499   TRINH KIEU. *The Functional and Conflict Orientations in
Oriental Social Thought and Their Consequences on National Development.* Brigham Young, 1975 (Ph.D. in Sociology). 289p. DAI 36, no.3 (Sept. 1975): 1833-A; UM
75-19,838. Deals with Confucian thought through the ages.

Taoism

See also entries 92, 108, 113, 1491, 1493, 1775, 1790, and 1792.

1500   BERGERON, Marie-Ina. *Wang Pi, philosophe du "Non-Avoir."
Etude de la philosophie de Wang Pi, à partir du Tcheou
Yi lio-li, "Introduction sommaire au Tcheou-Yi," avec*

*l'aide des commentaires de Wang Pi sur le Yi king et le
Tao-tö king. Traduction du Tcheou Yi lio-li.* [French:
Wang Pi, Philosopher of Wu-yu (Non-Being). A Study of
the Philosophy of Wang Pi, Based on His Chou i lüeh li
and on His Commentaries on the I-ching and the Tao te
ching. A Translation of the Chou i lüeh li.] Paris IV
(Paris-Sorbonne), 1971 (Doctorat de 3e cycle ès lettres).
225p. A copy is available at the Bibliothèque de la Sorbonne, library catalogue no. I 1594-4°.

1501 BINGHAM, Irwin Drake, Jr. *Communication and the Tao: A
Study of the Communication Theory Implicit in the Taoist
and Buddhist Traditions of China.* Southern Illinois,
1971 (Ph.D. in Speech). 157p. DAI 32, no.9 (Mar. 1972):
5380-A; UM 72-10,233.

1502 DOUB, William Coligny (II). *A Taoist Adept's Quest for
Immortality: A Preliminary Study of the Chou-shih Ming-
t'ung chi by T'ao Hung-ching (A.D. 456-536).* Washington
(Seattle), 1971 (Ph.D. in Asian Languages and Literature).
210p. DAI 32, no.3 (Sept. 1971): 1608-A; UM 71-24,030.

1503 HOMANN, Rolf. *Die wichtigsten Körpergottheiten im Huang-
t'ing ching.* [German: The Most Important Corporeal Dei-
ties in the Huang t'ing ching.] Tübingen, 1971 (Dr.,
Fachbereich Altertums- und Kulturwissenschaft). Published as Die wichtigsten...Huang t'ing ching (Göppingen:
Kümmerle, 1971. 168p. [Göppinger akademische Beiträge,
27]). On a taoist work from the T'ang period.

1504 KOJIMA, Hajime. *Der Text Chuang-tzu (Sōshi) in der Deu-
tung des Philosophen Mitsuji Fukunaga.* [German: The Text
of Chuang-tzu (Japanese: Sōshi) as Interpreted by the
Philosopher Mitsuji Fukunaga (1918-).] Würzburg, 1971
(Dr., Philosophische Fakultät). Published as Der Text...
Mitsuji Fukunaga (Würzburg, 1971. 182p.).

1505 SAILEY, Jay. *The Master Who Preserves His Simplicity: A
Study of the Chinese Philosopher Ko Hung, 283-343 A.D.*
Stanford, 1971 (Ph.D. in Asian Languages). 722p. DAI
32, no.3 (Sept. 1971): 1486-A; UM 71-23,555. Focuses on
the Wai p'ien ("Outside Chapters") of the Pao p'u tzu by
this Taoist thinker.

1506 SASO, Michael Raleigh. *Folk-Religion and Folklore in
Taiwan: A Study of Popular Taoism.* London, 1971 (Ph.D.
in Arts, School of Oriental and African Studies). viii,
261p. Published as Taoism and the Rite of Cosmic Renewal
(Pullman: Washington State University Press, 1972. 120p.).

1507 KANDEL, Barbara. *Wen Tzu. Ein Beitrag zur Problematik
und zum Verständnis eines taoistischen Textes.* [German:

Wen Tzu: A Contribution to the Problems of a Taoist Text
and to Its Understanding.] Wurzbürg, 1972 (Dr., Philosophische Fakultät). Published as Wen Tzu...Textes
(Bern & Frankfurt a.M.: Lang, 1974. vii, 362p. [Würz-
burger Sino-Japonica, 1]).

1508 KAPLAN, Charles David. *Method as Phenomenon: The Case
of the I Ching*. California (Los Angeles), 1973 (Ph.D.
in Sociology). 187p. DAI 34, no.7 (Jan. 1974): 4432-A;
UM 73-32,065.

1509 LIE, Hwa-Sun. *Der Begriff Skandalon im Neuen Testament
und der Wiederkehrgedanke bei Laotse*. [German: The Con-
cept of Skandalon in the New Testament and the Idea of
Return in the Works of Lao-tzu.] Frankfurt, 1973 (Dr.,
Fachbereich Religionswissenschaft). Published as Der Be-
griff...Laotse (Bern & Frankfurt: Lang, 1973. 252p.
[Europäische Hochschulschriften: Reihe 23, Theologie;
Bd.24]).

1510 McCREERY, John Linwood. *The Symbolism of Popular Taoist
Magic*. Cornell, 1973 (Ph.D. in Anthropology). 258p.
DAI 34, no.10 (Apr. 1974): 4802-B; UM 74-6319. Formu-
lates a structural analysis of several rituals that con-
stitute the repertoire of a Taoist magician in Taiwan.

1511 MAJOR, John Stephen. *Topology and Cosmology in Early Han
Thought: Chapter Four of the Huai-nan-tzu*. Harvard, 1973
(Ph.D. in History and East Asian Languages). v, 194p.
Available at the Harvard University Archives, Pusey Li-
brary, call no.HU 90.10589.

1512 SIE-GRABOWSKI, Jerzy. *Ying Shao i jego Feng-su tong-yi*.
[Polish: Ying Shao and His Work Feng su t'ung i.] Uni-
wersytet Warszawski, 1973 (Rozprawa doktorska, Institut
Orientalistyczny). The Feng su t'ung i (Compendium of
Customs), written ca.175 A.D., is an encyclopedia of
folklore containing biographies of Taoist immortals.

1513 GIRARDOT, Norman John. *The Theme of Chaos (hun-tun) in
Early Taoism*. Chicago, 1974 (Ph.D. in History of Reli-
gions). 447p. Order copies from the Photoduplication
Department, Joseph Regenstein Library, University of
Chicago.

1514 HICKS, Gail Frances. *Creativity and Body Awareness*.
Washington State, 1974 (Ph.D. in Psychology). 184p. DAI
35, no.6 (Dec. 1974): 2991-B; UM 74-28,882. Includes the
application of Taoism and Zen.

1515 LLOYD, Alicia Dawn. *A Rhetorical Analysis of the Tao-te-
ching: Some Taoist Figures of Speech*. Ohio State, 1974

(Ph.D. in East Asian Languages and Literatures).   192p.
DAI 35, no.8 (Feb. 1975): 5353-A; UM 75-3128.

1516   SWANSON, Gerald William. *The Great Treatise: Commenta-
       tory Tradition to the Book of Changes*. Washington (Se-
       attle), 1974 (Ph.D. in Asian Languages and Literature).
       332p. DAI 35, no.8 (Feb. 1975): 5367-A; UM 75-4056. On
       the largest of the seven commentaries to the I Ching.

1517   WU, Sing Chow. *A Study of the Taoist Internal Elixir:
       Its Theory and Development*. St. John's, 1974 (Ph.D. in
       Asian History). 267p. DAI 35, no.8 (Feb. 1975): 5270-A;
       UM 75-3282. Covers developments from the Former Han Dy-
       nasty to the early twentieth century.

1518   SIEH, Su-choan Stephen. *The Unity of Heaven and Man in
       the Chuang Tzu*. Temple, 1975 (Ph.D. in Religion).   305p.
       DAI 36, no.6 (Dec. 1975): 3809-A; UM 75-28,246.

1519   TUNG, Gea. *Metaphor and Analogy in the I Ching*. Clare-
       mont, 1975 (Ph.D. in Religion). 150p. DAI 37, no.1
       (July 1976): 388-A; UM 76-15,791.

SCIENCE AND TECHNOLOGY

Earth Sciences

See also entries 297 and 357 as well as the section--within
the Appendix--entitled "Science and Technology" (pp.256-57).

1520   BARTHEL, Hellmuth. *Versuch einer ersten Gesamtdarstel-
       lung von Klima und Bodengefrornis in der Mongolischen
       Volksrepublik*. [German: Attempt at an Initial Overall
       Presentation of the Climate and the Permafrost in the
       Mongolian People's Republic.] Technische Universität
       Dresden, 1971 (Dr., Sektion Geodäsie). v, 212, ix p.

1521   CHIN, Ping-chuen. *Rainfall in Hong Kong*. Hong Kong,
       1971 (Ph.D. in Geography and Geology). 428p.

1522   DON, Jerzy. *Geologia Ałtaju Mongolskiego w dorzeczu
       Choit-Cenchergoł*. [Polish: The Geology of the Mongolian
       Altai in the Hoyt Tsenher Gol River Basin.] Uniwersytet
       Wrocławski im. B. Bieruta, 1972 (Doktor habilitowany,
       Wydz. Nauk Przyrodniczych).

1523   DUMICZ, Marian. *Tektonika Ałtaju Mongolskiego i Kotliny
       Wielkich Jezior w regionie Kobdo*. [Polish: Tectonics of
       the Mongolian Altai and the Valleys of the Great Lakes
       in the Hovd Region.] Uniwersytet Wrocławski im. B.

Bieruta, 1972 (Doktor habilitowany, Wydz. Nauk Przyrod-
niczych).

1524   KO, Dip-shin Phyllis. *Triterpewoid and Other Constitu-
ents from the Leaves of Some Castanposis and Lithocarpus
Species of the Hong Kong Fagaceae.* Hong Kong, 1972
(Ph.D. in Chemistry). 214p.

1525   SŁOWAŃSKI, Władysław Wawrzyniec Walenty. *Kenozoik okolic
rzeki Czono-Charajch (Mongolia Zachodnia).* [Polish:
Cenozoic River Regions of "Czono-Charajch" (Western Mongolia).] Instytut Geologiczny w Warszawie, 1972 (Rozprawa doktorska).

1526   STEPHENSON, Francis Richard. *Some Geophysical, Astrophy-
sical and Chronological Deductions from Early Astronomical Records.* Newcastle upon Tyne, 1972 (Ph.D. in Geophy-
sics and Planetary Physics). 204p. Includes records
within the astronomical treatises of the Ch'ien Han shu,
Hou Han shu and Chin shu.

1527   BALLA, Zoltán. *A keletmongóliai Dél-Keruleni kiemelkedés
mezozoikuma.* [Hungarian: The Mesozoic of the South Keru-
len Eminence in Eastern Mongolia.] Magyar Tudományos
Akadémia, 1974 (kand.).

1528   TATHAM, Robert Haines. *Geologic Inferences from Seismic
Surface Wave Analysis of Small Magnitude Earthquakes and
V_p/V_s as a Direct Hydrocarbon Indicator.* Columbia, 1975
(Ph.D. in Geological Sciences). 149p. DAI 36, no.12
(June 1976): 6033-34-B; UM 76-12,790. Part of this dis-
sertation studies earthquakes which occurred in Tibet.

1529   TUNG, James Ping-ya. *The Surface Wave Study of Crustal
and Upper Mantle Structures of Mainland China.* Southern
California, 1975 (Ph.D. in Geology). xix, 331p. DAI 36,
no.11 (May 1976): 5485-86-B; Order copies directly from
the University of Southern California Library.

1530   WANG, Chwan-chau. *Phosphorus Test Evaluations of Sugar-
cane Soils in Taiwan.* Michigan State, 1975 (Ph.D. in
Crop and Soil Sciences). 86p. DAI 36, no.3 (Sept.
1975): 1019-B; UM 75-20,901.

Engineering and Technology

See also entry 265.

1531   FLESSEL, Klaus. *Der Huang-ho und die historische Hydro-
technik in China unter besonderer Berücksichtigung der
Nördlichen-Sung-Zeit. Mit einem Ausblick auf den vergleich-*

baren Wasserbau in Europa. [German: The Huang-ho (Yellow River) and Historical Hydrotechnology in China, Particularly during the Northern Sung Period. With a Survey of Comparable Hydraulic Engineering Works in Europe.] Tübingen, 1971 (Dr.). 255p.

1532 KO, King-lim Pius. *Characteristics of Monsoon and Typhoon Winds in Hong Kong from an Engineering Viewpoint.* Hong Kong, 1972 (Ph.D. in Civil Engineering). 127p.

1533 LEE, Rensselaer Wright (III). *The Politics of Technology in Communist China.* Stanford, 1973 (Ph.D. in Political Science). 305p. DAI 34, no.3 (Sept. 1973): 1331-32-A; UM 73-20,491. On Chinese efforts to pursue a uniquely indigenous path of technological development.

1534 SAKATA, Hiroe. *Analysis of a Flood Control Plan for Rice Fields in Asian Countries.* California (Berkeley), 1974 (D.Eng.). x, 216p. Order copies from the Library Photographic Service, General Library, University of California at Berkeley. This plan has applicability to flood basin development planning in China even though it does not focus on any specific country.

History of Science

See also entries 445, 625, 1531, and 1543.

1535 BUCK, Peter Stephen. *Orientations toward Occidental Knowledge: Comparative Perspectives on the Science Society of China, 1914-1937.* Harvard, 1972 (Ph.D. in History of Science). iv, 266p. Available at the Harvard University Archives, Pusey Library, call no. HU 90.10115.5.

Life Sciences

See also entries 922, 1799, 1800, and 1801, as well as the section entitled "Health, Medicine, and Social Welfare" (pp.53-55).

1536 CHUANG, Ching-chang. *Moss Flora of Taiwan (Exclusive of Pleurocarpi).* British Columbia, 1971 (Ph.D. in Botany). 249p. DAI 32, no.10 (Apr. 1972): 5647-B; Order copies directly from the Canadian Theses Division, National Library of Canada at Ottawa.

1537 KING, Edgar George, Jr. *Biology of the Formosan Subterranean Termite,* Coptotermes formosanus, *Shiraki, with Primary Emphasis on Young Colony Development.* Louisiana

State, 1971 (Ph.D. in Entomology).   222p.   DAI 32, no.5
(Nov. 1971): 2776-B; UM 71-29,377.

1538   SCHERPE, Wolf-Peter. *Beobachtungen am Verhalten des chinesischen Wasserrehs (Hydropotes inermis, Swinhoe), des
indischen Muntjaks (Muntiacus muntjak muntjak, Zimmermann) und des chinesischen Muntjaks (Muntiacus muntjak
reevesi, Ogilby)*.   [German: Observations on the Behavior
of the Chinese Water Deer (Hydropotes inermis, Swinhoe),
the Indian Muntjac [a small deer] (Muntiacus muntjak muntjak, Zimmermann) and the Chinese Muntjak (Muntiacus muntjak reevesi, Ogilby).]   Freie Universität Berlin, 1971
(Dr., Fachbereich Veterinärmedizin).   195p.

1539   TENORIO, JoAnn Marie. *A Revision of the Celyphidae (Dip-
tera) of the Oriental Region*. Hawaii, 1971 (Ph.D. in
Entomology).   x, 181p.   Order copies from the Interlibrary Loan Department, University of Hawaii Library.   Geographical coverage includes South China and Taiwan.

1540   PASCHAL, Eugene Hamer (II). *Heterosis and Combining
Ability in Exotic Soybean Germplasm*. Purdue, 1973 (Ph.D.
in Agronomy).   63p.   DAI 34, no.6 (Dec. 1973): 2415-B;
UM 73-28,124.   Agronomic experiments using soybeans of
Chinese, Manchurian, Korean, and American origin formed
the basis of Paschal's research.

1541   CUNDALL, David Langdon. *The Cranial Osteology and Myolo-
gy of the Green Snakes, Genus Opheodrys*. Arkansas, 1974
(Ph.D. in Zoology).   224p.   DAI 35, no.6 (Dec. 1974):
3109-10-B; UM 74-28,078.   Three of the six species of
these snakes are found in south China and other parts of
Asia.

1542   FUJII, Jack Koji. *Effects of an Entomogenous Nematode,
Neoaplectana carpocapsae Weiser, on the Formosan Subterranean Termite, Coptotermes formosanus Shiraki with Ecological and Biological Studies on C. formosanus.* Hawaii,
1975 (Ph.D. in Entomology).   179p.   DAI 37, no.1 (July
1976): 62-B; UM 76-16,433.

Mathematical and Calendrical Sciences

See also entries 253, 288, and 920.

1543   LIBBRECHT, Ulrich J. *Chinese Mathematics in the Thir-
teenth Century: The Shu-shu chiu-chang of Ch'in Chiu-shao*.
Leiden, 1971 (Dr. en Letteren).   2 vols.   Published as
Chinese...Ch'in Chiu-shao (Cambridge, Mass.: MIT Press,

1973. xxxi, 555p. [M.I.T. East Asian science series,
vol.1]).

1544 TURBAN, Helga. *Das Ching-Ch'u sui-shih chi. Ein chine-*
sischer Festkalender. [German: The Ching-Ch'u sui-shih
chi: A Chinese Calendar of Holidays.] München, 1971
(Dr., Philosophische Fakultät). Published as Das Ching-
Ch'u...Festkalender (Augsburg: Dissertationsdruck W.
Blasaditsch, 1971. 199p.). Based on a work by Tsung Lin
(ca.500-563 A.D.).

1545 BAZIN, Louis. *Les calendriers turcs anciens et médié-*
vaux. [French: Ancient and Medieval Turkish Calendars.]
Paris III (Sorbonne-Nouvelle), 1972 (Doctorat d'Etat ès
lettres). Published as Les calendriers...médiévaux
(Lille: Service de Reproduction des Thèses, Université
de Lille III, 1974. 800p.). Includes chapters about
the Chinese influence upon the calendars of the Turkish-
speaking peoples and about Uighur calendrical science.

1546 SCHUH, Dieter. *Untersuchungen zur Geschichte der tibeti-*
schen Kalenderrechnung. [German: Investigations into
the History of Tibetan Calendrical Computations.] Bonn,
1972 (Dr., Philosophische Fakultät). Published as Untersuchungen...Kalenderrechnung (Wiesbaden: Steiner, 1973.
164 + 239p. [Verzeichnis der orientalischen Handschriften in Deutschland, Suppl.-Bd. 16]).

1547 STEWART, Joe David. *Mesoamerican and Eurasian Calendars.*
Calgary, 1974 (Ph.D. in Archaeology). x, 304p. Order
copies directly from the Canadian Theses Division, National Library of Canada at Ottawa; available only in
microfiche format, fiche no.21354, @ $2.00. This disser-
tation includes coverage of Chinese, Mongolian and Tibetan calendars.

SOCIOLOGY

General and Historical Studies

See also entry 1575 as well as the two sections entitled "Overseas Chinese Communities" (pp.161-81 and pp.247-51).

1548 BERGESEN, Albert James. *The Social Origins of Political*
Witch-Hunts: A Cross-National Study of Deviance. Stanford, 1974 (Ph.D. in Sociology). 131p. DAI 35, no.3
(Sept. 1974): 1754-55-A; UM 74-20,173. China is one of
twenty-six countries covered in this cross-national study.

1549 DEYO, Frederic C. *Ethnicity, Organization, and Work Values: A Comparative Study of Thai and Chinese Industry.* Chicago, 1974 (Ph.D. in Sociology). 159p. Order copies from the Photoduplication Department, Joseph Regenstein Library, University of Chicago. Related publication by the author: Organization and Its Socio-Cultural Setting: A Case Study of Structural Compensation in an Atomistic Society (Singapore: Dept. of Sociology, University of Singapore, 1975. 31p. [Working papers, no.41]).

1550 FARR, Grant Michael. *Stratification in Non-Industrial Societies.* Washington (Seattle), 1974 (Ph.D. in Sociology). 177p. DAI 36, no.6 (Dec. 1975): 4035-A; UM 75-28,345. Based on data from the Ethnographic Atlas (Murdock, 1967), which includes information on 1200 societies, among them several in mainland China and Taiwan.

1551 YU, Elena Siok-hue. *Achievement Motive, Familism, and Hsiao: A Replication of McClelland-Winterbottom Studies.* Notre Dame, 1974 (Ph.D. in Sociology and Anthropology). 244p. DAI 35, no.1 (July 1974): 593-A; UM 74-14,942. The subjects were Chinese teenagers.

1552 VIGDERHOUS, Gideon. *Socio-Demographic Determinants of Suicide and Homicide: A Multivariate Cross-Cultural Investigation.* Illinois, 1975 (Ph.D. in Sociology). 231p. DAI 36, no.5 (Nov. 1975): 3154-55-A; UM 75-24,424. Covers 55 countries including the Republic of China, Hong Kong, and the heavily Chinese-populated Republic of Singapore.

1553 WOON, Yuen Fong. *Social Organization of South China 1911-1949: The Case of the Kwaan Lineage of Hoi-p'ing.* British Columbia, 1975 (Ph.D. in Sociology). viii, 447p. DAI 36, no.12 (June 1976): 8323-A; Order copies directly from the Canadian Theses Division, National Library of Canada at Ottawa; available only in microfiche format, fiche no.26031, @ $5.00.

Hong Kong

1554 JOHNSON, Graham Edwin. *Natives, Migrants, and Voluntary Associations in a Colonial Chinese Setting.* Cornell, 1971 (Ph.D. in Sociology). 448p. DAI 32, no.1 (July 1971): 550-A; UM 71-18,906. Deals with the rapidly growing town of Tsuen Wan in the New Territories of Hong Kong.

1555 GEPFORD, William George. *The Missionary as Agent of Change in Hong Kong.* San Francisco Theological Seminary, 1973 (Ph.D.).

1556 ROSEN, Sherry. *Mei Foo Sun Chuen: Middle Class Chinese Families in Transition*. Harvard, 1975 (Ph.D. in Sociology and East Asian Languages). iii, 284p. Available at the Harvard University Archives, Pusey Library, call no. HU 90.11032.10. On a suburb of Hong Kong.

People's Republic of China

See also entry 169.

1557 WHYTE, Martin King. *Small Groups and Political Rituals in Communist China*. Harvard, 1971 (Ph.D. in Sociology). ii, 515p. Available at the Harvard University Archives, Pusey Library, call no.HU 90.10091. Published as Small Groups and Political Rituals in China (Berkeley: University of California Press, 1974. viii, 271p. [Michigan studies on China]).

1558 WONG, Paul. *Organizational Leadership in Communist China*. California (Berkeley), 1971 (Ph.D. in Sociology). xvii, 403p. Order copies from the Library Photographic Service, General Library, University of California at Berkeley. Published as China's Higher Leadership in the Socialist Transition (New York: Free Press; London: Collier Macmillan, 1976. 310p.).

1559 SALAFF, Janet Weitzner. *Youth, Family, and Political Control in Communist China*. California (Berkeley), 1972 (Ph.D. in Sociology). viii, 462p. Order copies from the Library Photographic Service, General Library, University of California at Berkeley.

1560 WEINER, Lee Joel. *The Professional Revolutionary: Notes on the Initiation and Development of Careers in Revolution Making*. Northwestern, 1975 (Ph.D. in Sociology). 149p. DAI 36, no.11 (May 1976): 7686-A; UM 76-11,931. Weiner's case materials were drawn from the Chinese Communist Party and the American SDS/Weatherman organization.

Republic of China

For demographic studies, *see* the two sections entitled "Demography, Population, and Family Planning" (pp.23-25 and pp.226-27).

1561 CHANG, Chung-wu. *A Sociological Study of Changes in Land Tenure Status in Taiwan: A Study of Kwansi Community*.

Louisiana State, 1971 (Ph.D. in Sociology). 108p. DAI 32, no.12 (June 1972): 7111-A; UM 72-17,751.

1562 HUANG, Ta-chou. *Rural-Urban Migration in Taiwan*. Cornell, 1971 (Ph.D. in Development Psychology). 97p. DAI 32, no.8 (Feb. 1972): 4722-A; UM 72-8867.

1563 OLSEN, Nancy Johnston. *The Effect of Household Composition on the Child Rearing Practices of Taiwanese Families*. Cornell, 1971 (Ph.D. in Human Development and Family Studies). 215p. DAI 32, no.3 (Sept. 1971): 1659-A; UM 71-22,993.

1564 OLSEN, Stephen Milton. *Family, Occupation, and Values in a Chinese Urban Community*. Cornell, 1971 (Ph.D. in Sociology). 289p. DAI 32, no.9 (Mar. 1972): 5363-64-A; UM 72-8982. Studies residents of Taipei.

1565 KUMBHAT, Manmohan Chand. *Subjective Aspects of Class Structure: A Cross-National Analysis*. Pennsylvania, 1972 (Ph.D. in Sociology). 207p. DAI 33, no.4 (Oct. 1972): 1851-A; UM 72-25,609. Includes the Republic of China.

1566 LO, Rong-rong. *Marriage Patterns and Modernization in Taiwan*. Minnesota, 1972 (Ph.D. in Sociology). 395p. DAI 33, no.10 (Apr. 1973): 5840-41-A; UM 73-10,670. Studies residents of the Taichung area.

1567 YEH, Chii-jeng. *Structure Influence of Personal and Relational Attributes on Information Flow in Two Taiwan Villages*. Missouri, 1973 (Ph.D. in Sociology). 280p. DAI 34, no.11 (May 1974): 7354-55-A; UM 74-10,008.

1568 KIANG, Yu-lung. *Bestimmende Faktoren der Abwanderung vom Land in Entwicklungsländern*. [German: Factors Determining Out-Migration from the Countryside in Developing Countries.] Göttingen, 1974 (Dr., Landwirtschaftliche Fakultät). Published as Determinants of Migration from Rural Areas, a Case Study of Taiwan: A Contribution to the Formulation of Migration Models, Taking as Example the Rural Regions of Taipei and Taichung (Saarbrücken: Verlag d. SSIP-Schriften, 1975. 139p. [Sozialökonomische Schriften zur Agrarentwicklung; 13]).

1569 SA, Sophie. *Family and Community in Urban Taiwan: Social Status and Demographic Strategy among Taipei Households, 1885-1935*. Harvard, 1975 (Ph.D. in Sociology and East Asian Languages). 390p. Available at the Harvard University Archives, Pusey Library, call no.HU 90.10892.

URBAN AND REGIONAL PLANNING

See also entry 241.

1570 PRYOR, Edward George. *An Assessment of the Need and Scope for Urban Renewal in Hong Kong.* Hong Kong, 1971 (Ph.D. in Geography and Geology). 358p.

1571 KWOK, Reginald Ying-wang. *Urban-Rural Planning and Housing Development in the People's Republic of China: Regional and Local Planning in a Developing Socialist Nation.* Columbia, 1973 (Ph.D. in Architecture, Architectural Technology and Urban Planning). 448p. DAI 35, no. 7 (Jan. 1975): 4746-A; UM 74-29,610.

1572 WU, Chung-Tong. *Societal Guidance and Development: A Case Study of Hong Kong.* California (Los Angeles), 1973 (Ph.D. in Urban Planning). 400p. DAI 34, no.6 (Dec. 1973): 3610-11-A; UM 73-29,002. This examination of economic and social development since 1949 includes case studies relating to the provision of industrial land, the revision of land rents, and loans to small industries.

1573 SCHINZ, Alfred. *Chinesischer Städtebau in der Mandschudynastie 1644-1911; dargestellt am Beispiel der Ting-Stadt Hsinchu in Taiwan.* [German: Chinese Town Planning under the Manchu Dynasty (1644-1911): Described in the Example of the Ch'ing Period City Hsinchu in Taiwan.] Technische Universität München, 1975 (Dr., Fachbereich Architektur). 2 vols.

Appendix

Dissertations Completed between 1945 and 1970

The following 228 dissertations were accepted by
institutions of higher learning around the world
between 1945 and 1970. Comprehensive bibliographical information about them was received too late
to permit their inclusion in the predecessor to
this volume: *Doctoral Dissertations on China: A
Bibliography of Studies in Western Languages,
1945-1970* (Seattle: University of Washington
Press, 1972). The entries are divided into major
subject categories, and within each listing the
entries appear in chronological order by year of
completion. Cross-references to many of these
dissertations may be found throughout the entire
bibliography.

ANTHROPOLOGY AND SOCIOLOGY

1574 AIGNER, Jean Stephanie. *The Archaeology of Pleistocene
China.* Wisconsin, 1969 (Ph.D. in Anthropology). 518p.
DAI 32, no.11 (May 1972): 6173-74-B; UM 72-11,224.

1575 ZINGERLE, Arnold. *Max Weber und China: Herrschafts-
und religionssoziologische Grundlagen zum Wandel der
chinesischen Gesellschaft.* [German: Max Weber and China: The Religio-sociological Bases for Change in Chinese Society.] Bochum, 1970 (Dr., Abteilung für Sozialwissenschaft). Published as Max Weber...Gesellschaft
(Berlin: Duncker und Humblot, 1972. 180p. [Soziologi-
sche Schriften, Bd.9]).

ART AND ARCHITECTURE

1576 GYLLENSVÄRD, Bo. *T'ang Gold and Silver.* Stockholm,

1957 (Akad. avh.). Published as T'ang Gold and Silver (Göteborg: Elanders, 1957. viii, 370p.). Also published as The Museum of Far Eastern Antiquities [Stockholm]. Bulletin, no.29 (1957). On gold and silversmithing during the T'ang period.

1577   FUX, Herbert. *Zur Frage des islamischen Einflusses auf das frühe chinesische Blau-Weiss.* [German: On the Question of Islamic Influence upon Early Chinese Blue and White Porcelain.] Wien, 1959 (Dr., Kunsthistorisches Institut). 237p. Deals with the 1300s and the 1400s.

1578   SCHULZ, Alexander. *Hsi Yang Lou. Untersuchung zu den "Europäischen Bauten" des Kaisers Ch'ien-lung.* [German: Hsi Yang Lou: Studies of the "European Buildings" of the Emperor Ch'ien-lung.] Würzburg, 1966 (Dr.). Published as Hsi Yang Lou...Ch'ien-lung (Isny im Allgäu, 1966. 98p. + 24 plates). On the European influence upon Chinese architecture during the Ch'ing period.

1579   KLIMBURG, Max. *Die Entwicklung des 2. indo-iranischen Stils von Kutscha. Untersuchung zur buddhistischen Wandmalerei in Mittelasien.* [German: The Development of the Second Indo-Iranian Style of Kucha: Investigations of Buddhist Wall Painting in Central Asia.] Wien, 1969 (Dr., Philosophische Fakultät). 163p. On 5th-6th century art from a town and oasis in present-day Sinkiang.

1580   LEDDERHOSE, Lothar. *Die Siegelschrift (Chuan-shu) in der Ch'ing-Zeit. Ein Beitrag zur Geschichte der chinesischen Schriftkunst.* [German: The Seal Script (chuan-shu) during the Ch'ing Period: A Contribution to the History of Chinese Calligraphy.] Heidelberg, 1969 (Dr.). Published as Die Siegelschrift...Schriftkunst (Wiesbaden: Steiner, 1970. 267p. + 59 plates [Studien zur ostasiatischen Schriftkunst, 1]).

1581   SIMONET, Jean-Marie. *La suite au "Traité de Calligraphie" de Jiang Kui (1155-1221).* [French: The Hsu Shu-p'u of Chiang K'uei (1155-1221) on Calligraphy.] Paris, 1969 (Doctorat de 3e cycle ès lettres). 311p. A copy is available at the Bibliothèque de la Sorbonne, library catalogue no. I 1081-4°.

1582   BRINKER, Helmut. *Die Zen-buddhistische Bildnismalerei in China und Japan von dem Anfängen bis zum Ende des 16. Jahrhunderts; eine Untersuchung zur Ikonographie, Typen- und Entwicklungsgeschichte.* [German: The Zen Buddhist Portrait Painting in China and Japan from Its Beginnings until the End of the 16th Century: An Investigation

into Its Iconography, Its Typology, and Its Development.] Heidelberg, 1970 (Dr.). Published as Die Zen-
buddhistische...Entwicklungsgeschichte (Wiesbaden:
Steiner Verlag, 1973. x, 279p.).

1583   CHEN, Tsing-fang. *La calligraphie chinoise et la pein-
ture contemporaine.* [French: Chinese Calligraphy and
Contemporary Painting.] Paris, 1970 (Doctorat d'Université ès lettres). 3 vols. (618p., viii p., 78 plates).
A copy is available at the Bibliothèque de la Sorbonne,
library catalogue no. W Univ. 1970 (47)-4°.

CHINA AND CHINESE CIVILIZATION ABROAD

1584   KAISER, Elgrid. *Der Wortschatz des Marco Polo.* [Ger-
man: The Vocabulary of Marco Polo.] Wien, 1967 (Dr.,
Philosophische Fakultät). 272p. On the vocabulary
found within his published writings.

1585   RABATSCH, Elfriede. *Der pazifische Raum im Weltbild der
Europäer des sechzehnten Jahrhunderts.* [German: The Eu-
ropean Conceptions of the Pacific Region and Their Image
of the World during the Sixteenth Century.] Wien, 1968
(Dr., Philosophische Fakultät). 2 vols. Includes the
European image of and knowledge about China.

1586   ESIN, Emel. *Le dragon dans l'iconographie turque.*
[French: The Dragon in Turkish Iconography.] Paris,
1969 (Doctorat d'Université ès lettres). 335p. A copy
is available at the Bibliothèque de la Sorbonne, library catalogue no. W Univ. 1969 (10)-4°. Includes the
Chinese influence upon Turkish art.

1587   HULIN, Michel. *Hegel et l'Orient.* [French: Hegel and
the Orient.] Paris, 1969 (Doctorat de 3e cycle ès lettres). vi, 145, 95, ix p. Abstracted in Université
de Paris. Faculté des Lettres et Sciences Humaines.
Positions des thèses de troisième cycle soutenues devant
la Faculté en 1969, pp.362-63. A copy is available at
the Bibliothèque de la Sorbonne, library catalogue no.
I 1147-4°. Studies this early 19th century German philosopher's ideas regarding China and India.

1588   KANG, Koo-Chin. *Law in North Korea: An Analysis of So-
viet-Chinese Influences Thereupon.* Harvard, 1969
(L.L.D.). viii, 769p. Available at the Harvard University Law School library, call no. KOR-DR 980 KAN.

1589   LIE, Hiu. *Die Mandschu-Sprachkunde in Korea; mit beson-*

derer Berücksichtigung des Mandschustudiums im 18. Jhr.
[German: Manchu Language Studies in Korea: With Particular Consideration of Manchu Studies during the 18th
Century.] Göttingen, 1969 (Dr., Philosophische Fakultät). Published as <u>Die Mandschu-Sprachkunde in Korea</u>
(Bloomington: Indiana University, 1972. 275p. [Indi-
ana University publications. Uralic & Altaic series,
114]).

1590   ADDAZIO, Louis Carmine. *The Effects of an Asian Studies
Program on the Social Distance between Tenth-Grade Students and Selected Ethnic Groups.* Connecticut, 1970
(Ph.D. in Education). 180p. DAI 31, no.12 (June 1971):
6391-A; UM 71-15,953.

1591   DUFFY, Christopher Gregory. *The Development of Non-
Western Area Studies Programs at Selected Accredited
Private Liberal Arts Colleges.* Indiana, 1970 (Ed.D.).
145p. DAI 31, no.6 (Dec. 1970): 2702-A; UM 70-25,187.
Covers colleges in Ohio, Indiana and Illinois.

1592   HUE, Bernard. *L'Asie dans l'oeuvre de Claudel: expéri-
ences, influences.* [French: Asia in the Works of Paul
Claudel (1868-1955): Experiences, Influences.] Rennes,
1970 (Doctorat de 3e cycle en littérature comparée).
331p. This French author wrote extensively about China.

1593   WEBB, Glenn Taylor. *Japanese Scholarship behind Momo-
yama Painting and Trends in Japanese Painting <u>ca.</u> 1500-
1700 as Seen in the Light of a Stylistic Reexamination
of the Nature of Chinese Influence on Kano Painters and
Some of Their Contemporaries.* Chicago, 1970 (Ph.D. in
Art). 294p. Order copies from the Photoduplication
Department, Joseph Regenstein Library, University of
Chicago.

DEMOGRAPHY, POPULATION, AND FAMILY PLANNING

1594   BOWER, Leonard George. *Population Growth, Economic
Growth, and Family Planning Programs in Less Developed
Countries.* Duke, 1969 (Ph.D. in Economics). 261p.
DAI 31, no.1 (July 1970): 12-13-A; UM 70-11,666.
Covers many countries including the Republic of China
and Hong Kong.

1595   ROSE, Donald Kenneth. *Some Demographic Changes and
Their Relationship to the Pace and Sustainability of
Economic Growth in Underdeveloped Countries: An Empiri-
cal Study.* Colorado, 1969 (Ph.D. in Economics). 209p.

DAI 30, no.4 (Apr. 1970): 4096-A; UM 70-5888. Includes the Republic of China.

ECONOMY (since 1949)

1596 JAIN, Netra Pal. *Rural Reconstruction in India and China.* Allahabad, 1966 (D.Phil.). Published as Rural Reconstruction in India and China: A Comparative Study (New Delhi: Writers & Publishers Corp., 1970. xx, 370p.). On agriculture.

1597 OBERLÄNDER, Richard. *Die Stellung der Landwirtschaft im System der chinesischen Volkswirtschaft und ihre Widerspiegelung in den Theorien der chinesischen Ökonomen.* [German: The Place of Agriculture in the Chinese Economy and Its Reflection in the Theories of Chinese Economists.] Leipzig, 1968 (Dr.). vi, 206, xxxiv p.

1598 THORNBLADE, James Barnard. *Cotton Textile Exports from the Less-Developed Countries: The Competitive Challenge to the American Textile Industry.* Massachusetts Institute of Technology, 1968 (Ph.D. in Economics). xi, 279p. Order copies from the Microreproduction Laboratory, Massachusetts Institute of Technology. Includes information about textiles produced in Hong Kong and the Republic of China.

1599 WESEMANN, Kurt. *Probleme der proportionalen Entwicklung von Industrie und Landwirtschaft in China.* [German: Problems of Proportionate Development of Industry and Agriculture in the People's Republic of China.] Humboldt-Universität Berlin, 1968 (Dr.). 515p.

1600 CHEN, Ting-an. *Zum Problem der Importsubstitution und der Exportdiversifikation der unterentwickelten Volkswirtschaften unter besonderer Berücksichtigung Asiens.* [German: On the Problem of Import Substitution and Export Diversification in Underdeveloped National Economies with Particular Consideration of Asia.] Münster, 1969 (Dr., Rechts- und Staatswissenschaftliche Fakultät). Published as Zum Problem...Asiens (Münster, 1969. x, 312p.). This is a general study that includes consideration of the Republic of China.

1601 SOH, Ling-sing François. *Le développement économique de Formose depuis 1950.* [French: The Economic Development of Formosa since 1950.] Paris, 1969 (Doctorat de l'Université en droit). 241p. A copy is available at the Bibliothèque de la Sorbonne.

1602   TJIU, Mau-Ying. *Die Agrarreform Taiwans und ihre Aus-
       wirkungen auf die wirtschaftliche Entwicklung.* [German:
       Taiwan's Agrarian Reform and Its Effects upon Economic
       Development.] Göttingen, 1969 (Dr., Landwirtschaftliche
       Fakultät). Published as Die Agrarreform...Entwicklung
       (Frankfurt: DLG-Verlag, 1968. x, 157p. [Zeitschrift
       für ausländische Landwirtschaft. Materialsammlungen,
       9]).

1603   CHEN, Chaw-ming. *Untersuchung der Anwendungsmöglich-
       keit von Repräsentativaufnahmen in künstlichen Bestän-
       den; dargestellt am Beispiel von Waldaufnahmen in Tai-
       wan.* [German: Investigation of the Possibility of Rep-
       resentative Surveys in Cultivated Stands of Trees: A
       Case Study of Forest Surveys in Taiwan.] Freiburg i.B.,
       1970 (Dr., Forstwirtschaftliche Fakultät). iv, 94 + 23p.

1604   CROOK, Frederick William. *An Analysis of Work-Payment
       Systems Used in Chinese Mainland Agriculture, 1956 to
       1970.* Fletcher School of Law and Diplomacy, 1970
       (Ph.D.). 444p. DAI 32, no.7 (Jan. 1972): 3519-A; UM
       72-2226.

1605   ESPY, John Lee. *The Strategies of Chinese Industrial
       Enterprises in Hong Kong.* Harvard, 1970 (D.B.A.). 284p.
       Available at the Harvard University Business School Ar-
       chives, Baker Library.

1606   LEHMANN, Hubert. *Wirtschaftsordnung und Entwicklungs-
       politik in Taiwan.* [German: Economic Conditions and
       Economic Policy in Taiwan.] Ruhr-Universität Bochum,
       1970 (Dr., Abteilung für Wirtschaftswissenschaft). Pub-
       lished as Wirtschaftsordnung...Taiwan (Bochum, 1970.
       ix, 325p.).

1607   OH, Moonsong. *The Role of International Corporations
       in the Transfer of Technology to Developing Countries.*
       Pennsylvania, 1970 (Ph.D. in Business and Applied Eco-
       nomics). 291p. DAI 31, no.6 (Dec. 1970): 2585-A; UM
       70-25,710. Includes Hong Kong and the Republic of China.

1608   RAQUIBUZZAMAN, Mohammad. *An Economic Appraisal of the
       Sugar Policies of Developed Countries and the Implica-
       tions of These Policies to Developing Countries.* Cor-
       nell, 1970 (Ph.D. in Agricultural Economics). 262p.
       DAI 31, no.3 (Sept. 1970): 899-900-A; UM 70-14,399.
       Includes the Republic of China.

1609   REYNOLDS, Stephen Eugene. *Concentration of Trade and
       the Instability and Growth of Exports: Developing Asia.*
       Wisconsin, 1970 (Ph.D. in Economics). 380p. DAI 31,

no.4 (Oct. 1970): 1458-59-A; UM 70-13,935. Includes
consideration of the Republic of China during the 1960s.

1610 VOSS, Werner. *Die wirtschaftliche Entwicklung der
Volksrepublik China; Darstellung und Prognose. Eine
statistische Untersuchung.* [German: The Economic Development of the People's Republic of China: A Description
and Forecast. A Statistical Investigation.] Heidelberg, 1970 (Dr., Philosophische Fakultät). Published
as Die wirtschaftliche...Untersuchung (Freiburg i.B.:
Haufe, 1971. vii, 281p. [Institut für International
Vergleichende Wirtschafts- und Sozialstatistik an der
Universität Heidelberg, Schriftenreihe, Bd.10]).

1611 YADAV, Gopal Ji. *The Discriminatory Aspects of Canada's
Imports of Manufactured Goods from the Less Developed
and the Developed Countries.* Queen's University at
Kingston, 1970 (Ph.D. in Economics). xiv, 227p. Order
copies directly from the Canadian Theses Division, National Library of Canada at Ottawa; available only in
microfilm format, film no.5754, @ $2.50. A highly the-
oretical study that deals in part with the Republic of
China.

EDUCATION (since 1949)

1612 VASWANI, Hari Valiram. *A Study of the Problems of For-
eign Students at the Berkeley Campus of University of
California.* California (Berkeley), 1950 (Ed.D.). 160p.
Deals in part with Chinese students.

1613 MOORE, Forrest G. *Factors Affecting the Academic Success of Foreign Students in American Universities.*
Minnesota, 1953 (Ed.D.). 565p. DA 14, no.3 (Mar. 1954):
492-93; UM 7252. Chinese students are extensively discussed.

1614 HOUNTRAS, Panos Timothy. *Factors Associated with the
Academic Achievement of Foreign Graduate Students at
the University of Michigan from 1947 to 1949.* Michigan,
1955 (Ph.D.). 147p. DA 15, no.5 (May 1955): 762-63;
UM 11,297. Includes Chinese students at Michigan.

1615 MURASE, Kenneth. *International Students in Education
for Social Work.* Columbia, 1961 (D.S.W.). 371p. DA
22, no.2 (Aug. 1961): 673-74; UM 61-1083. Includes
Chinese students.

1616 LIN, Ching-jiang. *A Comparative Study of Some Aspects*

of the Educational Systems of England and the Republic
of China. Liverpool, 1968 (Ph.D. in Education). 549p.

1617 DAS, Man Singh. *Effect of Foreign Students' Attitudes*
toward Returning to the Country of Origin on the Nation-
al Loss of Professional Skills. Oklahoma State, 1969
(Ph.D. in Sociology). 257p. DAI 37, no.8 (Feb. 1971):
4282-A; UM 70-21,368. Published as Brain Drain Controversy and International Students (Lucknow: Lucknow Publishing House, 1972. 119p.). Includes Chinese students.

1618 FORD, Charles Christopher. *A Case Study of the Adapta-*
tional Patterns of Asian Graduate Students in Education
at Michigan State University. Michigan State, 1969
(Ph.D. in Education). 106p. DAI 31, no.3 (Sept. 1970):
1034-A; UM 70-15,031. A study of fifteen students from
eight countries including the Republic of China.

1619 KEATS, Daphne Mavis. *A Cross-Cultural Study of the De-*
velopment of Cognitive Structure in University Students,
with Particular Reference to Asian Students in the Uni-
versity of Queensland. Queensland, 1969 (Ph.D. in Education). viii, 342 + 273p. (2 vols.). Published as
Back in Asia: A Follow-up Study of Australian-Trained
Asian Students (Canberra: Department of Economics, Research School of Pacific Studies, Australian National
University, 1969. ix, 190p.). Includes students from
Hong Kong and students of Chinese ancestry from Singapore.

1620 SCHNEIDER, Robert Moren. *Perceptions of the Role of the*
Agricultural Equipment Industry in the Agricultural
Mechanization Education of Developing Countries. Mich-
igan State, 1969 (Ph.D. in Secondary Education and Cur-
riculum). 144p. DAI 31, no.3 (Sept. 1970): 1161-A;
UM 70-15,126. Includes the Republic of China.

1621 DE VINCENZO, Doris Kremsdorf. *Socio-Cultural Relocation*
and Changes in Anxiety and Attitudes toward the United
States as Host Country among Exchange Visitor Nurses.
New York, 1970 (Ph.D., School of Education). 139p.
DAI 31, no.7 (Jan. 1971): 4155-B; UM 70-26,415. 83% of
the subjects were of Asian nationality; some were from
the Republic of China.

1622 ELLAKANY, Farouk Abdelhamid Ahmed. *Prediction of Aca-*
demic Achievement of Foreign Students at Iowa State Uni-
versity 1969-1970. Iowa State, 1970 (Ph.D. in Education). 81p. DAI 31, no.4 (Oct. 1970): 1575-A; UM
70-18,884. Includes students from Hong Kong and the
Republic of China.

1623 HU, Shi-ming. *Interrelationship between Education and Political Ideology Exemplified in China: A Critical Analysis of Educational Policy and Curriculum Trends in the Chinese People's Republic (Mainland) and in the Republic of China (Taiwan) from 1949-1969.* Columbia (Teachers College), 1970 (Ed.D.). 318p. DAI 32, no.9 (Mar. 1972): 4837-A; UM 72-8823.

1624 LOZADA, Rhodelia Corazon Buenaventura. *Foreign Students at Purdue University: A Study of Selected Personal and Academic Characteristics in Relation to Current Experiences and Future Expectations.* Purdue, 1970 (Ph.D. in Education). 324p. DAI 31, no.8 (Feb. 1971): 3878-A; UM 71-2646. Includes students from Hong Kong and the Republic of China as well as students of Chinese ancestry from Singapore.

1625 NILAND, John Rodney. *The Brain Drain of Highly Trained Engineering Manpower from Asia into the United States.* Illinois, 1970 (Ph.D. in Labor and Industrial Relations). 195p. DAI 31, no.5 (Nov. 1970): 1957-58-A; UM 70-21,026. Published as The Asian Engineering Brain Drain: A Study of International Relocation into the United States from India, China, Korea, Thailand and Japan (Lexington, Mass.: Heath Lexington Books, 1970. xiv, 181p. [Studies in the social implications of science and technology]). Includes engineering graduate students from the Republic of China.

1626 SHEPARD, Nolan Edgbert. *The Acculturation of Foreign Students in Southern Colleges and Universities.* Mississippi, 1970 (Ph.D. in Education). 216p. DAI 31, no.6 (Dec. 1970): 2624-A; UM 70-24,337. Includes students from Hong Kong and the Republic of China.

GEOGRAPHY

1627 CHIAO, Joseph Wei. *Die chinesischen Ortsnamen unter besonderer Berücksichtigung der Provinzen Shansi und Szechwan: Typologie, Interpretation und Vergleich mit tibetischen Ortsnamen.* [German: Chinese Place Names with Particular Regard to the Provinces of Shansi and Szechwan: Typology, Interpretation and Comparison with Tibetan Place Names.] Wien, 1967 (Dr., Philosophische Fakultät). vi, 348p. Published as Die chinesischen Ortsnamen in Shansi und Szechwan: Typologie und Interpretation (Wien: Engelbert Stiglmayr, 1970. 138p. [Acta ethnologica et linguistica, Nr.19]).

1628   KLAUSING, Horst. *Probleme der Standortverteilung der Schwerindustrie in der Volksrepublik China 1949-1959. Eine Untersuchung an Hand von Primärquellen.* [German: Problems of the Geographical Distribution of Heavy Industry in the People's Republic of China, 1949-1959: An Investigation Based on Primary Sources.] Leipzig, 1968 (Dr.). 357p.

HEALTH, MEDICINE, AND SOCIAL WELFARE

1629   JAEGER, Thomas. *Beitrag zur gegenwärtigen Häufigkeit der Tuberkulose in verschiedenen europäischen und aussereuropäischen Ländern.* [German: Contribution to the Present Frequency of Tuberculosis in Various European and Non-European Countries.] Hamburg, 1967 (Dr., Medizinische Fakultät). Published as Beitrag...Ländern (Hamburg, 1967. 143p.). Includes consideration of Hong Kong, the People's Republic of China, the Republic of China, and Singapore (with its largely Chinese population).

1630   LAI, Chung-ling Éric. *Etude de l'assistance sociale à Hong Kong.* [French: A Study of Welfare Work in Hong Kong.] Paris, 1969 (Doctorat d'Université ès lettres). 274p. A copy is available at the Bibliothèque de la Sorbonne, library catalogue no. W Univ. 1969 (20)-4°.

1631   WONG, Ming. *Li Che-tchen (1518-1593) et le Pen-ts'ao kang-mou (Compendium général de la matière médicale, 1590): étude biographique, bibliographique, scientifique et méthodologique.* [French: Li Shih-chen (1518-1593) and the Pen ts'ao kang mu (General Compendium of Materia Medica, 1590): A Biographical, Bibliographical, Scientific and Methodological Study.] Tours, 1969 (Doctorat de 3e cycle ès lettres). ii, 59p.

1632   LAACKE, Hai Len Yvonne. *Ausgewählte Kapitel aus der traditionellen chinesischen Medizin.* [German: Selected Chapters from Traditional Chinese Medicine.] Erlangen-Nürnberg, 1970 (Dr., Medizinische Fakultät). Published as Ausgewählte...Medizin (Nürnberg? 1970? vi, 112p.).

HISTORY

1633   WEI, Kwei Sun. *Secret History of the Mongol Dynasty: Yuan-Chao-Pi-Shi.* Aligarh [India], 1950 (Ph.D.).

1634 BIELENSTEIN, Hans. *The Restoration of the Han Dynasty,*
      with Prolegomena on the Historiography of the Hou Han
      Shu. Stockholm, 1954 (Akad. avh.). Published as The
      Restoration...Hou Han Shu (Stockholm, 1954. 209p.
      [Museum of Far Eastern Antiquities. Bulletin, no.26]).

1635 PHILLIPS, Clifton Jackson. *Protestant America and the*
      Pagan World: The First Half Century of the American
      Board of Commissioners for Foreign Missions, 1810-1860.
      Harvard, 1954 (Ph.D. in History). 376p. Published as
      Protestant...1860 (Cambridge, Mass.: East Asian Research
      Center, Harvard University, 1969. ix, 370p. [Harvard
      East Asian monographs, 32]). Chapter 6 is entitled
      "China and the Far East".

1636 BROMAN, Sven. *Studies on the Chou Li.* Stockholm, 1961
      (Akad. avh.). Published as Studies on the Chou Li
      (Stockholm, 1961. 89p. [Museum of Far Eastern Antiqui-
      ties. Bulletin, no.33]). On the Rituals of Chou (one
      of the "Thirteen Classics"), a description of govern-
      mental organization in ancient China.

1637 HSIEH, Hon-Chun. *Les Belges et leurs relations cultu-*
      relles avec la Chine, 1900-1949. [French: The Belgians
      and Their Cultural Relations with China, 1900-1949.]
      Gent, 1963 (Doctoraat en Diplomatieke wetenschappen).

1638 WESTON, Rubin Francis. *The Influence of Racial Assump-*
      tions on American Imperialism, 1893-1946. Syracuse,
      1964 (D.S.S.). 484p. DA 25, no.7 (Jan. 1965): 4094-95;
      UM 64-8867. Includes American perceptions of the Chi-
      nese.

1639 FERENCZY, Mária. *A középkori északi-kinai nomád államok*
      történetéhez. [Hungarian: Towards the History of the
      Medieval Nomadic States of North China.] Eötvös Lóránd
      Tudományegyetem, 1966 (Dr.U. in China Studies).

1640 POUDEL, Bishnu Prasad. *Nepal's Relations with Tibet,*
      1792-1856. Indian School of International Studies,
      1966 (Ph.D.).

1641 EIKEMEIER, Dieter. *Elemente im politischen Denken des*
      Yŏn'am Pak Chiwŏn (1737-1805). Ein Beitrag zur Ge-
      schichte der kulturellen Beziehungen zwischen China und
      Korea. [German: Elements in the Political Thought of
      Yŏn'am Pak Chi-wŏn (1737-1805): A Contribution to the
      History of the Cultural Relations between China and Ko-
      rea.] Bochum, 1967 (Dr., Abteilung für Geschichtswis-
      senschaft). Published as Elemente...Korea (Leiden:
      Brill, 1970. xii, 256p. [Monographies du T'oung Pao,

8]). Includes this educated Korean's view of 18th century Confucianism and his opinions about the legitimacy of the Ch'ing dynasty.

1642 SCHUSTA, Guenter. *Österreich-Ungarn und der Boxeraufstand.* [German: Austria-Hungary and the Boxer Uprising.] Wien, 1967 (Dr., Philosophische Fakultät). vi, 211p.

1643 STUMPFELDT, Hans. *Staatsverfassung und Territorium im antiken China; über die Ausbildung einer territorialen Staatsverfassung.* [German: Constitution and Territory in Ancient China: On the Development of a Territorial Constitution.] Freiburg i.B., 1967 (Dr., Philosophische Fakultät). Published as Staatsverfassung...Staatsverfassung (Düsseldorf: Bertelsmann Universitätsverlag, 1970. 428p. [Freiburger Studien zu Politik und Gesellschaft überseeischer Länder, 8]).

1644 HONG, Soohn-Ho. *La question coréenne face aux conflits sino-japonais de 1894 à 1895.* [French: The Korean Question and the Sino-Japanese War of 1894-1895.] Paris, 1968 (Doctorat d'Université ès lettres). 374p. A copy is available at the Bibliothèque de la Sorbonne, library catalogue no. W Univ. 1968 (51)-4°.

1645 SCHLEGEL, Dietlinde. *Hao Ching (1222-1275), ein chinesischer Berater des Kaisers Kublai Khan.* [German: Hao Ching (1222-1275), a Chinese Counsellor of Emperor Kublai Kahn.] München, 1968 (Dr.). 209p.

1646 HAMMETT, Hugh Bernard. *Hilary Abner Hubert: A Southerner Returns to the Union.* Virginia, 1969 (Ph.D. in History). 385p. DAI 31, no.1 (July 1970): 325-A; UM 70-8036. Includes brief information about Hubert's attention to the Sino-Japanese War (1894-95) while serving as United States Secretary of the Navy.

1647 KEIGHTLEY, David Noel. *Public Work in Ancient China: A Study of Forced Labor in the Shang and Western Chou.* Columbia, 1969 (Ph.D. in Political Science). 427p. DAI 32, no.12 (June 1972): 6870-71-A; UM 72-15,577.

1648 LIU, Joseph. *She Ke-fa (1601-1645) et le contexte politique et social de la Chine au moment de l'invasion mandchoue.* [French: Shih K'o-fa (1601-1645) and Political and Social Conditions in China at the Time of the Manchu Invasion.] Paris, 1969 (Doctorat d'Université ès lettres). 204p. A copy is available at the Bibliothèque de la Sorbonne, library catalogue no. W Univ. 1969 (7)-4°.

1649   MAZOYER, Bernard. *Evolution politique, économique et
       sociale de la Chine de 1911 à 1967.* [French: The Polit-
       ical, Economic and Social Evolution of China, 1911–
       1967.]   Lyon, 1969 (Doctorat de 3ᵉ cycle ès lettres).
       131p.

1650   NIEH, Yu-hsi. *Die Entwicklung des chinesisch-japani-
       schen Konfliktes in Nordchina und die deutschen Vermitt-
       lungsbemühungen, 1937–1938.* [German: The Development
       of the Sino-Japanese Conflict in North China and the
       German Mediation Efforts in 1937–1938.]   Bonn, 1969
       (Dr., Philosophische Fakultät).   Published as Die Ent-
       wicklung...1938 (Hamburg: Institut für Asienkunde, 1970.
       217p.   [Mitteilungen des Instituts für Asienkunde Ham-
       burg, Nr.33]).

1651   OKAMOTO, Saë. *La crise politique et morale des manda-
       rins du Sud à l'époque de transition (1640–1660).*
       [French: The Political and Moral Crisis of the Mandarins
       in South China during the Age of Transition (1640–1660).]
       Paris, 1969 (Doctorat d'Université ès lettres).   135p.
       A copy is available at the Bibliothèque de la Sorbonne,
       library catalogue no. W Univ. 1969 (51)–4°.

1652   PUYRAIMOND, Guy. *Les événements anti-étrangers du Yang-
       zi (mai-septembre 1891).* [French: Anti-Foreign Occur-
       rences in the Yangtze Valley, May–September 1891.]   Pa-
       ris, 1969 (Doctorat de 3ᵉ cycle ès lettres).   vi, 120p.
       + 41p. (2 vols.).   A copy is available at the Biblio-
       thèque de la Sorbonne, library catalogue no. I 1065
       (1–2)–4°.

1653   SALOMON, Hilel Benami. *China's Policy toward Outer Mon-
       golia, 1912–1920.*   Columbia, 1969 (Ph.D. in Political
       Science).   342p.   DAI 33, no.1 (July 1972): 260-A; UM
       72-19,086.

1654   THIELE, Dagmar. *Der Abschluss eines Vertrages, Diploma-
       tie zwischen Sung- und Chin-Dynastie: 1117–1123.* [Ger-
       man: The Conclusion of a Treaty: Diplomacy between the
       Sung and Chin Dynasties, 1117–1123.]   München, 1969
       (Dr., Philosophische Fakultät).   Published as Der Ab-
       schluss...1117–1123 (Wiesbaden: Steiner, 1971.   289p.
       [Münchener ostasiatische Studien, Bd.6]).

1655   WEIGAND, Jörg. *Staat und Militär im altchinesischen Mi-
       litärtraktat Wei Liao Tzu.* [German: The State and the
       Military in the Ancient Chinese Military Treatise Wei
       liao tzu.]   Würzburg, 1969 (Dr., Philosophische Fakul-
       tät).   Published as Staat...Wei Liao Tzu (Würzburg,
       1971.   167p.).

1656   CHU, Cheng. *Contribution des Jésuites à la défense na-*
       tionale de la Chine des Ming face aux Man-Qing (1616-
       1644). [French: The Contribution of the Jesuits to the
       National Defense of Ming China against the Manchus,
       1616-1644.] Paris IV (Paris-Sorbonne), 1970 (Doctorat
       de 3e cycle ès lettres). 173, liii p. Abstracted in
       Université de Paris. Faculté des Lettres et Sciences
       Humaines. Positions des thèses de troisième cycle sou-
       tenues devant la Faculté en 1970, pp.467-68. A copy is
       available at the Bibliothèque de la Sorbonne, library
       catalogue no. I 1526-In-4°.

1657   CHUNG, Tan. *Manchu Government Policy vis-à-vis Sino-*
       Indian Trade 1757-1842. Delhi, 1970 (Ph.D.). Abstrac-
       ted in Indian Dissertation Abstracts, 1, no.3 (July-
       Sept. 1973): 182-84.

1658   CREAN, Eileen Marie. *The Governor-Generalship of Turke-*
       stan under K.P. von Kaufmann, 1867-1882. Yale, 1970
       (Ph.D. in History). 290p. DAI 31, no.6 (Dec. 1970):
       2838-A; UM 70-25,253. Includes some information about
       von Kaufmann and the Sino-Russian controversy over Ili,
       1871-1881.

1659   DIETRICH, Craig. *Cotton Manufacture and Trade in China*
       (ca. 1500-1800). Chicago, 1970 (Ph.D. in Far Eastern
       Languages and Civilizations). 274p. Order copies from
       the Photoduplication Department, Joseph Regenstein Li-
       brary, University of Chicago.

1660   FEIG, Konnilyn Gay. *The Northwest and America's Inter-*
       national Relations, 1919-1941: A Regional Study of the
       Domestic Formulation of Foreign Policy. Washington
       (Seattle), 1970 (Ph.D. in History). 715p. DAI 31, no.
       10 (Apr. 1971): 5316-17-A; UM 71-8487. Includes the
       views that congressmen from Idaho, Oregon and Washing-
       ton had of American Far Eastern policies.

1661   GREINER, Peter. *Die Brokatuniform-Brigade (chin-i wei)*
       der Ming-Zeit von den Anfängen bis zum Ende der T'ien-
       shun-Periode (1368-1464). [German: The "Brocade-Uniform
       Guard" (i.e., Imperial Guard) (chin-i wei) of the Ming
       Dynasty from Its Beginnings to the End of the T'ien-shun
       Period (1368-1464).] Bochum, 1970 (Dr., Abteilung für
       Ostasienwissenschaft). Published as Die Brokatuniform-
       Brigade...(1368-1464) (Wiesbaden: Harrassowitz, 1975.
       vii, 272p. [Veröffentlichungen des Ostasien-Instituts
       der Ruhr-Universität Bochum, 12]).

1662   KOLATCH, Jonathan. *The Development of Modern Sports*
       and Physical Culture in China. Columbia, 1970 (Ph.D.).

343p.   DAI 33, no.10 (Apr. 1973): 5655-A; UM 73-8961.
Published as Sports, Politics, and Ideology in China
(New York: Jonathan David Publishers, 1972. xix, 254p.).

1663   KURGAN-VAN HENTENRYK, Regine. *Leopold II et les groupes*
financiers en Chine: la politique royale et ses pro-
longements (1895-1914). [French: Leopold II and the Financial Groups in China: Royal Policy and Its Consequences (1895-1914).] Université libre de Bruxelles,
1970 (Doctorat en histoire). Published as Leopold II...
1914 (Bruxelles: Palais des Académies, 1972. 969p.
[Académie royale de Belgique. Mémoires de la Classe des
Lettres. Collection in-8°. 2 ser., t.61, fasc.2]).

1664   LEWIN, Günter. *Die ersten fünfzig Jahre der Song-Dynas-*
tie in China. Beitrag zu einer Analyse der sozialöko-
nomischen Formation während der ersten 50 Jahre der chi-
nesischen Song-Dynastie (960-ca.1010). [German: The
First Fifty Years of the Sung Dynasty in China: A Contribution to an Analysis of the Socioeconomic Formation
of the Chinese Sung Dynasty during Its First 50 Years
(960-ca.1010).] Leipzig, 1970 (Dr., Sektion Afrika- und
Nahostwissenschaften). Published as Die ersten...(960-
ca.1010) (Berlin: Akademie-Verlag, 1973. 355p. [Ver-
öffentlichungen des Museums für Völkerkunde zu Leipzig,
H.23]).

1665   LI, Lincoln. *The Japanese Army in North China: Prob-*
lems of Political and Economic Control, July 1937 to
December 1941. Australian National, 1970 (Ph.D. in Far
Eastern History). v, 388p. Published as The Japanese
Army in North China: Problems of Political and Economic
Control (New York: Oxford University Press, 1975. 278p.
[East Asian historical monographs]).

1666   LØTVEIT, Trygve. *The Central Chinese Soviet Area: Some*
Aspects of Its Organisation and Administration, November
1931-October 1934. Leeds, 1970 (Ph.D. in Chinese Studies). iii, 467p. Published as Chinese Communism 1931-
1934: Experience in Civil Government (Lund, Sweden: Studentlitteratur, 1970. 290p. [Scandinavian Institute
of Asian Studies, monograph no.16]).

1667   LOMBARD-SALMON, Claudine. *Un exemple d'acculturation*
chinoise: la province du Gui zhou (Kouei-tcheou) au
XVIIIème siècle. [French: An Example of Chinese Acculturation: The Province of Kweichou during the Eighteenth
Century.] Paris, 1970 (Doctorat d'Etat ès lettres).
ix, 419 + 199p. A copy is available at the Bibliothèque
de la Sorbonne. Published as Un exemple...siècle

(Paris: Ecole française d'Extrême-Orient, 1972. 461p.
[Publications de l'Ecole française d'Extrême-Orient,
84]).

1668 MOORE, Jamie Wallace. *The Logic of Isolation and Neu-
trality: American Foreign Policy 1933-1935*. North Carolina, 1970 (Ph.D. in History). 400p. DAI 31, no.9
(Mar. 1971): 4684-A; UM 71-3583. Published as The New
Deal and East Asia: The Basis of American Policy
(Charleston, S.C.: The Citadel, 1973. 56p. [The Citadel monograph series, 11]). Includes an assessment of
conditions in China during the mid-1930s.

1669 ROSSABI, Morris. *Ming China's Relations with Hami and
Central Asia, 1404-1513: A Reexamination of Traditional
Chinese Foreign Policy*. Columbia, 1970 (Ph.D. in Political Science). 402p. DAI 33, no.11 (May 1973):
6262-63-A; UM 73-8980. Related publication by the author: China and Inner Asia: From 1368 to the Present
Day (New York: Pica Press; London: Thames and Hudson,
1975. 320p.).

1670 ROUX, Alain. *Le mouvement ouvrier à Shanghai de 1928 à
1930*. [French: The Workers' Movement in Shanghai, 1928-
1930.] Paris IV (Paris-Sorbonne), 1970 (Doctorat de 3e
cycle ès lettres). 433p. Abstracted in Université de
Paris. Faculté des lettres et sciences humaines. Positions des thèses de troisième cycle soutenues devant la
Faculté en 1970, pp.485-86. A copy is available at the
Bibliothèque de la Sorbonne, library catalogue no.
I 1525-in-4°.

1671 SCHWARZ, Rainer. *Die Revolutionierung des Chinesischen
Seeleuteverbandes*. [German: The Revolutionizing of the
Chinese Seamen's Association.] Deutsche Akademie der
Wissenschaften Berlin, 1970 (Dr.). 230p.

1672 SEIBT, Peter. *Engagement und Indifferenz in der amerikanischen Chinapolitik 1941-1950*. [German: Engagement
and Indifference in American China Policy, 1941-1950.]
Tübingen, 1970 (Dr., Philosophische Fakultät). Published as Engagement...1950 (Tübingen: Spangenberg,
1970. iii, 178p.).

1673 URAY, Géza. *Tanulmányok a királykori és a kései tibeti
történetírás kapcsolatáról: A Királyi Évkönyvek és az
Ótibeti Krónika maradványai Dpa'-bo Gcug-lag-'phreṅ-ba
Mkhas-p'ai dga'-ston-jában*. [Hungarian: Studies on the
Relationship of the Historiography of the Royal and Late
Tibetan Ages: Fragments of the Royal Annals and the Old
Tibetan Chronicles Found within the Mkhas-p'ai dga'-ston

by Dpa'-bo Gcug-lag-'phreṅ-ba.] Magyar Tudományos Akadémia, 1970 (Kandidátusi értekezés). 187p. Available
from the library of the Hungarian Academy of Sciences
in Budapest. Several papers based on the thesis have
been published in various European journals. The Mkhas-
pa'i dga'-ston was written between 1545 and 1565.

1674 WOODARD, Nelson Eugene. *Postwar Reconstruction and In-*
ternational Order: A Study of the Diplomacy of Charles
Evans Hughes, 1921-1925. Wisconsin, 1970 (Ph.D. in History). 391p. DAI 31, no.10 (Apr. 1971): 5343-A; UM
70-22,683. Deals in part with issues involving China
at the Washington conference (1921-22).

1675 WOU, Odoric Ying-kwong. *Militarism in Modern China as*
Exemplified in the Career of Wu P'ei-fu, 1916-1928.
Columbia, 1970 (Ph.D. in Political Science). 362p.
DAI 32, no.9 (Mar. 1972): 5169-A; UM 72-10,472.

INTERNATIONAL ECONOMIC AND POLITICAL RELATIONS
(since 1949)

1676 STEINBERG, Blema Solomon. *India's Neutralism in Theory*
and Practice. McGill, 1961 (Ph.D. in Economics and Political Science). v, 459p. Deals in part with India's
relations with the People's Republic of China.

1677 LAL, Gopal. *India's Trade Relations with South East*
Asia and the Far East since Independence. Bhagalpur,
1963 (D.Phil.). ii, 304, xxiii p.

1678 RAJBALAK, R. P. *Nepal's Trade Relations with India and*
Tibet. Patna, 1965 (Ph.D.).

1679 RAJHANS, Gauri Shanker. *A Study of External Forces on*
India-China Relations, 1949-1962. Bihar, 1967 (Ph.D.).

1680 RÖPER, Erich. *Die Formosa-Frage. Ein Beitrag zur Be-*
stimmung der völkerrechtlichen Stellung der chinesischen
Nationalregierung und des kommunistischen China. [Ger-
man: The Question of Formosa: Determining the Respective
International Legal Positions of the Nationalist Chinese
Regime and of the People's Republic of China.] Würzburg, 1967 (Dr.). 320p.

1681 SYMPSON, Patricia Colway. *The Kashmir Dispute in World*
Politics. St. John's, 1968 (Ph.D. in Political Science). 276p. DA 29, no.9 (Mar. 1969): 3202-A; UM
69-4139. Focuses on the involvement of the United Nations, the People's Republic of China and the U.S.S.R.

in this dispute between India and Pakistan.

1682 VENNING, Corey Brown. *Joseph Alsop: The Man and the Mirror*. Chicago, 1968 (Ph.D. in Political Science). iv, 379p. Order copies from the Photoduplication Department, Joseph Regenstein Library, University of Chicago. This examination of Alsop's journalistic writings about U.S. foreign policy and related matters includes coverage of Sino-American relations during the 1940s, Chinese economic development, the question of Taiwan, and the People's Republic of China.

1683 FREEDMAN, Robert Owen. *The Soviet Union's Utilization of Economic Pressure as an Instrument of Its Foreign Policy toward Other Communist Nations*. Columbia, 1969 (Ph.D. in Political Science). ii, 285p. Published as Economic Warfare in the Communist Bloc: A Study of Soviet Economic Pressure against Yugoslavia, Albania, and Communist China (New York: Praeger, 1970. xvi, 192p. [Praeger special studies in international economics and development]).

1684 HOLMES, Robert Alexander. *Chinese Foreign Policy toward Burma and Cambodia: A Comparative Analysis*. Columbia, 1969 (Ph.D. in Political Science). 486p. DAI 33, no.1 (July 1972): 379-A; UM 72-19,065.

1685 HORN, Robert Chisolm (III). *Soviet-Indonesian Relations, 1956-1966: A Case Study of Soviet Foreign Policy*. Fletcher School of Law and Diplomacy, 1969 (Ph.D.). ix, 649p. Includes coverage of Djakarta-Moscow-Peking relations.

1686 PARK, Tong-Whan. *Asian Conflict in Systemic Perspective: Application of Field Theory (1955 and 1963)*. Hawaii, 1969 (Ph.D. in Political Science). 202p. DAI 31, no.4 (Oct. 1970): 1868-A; UM 70-19,512. Published as Asian...1963 (Honolulu: Dimensionality of Nations Project, Dept. of Political Science, University of Hawaii, 1969. vii, 110p. [Research report no.35]). Attempts to predict conflict and cooperative behavior between any pair of Asian countries including the People's Republic of China and the Republic of China.

1687 SPAULDING, Wallace Holmes. *Ceylon's Relations with the Communist Bloc, 1956-1965: The Role of Ideological Affinity in the Making of Foreign Policy*. Pennsylvania, 1969 (Ph.D. in International Relations). 310p. DAI 30, no.6 (Dec. 1969): 2596-A; UM 69-21,431. Includes Ceylonese trade with the People's Republic of China.

1688   TURNER, Jack Justin. *Arab-Asian Positive Neutralism and United States Foreign Policy.* Kentucky, 1969 (Ph.D. in Political Science). 392p. DAI 30, no.8 (Feb. 1970): 3532-A; UM 70-2604. Includes information about Communist Chinese policies during the 1950s and the 1960s.

1689   YANG, Alexander Ching-an. *The Policy-Making Process in Japan's Policy toward the People's Republic of China: The Making of the Liao-Takasaki Trade Agreement of November 1962.* Columbia, 1969 (Ph.D. in Political Science). 345p. DAI 33, no.7 (Jan. 1973): 3747-A; UM 72-33,449.

1690   AUROUSSEAU, Jean-Pierre. *Les relations sino-japonaises de 1945 à 1952.* [French: Sino-Japanese Relations, 1945-1952.] Paris IV (Paris-Sorbonne), 1970 (Doctorat de 3e cycle ès lettres). i, 188p. A copy is available at the Bibliothèque de la Sorbonne, library catalogue no. I 1522-in-4°.

1691   BARTEL, Ronald Francis. *Attitudes toward Limited War: An Analysis of Elite and Public Opinion during the Korean Conflict.* Illinois, 1970 (Ph.D. in Political Science). 390p. DAI 31, no.9 (Mar. 1971): 4863-A; UM 71-5037. Includes American perceptions of Communist China as the real enemy in the Korean War.

1692   BETTATI, Mario. *Les thèmes du conflit sino-soviétique.* [French: The Themes of the Sino-Soviet Conflict.] Nice, 1970 (Doctorat d'Etat en droit). 457p. Published as Le conflit sino-soviétique (Paris: A. Colin, 1971. 2 vols. [Collection U2, 174-175]).

1693   LIU, Leo Yueh-yun. *Communist China as a Nuclear Power: Its Effects on the International Political System.* Alberta, 1970 (Ph.D. in Political Science). vii, 207p. Order copies directly from the Canadian Theses Division, National Library of Canada at Ottawa; available only in microfilm format. Published as China as a Nuclear Power in World Politics (New York: Taplinger; London: Macmillan, 1972. 125p.).

1694   NIZAMI, Taufiq Ahmed. *The Attitude of the Communist Party of India towards India's Foreign Policy.* Aligarh Muslim, 1970 (Ph.D.). Abstracted in Indian Dissertation Abstracts 1, no.2 (Apr./June 1973): 120-122. Deals extensively with India's policy towards the People's Republic of China.

1695   OSMER, Harold Henry. *United States Religious Press Response to the Containment Policy during the Period of the Korean War.* New York, 1970 (Ph.D., School of Education). 266p. DAI 31, no.5 (Nov. 1970): 2318-A; UM 70-21,144. Includes the American response to Chinese Communist intervention in the Korean War.

1696 RAABE, Francis Conrad. *The China Issue in Canada: Politics and Foreign Policy.* Pennsylvania State, 1970 (Ph.D. in Political Science). 362p. DAI 32, no.2 (Aug. 1971): 1052-53-A; UM 71-21,790. On Canada's relations with the People's Republic of China, 1949-1969.

1697 SZENBERG, Michael. *The Economics of the Israeli Diamond Industry.* City University of New York, 1970 (Ph.D. in Economics). 259p. DAI 31, no.11 (May 1971): 5622-23-A; UM 71-12,200. Published as The Economics... Industry (New York: Basic Books, 1973. xxi, 183p.). Includes some information about Israeli sales of finished diamonds to Hong Kong.

1698 VIDYA, Nand. *British India and Her Himalayan Neighbors: Sikkim, Tibet and Bhutan (1890-1910).* Magadh, 1970 (Ph.D.). Abstracted in Indian Dissertation Abstracts 1, no.2 (Apr./June 1973): 131-32.

LANGUAGE AND LINGUISTICS

1699 KALLGREN, Gerty. *Studies in Sung Time Colloquial Chinese as Revealed in Chu Hi's Ts'üanshu.* Stockholm, 1958 (Akad. avh.). Published as Studies...Ts'üanshu (Stockholm, 1958. 165p. [Museum of Far Eastern Antiquities. Bulletin, no.30]). On the Chüan shu by Chu Hsi (1130-1200).

1700 RÓNA-TAS, András. *Tibeto-Mongolica: The Tibetan Loanwords of Monguor and the Development of the Archaic Tibetan Dialects.* Magyar Tudományos Akadémia [Budapest, Hungary], 1962 (kand.). Published as Tibeto-Mongolica ...Dialects (The Hague: Mouton, 1966. 232p. [Indo-Iranian monographs, 7]).

1701 KAŁUŻYŃSKI, Stanisław. *Mongolische Elemente in der jakutischen Sprache.* [German: Mongolian Elements in the Yakut Language.] Uniwersytet Warszawski, 1963 (Doktor habilitowany, Wydz. Filologiczny). Published as Mongolische...Sprache (Warszawa: Państwowe Wydawn. Naukowe, 1961. 169p. [Prace orientalistyczne, t.10]).

1702 LEE, Mercedes. *Laut und Sinn in der chinesischen Sprache.* [German: Sound and Meaning in the Chinese

Language.] Wien, 1966 (Dr., Philosophische Fakultät).
138, vi p.

1703 WEIDMANN, Horst. *Untersuchung zu Vorkommen und Funktion
der grammatischen Formen zum Ausdruck kausaler Beziehungen in den Texten des Meng-tzu und Mo-tzu. Ein Beitrag
zur Grammatik des klassischen Chinesisch.* [German:
Studies of the Occurrence and Function of the Grammatical Forms Expressing Causal Relationships in the Texts
of Mencius and Mo Tzu: A Contribution to the Grammar of
Classical Chinese.] Freiburg i.B., 1967 (Dr., Philosophische Fakultät). iv, 199p.

1704 STUMPF, Peter. *Der Gebrauch der Demonstrativ-Pronomina
im tocharischen.* [German: The Use of the Demonstrative
Pronouns in the Tocharian Language.] Frankfurt a.M.,
1968 (Dr., Philosophische Fakultät). Published as Der
Gebrauch...Tocharischen (Wiesbaden: Harrassowitz, 1971.
xix, 158p.).

1705 DELLINGER, David Whitley. *Akha: A Transformational Description.* Australian National, 1969 (Ph.D. in Linguistics). xi, 271p. A grammatical study of a Tibeto-Burman language that is spoken in Yünnan.

1706 RICHTER, Gunnar. *Zu den zweisilbigen Verb-Objekt-Kon-
struktionen im modernen Chinesisch.* [German: On the
Two-Syllable Verb-Object Constructions in the Modern
Chinese Language.] Humboldt-Universität Berlin, 1969
(Dr., Philosophische Fakultät). 106p.

1707 SCHMIDT, Claus-Peter. *Maskuline Genuskongruenz beim
Plural der Substantiva alternantia im Tocharischen.*
[German: Masculine Gender Agreement in the Plurals of
Alternating Nouns in Tocharian.] Frankfurt, 1969 (Dr.,
Philosophische Fakultät). Published as Maskuline...To-
charischen (Frankfurt a.M., 1972. xiv, 132p.).

1708 ZIEME, Peter. *Untersuchungen zur Schrift und Sprache
der manichäisch-türkischen Turfantexte.* [German: Studies of the Script and Language of the Manichaean-Turkish
Turfan Texts.] Humboldt-Universität Berlin, 1969 (Dr.,
Sektion Asienwissenschaft). x, 290p. On the medieval
texts discovered in present-day Sinkiang.

1709 BEUTEL, Helga. *Zur Problematik der Elementarsätze und
der Kernsätze im modernen Chinesisch.* [German: On the
Problems of Elementary and Core Sentences in Modern Chinese.] Humboldt-Universität Berlin, 1970 (Dr., Gesell-
schaftswissenschaftliche Fakultät). 150, vi p.

1710 CHU, Cheng-hsi. *The Structures of Shr̀ and Yŏu in*

Mandarin Chinese. Texas, 1970 (Ph.D. in Linguistics).
213p. DAI 32, no.6 (Dec. 1971): 3281-A; UM 72-2318.

1711 WANG, Peter Chin-tang. *A Transformation Approach to*
Chinese Ba and Bei. Texas, 1970 (Ph.D. in Linguistics).
130p. DAI 32, no.7 (Jan. 1972): 3983-A; UM 72-2435.

LAW AND THE JUDICIAL SYSTEM

1712 LIN, Chü-chih. *Elterliche Gewalt im deutschen, japani-*
schen, und chinesischen Recht. [German: Parental Authority in German, Japanese and Chinese Law.] München,
1967 (Dr.). Published as Elterliche...Recht (München:
Foto-Druck, 1966. vi, 82p.).

1713 LUBMAN, Stanley B. *Chinese Communist Legal Institu-*
tions: Two Essays. Part I: "Mao and Mediation: Politics
and Dispute Resolutions in Communist China." Part II:
"Form and Function in the Chinese Criminal Process."
Columbia, 1969 (J.S.D.). Part I was published in the
California Law Review 55, no.5 (Nov. 1967): 1284-1359;
part II appeared in the Columbia Law Review 69, no.4
(Apr. 1969): 535-575.

1714 SHA, Zui-chi. *Parlament und Regierung im Licht des chi-*
nesischen Verfassungsrechts; entwicklungsgeschichtlich
dargestellt. [German: Parliament and Government in the
Light of Chinese Constitutional Law: A Developmental
Perspective.] Wien, 1969 (Dr., Rechts- und Staatswissenschaftliche Fakultät). vi, 161p. Related publication by the author: Chung-hua min kuo hsien fa piao
chieh. By Jui-chih Hsieh [i.e., Zui-chi Sha] (Taipei,
1974. 202p.).

1715 CHENG, Chung-mo. *Geschichtliche Entwicklung und Charak-*
teristik des chinesischen Verwaltungsrechts. [German:
Historical Development and Characteristics of Chinese
Administrative Law.] Wien, 1970 (Dr., Rechts- und
Staatswissenschaftliche Fakultät).

1716 PFEFFER, Richard Monroe. *Understanding Business Con-*
tracts in Communist China, 1949-1963. Harvard, 1970
(Ph.D. in Political Science). i, 210p. Available at
the Harvard University Archives, Pusey Library, call no.
HU 90.9831. Published as Understanding Business Con-
tracts in China, 1949-1963 (Cambridge, Mass.: East
Asian Research Center, Harvard University, 1973. xv,
147p. [Harvard East Asian monographs, 53]).

1717   SENGER, Harro von. *Kaufverträge im traditionellen Chi-
       na.* [German: Sales Contracts in Traditional China.]
       Zürich, 1970 (Dr., Rechts- und Staatswissenschaftliche
       Fakultät). vi, 223p. Published as <u>Kaufverträge...Chi-
       na</u> (Zürich: Schulthess, 1970. 222p. [Zürcher Beiträge
       zur Rechtswissenschaft, n.F., Heft 337]).

1718   SHIH, Jhy-mou. *Die Abwicklung des Seefrachtvertrages
       und die Haftung des Reeders im deutschen und chinesi-
       schen Recht.* [German:Settlement of the Bill of Lading
       and the Liability of the Shipowner in German and Chi-
       nese Law.] Frankfurt a.M., 1970 (Dr., Rechtswissen-
       schaftliche Fakultät). Published as <u>Die Abwicklung...
       Recht</u> (Bamberg, 1970. 261p.).

LIBRARIES

1719   ANDERSON, James Doig. *A Comparative Study of Methods
       of Arranging Chinese Language Author-Title Catalogs in
       Large American Chinese-Language Collections.* Columbia,
       1970 (D.L.S.). 151p. DAI 33, no.7 (Jan. 1973): 3683-A;
       UM 72-33,402.

LITERATURE

1720   KALVODOVÁ, Dana. *Ting Ling, Život a dílo.* [Czech: Ting
       Ling, Her Life and Work.] Doktorská práce University
       Karlovy (Praha), 1952. On a 20th century writer.

1721   STEININGER, Hans. *Kuan Yin-tzu im Spiegel der literar-
       historischen Kritik. Der Streit der Meinungen um den
       Text und den Mann Kuan Yin-tzu mit Beiträgen zur Ar-
       beitsweise der chinesischen literarhistorischen Kritik
       und einem Ausblick auf die neun Kapitel des Traktates.*
       [German: Kuan Yin-tzu as Seen in Literary-Historical
       Criticism. The Controversy of Opinions about the Text
       and the Man Kuan Yin-tzu with Contributions to the Func-
       tion of Criticism in the Area of Chinese Literary His-
       tory and a Conspectus of the Nine Chapters of the Trac-
       tate.] Erlangen-Nürnberg, 1960 (Habilitationsschrift).
       171p.

1722   TAGORE, Amitendra Nath. *Left Wing Literary Debates in
       Modern China, 1918-1937.* Visva-Bharati, 1962 (Ph.D.).
       Published as <u>Literary Debates in Modern China, 1918-
       1937</u> (Tokyo: Centre for East Asian Cultural Studies,

1967. xiv, 280p. [East Asian cultural studies series,
11]).

1723 GRUNER, Fritz. *Der literarisch-künstlerische Beitrag
Mao Duns zur Entwicklung des Realismus der neuen chinesischen Literatur.* [German: The Literary and Artistic
Contribution of Mao Tun to the Growth of Realism in Modern Chinese Literature.] Leipzig, 1967 (Habilitationsschrift). v, 274p.

1724 KOTZENBERG, Heike. *Der Dichter Pao Chao (✝466). Untersuchung zu Leben und Werk.* [German: The Poet Pao Chao
(Died 466 A.D.): A Study of His Life and Work.] Bonn,
1970 (Dr., Philosophische Fakultät). Published as Der
Dichter...Werk (Bonn, 1971. 187p.).

1725 LEIMBIGLER, Peter. *Mei Yao-ch'en (1002-1060). Versuch
einer literarischen und politischen Deutung.* [German:
Mei Yao-ch'en (1002-1060): Attempt at a Literary and Political Interpretation.] Bochum, 1970(?). Published
as Mei Yao-ch'en...Deutung (Wiesbaden: Harrassowitz,
1970. vii, 158p. [Veröffentlichungen des Ostasien-Instituts der Ruhr-Universität Bochum, 6]).

1726 McDOUGALL, Bonnie Suzanne. *The Introduction of Western
Literary Theories into China, 1919-1925.* Sydney, 1970
(Ph.D. in Oriental Studies). vii, 396p. Published as
The Introduction...1925 (Tokyo: Centre for East Asian
Cultural Studies, 1971. 368p. [East Asian cultural
studies series, nos.14-15]).

MASS COMMUNICATIONS AND JOURNALISM

1727 WONG, Soon-Chong. *L'étude du contenu des journaux de
Singapour quant à la place des informations d'origine
étrangère, et spécialement chinoise, dans cette presse.*
[French: A Study of the Contents of Newspapers in Singapore with Regard to the Place of Information of Foreign Origin, Especially Chinese, in This Press.] Strasbourg, 1970 (Doctorat de 3e cycle en journalisme). 311p.

MUSIC

1728 KARA, György. *Egy keleti mongol regős énekei és nyelve.*
[Hungarian: The Songs and Language of an Oriental Mongolian Minstrel.] Magyar Tudományos Akadémia, 1965
(kand.). 407p.

1729 GIMM, Martin. *Das Yüeh-fu tsa-lu des Tuan An-chieh.*
      Studien zur Geschichte von Musik, Schauspiel, und Tanz
      in der T'ang-Dynasty. [German: The Yüeh fu tsa lu of
      Tuan An-chieh: Studies in the History of T'ang Music,
      Drama, and Dance.] Köln, 1967 (Dr., Philosophische Fa-
      kultät). Published as Das Yüeh-fu tsa-lu...T'ang-Dynas-
      ty (Wiesbaden: Harrassowitz, 1966. 631p. [Asiatische
      Forschungen; 19]).

1730 SCHÖNFELDER, Gerd. *Die Peking-Oper "Yue mu ci zi" und*
      ihre schlagrhythmische und formstrukturelle Gestalt.
      [German: The Peking Opera Yüeh-mu ch'i tzu and Its
      Rhythmical and Structural Form.] Leipzig, 1969 (Dr.,
      Sektion Kulturwissenschaft und Germanistik). xviii,
      176p. Published as Die Musik der Peking-Oper (Leipzig:
      Deutscher Verlag für Musik, 1972. 287p.).

OVERSEAS CHINESE COMMUNITIES

1731 MELDRUM, George Weston. *The History of the Treatment*
      of Foreign and Minority Groups in California, 1830-1860.
      Stanford, 1948 (Ph.D. in History). 437p. Chinese immi-
      grants are discussed on pages 355-385.

1732 FISHER, Lloyd Horace. *The Harvest Labor Market in Cal-*
      ifornia. Harvard, 1949 (Ph.D.). Published as The Har-
      vest...California (Cambridge, Mass.: Harvard University
      Press, 1953. viii, 183p. [Wertheim publications in in-
      dustrial relations]). Includes Chinese laborers.

1733 HEILMAN, Grace Elizabeth. *The Early History of the La-*
      bor Movement in Los Angeles. Pennsylvania, 1949 (Ph.D.
      in History). 486p. Chapter 6 examines anti-Chinese
      agitation in 1885 and 1886.

1734 DAVISON, Stanley Roland. *The Leadership of the Recla-*
      mation Movement, 1875-1902. California (Berkeley), 1950
      (Ph.D. in History). iv, 267p. Includes coverage of
      the reclamation work in California undertaken by the
      Chinese.

1735 KENNEDY, Chester Barrett. *Newspapers of Californian*
      Northern Mines, 1850-1886: A Record of Life, Letters
      and Culture. Stanford, 1950 (Ph.D. in English). xiii,
      641p. Includes information about the Chinese in Cali-
      fornia.

1736 LAU, James Brownlee. *Attitude Change as Related to*
      Change in Perception of the Group Norm. Michigan, 1954

(Ph.D. in Social Psychology). 135p. DA 14, no.7 (July
1954): 1108; UM 8328. Includes American Caucasian attitudes toward Chinese Americans.

1737 FAHEY, Frank Michael. *Denis Kearney: A Study in Dema-*
goguery. Stanford, 1956 (Ph.D. in History). 330p. DA
16, no.3 (Mar. 1957): 611-12; UM 19,923. Includes this
Californian's anti-Chinese speeches, 1877-1880.

1738 THOMPSON, John. *The Settlement Geography of the Sacra-*
mento-San Joaquin Delta, California. Stanford, 1958
(Ph.D. in Geography). 636p. DA 19, no.2 (Aug. 1958):
295-96; UM 58-2516. Includes reclamation work undertaken by the Chinese during the 1800s.

1739 CHING, James Christopher. *A History and Criticism of*
Political Speaking in the Hawaiian Kingdom: 1874-1891.
Missouri, 1962 (Ph.D. in Speech and Dramatic Art). 290p.
DA 23, no.12 (June 1963): 4782; UM 63-1550. Contains a
section on anti-Chinese speeches.

1740 SMITH, Duane A. *Mining Camps and the Settlement of the*
Trans-Mississippi Frontier, 1860-1890. Colorado, 1964
(Ph.D. in History). 367p. DA 25, no.12 (June 1965):
7233; UM 65-4272. Includes information about the Chinese. Published as Rocky Mountain Mining Camps: The Urban Frontier (Bloomington: Indiana University Press,
1967. xii, 304p.).

1741 SAKUMOTO, Raymond Eiji. *Social Areas of Honolulu: A*
Study of the Ethnic Dimensions in an Urban Social Struc-
ture. Northwestern, 1965 (Ph.D. in Sociology). 166p.
DA 26, no.6 (Dec. 1965): 3523-24; UM 65-12,159. Includes Chinese Americans.

1742 TAHER, Mohommod. *Asians in New Zealand: A Geographical*
Review and Interpretation. Auckland, 1965 (Ph.D. in Ge-
ography). xv, 350p. Request copies from the Reference
Librarian, University of Auckland, Private Bag, Auck-
land, New Zealand. Taher is concerned with Chinese,
Indians and Lebanese.

1743 DAWS, Alan Gavan. *Honolulu--The First Century: Influ-*
ences in the Development of the Town to 1876. Hawaii,
1966 (Ph.D.). 799p. DA 27, no.6 (Dec. 1966): 1751-A;
UM 66-13,696. Includes information about Honolulu's
Chinese population, Chinese immigration problems, and
anti-Chinese sentiments.

1744 SINKLER, George. *The Racial Ideas of American Presi-*
dents: From Lincoln to Theodore Roosevelt. Columbia
(Teachers College), 1966 (Ed.D.). 480p. DA 27, no.5

(Nov. 1966): 1307-A; UM 66-10,316.   Includes their views of the Chinese.

1745   FARMER, George Luther. *Majority and Minority Americans: An Analysis of Best Selling American Fiction from 1926-1966.* Southern California, 1968 (Ed.D.).   243p.   DA 28, no.11 (May 1968): 4457-58-A; UM 68-7180.   Includes perceptions of the Chinese in American literature.

1746   LEINENWEBER, Charles Robert. *Immigration and the Decline of the Internationalism in the American Working Class Movement, 1864-1919.* California (Berkeley), 1968 (Ph.D.).   257p.   DAI 30, no.3 (Sept. 1969): 1257-58-A; UM 69-14,938.   Includes brief information relating to Chinese immigration into the United States.

1747   LUCKINGHAM, Bradford Franklin. *Associational Life of the Urban Frontier: San Francisco, 1848-1856.* California (Davis), 1968 (Ph.D. in History).   247p.   DA 29, no. 7 (Jan. 1969): 2185-86-A; UM 69-858.   Deals in part with San Francisco's Chinese population.

1748   OLSEN, Barton Clark. *Lawlessness and Vigilantes in America: An Historical Analysis Emphasizing California and Montana.* Utah, 1968 (Ph.D. in History).   252p.   DA 29, no.8 (Feb. 1969): 2654-A; UM 69-3509.   Includes anti-Chinese activities in California.

1749   RAMALINGAM, Sarojini Thevi. *Investigations of Variations in Blood and Urinary Amino Acids in Humans in Relation to Age, Different Ethnic Groups and Pathological Conditions.* Singapore, 1968 (Ph.D. in Biochemistry).   xvii, 211p.   The subjects included Chinese residents of Singapore.

1750   CHONG, Tong-mun. *The Study of Bronchial Asthma in Children in Singapore and Their Management by Hypnotherapy.* Singapore, 1969 (M.D.).   iv, 120p.   Involved Chinese.

1751   GOH, Yoon-fong. *Trade and Politics in Banjarmasin, 1700-1747.* London, 1969 (Ph.D. in Arts, School of Oriental and African Studies).   349p.   Includes the activities of the Chinese traders who congregated in this southern Borneo port.

1752   KNIGHT, Franklin. *Cuban Slave Society on the Eve of Abolition, 1838-1880.* Wisconsin, 1969 (Ph.D. in History).   367p.   DAI 30, no.3 (Sept. 1969): 1096-97-A; UM 69-9696.   Published as <u>Slave Society in Cuba during the Nineteenth Century</u> (Madison: University of Wisconsin Press, 1970.   xxi, 228p.).   Includes the Chinese in Cuba.

1753   LIGHT, Ivan Hubert. *Sociological Aspects of Self-Employment and Social Welfare among Chinese, Japanese, and Negroes in Northern, Urban Areas of the United States, 1900-1940.* California (Berkeley), 1969 (Ph.D. in Sociology). xvii, 453p. Order copies from the Library Photographic Service, General Library, University of California at Berkeley. Published as Ethnic Enterprise in America: Business and Welfare among Chinese, Japanese, and Blacks (Berkeley: University of California Press, 1972. 209p.).

1754   LOTCHIN, Roger Williams. *A History of San Francisco, 1846-1856.* Chicago, 1969 (Ph.D. in History). 807p. Order copies from the Photoduplication Department, Joseph Regenstein Library, University of Chicago. Includes the Chinese in San Francisco.

1755   POURTIER, Roland. *Les régions littorales du Cambodge.* [French: The Coastal Regions of Cambodia.] Paris, 1969 (Doctorat de 3ᵉ cycle ès lettres). 152p. Abstracted in Université de Paris. Faculté des Lettres et Sciences Humaines. Positions des thèses de troisième cycle soutenues devant la Faculté en 1969, pp.276-77. A copy is available at the Bibliothèque de la Sorbonne, library catalogue no. I 1176-4°. Pourtier pays particular attention to the active Chinese community living there.

1756   ABBOTT, Kenneth Albert. *Cultural Change, Psychosocial Functioning, and the Family: A Case Study in the Chinese-American Community of San Francisco.* California (Berkeley), 1970 (D.S.W.). 386p. DAI 32, no.2 (Aug. 1971): 1077-A; UM 71-20,755. Published as Harmony and Individualism: Changing Chinese Psychosocial Functioning in Taipei and San Francisco (Taipei: Oriental Cultural Service, 1970. xiv, 374p. [Asian folklore and social life monographs, 12]).

1757   ARAFAT, Ibtihaj Said. *The Foreign Stock and the Native Stock in the United States: A Demographic Profile.* Oklahoma State, 1970 (Ph.D. in Sociology). 138p. DAI 31, no.11 (May 1971): 6171-A; UM 71-11,091. Includes Chinese Americans.

1758   DA COSTA, Joel Luis. *Chronic Obstructive Lung Diseases in Singapore.* Singapore, 1970 (M.D.). v, 267p. 96% of the patients Da Costa studied were ethnically Chinese.

1759   DE KONINCK, Rodolphe. *Chinese Farmers of Singapore: A Study in Social Geography.* Singapore, 1970 (Ph.D. in Geography). xxi, 331p.

1760 LICHLITER, William F. *Political Reflections of an Age:*
      The New York Graphic Weeklies during the 1880's. Bran-
      deis, 1970 (Ph.D. in the History of American Civiliza-
      tion). 457p. DAI 31, no.6 (Dec. 1970): 2849-A; UM
      70-24,649. Contains some information about American
      opinion of the Chinese in the West.

1761 MANN, Ralph Emerson (II). *The Social and Political*
      Structure of Two California Mining Towns, 1850-1870.
      Stanford, 1970 (Ph.D. in History). 206p. DAI 31, no.8
      (Feb. 1971): 4091-92-A; UM 71-2802. Includes informa-
      tion about the Chinese.

1762 MARUTANI, Herbert Katsuyuki. *Labor-Management Relations*
      in Agriculture: A Study of the Hawaiian Sugar Industry.
      Hawaii, 1970 (Ph.D. in Agricultural Economics). viii,
      153p. Order copies from the Interlibrary Loan Depart-
      ment, University of Hawaii Library. Includes Asian
      Americans in Hawaii.

1763 NANN, Richard Chun. *Urban Renewal and Relocation of*
      Chinese Community Families. California (Berkeley), 1970
      (D.S.W.). 132p. DAI 32, no.2 (Aug. 1971): 1104-A; UM
      71-20,757. On Chinese families living in Vancouver,
      British Columbia, Canada.

1764 PALUCH, Ryszard. *Analyza antropologiczna ludności poch-*
      odzenia tatarskiego zamieszkałej w województwie biało-
      stochim. [Polish: An Anthropological Analysis of People
      of Tartar Descent Living in the Bialystok Area (in
      Northeastern Poland).] Uniwersytet Wrocławski im. B.
      Bieruta, 1970 (Rozprawa doktorska, Wydz. Nauk Przyrod-
      niczych).

1765 WONG, P. C. N. *An Epidemiologic Study of the Long Limb*
      Bones, the Vertical Column and the Calcaneum: A Singa-
      pore Population Study. Singapore, 1970 (M.D. in Ortho-
      paedic Surgery). 75% of Wong's subjects were ethnically
      Chinese.

                    POLITICS AND GOVERNMENT

1766 ABDUSHAH, Abdi A. *An Exploration in Developmental The-*
      ory: Resocialization and Political Development. Oregon,
      1969 (Ph.D. in Political Science). 252p. DAI 31, no.3
      (Sept. 1970): 1353-A; UM 70-15,328. Includes a study
      of students from China.

1767 CHANG, Parris Hsu-cheng. *Patterns and Processes of*

*Policy-Making in Communist China 1955-1962: Three Case
Studies.* Columbia, 1969 (Ph.D. in Political Science).
385p. DAI 33, no.1 (July 1972): 368-69-A; UM 72-19,047.
Published as <u>Power and Policy in China</u> (University Park:
Pennsylvania State University Press, 1975. 276p.).

1768   LIN, Chiang-chang. *Le gouvernement de la Chine populaire.* [French: The Government of the People's Republic
of China.] Paris, 1969 (Doctorat d'Université en droit).
204p. A copy is available at the Bibliothèque Cujas de
Droit et des Sciences Economiques, library catalogue no.
DZ 1969/84.

1769   MOSELEY, George Van Horn (III). *Policy toward Ethnic
Minorities on the Southern Frontier of the People's Re-
public of China.* Oxford, 1970 (D.Phil. in Social Stud-
ies). 272p. Published as <u>The Consolidation of the
South China Frontier</u> (Berkeley: University of California
Press, 1973. x, 192p.).

1770   PASIERBSKY, Fritz. *Zur Politsprache im modernen China.
Sprache, Denken, Wirklichkeit bei Mao Tse-tung.* [German:
On Political Language in Modern China: Mao Tse-tung and
Language, Thought, and Reality.] Bochum, 1970 (Dr., Ab-
teilung für Ostasienwissenschaft). Published as <u>Zur
Politsprache...Mao Tse-tung</u> (Wiesbaden: Harrassowitz,
1971. 137p. [Veröffentlichungen des Ostasien-Instituts
der Ruhr-Universität Bochum, 7]).

1771   TRUHART, Peter. *Drei Systeme der allgemeinen Kontrolle
der Staatsverwaltung durch besondere Organe der Verfas-
sung; die Systeme des Parlamentsbeauftragten (Ombudsman), der "Allgemeinen Aufsicht" durch die Staatsanwalt-
schaft in den sozialistischen Staaten und des Kontroll-
rats der Republik China (Taiwan).* [German: Three Systems for General Supervision of Public Administration
through Specific Constitutional Organs: The System of
Parliamentary Representatives (Ombudsman), the "General
Inspection" through the Public Prosecutor's Office in
the Socialist States, and the Control Council of the Republic of China (Taiwan).] Bonn, 1970 (Dr., Rechts-
und Staatswissenschaftliche Fakultät). Published as
<u>Drei...Taiwan</u> (Bonn, 1970. xlvii, 150p.).

RELIGION AND PHILOSOPHY

1772   CHOU, Hsiang-kuang. *An Outline of the History of Buddhism in China.* Delhi, 1955 (Ph.D.). Published as <u>A</u>

History of Chinese Buddhism (Allahabad: Indo-Chinese
Literature Publications, 1955. 264p.).

1773 DHAR, Satchidananda. *A Survey of the Avadana Literature
with Special Reference to Sumagadhavadana from Indian
and Tibetan Sources.* Calcutta, 1956 (Ph.D.).

1774 BRUNNER, Paul. *L'euchologe de la mission de Chine; Edi-
tio princeps 1628 et développements jusqu'à nos jours.
Contribution à l'histoire des livres de prières.*
[French: The Euchology of the China Mission; First Edition 1628 and Developments up to the Present Time. Contribution to the History of Prayer Books.] Trier, 1960
(Dr., Theologische Fakultät). Published as L'euchologe
...prières (Münster: Aschendorff, 1964. xii, 368p.
[Missionswissenschaftliche Abhandlungen und Texte, 28]).

1775 RHEE, Kyu Ho. *Dialektik des Yih Ging im Lichte der
abendländischen Dialektik.* [German: Dialectic of the
I Ching in Light of Western Dialectic.] Tübingen, 1962
(Dr.). 160p.

1776 HAHN, Michael. *Jñanasrimitras Vrttamalastuti. Eine
Beispielsammlung zur altindischen Metrik. Nach der ti-
betischen Tanjur herausgegeben, übersetzt, und erläutert.*
[German: Jñanasrimitra's Vrttamalastuti: An Illustrative
Collection of Early Indian Prosody, Edited in Accordance
with the Tibetan Tanjur, Translated, and Interpreted.]
Marburg, 1967 (Dr., Philosophische Fakultät). 189 +
209p.

1777 HUNG, Lien-te. *Hu Shih und die Politik des republikan-
ischen China; die Staats-, Rechts- und Kulturphilosophie
des Hu Shih.* [German: Hu Shih and the Politics of Republican China: His Philosophy about State, Law, and
Culture.] Wien, 1967 (Dr., Rechts- und staatswissenschaftliche Fakultät). 232p.

1778 CHATTOPADHYAY, Aloka. *Atisa and Tibet: Life and Works
of Kipankar Srijanana in Relation to the History and Religion of Tibet.* Calcutta, 1968 (Ph.D.).

1779 FIEDELER, Frank. *Hua-Shu, das Buch des Verwandelns.
Darstellung der Lehre und Übersetzung des Textes. Ein
Beitrag zum Verständnis chinesischer Philosophie.*
[German: Hua shu, the Book of Transformation: A Presen-
tation of Its Teachings and a Translation of Its Text.
A Contribution to the Understanding of Chinese Philoso-
phy.] Erlangen-Nürnberg, 1968 (Dr.). Published as Hua-
Shu...Philosophie (Würzburg, Vervielfältigung: E. Schmitt
und M. Meyer, 1967? 271p.).

1780 IIDA, Shotaro. *An Introduction to Svātantrika-Mādhyami-
ka.* Wisconsin, 1968 (Ph.D. in Indian Studies). 320p.
DA 29, no.12 (June 1969): 4547-48-A; UM 68-17,903. This
investigation of the system propounded by Bhāvaviveka
(ca.490-570) includes a study of Buddhist thought within the Tibetan tradition.

1781 NAUNDORF, Gert. *Aspekte des anarchischen Gedankens in
China. Darstellung der Lehre und Übersetzung des Textes
Wu Neng Tzu.* [German: Aspects of the Anarchic Thought
in China: A Presentation of the Teachings and a Transla-
tion of the Text Wu neng tzu.] Würzburg, 1968 (Dr.,
Philosophische Fakultät). Published as Aspekte...Wu
Neng Tzu (Würzburg, 1972. 202p.).

1782 STEINFELD, Erich. *Die menschlichen Beziehungen in der
Sicht der Philosophen Mo-tzu, Meng-Tzu und Hsün-Tzu.*
[German: Human Relations as Seen by the Philosophers Mo-
tzu, Mencius (Meng-tzu), and Hsün-tzu.] Mainz, 1968
(Dr., Philosophische Fakultät). Published as Die sozialen Lehren der altchinesischen Philosophen Mo-Tzu,
Meng-Tzu und Hsün-Tzu (Berlin: Akademie-Verlag, 1971.
iv, 186p. [Schriften zur Geschichte und Kultur des alten Orients, 2]).

1783 HSIA, Tao-chen. *La pensée économique de Kuan-Tze.*
[French: The Economic Thought of Kuan-tzu.] Paris, 1969
(Doctorat d'Université ès lettres). 127p. A copy is
available at the Bibliothèque de la Sorbonne, library
catalogue no. W Univ. 1969 (71)-4°.

1784 KÜNSTLER, Mieczysław Jerzy. *Ma Jong: vie et oeuvre.*
[French: Ma Jung (79-166 A.D.): His Life and His Works.]
Uniwersytet Warszawski, 1969 (Doktor habilitowany, Wydz.
Filologii Obcych). Published as Ma Jong...oeuvre (Warszawa: Państwowe Wydawn. Naukowe, 1969. 223p. [Disser-
tationes Universitatis Varsoviensis, 35]). Includes an
annotated translation and analysis of Ma Jung's Kuang-
ch'eng sung.

1785 LAM, Shui-fook. *Der Ursprung der chinesischen Tanzmas-
ken im Exorzismus.* [German: The Origin of Chinese Dance
Masks in Exorcism.] Köln, 1969 (Dr., Philosophische
Fakultät). vi, 131p.

1786 MORITZ, Ralf. *Hui Shi und die Entwicklung des philo-
sophischen Denkens im alten China.* [German: Hui Shih
and the Development of Philosophical Thought in Ancient
China.] Leipzig, 1969 (Dr., Sektion Afrika- und Nahostwissenschaft). 319p. Published as Hui Shi...China
(Berlin: Akademie-Verlag, 1973. vii, 203p. [Schriften

zur Geschichte und Kultur des alten Orients, 12]). On a 4th century B.C. dialectician famous for his Ten Paradoxes.

1787 RUEGG, David Seyfort. *Le traité sur le Tathāgatagarbha de Bu Ston Rin Chen Grub: traduit du "De bžin gšegs pa'i snin po gsal žin mdzes par byed pa'i rgyan".* [French: The Treatise on the Tathāgatagarbha of Bu-stoń Rin-chen-grub (1290-1364): Translated from the De bžin gšegs pa'i snin po gsal žin mdzes par byed pa'i rgyan.] Paris, 1969 (Doctorat d'Etat ès lettres). Thèse complementaire. various pagings. Published as Le traité... rgyan (Paris: Ecole française d'Extrême-Orient, 1973. 162p.).

1788 SANDER, Lore. *Paläographisches zu den Sanskrithandschriften der Berliner Turfansammlung.* [German: Palaeographic Investigations of the Sanskrit Manuscripts in the Turfan Collection in Berlin.] Göttingen, 1969 (Dr., Philosophische Fakultät). Published as Paläographisches ...Turfansammlung (Wiesbaden: Steiner, 1968. x, 203p. [Verzeichnis der orientalischen Handschriften in Deutschland. Supplementband, 8]). On the manuscripts from eastern Sinkiang brought to Germany by 4 Royal Prussian Expeditions to Turfan (1902-1914) and now in the possession of the East German Academy of Sciences.

1789 TAI, Tong-schung. *Der chinesische Legalismus (Fa chia) unter besonderer Berücksichtigung seiner rechtspositivistischen Elemente.* [German: The Chinese Legalist School (Fa chia) with Particular Consideration of Its Positive Law Elements.] Mainz, 1969 (Dr., Rechts- und Wirtschaftswissenschaftliche Fakultät). xviii, 146p.

1790 WOO, Kwan-Yue Peter. *Begriffsgeschichtlicher Vergleich zwischen Tao, hodos und logos bei Chuang-tzu, Parmenides und Heraklit.* [German: A Historical Comparison of the Concepts of Tao, Hodos and Logos among the Philosophers Chuang-tzu, Parmenides and Heraclitus.] München, 1969 (Dr., Philosophische Fakultät). 257p.

1791 BLONDEAU, Anne-Marie. *Le lHa-'dre bka'-than: édition critique et traduction.* [French: The lHa-'dre bka'-than: A Critical Edition and Translation.] Paris, 1970 (Doctorat de 3e cycle ès lettres). 139p. A copy is available at the Bibliothèque de la Sorbonne. On a medieval Tibetan religious text.

1792 BYUN, Kyu-Yong. *Tao et Logos: un essai sur la structure de la pensée philosophique dans le taoïsme primitif et chez les présocratiques.* [French: Tao and Logos: An

Essay on the Structure of Philosophical Thought in Prim-
itive Taoism and among the Pre-Socratic Philosophers.]
Toulouse, 1970 (Doctorat de 3e cycle en philosophie).
756p.

1793 DURT, Hubert. *La version chinoise de l'introduction
historique de la Samantapasadika: traduction du chapitre
introductif du Chan kein liu p'i-p'o-cha et notes sur
les rapports entre ce texte et la tradition pali concernant l'histoire du bouddhisme ancien en Inde et à
Ceylan.* [French: The Chinese Version of the Historical
Introduction of the Samantapasadika: Translation of the
Introductory Chapter of the Shan chien lü p'i p'o sha
and Notes on the Relations between This Text and Pali
Tradition Concerning the History of Ancient Buddhism in
India and Ceylon.] Louvain, 1970 (Doctorat en philologie et histoire). 520p.

1794 KNAACK, Peter. *Die Religionen Chinas, dargestellt in
den Werken der französischen Jesuitenmissionare des 17.
und 18. Jh.* [German: The Religions of China as Represented in the Works of the 17th and 18th Century French
Jesuit Missionaries.] Wien, 1970(?). (Dr., Philosophische Fakultät).

1795 TERJÉK, József. *A tibeti 'Jans-blun sutra tunhuangi'
töredékei.* [Hungarian: Fragments of the Tibetan 'Jans-
blun Sutra from Tun-huang.] Eötvös Lóránd Tudományegyetem, 1970 (Dr.U. in Inner Asian Studies).

SCIENCE AND TECHNOLOGY

1796 HANSON-LOWE, John Bokenham. *Contributions to the Clima-
tology and Geomorphology of Sino-Tibet and Central China.* London, 1949 (Ph.D. in Geography). This dissertation consists of five printed pages and two supplementary papers.

1797 GRADZIŃSKI, Ryszard. *Sedymentacja górnokredowych osa-
dów kotliny Nemegt na pustyni Gobi, zawierajacych szczat-
ki dinozaurów.* [Polish: Chalk-Sediments in the Nemegt
Basin of the Gobi Desert Found in Dinosaur Tracks.]
Uniwersytet Jagielloński w Krakowie, 1968 (Doktor habilitowany, Wydz. Biologii i Nauk o Ziemi).

1798 KOZŁOWSKI, Stefan. *Badania geologiczne nad rozwojem
plutonizmu i wulkanizmu na obszarze gór Chasagtu w
Zachodniej Mongolii.* [Polish: Geological Investigations
of the Development of Plutonization and Vulcanization

in the Ch'a-sa-t'u Region of Western Mongolia.] Akade-
mia Gŏrniczo-Hutnicza im. S. Staszica w Krakowie, 1969
(Doktor habilitowany, Wydz. Geologiczno-Poszukiwawczy).

1799 BACON, James Patterson, Jr. *Local and Latitudinal Vari-*
ations in Reptile and Amphibian Community Structure in
East Asia. Chicago, 1970 (Ph.D. in Biology). 141p.
Order copies from the Photoduplication Department, Joseph Regenstein Library, University of Chicago.

1800 GROSSER, Dietger. *Beitrag zur Histologie und Klassifi-*
kation asiatischer Bambusarten. [German: A Contribution
to the Histology and Classification of Asian Species of
Bamboo.] Hamburg, 1970 (Dr., Fachbereich Biologie).
Published as Beitrag...Bambusarten (Hamburg: Wiedebusch,
1971. 321p. [Mitteilungen der Bundesforschungsanstalt
für Forst- und Holzwirtschaft Reinbek bei Hamburg, Nr.
85. Holzbiologie]). Investigates 52 species of bamboo
in the Republic of China and other Asian countries.

1801 NEGELE, Rolph-Dieter. *Morphologische und histologische*
Untersuchungen an Kauplatten, Schlundzähnen und Weber-
schen Knöchelchen bei ostasiatischen Cypriniden (Cteno-
pharyngodon idella Val., Hypophthalmichthys molitrix
Val., Hypophthalmichthys nobilis Rich.). [German: Mor-
phological and Histological Investigations of the Mas-
ticatory Plates, Pharyngeal Teeth and Weberian Ossicles
among East Asian Cyprinidae (Ctenopharyngodon idella
Val., Hypophthalmichthys molitrix Val., Hypophthalmichthys nobilis Rich.).] München, 1970 (Dr., Tierärztliche
Fakultät). vi, 56p.

1802 SZTUK, Teodor. *Dynamika i chemizm wód podziemnych dor-*
zecza Charchiry na tle budowy geologicznej (Zachodnia
Mongolia). [Polish: The Dynamics and Chemistry of Un-
derground Waters in the Charchira Basin (Western Mongolia) with a Study of Its Geological Structure.] Poli-
technika Wrocławska, Inst. Geotechniki, 1970 (Rozprawa
doktorska).

TABLE 1

THE DISTRIBUTION OF DISSERTATIONS ON CHINA BY COUNTRY AND BY YEAR (1945-1975)

COUNTRY/YEAR	'45	'46	'47	'48	'49	'50	'51	'52	'53	'54	'55	'56	'57	'58	'59	'60	'61	'62	'63	'64	'65	'66	'67	'68	'69	'70	'71	'72	'73	'74	'75	TOTAL
AUSTRIA	1			2		1	1	1			1					1	1								2	2	1	1	2	1		29
BELGIUM															2																	7
DENMARK													1	1										1	1							4
FRANCE	1	3	4	8	5	8	6	6	5	6	3	6	6	6	6	2	2	7	3	12	8	7	4	14	18	11	12	11	14	21	11	235
GERMANY (WEST)	1	2	1	4	11	11	3	1	3	8	7	3	9	5	2	8	8	6	9	9	6	10	15	9	16	17	31	27	20	19	10	279
GREAT BRITAIN		2	1	3	5	5	5	2	4	7	7	9	7	2	2	7	4	6	6	5	10	6	10	17	13	9	8	24	12	16	13	218
NETHERLANDS	1	1	2	2						1	1		2	1	1	1	1	1	1	1	1	2			2	2	1		2	3	2	26
SWEDEN																									1	1	1	2	1	1		12
SWITZERLAND		2				1	3	1	1	1	1			1	1	2	3	2	1		1	2	3	2		1	1	5	2	6	1	35
VATICAN CITY						1	1		1		1			1	1		2	2	1	1			2		2	1	2					16
SUB-TOTAL	3	9	10	16	18	26	20	14	13	21	17	22	25	14	17	18	19	22	21	24	20	28	39	41	52	45	59	71	49	61	47	861
CZECHOSLOVAKIA								1	1		1	4	1	1	1		1	1	1	1		5		4	4	3	3		1	1		21
GERMANY (EAST)				2		4	1	1	1					1	2	2	3	4	2	3	5	2	7	4	4	2	2	3				63
HUNGARY						1										1		1			1	1		1	1	3		4	1	1		11
POLAND			2			1	2	1		1			1			1		1	2	1	2	5		3	2	3		3	7	2		22
SUB-TOTAL			2			5	1	2	1	1	1	4	1	3	3	4	4	7	5	5	8	8	7	9	7	8	5	10	8	2		117
AUSTRALIA																	1	1	1	1	3	4	2	4	5	7	4	5	3	5	3	50
CANADA	1													1		2	2			1	1		1	1	1	3	3	5	5	3	3	29
HONG KONG	1																					1	1	1	3	2	6	3	2			16
INDIA						1	1	1			2							2	1	4	3	2	1	1	3	3	2		2			27
ISRAEL																1																1
MALAYSIA																					1	1										2
NEW ZEALAND																					1											1
PHILIPPINES																						1	1	1	1		1			1		5
SINGAPORE					1	1	1				2	1														3						6
SOUTH AFRICA	1																															1
UNITED STATES	21	29	22	34	34	43	40	39	51	49	42	28	28	27	39	30	42	54	57	64	70	99	106	120	138	174	202	237	243	263	260	2685
GRAND TOTAL	26	39	32	52	52	75	61	56	65	70	62	55	55	45	59	51	68	86	85	98	107	142	157	178	207	282	245	332	311	335	313	3801

Note: This table contains statistical data for dissertations on China as defined within the scope of this bibliography, i.e., dissertations dealing in whole or in part with China before and after 1949 as well as with Hong Kong, Mongolia, Tibet, and the overseas Chinese communities. It both incorporates data appearing in Appendix A--"Provenance of Dissertations by Country and Year"--within Doctoral Dissertations on China... 1945-1970 and updates the information there. Statistics for doctoral research in the U.S.S.R., however, have been excluded; and the records for theses written in various European and Asian countries during 1974 and 1975 are incomplete.

TABLE 2

THE DISTRIBUTION OF AMERICAN DISSERTATIONS BY DEGREE-AWARDING INSTITUTION (1971-1975)

Institution	No.	Institution	No.	Institution	No.
Akron	1	Georgetown	20	Pittsburgh	9
Alabama	2	Georgia	4	Princeton	15
American	17	Harvard	78	Princeton Theological Seminary	4
Arizona	7	Hawaii	28	Purdue	3
Arizona State	5	Howard	3	Rensselaer Polytechnic Institute	1
Arkansas	1	Idaho	20	Rice	2
Boston College	1	Illinois	1	Rochester	3
Boston University	6	Illinois Institute of Technology	1	Rutgers	6
Brigham Young	5	Indiana	34	St. John's	13
Brown	10	Iowa	7	Saint Louis	2
Bryn Mawr	1	Iowa State	1	San Francisco Theological Seminary	1
California (Berkeley)	85	Johns Hopkins	4	Santa Clara	1
California (Davis)	7	Johns Hopkins (SAIS)	1	South Carolina	6
California (Irvine)	3	Kansas	7	Southern Baptist Theological Seminary	1
California (Los Angeles)	24	Kent State	4	Southern California	20
California (Riverside)	1	Kentucky	5	Southern Illinois	14
California (San Francisco)	1	Louisiana State	2	Stanford	46
California (Santa Barbara)	4	Loyola University of Chicago	1	State University of New York (Albany)	1
California Institute of Asian Stud.	1	Marquette	2	State University of New York (Binghamton)	1
California School of Professional Psychology	2	Maryland	7	State University of New York (Buffalo)	3
Carnegie-Mellon	2	Massachusetts	8	Syracuse	10
Case Western Reserve	3	Massachusetts Institute of Tech.	4	Temple	5
Catholic University of America	2	Michigan	49	Tennessee	8
Chicago	48	Michigan State	18	Texas	3
Cincinnati	1	Minnesota	15	Texas Christian	1
City University of New York	3	Mississippi	1	Texas Tech	1
Claremont	14	Missouri	8	Tulane	2
Colorado	9	Nebraska	4	Union Theological Seminary	6
Colorado State	1	New Mexico	6	United States International University	2
Columbia	54	New School for Social Research	2	Utah	5
Columbia (Teachers College)	10	New York	14	Utah State	1
Connecticut	2	North Carolina	10	Vanderbilt	3
Cornell	32	North Dakota	1	Virginia	12
De Paul	1	North Texas State	1	Washington University (St. Louis)	2
Delaware	1	Northern Colorado	7	University of Washington (Seattle)	36
Denver	5	Northern Illinois	1	Washington State	4
Duke	5	Northwestern	10	Wayne State	2
Emory	2	Notre Dame	2	West Virginia	1
Fletcher School of Law & Diplomacy	5	Ohio State	21	Wisconsin	47
Florida	6	Oklahoma	6	Wright Institute	1
Florida State	6	Oklahoma State	1	Wyoming	1
Fordham	9	Oregon	12	Yale	25
Fuller Theological Seminary	2	Oregon State	1	Yeshiva	3
George Peabody Teachers College	6	University of the Pacific	1		
George Washington	14	Pennsylvania	15	TOTAL	1205
		Pennsylvania State	8		

Availability of Dissertations

American Doctoral Research

Over 30,000 American doctoral dissertations are presently
sent to University Microfilms International in Ann Arbor,
Michigan for publication each year.[1] Within weeks of their
receipt, master negatives are prepared from the typescripts,
and microfilm as well as xerographic ("xerox") copies are made
available for purchase. Within three to six months, six hundred word summaries of the theses written by the dissertation
authors also appear in print within the monthly journal *Dissertation Abstracts International* (DAI).[2] Together with several thousand titles which are not received by University Microfilms International, these dissertations gradually find
their way into standard and specialized bibliographical refer-

---

1. In 1974, a total of 33,826 doctoral degrees were conferred at American educational institutions. (See Table no.
247, "Earned Degrees Conferred by Field of Study, Level of Degree, and Sex: 1972 to 1974", in U.S. Bureau of the Census.
Statistical Abstract of the United States: 1976 [97th annual
edition]. Washington, D.C.: Government Printing Office, 1976.
p.147.) This number has been rising year after year, and current estimates are that 35-36,000 doctoral degrees will be
awarded in 1977.

2. Known as *Dissertation Abstracts* before July 1969 and
as *Microfilm Abstracts* from the year of its inception through
1951, this periodical is compiled and edited by University Microfilms International and is published in two parts: Humanities (A) and Sciences (B). It is found in most American college and university libraries and in many academic institutions elsewhere throughout the world. Parts A and B contain
primarily (but not exclusively) American and Canadian dissertation abstracts. Part C--a quarterly publication inaugurated
in the autumn of 1976--is limited to abstracts of dissertations submitted to European institutions of higher learning.

261

ence works. They are automatically listed in the annual volumes of *American Doctoral Dissertations*, compiled on behalf of the Association for Research Libraries, as well as in University Microfilms International's multivolume *Comprehensive Dissertation Index 1861-1972* and in its annual supplements. Other bibliographies provide retrospective coverage for doctoral research specifically on East Asia. These include not only the present book and its "parent volume" *Doctoral Dissertations on China: A Bibliography of Studies in Western Languages, 1945-1970,*[3] but also *American Doctoral Dissertations on Asia 1933-1966* (useful for its coverage of research about China completed before 1945),[4] *Japan and Korea: An Annotated Bibliography of Doctoral Dissertations in Western Languages, 1877-1969,*[5] and *Doctoral Dissertations on Japan and Korea, 1969-1974: A Classified Bibliographical Listing of International Research.*[6] The semiannual listings found in the *Asian Studies Professional Review* and its successor *Doctoral Dissertations on Asia: An Annotated Bibliographical Journal of Current International Research*, in turn, offer information about the latest dissertations as well as about in-progress doctoral research.[7] By consulting these works, interested faculty members, librarians and students can easily determine what theses have been written on topics of relevance to them in a variety of academic fields.

---

3. Compiled and edited by Leonard H.D. Gordon and Frank J. Shulman. Seattle: University of Washington Press, 1972. xix, 317p. (Association for Asian Studies, Reference series, no.1) This volume contains 2217 entries.

4. By Curtis Stucki. Ithaca, N.Y.: Southeast Asia Program, Department of Asian Studies, Cornell University, 1968. 304p. (Its Data paper, no.71)

5. Compiled and edited by Frank J. Shulman. Chicago: American Library Association; London: Frank Cass, 1970. xix, 340p. It contains 2562 numbered entries and an addenda.

6. Compiled and edited by Frank Joseph Shulman. Ann Arbor, Mich.: University Microfilms International, 1976. x, 78p. Containing 1316 entries and two appendixes, this reference work is currently available free of charge upon request from the publisher.

7. An ongoing column of in-progress dissertations and recently completed theses appeared in each issue of the *Asian Studies Professional Review* between fall 1971 and spring 1974. Since winter 1975, it has been continued in the form of a new periodical published by the Association for Asian Studies under the title *Doctoral Dissertations on Asia: A Bibliographical Journal of Current International Research*.

The procedure for getting hold of copies of unpublished dissertation typescripts, however, is not necessarily easy for interested individuals--especially if they lack appropriate guidance. With the single exception of the Library of Congress, which obtains them through copyright, American libraries today do not regularly acquire large numbers of dissertations for their general collections. Furthermore, because of prohibitive administrative costs, the possible inconvenience to readers on their own campuses, and the potential of damage to borrowed volumes, only a few universities maintain a policy of lending copies of their dissertations to people at other institutions through interlibrary loan whenever the same items are commercially available.[8] For these reasons, the following guide should be useful not only as a brief statement about the availability of dissertations from University Microfilms International but also as a summary of the current policies of those schools which regularly award doctorates for research on East Asia but which do not promptly send all such dissertations to University Microfilms. The information below was initially gathered and published during the winter of 1975,[9] and it has been updated and revised specifically for readers of this volume.

UNIVERSITY MICROFILMS INTERNATIONAL: More than 250 universities now participate in this cooperative dissertation microfilming program inaugurated in the late 1930s. The involvement of such institutions as Cornell University, Indiana University, The University of Michigan, New York University, Stanford University, the University of Washington, and Yale University enables University Microfilms to provide coverage for 85-90% of all current American doctoral research.[10] At the present time, copies of 35mm positive (i.e., black on

---

8. Duke University, Indiana University, Michigan State University, the University of Virginia, and the University of Washington are among the handful of institutions with established programs in Asian Studies that do lend their recent dissertations under varying conditions.

9. See "The Availability of Recently Completed American Doctoral Dissertations with Particular Reference to Work on East Asia." Association for Asian Studies. Committee on East Asian Libraries. *Newsletter*, no.46 (March 1975): 56-64.

10. A comprehensive, up-to-date listing of these universities together with the dates when they began sending in dissertations for microfilming appears in each monthly issue of *Dissertation Abstracts International*.

white) microfilm made at a reduction of 15-20x and paperbound
xerographic copies reproduced at about 2/3 their original size
are available on demand. For individuals associated with universities, colleges and high schools (this includes their libraries, departments, faculty, staff, and students), the prices of single copies are as follows: For microfilm copies--
$7.50 (within the U.S.), $8.25 (for orders from Canada and
Mexico), and $11.50 (for orders from all other countries).
For paperbound xerographic copies--$15.00 (within the U.S.),
$16.50 (for orders from Canada and Mexico), and $23.00 (for
orders from all other countries). Clothbound xerographic
copies of dissertations may be ordered for an additional $3.00
per volume. (Shipping and handling are extra except in the
case of prepaid orders from individuals in North America.)[11]
All orders should contain the author's name, the dissertation
title, the order number which appears for each thesis in *Dissertation Abstracts International* (indicated by the prefix
"UM" within the present bibliography), the format and type of
binding desired, and the customer's name and mailing address.
Orders from individuals and institutions in the United States,
Canada and Latin America should be sent to University Microfilms International, Dissertation Copies, Post Office Box
1764, Ann Arbor, Michigan 48106. All orders originating from
Africa, Asia, Australasia and Europe as well as those which
are to be mailed to destinations in the Eastern hemisphere
must be placed with University Microfilms International,
18 Bedford Row, London WC1R 4EJ, England. Prices are subject
to change without advance notice in all cases. Publication
through University Microfilms, it should be remembered, does
not preclude other forms of publication, and many dissertations also eventually appear as books and/or articles.[12]

---

11. Individuals within the United States who are not associated with an educational institution are charged $10.00
and $20.00 respectively for microfilm and for xerographic cop-
ies. In Canada and Mexico, in turn, the prices are $11.00
and $22.00. And elsewhere: $11.50 and $23.00.

12. There is a widely held misconception that a legal contract exists between University Microfilms International and
each cooperating institution. In reality, all agreements for
the microfilming and publication of dissertations through
University Microfilms are concluded with the degree recipients, whose home institutions handle much of the paperwork and
verify that their theses have been successfully defended for
the doctorate. Many individuals retain the copyright to their
research and publish some or all of their doctoral work
through conventional channels after their dissertations have
been microfilmed and made commercially available.

UNIVERSITY OF CALIFORNIA AT BERKELEY: Berkeley joined
the University Microfilms' microfilming program in 1962 and
for several years automatically sent all new dissertations to
Ann Arbor. The university discontinued this arrangement between fall 1970 and fall 1975, however, and most Berkeley theses listed in this bibliography must therefore be ordered directly from the Library Photographic Service, The General Library, University of California, Berkeley, CA 94720. (They
are available in both microfilm and xerographic form; their
cost varies with the number of pages involved.) Abstracts for
them did not appear in *Dissertation Abstracts International*
or in any other publication. Those summaries which were published represent only the small number of Berkeley Ph.D. recipients who chose to join the University Microfilms International program on their own during this five-year period.
Restrictions have seldom been placed on the availability of
Berkeley theses, and then only under stringent circumstances
(usually for reasons of copyright intent). For details regarding the purchase of dissertations and for a current price
list, write directly to the Library Photographic Service; for
other information about Berkeley doctoral research, contact
the General Reference Service at The General Library.

UNIVERSITY OF CALIFORNIA AT SANTA BARBARA: On the
average, only twenty percent of Santa Barbara Ph.D. recipients
request that their dissertations be forwarded to University
Microfilms International for publication. All other dissertations, however, are available on interlibrary loan and copies
may be purchased at a cost of 10¢ per page (plus handling and
postage) provided that the author gives his permission. Requests should be directed to the Department of Special Collections, The Library, University of California, Santa Barbara,
CA 93106. For further information regarding the university's
policies, contact the Administrative Service Officer, Graduate
Division, Administration Building, University of California
at Santa Barbara.

UNIVERSITY OF CHICAGO: Since 1948 Chicago has required
that all dissertations be microfilmed by the university's photoduplication department in lieu of formal publication and
that a positive microfilm copy be deposited at the Library of
Congress. An alphabetical, unannotated listing of these works
(together with new M.A. theses) is published annually in pam-
phlet form.[13] Since autumn 1974, seventeen departments and

---

13. Formally known as *Supplementary List* [number] *of Doctoral Dissertations and Master's Theses through* [date] *and*

professional schools at Chicago have also required the publication of a six hundred word summary in *Dissertation Abstracts
International*.[14] In all cases, however, the dissertation
typescripts themselves continue to be available for purchase
in positive microfilm and in unbound xerographic form only
from the Department of Photoduplication, The Joseph Regenstein
Library, The University of Chicago, 1100 East 57th Street,
Chicago, IL 60637.[15] Most microfilms presently sell for under
$5.00, but prices vary according to the length of the thesis
and, in the case of xerographic copies, also according to the
size of the paper on which the customer requests that his copy
be printed. Only dissertations written before 1948 may be
borrowed on interlibrary loan. For further information, write
to the reference department of the Regenstein Library.

COLUMBIA UNIVERSITY/TEACHERS COLLEGE: Since 1952 Columbia has been promptly sending the majority of its dissertations to University Microfilms International. Doctoral degree
recipients, however, are permitted to withhold their theses
from microfilming for a maximum of two years.[16] These dissertations are not available without the author's consent; like
other theses, they normally may not be borrowed on interlibrary loan. Commercially published dissertations have always

---

Miscellaneous Long Run Serials on Film, this list is published
by the Department of Photoduplication. Copies of all in-print
and forthcoming numbers are available free of charge upon request to institutions, but not to individuals.

14. The seventeen departments and professional schools involved include Business, Education, Far Eastern Languages,
History, Law, Music, Sociology, and South Asian Languages.
Among the thirty-six departments which have no abstract publication requirement are Anthropology, Art, Economics, Geography, Linguistics, and Political Science as well as the Divinity and Library Schools. Few Chicago theses are ever placed
under restricted access.

15. The sole exception is the Geography Department, whose
doctoral dissertations are available in planographed form and
may be ordered directly from that department.

16. Certain dissertations are entirely withheld from microfilming while others are sold by University Microfilms International only upon receipt of the author's written permission. The addresses of all Ph.D. recipients may be obtained
from the Office of the Dissertation Secretary at Columbia.
Abstracts in *Dissertation Abstracts International* for theses
whose sales are restricted also contain the authors' respective addresses.

been acceptable for the completion of doctoral degree requirements, and until September 1974 they could be submitted under
the so-called author publication option (with copies available
through the Photographic Services Department, 110 Butler Library, Columbia University). Since then, all authors have
been required to submit an abstract for publication in *Dissertation Abstracts International*. As in the case of the University of Chicago, Columbia University publishes an annual booklet listing new dissertations. It is arranged by academic
department, indexed by author, and indicates which theses have
been withheld from microfilming.[17] While these booklets list
dissertations accepted specifically for the Ph.D. degree in
Education (prepared under a Columbia University/Teachers College "joint program"), however, they omit Ed.D. dissertations
since the latter are on file only at the Teachers College Library. Inquiries about all Education theses, it should be
noted, must be addressed to the Teachers College Library, 525
West 120th Street, New York, NY 10027. For further information about all other Columbia University dissertations, write
directly to the Office of the Dissertation Secretary, 105 Low
Memorial Library, Columbia University, New York, NY 10027.

THE FLETCHER SCHOOL OF LAW AND DIPLOMACY, TUFTS
UNIVERSITY: Fletcher has never participated in the University Microfilms International program and abstracts of its
recent dissertations do not regularly appear in any publication. The typescripts of Fletcher theses may be borrowed on
interlibrary loan, however, and arrangements can be made for
purchasing a copy if the author's written authorization has
been secured. For further information, write directly to the
Edwin Ginn Library, The Fletcher School of Law and Diplomacy,
Tufts University, Medford, MA 02155.

HARVARD UNIVERSITY: Since 1972 and 1975 respectively, the
School of Business Administration and the School of Education
have fully participated in the University Microfilms International program. With the exceptions of Astronomy and Chemistry,

---

17. Through the 1970-1971 annual issue, the booklet was
known as *Masters' Essays and Doctoral Dissertations*. Since
then it has simply been called *Doctoral Dissertations*. Copies
are supplied to interested individuals and institutions upon
request. Applications for a particular booklet or for having
one's name placed on the annual mailing list should be sent
to the Gifts and Exchange Division, 103 Butler Library, Columbia University, New York, NY 10027.

however, none of the university's departments have ever had
their dissertations sent to Ann Arbor for publication, and abstracts of theses do not regularly appear in print.[18] Furthermore, certain departments and programs--e.g., History;
History and East Asian Languages; History of Science--automat-
ically limit access to their dissertations to Harvard University faculty members associated with those same departments
and to individuals securing the authors' written consent during the five-year period following the award of the Ph.D. degree. In June 1974, the Harvard University Archives (Pusey
Library) also discontinued its long-established policy of
lending the second copies of doctoral dissertations and senior
honors theses to all other institutions except for members of
the Research Libraries Group: Columbia University, the New
York Public Library, and Yale University. Nevertheless, positive microfilm copies (at 10¢ per page) and xerographic copies
(at 15¢ per page) of unrestricted dissertations may easily be
purchased from the Photographic Department in Widener Library.
Price estimates and the current addresses of Ph.D. recipients
(supplied on request whenever an individual must secure the
author's written consent) as well as further details about
current policies may be obtained directly from the Photographic Department, Widener Library, Cambridge, MA 02138. Inquiries must be made in person or by mail.

UNIVERSITY OF HAWAII: Hawaii has been a cooperating institution in the University Microfilms International program
since 1960, but since 1970, Ph.D. recipients have had the option of withholding their dissertations permanently from that
publisher. As a consequence, only a selection of the theses
submitted to Hawaii are both abstracted in *Dissertation Abstracts International* and sold by University Microfilms.[19]
Since 1974, moreover, participation in the microfilming program for a number of other doctoral students has meant merely
the publication of their thesis summaries in *Dissertation*

---

18. As in the case of students fulfilling their doctoral
requirements at institutions discussed elsewhere within this
guide, Harvard University Ph.D. recipients may take the initiative of making their dissertations available through University Microfilms International. A case in point is *Peking
Drumsinging* by Catherine Stevens (entry 1140 within this bibliography), which was abstracted in the October 1975 issue of
Dissertation Abstracts International.

19. Approximately half of the dissertations dealing specifically with East Asia and with the Asian American community
of Hawaii are sent to University Microfilms International.

Abstracts International. All such non-University Microfilms dissertations must be ordered directly from the Interlibrary Loan Department, University of Hawaii Library, 2550 The Mall, Honolulu, HI 96822. Xerographic copies are currently 10¢ per page plus postage; microfilms are less. Prepayment is required for all foreign orders. The university lists its dissertations in *Current Hawaiiana*, a quarterly bibliography issued by the Hawaiian Collection of the University of Hawaii Library, as well as in its commencement programs. For further information, write directly to the University of Hawaii Library.

MASSACHUSETTS INSTITUTE OF TECHNOLOGY (M.I.T.):

M.I.T. has never participated in the University Microfilms International program, and while it has not established a formal area studies program focusing on Asia, important dissertations on China and Japan have been submitted in recent years to such departments as Linguistics, Political Science, and Sociology. These dissertations are listed in a university publication, copies of which are sent to other academic libraries upon request.[20] There are no provisions for publishing thesis abstracts or for making the dissertations themselves available through interlibrary loan. Positive microfilm copies (currently at 6¢ per page) and xerographic copies (currently at 25¢ per page), however, may be ordered directly from the Microreproduction Laboratory, Room 14-0551, Massachusetts Institute of Technology, Cambridge, MA 02139.[21] For more information, write directly to the Institute Archives, Room 14N-118, Massachusetts Institute of Technology, Cambridge, MA 02139.

SCHOOL OF ADVANCED INTERNATIONAL STUDIES (SAIS), THE JOHNS HOPKINS UNIVERSITY:

Approximately two-thirds of all SAIS dissertations are sent to University Microfilms International. These titles are not available through interlibrary loan.[22] All other SAIS dissertations are available

---

20. Issued three times each year under the titles *Graduation Exercises* (June) and *Degrees Awarded* (February and September), this publication may be requested through the Exchange and Gifts Section, M.I.T. Libraries, Room 14SM-28, Massachusetts Institute of Technology, Cambridge, MA 02139.

21. The maximum charge for a 35mm positive microfilm is currently $10.50. For a xerographic copy of a thesis, it is $48.00.

22. The maximum delay in the case of theses temporarily withheld from microfilming is two to three years.

only through interlibrary loan from the SAIS library, except where the author has withheld permission for his dissertation to be seen pending its publication. There is no periodical containing abstracts for the dissertations which are not commercially available, nor are the typescripts themselves on sale at SAIS. For further information, write directly to the Library, School of Advanced International Studies, The Johns Hopkins University, 1740 Massachusetts Avenue, N.W., Washington, DC 20036.

UNIVERSITY OF SOUTHERN CALIFORNIA: Since summer 1975, the University of Southern California has not been sending its dissertations to Ann Arbor for microfilming even though it has continued to have the authors' abstracts published in *Dissertation Abstracts International*.[23] Except for theses completed for the Ed.D. degree, these dissertations are generally not available through interlibrary loan. Nevertheless, in all cases, microfilm and xerographic copies are available for purchase from the Photoduplication Department, University of Southern California Library, University Park, Los Angeles, CA 90007. Prices vary according to the type of copy desired and the length of the thesis typescript; there is a minimum charge of $2.50. Write directly to the Photoduplication Department for a complete price list.

There are a number of additional institutions of higher learning that do not cooperate in what has become essentially the national microfilming and publication program for dissertations, but theses dealing with East Asia are infrequently submitted to any of them.[24] Certain departments of cooperating

---

23. Copies of all theses submitted to the University of Southern California between 1959 and mid-1975--among them, most of the items listed within this bibliography--are currently available for purchase from University Microfilms International.

24. Many of the institutions in question, as the following list suggests, are schools of theology: Aquinas School of Theology, Atlanta University, Bob Jones University, Chicago Theological Seminary, Dropsie University, Hebrew Union College, Iliff School of Theology, Indiana University at Indianapolis, Jewish Theological Seminary of America, Middlebury College, Ner Israel Rabbinical College, New Mexico Institute of Mining and Technology, University of Oregon Medical School, Peabody Institute of Baltimore, Providence College, University of Puerto Rico, St. Mary of the Lake Seminary, San Diego State

universities such as the Law and Medical Schools of Yale University, the School of Industrial Labor Relations at Cornell University, and the University of California's Medical School (in San Francisco) also have never participated.

While the large majority of American universities now fully cooperate with University Microfilms International, it is important to keep in mind the fact that these same schools accepted several hundred dissertations on East Asia before joining the microfilming program.[25] If they were never published in book or article form, then (with some exceptions) these works are available only from the libraries where they were deposited. Accordingly, inquiries about many of the theses listed in the Appendix to this volume--especially those written during the late 1940s and in the 1950s--must be sent directly to the institutions that accepted them. The policies of American universities regarding the provision of interlibrary loan service and the sale of copies for all theses which fit into this category vary from one school to another.

Finally, it should be noted that the Library of Congress does have positive microfilm copies of all dissertations which are available from University Microfilms International regardless of whether they have been copyrighted or not. The Library has also acquired all University of Chicago dissertations on microfilm since 1955 together with a few theses from elsewhere. These may readily be consulted in the Library's Microform Reading Room, but they normally are not available on loan.

College, San Francisco Theological Seminary, Smith College, Spertus College of Judaica, Thomas Jefferson University, and Woodstock College. For a complete listing, see the latest issue of the annual bibliography *American Doctoral Dissertations*.

25. As noted above, the calendar year in which a university began to send its dissertations to University Microfilms International is prominently stated together with its name in the list of cooperating institutions published within each issue of *Dissertation Abstracts International*.

Asian, Australian, Canadian, and European Doctoral Research

The following guide outlines the availability of dissertations on a country by country basis. Readers interested in
detailed information about the differing structures of higher
education within European countries and their corresponding
degrees are advised to consult the "Survey of European Higher
Educational Practices" in the latest issue of volume C--"European Abstracts"--of *Dissertation Abstracts International.*

AUSTRALIA: For copies of dissertations submitted to the
Australian National University, write to: The Library, Australian National University, P.O. Box 4, Canberra, A.C.T. 2600.
In some cases access is restricted to staff and students of
the Australian National University for a period of five years
following the completion of a thesis, and such theses may
be consulted and borrowed by others only if the author gives
his written permission. The author's permission, moreover,
must be secured before photocopies of a dissertation can be
sold. Copies are available at cost, and for microfilms this
will usually be between Aust. $8.00 and $15.00 while xerographic copies will be about three times as much. Copies are not
usually supplied directly to researchers; applications should
therefore be made through the library of a university or research institution. For information about the availability of
dissertations submitted to other Australian universities, write
to the library of the institution in question.

AUSTRIA: Dissertations submitted to the Universität Wien
(University of Vienna) are normally available either from (1)
Die Universitätsbibliothek der Universität Wien, A-1010 Wien,
Dr. Karl Lueger-Ring 1; or (2) Die Österreichische National-
bibliothek [National Library of Austria], A-1010 Wien, Josefs-
platz 1. Theses accepted by other Austrian academic institutions may be found at their respective libraries as well as at

the National Library in Vienna. Interlibrary loan service is available for Austrian dissertations in general (according to the *Gesamtverzeichnis österreichischer Dissertationen*).

BELGIUM: Write directly to the general library of the university to which the dissertation has been submitted.

CANADA: Since the mid-1960s, the National Library of Canada has undertaken efforts to microfilm completed Canadian doctoral research in all subject areas. Coverage is becoming increasingly comprehensive, and most theses listed within the present bibliography may be ordered directly from the Canadian Theses Division, National Library of Canada, 395 Wellington, Ottawa, Ontario K1A ON4. They are available only in microform (either on microfilm or on microfiche, as indicated within each bibliographical entry), and pre-payment is mandatory in the case of orders from individuals. Interlibrary loan requests for the same may be addressed to the National Library's Reference Branch. Dissertations submitted to institutions which do not yet send theses to Ottawa for microfilming must be obtained directly from their respective university libraries. Most Canadian dissertations, it should be noted, are currently being abstracted in *Dissertation Abstracts International* (volumes A and B) within two years of their completion.

CZECHOSLOVAKIA: Write to the Filosofická fakulta University Karlovy, děkanát, Praha 1, Náměstí Krasnoarmějcu.

DENMARK: The one dissertation listed in this bibliography has been published and should be readily available at major academic libraries.

FRANCE: Most dissertations completed in Paris are available at the Bibliothèque de la Sorbonne, 47 rue des Ecoles, 75005 Paris or at the Bibliothèque Cujas de Droit et de Sciences Economiques, 2 rue Cujas, 75005 Paris. Address all inquiries to the "Service des Thèses" of those respective libraries. For all other French dissertations, write directly to the library of the university in question. Please note that *some* French dissertations may be purchased in microfiche format from the Bureau Européen de l'Association des Universités Partiellement ou Entièrement de Langue Française (AUPELF), 173 bd. Saint-Germain, 75272 Paris Cedex 06. Furthermore, since 1952, the Center for Research Libraries (5721 South Cottage Grove Avenue, Chicago, Illinois 60637) each year has received through the Ministry of Education of France copies of all *printed* doctoral dissertations from all French universities in all subject areas except medicine. These are available through interlibrary loan to individuals associated with American institutions holding memberships in the Center for Research Libraries.

GERMAN DEMOCRATIC REPUBLIC (EAST GERMANY): Write directly to the general library of the university to which the dissertation has been submitted.

FEDERAL REPUBLIC OF GERMANY (WEST GERMANY): Most dissertations are either available in printed form from the libraries of the universities to which they were submitted or are on sale from commercial publishers. Copies of the printed theses may also be found at many libraries outside of Germany, among them the Library of Congress in Washington and the Center for Research Libraries (5721 South Cottage Grove Avenue, Chicago, Illinois 60637). Microfilm copies of most unpublished dissertations, in turn, may be ordered directly from the libraries of the universities which have accepted them.

GREAT BRITAIN: In 1971, the British Library Lending Division at Boston Spa (Wetherby, West Yorkshire LS23 7BQ) inaugurated a program for increasing the availability of British doctoral research. Academic institutions are encouraged to send copies of their dissertations to Boston Spa, where they are microfilmed and listed in the *BLLD Announcement Bulletin*. When requests for these dissertations are subsequently received, the microfilms are enlarged xerographically and the resulting paper copies are sent out on interlibrary loan. With the exception of theses submitted to the Universities of Cambridge and Durham, moreover, paper copies of 35mm positive microfilms available at the British Library Lending Division may also be purchased. Every request, whether for a loan or for a retention copy, must be accompanied by a special copyright declaration form designed by the Standing Conference of National and University Libraries (SCONUL) and available from the BLLD. Whenever possible, the British Library Lending Division's accession number for pertinent thesis holdings has been included within the present bibliography. In spite of the BLLD's efforts, however, the majority of British dissertations remain available only at the libraries of the universities which have accepted them. In the case of the University of London, one copy is kept in the University Library and may be loaned to other approved libraries for consultation only within those libraries. Photocopies may not be made of the whole or any part of a thesis without the author's written permission. Interested readers should address all inquiries to: The Director of the University Library, Senate House, Malet Street, London WC1E 7HU. For information regarding the availability of theses submitted to other British institutions, write directly to the library of the university in question or consult the editorial note of the latest volume of the Association of Special Libraries and Information Bureaux (ASLIB)'s *Index to Theses Accepted for Higher Degrees by the Universities of Great Britain and Ireland and the Council for National Academic Awards* (London; published annually).

HONG KONG: Write to the library of the University of Hong Kong.

HUNGARY: Write to the general library of the university or institute to which the dissertation has been submitted.

INDIA: For dissertations submitted to the Indian School of International Studies and the Jawaharlal Nehru University, write to: The Librarian, Jawaharlal Nehru University, New Mehrauli Road, New Delhi 57. For dissertations accepted by other institutions, write directly to the general library of the university in question.

MALAYSIA: Write directly to the library of the University of Malaya in Kuala Lumpur.

NETHERLANDS: Most Dutch theses have been published and are available in the collections of many university libraries outside of The Netherlands, among them the Center for Research Libraries (5721 South Cottage Grove Avenue, Chicago, Illinois 60637) and the Library of Congress in Washington, D.C. In all other cases, write directly to the general library of the university to which the dissertation has been submitted.

NEW ZEALAND: Write to the Reference Librarian, The University of Auckland, Private Bag, Auckland.

PHILIPPINES: Write directly to the general library of the university to which the dissertation has been submitted.

POLAND: Write directly to the general library of the university or institute which has accepted the dissertation.

AVAILABILITY OF DISSERTATIONS

SINGAPORE: Write to the library of the University of Singapore.

SWEDEN: Most Swedish theses have been published and are available in the collections of many libraries outside of Scandinavia, among them the Library of Congress in Washington and the Center for Research Libraries (5721 South Cottage Grove Avenue, Chicago, Illinois 60637).   In all other cases, write directly to the general library of the university to which the dissertation has been submitted.

SWITZERLAND: Most Swiss theses have been published and are available in the collections of many libraries outside of Switzerland, among them the Library of Congress in Washington and the Center for Research Libraries (5721 South Cottage Grove Avenue, Chicago, Illinois 60637).   In all other cases, write directly to the general library of the university to which the dissertation has been submitted.

VATICAN CITY: Write directly to the library of the university to which the dissertation has been submitted.

Author Index

All numbers refer to entry numbers

AUTHOR INDEX

Institutional Index

Entries numbered from 1574 through 1802 refer to dissertations accepted by academic institutions *before* the year 1971. All numbers refer to entry numbers.

AUSTRALIA

THE AUSTRALIAN NATIONAL UNIVERSITY
Bucknall, 174; Chan, 668; Ching, 1481; Choi, 1153; Chow, 555; Dellinger, 1705; Fung, 497; Howard, 816; Hunter, 1114; Li, Lincoln, 1665; Li, Lin-nei Yeung, 926; Radtke, 1072; Rigby, 716; Rule, 1485; Shaw, 878; Tanaka, 1360; Wong, 32; Wu, 1156
UNIVERSITY OF NEW SOUTH WALES
Willis, 678
UNIVERSITY OF QUEENSLAND
Dignan, 691; Keats, 1619
UNIVERSITY OF SYDNEY
Davies, 175; Lee, 1007; McDougall, 1726

AUSTRIA

UNIVERSITÄT IN GRAZ (University of Graz)
Fussy, 111

HOCHSCHULE FÜR WELTHANDEL (WIEN) (Vienna School of Economics and Business Administration)
Stolz, 155
UNIVERSITÄT SALZBURG (University of Salzburg)
Wei, 1125
UNIVERSITÄT WIEN (University of Vienna)
Cheng, 1715; Chiao, 1627; Fux, 1577; Hsüeh, 1137; Hung, 1777; Kaiser, 1584; Klimburg, 1579; Knaack, 1794; Lee, Kya Ha, 532; Lee, Mercedes, 1702; Rabatsch, 1585; Schusta, 1642; Sha, 1714

BELGIUM

UNIVERSITÉ LIBRE DE BRUXELLES (Free University of Brussels)
Kurgan-Van Hentenryk, 1663
RIJKSUNIVERSITEIT TE GENT (State University of Ghent)
Hsieh, 1637

Modified Subject Index

This index is limited primarily to geographical, literary, and personal names appearing within the titles of the dissertations and in the accompanying annotations whenever they exist. Included are the names of non-Chinese who have lived in China, who have been influenced in some way by Chinese culture and civilization, or who have otherwise had some meaningful relationship with the Chinese world. Place names outside of China, Mongolia and Tibet (e.g., the resident communities of overseas Chinese), however, have been excluded. The names of cities and villages, it should be noted, usually appear twice: as main entries, and as sub-entries under the provinces in which they are located. All numbers refer to entry numbers.

About the Author

Frank Joseph Shulman is director of the East Asia
library collection at the University of Maryland
(College Park). Among his publications are several
reference works including *Japan and Korea: An Annotated Bibliography of Doctoral Dissertations in
Western Languages, 1877-1969* (1970), *The Allied
Occupation of Japan, 1945-1952: An Annotated Bibliography of Western-Language Materials* (1974),
and *East Asian Resources in American Libraries*
(1977). Mr. Shulman has also served as an assis-
tant editor of the Association for Asian Studies'
Bibliography of Asian Studies and as bibliographer/
librarian of The University of Michigan's Center
for Japanese Studies. He is currently working on
additional guides to doctoral research about Asia
and on a bibliography of book reviews about China,
Japan and Korea.

10/94